"Good evening. Wh█ █████████ sportsman and pow████████ ███████ Aronow?" asked Susan Lichtman of WTVJ Channel 4. The station reported that police had finally confirmed later in the evening that Aronow was the victim of a shooting.

Still on the scene, a WTVJ reporter recorded bystanders saying that Aronow's car had been ambushed by one or two men in a black Lincoln. They also interviewed a local boat salesman, who said he heard five rounds from a .45. "I shoot guns, I know the sound of a .45 caliber pistol," he said.

WCIX Channel 6 reported that the murder weapon might have been a machine gun. They also interviewed Aronow's friend Don Soffer, developer of Turnberry Isle, who described Aronow as "smart, charming, handsome, tough-as-nails, and liked by everyone he came in touch with."

WSVN Channel 7 reminded viewers that Aronow's boats had become popular with drug smugglers. But "in recent years, Aronow tried to help turn the tide on them by building highly powerful catamarans for the U.S. Customs Service."

JUST WHAT WAS THE TRUTH?

Other True Crime Cases by
Arthur Jay Harris
from Avon Books

FLOWERS FOR MRS. LUSKIN
UNTIL PROVEN INNOCENT

SPEED KILLS

ARTHUR JAY HARRIS

AVON BOOKS  NEW YORK

SPEED KILLS is a journalistic account of the actual 1987 murder investigation of Donald Aronow in Miami, Florida. The events recounted in this book are true. The scenes and dialogue have been reconstructed based on tape-recorded formal interviews, police department records, and published news stories. Quoted testimony has been taken verbatim from pretrial transcripts and other sworn statements.

Research for this story was originally published in *Boating* magazine.

AVON BOOKS
A division of
The Hearst Corporation
1350 Avenue of the Americas
New York, New York 10019

Copyright © 1998 by Arthur Jay Harris
Cover photos courtesy John Crouse
Published by arrangement with the author
Visit our website at http://www.AvonBooks.com
Library of Congress Catalog Card Number: 97-94326
ISBN: 0-380-78183-2

First Avon Books Printing: April 1998

AVON TRADEMARK REG. U.S. PAT. OFF. AND IN OTHER COUNTRIES, MARCA REGISTRADA, HECHO EN U.S.A.

Printed in the U.S.A.

WCD   10 9 8 7 6 5 4 3 2 1

The heroic spirit has fallen from grace. Time and technology have shrunk the number of acceptable outlets for the daring, aggressive nature that swung the sword and mapped the unknown, until it has come to be associated primarily with criminals.

—WINIFRED GALLAGHER
"HOW WE BECOME WHAT WE ARE"
THE ATLANTIC MONTHLY, SEPTEMBER 1994

The psychopath and the hero are twigs of the same branch.

—DAVID LYKKEN,
UNIVERSITY OF MINNESOTA
PSYCHOLOGY PROFESSOR AND RESEARCHER
QUOTED IN THE SAME STORY

How do I want to be remembered? You mean after I'm gone? Who gives a fuck?

—DON ARONOW
AUGUST 1985, TO *THE ROBB REPORT*
(WHICH EDITED HIS LANGUAGE FOR PUBLICATION)

Who Killed "The Don" of Powerboat Racing?

On an industrial street just behind Loehmann's that dead ends into Biscayne Bay, a place most Miamians don't know exists and would need a map to find, Brooklyn-born Donald Joel Aronow made his name and most of his fortune, and satisfied his whims in a way few men ever do. An immigrant's son, he built boats that went fast—very fast—and sold them to kings, princesses, presidents-for-life propped up by the U.S., CEOs, the CIA, fugitive financiers, oil-wealthy Arabs, the Mossad, big-league dopers, the people who tried to catch big-league dopers, current and to-be U.S. presidents, and every other type of rogue who could borrow a briefcase and stuff it with enough high-denomination dinars.

But that was not how he made money, he would tell you. Like the guy who was so impressed by a Remington razor that he bought the company, Aronow tried to impress you with his boats so you would buy *his* company. Then you'd sue him after you had.

His door was open to anyone, but he'd cut you off after a few minutes. His boats were gorgeous, but his office was ramshackle and disorganized. He didn't dress well. He owned a Rolls but hated it, and for years drove to work in a fire-engine-red Rabbit convertible, too cramped for his six-foot-plus-frame. But he had his priorities. He built a false wall in an office closet that led to a spiral staircase and an upstairs room where he entertained young ladies in a suite with a large bed, and a shower with more nozzles than most people would find necessary. His friends would one-up each other with stories about him. One said he saw Aronow ascend the stairs with three women, one after another, each one gorgeous. When he came down, he'd light a cigar and say with a big grin, "Nothin' like it."

"That's nothing," said another Aronow observer on N.E. 188th Street, Thunderboat Row. "I saw him one day with four. The oldest one was twenty-four." Not bad for a man pushing sixty, ethnic-swarthy with thick eyebrows, and half-blind. No wonder he always complained to his wife that he was too tired to do much in the evenings.

Aronow was the living, breathing personification of what his muscle boats could do for your flagging sex life. For a long time, his primary market was rich men in middle-age crises. His most famous boat company was called Cigarette—which became the generic name for all fast boats—and one blunt full-page ad for the company in a Spanish-language boat magazine said what was too vulgar to properly express in the English language: *"Mas que un objecto sexual . . . Una tigresa entre gatitos"*— "more than a sexual object . . . A tiger among kittens."

The chicks flocked. Satisfied Aronow customer Bill Wishnick volunteered a testimonial for a *Sports Illustrated* profile, circa 1970. "I was a married, out-of-shape, middle-aged businessman," he said. "Now I'm divorced, an ocean racer and a swinger. Seeing Don was the best thing that ever happened to me."

Aronow's most famous picture defined him: smirky grimace, ebullience in the deep lines of his forehead, both cotton sleeves badly ripped at the shoulders, his hand bracing an injured elbow that should have slowed him down at least the *six feet* he won the five-hundred-mile marathon by, but didn't.

Even beyond the last day of his life, Aronow's fans held the moment of that picture as who he would forever be.

No other sport, not even auto racing, causes as many fatalities as powerboat racing. Even beside that, oceangoing powerboaters give their bodies an incredible pounding each time their crafts bisect a choppy wave at high speed. In his career, Aronow broke his nose, an arm, a foot, and his sternum as he tried to control his boat while racing full throttle in the most dangerous seas. Sometimes his boat would lurch a hundred feet out of the water, then crash into the next wave. And for most of his racing years, he refused to wear a helmet.

Aronow was in his thirties and forties when he did all this to himself. What was he trying to prove by this adult ritual of passage? What childhood deficit was he trying to even the score with? Aronow's friendly competitors those years called him "that crazy Aronow," who won races not necessarily with the fastest boat, but because he was fearless in the worst of conditions. As he passed boats that prudently slowed down, he smiled. Other racers thought he had a death wish.

When Don was forty and his daughter Claudia sixteen, she wondered out loud, "I wonder what Daddy will be when he grows up."

By 1987, almost two decades had passed since his last race, and he was planning to make a comeback. Usually, older men don't put themselves in danger the way they might have as younger men. But Don Aronow had shown few signs of growing up even after age forty, so that rule might not have applied.

Aronow once described himself as "something of a juvenile delinquent" until he was seventeen.

"He was a juvenile delinquent when he was forty," said his longtime friend Dick Genth, himself a racer and boatbuilder. "He was a juvenile delinquent when he was shot." Genth remembered barroom brawls, free-for-alls, and a food fight with tortillas that Aronow instigated in a restaurant in Mexico. "Don was a big laugh," he said.

Eras can end in a single moment. The Flapper Twenties ended the instant the stock market bubble burst in 1929. A similar graphic truth that powerboating's—and Miami's—Go-Fast Eighties had met their sudden, sobering end February 3, 1987, was the sight of Don Aronow's blood pooling into the bucket seat of his gleaming white two-seater Mercedes, which idled at high rev a few hundred yards west of his last big-name boat company.

Don Aronow had sold pleasure boats to celebrate life. Murder was not supposed to be part of it.

In a time when Miami was Murder City, U.S.A., Aronow's was the city's scariest and most glaring. Up to then, Miami had oddly celebrated its dubious image. Those of us here knew that most of those statistics were rooted in drug deals gone sour, and if bad guys wanted to kill each other, *c'est la vie* in the big city. Meanwhile, *Miami Vice* reminded us that drug money had added wealth, elegance, and excitement to the city. And it was true.

But Aronow didn't have a reputation of involvement with criminals, although his murder certainly exuded those trappings.

The world was about to change anyway. The age of AIDS was arriving. The stock market free-fell 508 points on a single day later that year. Nancy Reagan had repeated "Just Say No" enough to make the message sink in. The public paired Cigarettes and smuggling. So did the Marine Patrol; Cigarettes headed for open water were routinely stopped, on no other suspicion than that they were Cigarettes. NBC canceled *Miami Vice*.

Later the same week that Aronow was killed, Carlos Lehder, the head of the Medellin cocaine cartel, was apprehended in Colombia and extradited to Florida to face federal charges.

The Go-Fast business quickly went limp. Nobody wanted them; they were too expensive, they ate too much fuel, they were beautiful relics of a lost time of excess and machismo.

Had Don Aronow died racing even one day before his murder, he would have gone out a hero. But on the closer scrutiny he got after he was gone, it turned out that what made Aronow great and glamorous were probably the same qualities that led to his premature death.

That is to say, if it *was* a premature death. Aronow might also have been on an inevitable collision course whose day of impact could not be put off much longer.

Did the pleasure machine mutiny and kill its creator?

When Elvis Presley died, songwriter Neil Young suggested in the medium that Presley had entered as a raw talent, then helped to corrupt, "It's better to burn out than to fade away."

1

February 3, 1987, began like most other perfect, warm, and sunny southern Florida winter days.

Don Aronow was less than a month shy of his sixtieth birthday. Nothing seemed to be wrong that morning, his wife, Lillian, said. He got up at seven, called his office, USA Racing Team, at about nine, and talked to his salesman, Jerry Engelman, who later said he reminded Aronow about an eleven o'clock meeting at Financial Federal Savings and Loan, of which Aronow was a member of the Board of Directors.

The bank was run by his friend and fellow boatbuilder Elton Cary. Cary's wife, Frances, shared half the stock with him, but after they divorced, Cary had enlisted Aronow to help him gain voting control of the board. Frances had since taken Cary, Aronow, and others to court, and at that moment the tide was turning in her favor.

After 9:30, Aronow left his house to check on the new Spanish-Mediterranean bay-front mansion on Miami Beach that he and Lillian had bought for $2.1 million and were paying hundreds of thousands of dollars—much of it in cash—to remodel. Built in 1929, the mansion had 9,900 square feet, eleven bedrooms, nine baths, and a private dock with the most stunning view in town—downtown Miami's new postmodern skyscrapers, almost all banks, buffered by miles of shimmering blue water. On both sides of the mansion were estates owned by English disco stars the Bee Gees. Don and Lillian planned to move in once the work was done.

But Mike Kandrovicz, Aronow's longtime jack-of-all-trades, said Aronow got a "threatening" phone call that morning at the new house. He was standing with Aronow when he got it. Aronow got nervous—extremely unusual for him, Kandrovicz said—and wouldn't discuss it.

At 10:30, Aronow called Engelman again and said he was on his way to the bank. Normally, those meetings ended at 1:30.

At almost two o'clock, on his way to his USA Racing Team office, he called his elder son, Michael, and got Michael's wife, Ellen. He was in a good mood, she said. He said he was supposed to have a meeting at the Apache Marina.

At the shop, Patty Lezaca, Aronow's office administrator, said she saw a car with dark-tinted windows drive into the parking lot. Kandrovicz said he saw it, too, and noted that it was black. Minutes later, Aronow arrived, bearing the mail. It was sometime after two o'clock. He went straight to his desk, stopping to berate Engelman about a boat engine order.

Within a few minutes came a foreshadow of what was to happen.

Someone entered the front door and walked in front of Engelman's desk. He was in his thirties, about Aronow's height—which was six feet, three inches—with collar-length, sandy blond hair, a blond moustache and sideburns, wearing a straw-colored hat, a red pull-over shirt, and Bermuda shorts. Nobody in the office had ever seen him before.

Could Lezaca help him? He asked to speak with Don Aronow, then looked right at him without recognizing him.

"What do you want?" Aronow asked.

He wasn't a boat buyer, Engelman could tell; he

looked more like a truck driver. Kandrovicz thought he looked like a bodyguard.

"I've been trying to get ahold of you," the man said. "I've left messages." He said he worked for a very rich man, with an Italian surname, who wanted to make an appointment to buy a boat.

"I never heard of him," Aronow answered.

Engelman could tell something else was happening, and he thought Aronow was trying to find out what the hell the guy was doing there. Then the conversation got weird.

He was proud of his boss, the man said. "He picked me up off the street when I was sixteen and took care of me. I'd even kill for my boss." Then he said his name was Jerry Jacoby.

Everyone in the office knew Jerry Jacoby, but this was not the same man. The Jacoby they knew—who was short—had won powerboat racing's world championship in 1981 and the U.S. championship in 1982. Also in 1982, he had organized a group that purchased Cigarette Racing Team from Aronow, although the deal had since resulted in litigation.

Aronow said he didn't make appointments, but told the man just to bring his boss to the business, and he could be there within ten minutes. Then Aronow asked him for identification.

"Jacoby" reached into his back pocket, stopped, then said he didn't have it with him. He had it in his car, he said, and went outside to find it, then never came back. For the moment, Engelman, Kandrovicz, and Lezaca didn't think anything more of the incident.

Aronow then returned some messages and called his old friend and protégé Bobby Saccenti at Apache Performance Boats to ask when he would pay the $16,000 balance of the $24,000 he owed Aronow for engines he had bought ten months earlier. Aronow told Saccenti he would stop by—diagonally across the street—to see him.

Minutes later, Aronow walked out of the office; then Ben Kramer called for him. Lezaca said he had left for the day.

In the previous year, Ben Kramer—another Aronow protégé—and his dad, Jack, had built Fort Apache Marina, a high-rise boat storage facility with a casual waterfront restaurant and wooden patio bar called Apache Landing, which was popular on weekends. It had brought some classy looks to a street that sold itself as a boulevard of wet dreams but was really just a bunch of gritty plants loud with buzz saws, its air heavy with the smell of lacquer and dusty with airborne fiberglass.

Ten minutes later, Aronow walked back in. He had been talking in the parking lot to Mike Peters, who had just started as a salesman for him the day before. Aronow then wrote down some numbers.

"Ben Kramer just called you," Lezaca told him. "I thought you had left."

"No, I'm leaving now," Aronow responded, not anxious to speak to him, it seemed to her. "I'll see you tomorrow." He added that after seeing Saccenti, he would be going home.

Another ten minutes later, Kramer called again. Lezaca explained what had just happened.

Meanwhile, Aronow drove across the street to Saccenti's shop and walked in back. There, he found Saccenti, Mike Britton—a marine supplier—and George Bacher, a sixty-seven-year-old man who had commissioned Saccenti to build him a boat. Aronow asked Britton if he could help him find a molding for a staircase at his new house and some trim work for one of his boats.

Britton and Aronow then walked to the street, where Aronow had parked his new 1987 white Mercedes 560 sports coupe next to Britton's blue-and-white 1986 Ford pickup. Britton drove out of his parking space forward, and Aronow backed up behind him.

That's when Britton saw a dark Lincoln Town Car with tinted windows, about ten yards away, in front of the construction site on the other side of the road from Apache Boats. It was parked half on the dirt-and-sand shoulder of the narrow street, facing east as Britton was about to head west. The driver's window was down, and Britton could see the driver looking at him.

Britton said the man was tall, in his thirties, had wavy, dark brown hair combed straight back, and was clean-shaven with a day or two's growth of facial hair. He was white but had a tanned complexion, and wore a white shirt.

At their closest, when they passed, they were just a few feet apart, keeping eye contact the entire time. Then Britton drove on to Fort Apache—a total trip of hardly fifty yards from Saccenti's.

Then he heard gunshots.

Britton finished parking his truck, then raced back toward Aronow. In a hurry, the Lincoln passed him, going west. It had turned around.

It was just before 3:30, when some of the boat shops sent their production workers home for the day. People swarmed into the street, as they would have had nothing happened.

By the time Britton got to the car, others had arrived. By happenstance, Bobby Saccenti's personal physician, Dr. Wesley King, was also present. He would have the other onlookers take Aronow out of the car and place him flat on the street; then he would begin CPR.

The car was sitting parallel in front of the painted sign on Saccenti's building that read APACHE. Britton found Aronow's driver's-side window nine-tenths down, the automatic transmission in neutral, and Aronow's foot pressed against the accelerator like a rock, forcing the engine to rev at its most shrill. Apparently, Aronow had stopped for a moment to kibitz with his killer.

3:31 P.M.
Metro-Dade Police Dispatch

Since the shooting had happened in an unincorporated part of Dade County (although its postal address was North Miami Beach), Metro-Dade Police received the 911 call that went out. Dispatch radioed a bulletin of a shooting at 3161 N.E. 188th Street and a BOLO—be on the lookout—for a dark Lincoln Continental that was being pursued by an observer of the shooting, who was driving a black 1986 Toyota pickup truck with the word "Cigarette" on the side.

Since Metro-Dade Police District 6 and a fire station next door were just two miles south, fire rescue and a fire engine arrived in two or three minutes. They found Aronow lying beside his car and began applying life support, including an oxygen mask. Meanwhile, Aronow's blood pooled underneath him, staining the road.

3:35 P.M.

OFFICER OSCAR PLASENCIA

The first police officer arrived. He was Oscar Plasencia, who was cruising on road patrol at about 163rd and Biscayne Boulevard when he heard the dispatch. Immediately, he called for backup.

Onlookers had already begun to gather. Plasencia's first actions were to clear room for the emergency workers, then secure the crime scene area by roping it off with yellow tape.

A minute later, Corporal Tim Williams arrived. As the two men pushed onlookers back, they began to ask around, "Did you see anything?"

George Bacher, who moments before had been talking to Aronow, approached Plasencia. He was holding a coffee-stained styrofoam cup containing six brass-colored spent bullet shells. He said he had heard the shooting and come over to the car. Looking down a few feet south of where Aronow was lying, he said he and Eddie Beato, a twenty-one-year-old Cigarette employee, noticed the shells. Bacher said he collected five of them into the cup using the legs of his eyeglasses so he wouldn't have to touch them with his hands—he said he had learned that from watching *Kojak*. But Beato had picked up one with his hands because he wanted to see what kind they were. The brand was Felco.

Plasencia took the cup and put it in his patrol car. He knew the two men were just trying to help; however, it would have been a bigger favor if they had left the evidence where it was and called an officer over to observe it.

The next witness Plasencia found was Mike Britton. He said he had seen the Lincoln's driver lower his window and fire five rounds into Aronow's Mercedes.

Another witness, twenty-five-year-old Michael Harrison, told Plasencia that he was in his vehicle traveling westbound in front of Aronow's car when he saw a black Lincoln Continental driving eastbound. He got a glimpse of the driver: he was dark complected, with dark, bushy hair and possibly a light beard—or just a couple days of growth.

3:40 P.M.

DETECTIVES GREG SMITH
AND JIM RATCLIFF

The first two homicide detectives on the scene were Greg Smith and Sergeant Jim Ratcliff. When they heard the dispatch call, they happened to be on Miami Gardens Drive—N.E. 186th Street—and N.E. 6th Avenue, on another case. In the few minutes it took them to arrive, a number of other uniformed officers and Northeast district detectives had also gotten there, and the crowd of onlookers had grown to about fifty.

Some of those officers already had blocked off the west end of 188th Street. Since the east end dead-ended into the Intracoastal Waterway, that meant that everyone on the street had to stay put—even though the work day was over.

Ratcliff found Oscar Plasencia, who described what he had learned in the previous ten minutes. Then Ratcliff radioed for a crime lab unit to respond.

Smith surveyed the crime scene. On the ground near the left front fender of the Mercedes he found four white shirt buttons and a lead pencil bearing a small amount of blood. He also wrote down descriptions and license plate numbers of five vehicles parked nearby, all of which turned out to be owned by factory workers.

Then he and Ratcliff began working the crowd to find additional witnesses.

First, Ratcliff found Cigarette Racing Team employee Lynda Kirkland, aged twenty-three, who had called 911, but she hadn't heard the shooting herself.

Next, Ratcliff talked to George Bacher. He said he had talked with Aronow, Britton, and Bobby Saccenti minutes before the shooting. When Aronow and Britton left in their vehicles, Bacher walked into Saccenti's warehouse, and that's when he heard either three or four gunshots.

Bacher said he quickly ran out to the street and saw Aronow slumped over his steering wheel. The Mercedes's passenger-side door was open, and he noticed a bullet hole in it.

4:15 P.M.
Mt. Sinai Medical Center
Miami Beach

Metro-Dade helicopter Air Rescue One arrived with Aronow at Mt. Sinai Medical Center. Lillian Aronow, his wife, had already been called by Patty Lezaca and told to go to the hospital. It was a short ride for Lillian, and she was there when the helicopter touched down.

Chief of emergency medicine Dr. Stuart Lerman immediately began heart massage and other attempts to revive Aronow. He had four gunshot wounds: to the front of the left shoulder, the rear of the left shoulder, his left side underneath the armpit, and his left wrist. Also, he had a graze wound to the right side of the chest, and cuts to the left cheek of his face. There was also extensive internal trauma to his lung and heart, and he had lost a lot of blood. His pulse was being supported artificially.

4:28 P.M.

Dr. Lerman pronounced the victim deceased.

4–5:30 P.M.
Crime Scene

SERGEANT JIM RATCLIFF

Ratcliff interviewed Jesus Haim, aged thirty-four, employed at Apache Boats, who said he heard six gunshots, then ran into the street in time to see a fleeing Lincoln Continental, a newer model, very dark blue or black. But he couldn't tell anything about who or even how many people were in it.

He said when he got to the Mercedes, the driver's window was open but the passenger door was closed.

Haim said he saw the shell casings on the ground, and—contradicting George Bacher—Haim said *he* picked up four of them. He was even able to describe where he had found each: one was directly south of the Mercedes, on the south swale of the street; two were seven feet behind (to the east of) the Mercedes; and one was on the north swale of the street.

Mario Alvarez, aged thirty, another Apache Boats employee who was inside working, said he heard either three or four shots. He said he and three or four other employees raced outside, and he saw a black, four-door Lincoln Continental, new, leaving the area.

Marcus Brown, aged thirty-seven, also working inside Apache Boats, said he heard six gunshots. He was standing next to a large exhaust fan with a louvered window that allowed him to see outside. He said he heard the shots, then immediately looked out the window and saw a black, late-model *Mercedes* sedan with dark-tinted windows approach Aronow's white Mercedes, then drive around it and leave westbound.

Inside the dark car he saw *two* silhouettes but couldn't describe them at all. He insisted that the dark car was either a 300 or 500 series Mercedes, because he owned a similar one.

David Peña, aged twenty-three, a Cigarette Racing Team employee, said he was crossing 188th Street about a hundred yards east of the occurrence when he heard five shots. He immediately looked west and saw Aronow's car, which he recognized.

He then saw a very dark blue or black Continental make a wide U-turn around Aronow's car, then go west-bound. He noticed the hubcaps: they had squared-off rims, as opposed to spokes. He also thought he had seen a sticker on the left side rear bumper of the Lincoln, although he couldn't describe it.

4:30 P.M.

DETECTIVE GREG SMITH

Smith interviewed Mike Britton, aged thirty-three. He said he had known Aronow for about eight years and had come to 188th Street to speak to Bobby Saccenti. He then briefly described what he had seen happen.

4:35 P.M.

DETECTIVE MIKE DeCORA

Mike DeCora had been at the medical examiner's office in downtown Miami when his sergeant, Mike Diaz, found him and assigned him to be lead detective on the case. Within a half hour, he arrived at 188th Street to find chaos, with the challenge of creating order out of it. Either on-scene already, or en route, were ten homicide detectives to conduct interviews or canvass the area, two homicide sergeants, two crime scene technicians, and a Dade County assistant state's attorney, Gary Rosenberg.

5 P.M.

BOLO RESPONSE

While Smith was interviewing Britton, a call came in from North Miami Police. Responding to a revised BOLO for a black Lincoln four-door driven by a white male, at about 4:45 they had spotted a black Lincoln

Town Car with a license tag that had a "Z" in it (which indicated a rented or leased car) driving south on Biscayne Boulevard at about N.E. 110th Street, about five miles from the crime scene. They followed it west for about five minutes until it looked like it might enter an I-95 ramp, then they requested backup officers and stopped it. The driver was a white male.

The driver said he hadn't been anywhere near N.E. 188th Street. He had left the Cricket Club on Biscayne and N.E. 114th Street and was on his way to pick up a friend at federal court in downtown Miami, then take him to Miami International Airport.

Archie Moore and Steve Parr were members of the same homicide team as Mike DeCora, all stationed at police headquarters west of downtown. On their way to the crime scene, DeCora ordered them to stop first at where the Lincoln had been detained. Then DeCora ordered Detective Paul Ohanesian, who was at the scene, to take Britton there.

5 P.M.

DETECTIVE MIKE DeCORA

On the street, DeCora found Patty Lezaca, aged forty-three, Aronow's secretary, who was in a panicky state. She described the Jerry Jacoby incident.

Then DeCora spoke to Ray Garcia, aged thirty-six, who said he had known Aronow for fifteen years, from horse racing. He had last seen Aronow the previous weekend at Hialeah race track, where Aronow had two horse trainers: Newcomb Green and J. R. Garrard. Garcia said Aronow had seemed to be in good spirits.

5:05 P.M.

DETECTIVE GREG SMITH

Smith found Miguel Fernandez, aged fifty-five, a fiberglass worker for Apache Boats, who didn't speak English well. He said he was working inside when he heard what sounded like four gunshots. Immediately, he raced out with three other workers—Jesus Haim, Mario Alvarez, and Marcus Brown—and they all ran to the white Mercedes. Fernandez said he didn't see a car leaving the scene.

5:20 P.M.

Michael Harrison, a stock room manager for Cigarette Racing Team, told Smith he was crossing 188th Street with David Peña—before the shooting—when he looked down the street and noticed both the Lincoln and Aronow's Mercedes in stationary positions. He also looked at his watch; it was 3:25, almost quitting time.

[However, that contradicted what Officer Oscar Plasencia had written down when he had interviewed Harrison. He said Harrison told him he was in his vehicle traveling westbound in front of Aronow's car when he saw a black Lincoln Continental driving eastbound, and that he got a glimpse of the driver.]

While crossing the street, Harrison told Smith, he heard about five gunshots, then saw the Lincoln—now he thought it was a black or dark blue Town Car—continue east, turn around the back of the Mercedes using the swale, and then go west, although not at a particularly high speed.

Harrison described the Lincoln as a four-door with dark-tinted windows. He said he got a glimpse of the license plate: it was a Florida tag with the letter "Z." He saw a bumper sticker, too, but he could only describe it as green, and on the left rear fender.

5:30 P.M.
500 N.W. 95th Street

When Mike Britton arrived at North Miami Police's traffic stop, he said it wasn't the same car; this car had chrome on the bottom of the doors, and wire wheels. Also, the white male didn't match the shooter: his complexion was too light; at five feet, six inches tall and 225 pounds, he was too short and too heavy, and he looked Latin, which was also wrong. Britton said the shooter was tall and slender, had a very high forehead, and his hair was combed back. Further, the man had a moustache and full beard—the most the shooter had was a day or so of growth.

5:30 P.M.
Mt. Sinai Medical Center

By the time Detective Danny Borrego arrived at Mt. Sinai, Lillian Aronow had already left. Borrego spoke with emergency room head nurse Leslie Thompson, who said she gave Mrs. Aronow her husband's wallet, containing $2,000 and credit cards. Then Borrego called DeCora to tell him Aronow was dead.

Borrego then went to see the body, lying on a gurney in the trauma room. Aronow's shirt was off, but he was wearing light gray slacks with a tan belt, light brown deck shoes, and gray Calvin Klein briefs. Borrego reached into Aronow's left rear pants pocket and found a key ring and comb. He wasn't wearing any jewelry.

Borrego took the keys and comb for evidence. He also impounded six tubes of blood the hospital had taken on admission.

5:30 P.M.
Crime Scene

Crime lab technicians Carl Barnett and Kim Haney arrived at the scene.

First, they noted Aronow's personal effects, left in the car: on the passenger seat was a well-worn tan leather portfolio, with a well-thumbed notebook inside; an expandable manila folder, with doodlings scrawled on it;

two copies of the *Daily Racing Form*, one dated February 3, another folded open to a page listing past performances for horses running in the next day's seventh race at Hialeah; unread copies of that day's *New York Times* and *Daily News*; a medium-weight zippered leather jacket, also tan-colored; a brown tweed sportcoat; and a bright red vinyl windbreaker. In the small foot space behind the passenger seat was a green brochure entitled "Financial Federal."

In the pocket area on the driver's-side door was a receipt for the visitors' parking lot at Mt. Sinai Medical Center—ironically, the place where he had just died.

When they opened the glove compartment, out spilled a box of Chooz antacid gum; a package of Mercedes-Benz owner's information; and about twenty (apparently losing) tote tickets from Calder race track, some for $100, some $300, some $600.

Inside the trunk were three boxed bottles of Bacardi silver label rum, two boxed bottles of Seagram's VO whiskey, and a set of orange jumper cables.

Barnett and Haney also attempted to reconstruct the angles at which some of the bullets had been fired.

Since six casing shells had been found, and the emergency room had located four bullets in the body, that left two bullets unaccounted for.

Using colored rods, they showed that one bullet had struck the plastic molding of the driver's-side rearview mirror, cracking it and part of the glass. That same bullet then struck Aronow on the left wrist, which was probably holding onto the steering wheel (possibly hitting his Rolex watch, which wasn't on the body or in evidence at the crime scene), then continued through the passenger-side door and exited. They found that projectile, in pretty good shape, outside the car.

The second missing bullet apparently had grazed Aronow's torso on the right side. It then continued into the backrest of the passenger seat, exited the side of that seat, then hit the passenger door. However, this one didn't have enough energy remaining to pierce metal; on the carpet in front of the passenger side rear seat, they found a deformed bullet.

5:45 P.M.
Mt. Sinai Medical Center

Crime scene investigators Tommy Stoker and Susan Bowman arrived at the hospital to photograph the victim and swab his hands with cotton and alcohol, for evidence.

6 P.M.

LOCAL NEWS

WTVJ Channel 4 had reporter Katrina Daniel live at the scene as dusk set in, but she admitted she didn't have much to say. Bystanders had told her the murder victim was Don Aronow, but police weren't confirming anything. One unidentified person told her he had heard four or five shots; as he pieced it together from what others had told him, a black Lincoln Town Car had pulled up to Aronow's white Mercedes as though to wave him down. That was when he heard the shots.

6:30 P.M.
Crime Scene

DETECTIVE STEVE PARR

When Detective Steve Parr arrived, DeCora asked him to interview Jerry Engelman. Engelman said he had worked for Aronow exactly one year and a day. The first thing he recalled was that on either the previous Friday or Saturday, a woman who said her name was Cynthia Anderson called the office and told him she worked for a wealthy man who wanted to meet Aronow so he could build him a racing boat for pleasure. She wanted to make an appointment for her boss but wouldn't give his name.

Engelman said he told her that Aronow didn't make

appointments; to see him, they should just call before leaving, and he would be there. Engelman said he could tell it was a long-distance call from a phone booth because he heard coins dropped in the phone.

When the man came in who said he was Jerry Jacoby, he said his boss wanted Aronow to build him a sixty-five-foot boat. Engelman replied that Aronow didn't build sixty-five-footers, would the man's boss be interested in a thirty-nine-footer? "Jacoby" answered that he didn't think so; however, his boss still wanted to meet Aronow. Could they make an appointment? Engelman told "Jacoby" what he had told Cynthia Anderson; have his boss call first, then come, and Aronow would meet him.

Responding to Parr's questions, Engelman said "Jacoby" might have mentioned his boss's name, but he couldn't remember it. The man was in the office for about fifteen minutes but didn't touch anything, nor did Engelman see his vehicle.

Parr asked to look at Aronow's telephone message pad and found something intriguing. On January 21, he had gotten a message from Jerry Jacoby, but with no return phone number.

6:40 P.M.

MIKE BRITTON
SWORN STATEMENT

Detectives Moore and Ohanesian took Britton to the nearby Metro-Dade Police substation. On tape, Britton contradicted himself on two major points from what he had told Officer Plasencia three hours earlier.

Britton had previously said that he had seen the Lincoln's driver lower his window and fire five rounds into Aronow's Mercedes.

Now he said, "I think I heard three shots. It could have been less or it could have been more, but for some reason I'm picking the number three. It just seems like there were three shots."

He also added that he hadn't seen the shooting himself; someone named Mike who worked for Cigarette saw it and told him what had happened. That described Mike Harrison, who hadn't mentioned that to Greg Smith.

"They saw this Lincoln Continental pull up alongside of Mr. Aronow's car. They saw a hand come out with a gun, fire into the vehicle proceeding then east, and going around the back of Mr. Aronow's car, turning north onto the grass and then heading west."

Britton said he had passed the Lincoln before the shooting and looked at its driver. Moore inquired if he saw anyone else inside.

"To my best knowledge, the car was empty other than the one occupant."

"Can you identify this person if you saw a picture or possibly a live lineup?"

"I honestly don't know, you know, it's very hard."

7:55 P.M.

JESUS HAIM
SWORN STATEMENT

Haim said he had heard either four or five shots. [Hours earlier, he had said he heard six.] "We took it for granted it was nothing, but we walked out anyway because we still heard an accelerating noise," he said. The "we" included Marcus Brown, Miguel Fernandez, and Mario Alvarez.

Haim said he first saw what he thought was a Lincoln passing Aronow's Mercedes on the passenger side, traveling west. All of them walked out to the car and found Aronow still conscious; then Haim ran back inside Apache Boats to call for rescue.

8:05 P.M.

MARIO ALVAREZ
SWORN STATEMENT

Alvarez said he heard either three or four gunshots. When he and his coworkers walked outside, they were "kidding around"; then they saw the black Lincoln go by. He said he couldn't see inside it.

Alvarez went back inside the shop to finish what he was doing, then "I heard a car going up in RPMs, and it was winding a lot." That's when he went to the white Mercedes and saw Aronow bleeding.

8:14 P.M.

MARCUS BROWN
SWORN STATEMENT

Brown was the closest of the fiberglass workers to the street. Instantly after hearing the shots, he looked through the ventilation window. The action happened just in front of him.

He said he heard six shots. "There were two shots, a short pause, and then four shots in rapid succession.

"I saw a white Mercedes-Benz coupe stopped in the street, just to the east of the driveway of Apache Boats, and I saw a black, late model Mercedes-Benz [which everyone else had identified as some sort of Lincoln] approach the rear of the white Mercedes and pull around it.

"It seemed to be just beginning to accelerate, but it accelerated rapidly as it went around the vehicle and then it went out of my field of vision. And I ran to the doorway of the glass shop, which has a large overhead door that goes out to the parking lot, to see what had happened." That parking lot was at the west edge of the building and led into the street.

"Did you see the occupants of that black vehicle?" Ratcliff asked.

"I saw two silhouettes," Brown said. But he couldn't

describe them at all, not even whether they were men or women.

"I ran to [Aronow's] vehicle. Before I reached the vehicle, someone reached in and turned off the ignition switch as the car was revving up because it was in neutral and the victim's foot evidently was jammed against the accelerator. Then, I believe, Jesus and Mario ran away from the car to go to inform somebody to call the police as quickly as possible. And I went to the victim's assistance. I raised his head up and felt his carotid artery to see if there was a pulse and I saw that he wasn't breathing normally. So I held his head up and depressed his tongue with my fingers.

"I spoke to him a couple of times. I encouraged him to breathe, and he responded. The guy was tough. I told him, 'Take a breath. Take a breath.' And I could tell it was a tremendous effort for him, and he did."

"Did the victim say anything to you at all?"

"No, he made a couple of sounds, like he was going to say something, but what he articulated was really unintelligible."

8:30 P.M.

GEORGE BACHER
SWORN STATEMENT

Bacher remembered nothing unusual about his last conversation with Aronow. In fact, they had kidded around.

Bacher then walked back into Apache's shop area to look at his boat, talked for a moment to a worker, walked away, and then heard shots. He thought it couldn't have been much more than a minute after he said "So long" to Aronow.

"It seemed like the first two were real quick, 'bang, bang' and then a split second or something, and then two, three or four more," he said.

[Earlier he had told Sergeant Ratcliff he had heard only three or four shots, total.]

Bacher then ran to the car, but Marcus Brown had gotten there first. Bacher opened the Mercedes passenger door so Aronow could get more air.

[That also contradicted what Ratcliff had written down earlier. Bacher had said that when he approached the Mercedes, the passenger door was open.]

"I saw shells lying on the street pavement, and I asked for people not to touch them. Jesus and Mario and I asked [someone around them] to get a piece of paper. We picked them up with the earpiece of my glasses, and Mario used a pen, and we got five or six shells and I gave them to a police officer," he said.

10:30 P.M.
Crime Scene

MIKE DeCORA

Still at the crime scene, Mike DeCora asked six detectives to canvass shopping centers near the scene to look for a dark-colored Lincoln with tinted windows and a green sticker on the left rear bumper. In addition, he asked that security patrols at the parking lots of both Miami and Fort Lauderdale airports also be alerted to look for the car.

Further, DeCora asked detectives to check Biscayne Boulevard from downtown north to the nearby Broward County line, and all of Collins Avenue, on Miami Beach. While cruising Biscayne Boulevard southbound in North Dade, Detective Borrego spotted a Lincoln that matched the description, except for the lack of a green bumper sticker. When he checked its tag number, he found it was a 1985 Town Car, titled to Ford Motor Credit Company. He made a note of it, but didn't stop it.

10:30 P.M.
Metro-Dade Police Headquarters

MICHAEL ARONOW

Mike Aronow, the victim's eldest son at thirty-seven, had learned of his father's murder earlier in the day when Patty Lezaca called him at his home on Long Island, New York. He immediately flew to Miami, and when he got there, he called the Metro-Dade Police homicide department, hoping to learn more.

Detective David Kosloske took the call and asked him to come to their offices.

When he arrived, with Elton Cary, Detective Sheldon Merritt interviewed Aronow, and Kosloske took Cary.

Mike was in a wheelchair. He explained that he had lost the use of his legs in a traffic accident while attending the University of Florida in the early '70s.

Since then, he said, he and his father had gotten involved in horse racing. Mike owned two horses himself and trained them at Belmont Park, in New York. But his father owned more than a hundred horses at a farm called Aronow Stables, in Ocala, Florida, and he frequently raced them at south Florida's three tracks: Calder, Hialeah, and Gulfstream. He was also a heavy gambler, usually betting $500 any time he'd place a bet. Often he used bookies; he'd give the bet to his confidant, Norman Moffett, who would contact the bookies for him.

In fact, earlier that day, in the third race at Hialeah, his father had probably made a big score, he said. A horse trained by Moffett had won, paying 33-to-1. Mike had also placed a winning bet on it.

[The horse's name was Lu Chano, and at Hialeah's windows it paid $44.60 to win, crossing the finish line two and a half lengths in front. (Perhaps Mike had gotten 33 to 1 from a bookmaker.) The morning line in the newspaper had been 8 to 1, but at post time, it was 21 to 1, the third-longest shot in a claiming race for maidens—horses that had never won before. The race went off at about two o'clock, an hour and a half before the murder.]

Merritt asked if Mike knew any other of his father's associates, and he answered Hal Halter, from New Orleans, who owned Halter Marine. Mike said his father had recently bought two very large boats from Halter for more than $100,000 each, which he planned to resell to a waiting buyer. But then the customer backed out of the deal, leaving Aronow holding the merchandise and upset. However, there was no way Halter could have been involved in his father's murder, he said.

Then Merritt pursued the *femme fatale* angle. Mike said his father had fooled around a little with an old girlfriend named Missy Holiday who lived at Turnberry Isle, an exclusive development minutes away by boat from 188th Street.

Mike said his father had dated Missy in the late '70s and early '80s, but they had since broken up. During that time, he married Lillian Crawford, who had recently inherited a million dollars of her own money. Mike didn't feel that Lillian could have had anything to do with his father's murder, either.

Mike said his father had seemed upset over something in the previous week or two, but he didn't know why. Earlier that day, he had told Mike's wife, Ellen, that he was supposed to have a meeting across the street at [Fort] Apache Marina, but Mike didn't know what for.

Merritt asked Mike if he felt [Fort] Apache Marina was somehow involved in the murder. To that, Mike answered strongly, yes.

But when Mike detailed Apache's corporate history, as he knew it, he got very confused. He said his father had owned Apache and sold it to Bobby Saccenti, who had once worked for him as a carpenter.

[The real story was that Saccenti owned Apache Performance Boats, but not Fort Apache Marina. Further, although Don Aronow had once owned the land on which both Apache Performance Boats and Fort Apache Marina stood, he had never owned any part of anything called Apache, of which—more confusingly—there was even a third separate entity, Apache Powerboats, in Hollywood.

That and Fort Apache Marina were both owned by Ben and Jack Kramer.]

Then Mike said Apache had changed hands back and forth several times between his father and other owners due to financial problems brought on by Saccenti. [That part was true, with two corrections: Mike was talking about Cigarette Racing Team, a company that *had* been started by his father, not Apache; and therefore it had nothing to do with Saccenti.] Mike said he had last heard that Apache [read: Cigarette] was since doing better because financiers from Cleveland had taken over.

Then Mike added that Ben Kramer, the principal owner of [Fort] Apache [Marina], was a small-time organized crime member.

Mike said his father had owned a number of boat companies—perhaps that warranted his confusion—but at the time of his death, he had only one, USA Racing Team. He estimated his father's net worth at $18–25 million.

Before ending the interview, Mike said he had been told that two separate people had called Mt. Sinai Hospital's emergency room wanting to know if his father was dead. Merritt answered that those callers might have been homicide detectives; however, he couldn't say for sure.

ELTON CARY

Meanwhile, Kosloske had been interviewing Elton Cary. He said he was a close friend of both Don and Lillian, had known Don since 1959, and had been a fellow boatbuilder until 1973. They talked two to three times a week and met once a week. Aronow was a member of the board of directors of two of Cary's companies: Financial Federal and General Insurance Corporation. Although Aronow had attended the weekly Financial Federal board meeting earlier in the day, that was unusual for him, he said.

11 P.M.

LOCAL NEWS

"Good evening. Who killed multimillionaire sportsman and powerboat designer Don Aronow?" asked Susan Lichtman of WTVJ Channel 4. The station reported that police had finally confirmed later in the evening that it was Aronow who was the victim, long after the station had gotten the same information from Mt. Sinai Hospital.

Still on the scene, Katrina Daniel reported bystanders saying that Aronow's car had been ambushed by one or two men in a black Lincoln. They also interviewed boat salesman Richard Conti, who said he heard five rounds from a .45. "I shoot guns; I know the sound of a .45-caliber pistol," he said.

Ray Garcia, interviewed earlier by the police, said, "He was a friend to everybody. I don't know anyone who would speak bad of him or had anything bad to say about him."

WCIX Channel 6 reported that the murder weapon might have been a machine gun. They also interviewed Aronow's friend Don Soffer, developer of Turnberry Isle, who described Aronow as "smart, charming, handsome, tough as nails, and liked by everyone he came in touch with.

"I guess when you're too much of a person, people get envious, and that's why these things happen," he said.

WSVN Channel 7's Michael Williams reminded viewers that Aronow's boats had become popular with drug smugglers, but "in recent years, Aronow tried to help turn the tide on them by building highly powerful catamarans for the U.S. Customs Service."

"He's bigger than life in the sense that when you talk about these boats, this sport, he is it," said Jay Busciglio.

"Don was the granddaddy of powerboat racing. We all held him in very, very high esteem," said Vic Spellberg.

11 P.M.
1717 North View Drive
Miami Beach

LILLIAN ARONOW

When DeCora and Steve Parr finally left the crime scene, they went to see Lillian Aronow at her home. Also there were Don's two other children from his previous marriage, twenty-eight-year-old David and thirty-four-year-old Claudia, who had both just arrived from the New York area.

DeCora asked that they speak to each of the family members alone. Lillian, aged thirty-six, invited the detectives into her living room. She said she and Don had been married eight years; before that, he had been married thirty years to Shirley, his first wife. They had lived together in Coral Gables, but now she lived out of town.

Lillian told them that for the previous month, they had gotten eight to ten hang-up calls a day, at all hours of the day and night—even more within the past two weeks. Something else disturbing her was that a man had called the hospital while she was there, asking if Don was alive or dead.

DeCora asked if her husband was much of a socializer. No, she said, he usually stayed home. Asked to list his closest friends, she named Dr. Bob Magoon, Elton Cary, and Jerry Jacoby.

DeCora also asked if she had any idea who was behind the murder. She named Ben Kramer. It was just a gut feeling, she said; she couldn't prove it, mainly because Don had kept her away from all his business matters, but she just didn't like him.

DAVID ARONOW

DeCora then turned to David Aronow. He said he was living in Lakewood, New Jersey, and owned a construction company that built houses. His father had helped him get started in the business, but about seven years before, they had fought, and David moved away. However, he said, in the last two years they had begun speaking and become close again.

David volunteered that his father had a reputation as a ladies' man, and as far as he knew, it was true. He had had affairs with women while he was still married to David's mother. After they were divorced, his father even bragged to him about the various women he was seeing. But he knew of no problems between Lillian and Shirley, nor was there any friction between himself and Lillian.

DeCora asked David if he knew any reason why his father might have been murdered, or by who. He didn't know, he said.

CLAUDIA ARONOW CAMPBELL

Claudia lived in New York City. She said the last time she had talked to her father was a week prior, when she was making plans for her son's bar mitzvah. She said that the last time she had been in Miami, within the last few months, she had stayed with her dad and Lillian and seen no problems.

But her father did have a reputation for having affairs, although she didn't know of any at present. She told DeCora that people were very jealous of his lifestyle and business sense, and that he had seemed to be intrigued with underworld-type people. He liked living on the edge, cheating death, she said. But she had no idea of who specifically would have murdered him.

2 A.M.
(FEBRUARY 4)
Alexander Hotel, Miami Beach

MICHAEL AND DAVID ARONOW

At two in the morning, Mike called Detective Merritt back and asked him to come to his hotel room to talk further. Merritt and Steve Parr came.

Mike was there with his brother, David. He wanted to

talk more about Apache and a specific transaction between them and his father.

Mike did most of the talking. He said that people in Apache were definitely involved in narcotics smuggling. One of the times Apache had bought back the marina from his father [again, Mike was vague or confused on the actual transaction, as well as which Apache entity], Apache paid in cash that smelled of marijuana and had sand on it.

Mike described the deal; approximately a million dollars in cash had passed under the table. He didn't know what his father had done with the cash, nor whether he had had any numbered bank accounts.

He wasn't sure if it was Apache or his father, but someone hadn't made out as they had expected in the transaction, and hard feelings over money had followed.

2

The lead banner headline in the morning *Miami Herald* was BOAT-RACING LEGEND ARONOW SHOT TO DEATH.

"Offshore powerboat pioneer Don Aronow, a legend of speed at sea, was murdered Tuesday on a North Dade street lined with boat-manufacturing companies he founded."

The story quoted Patty Lezaca, Aronow's secretary:

"I've been with him so long, I'd know if there were any problems. . . . To me, Mr. Aronow had a good heart. I can't say anything bad about him. He had no enemies."

Mike Thaler, who told the *Herald* he used to do odd jobs around Aronow's boat shops, said, "You can't say 'powerboats' without using his name. He is the one who started it all. He is powerboat-racing."

A spokeswoman for the U.S. Attorney's Office in Miami, Ana Barnett, said, "It sure sounds like a hit to me."

The banner headline of the newsstand edition of the afternoon *Miami News* read VICE PRESIDENT, MECHANICS GRIEVE FOR ARONOW. It reported that Vice President George Bush was a speedboat-racing fan who knew Aronow personally.

" 'The vice president contacted Aronow's wife and expressed his and Barbara's sympathies,' Bush's press spokesman Steve Hirt told *The Miami News* last night. 'He was concerned over the tragic and violent death and expressed his hope that those responsible would be brought to justice quickly.' "

Later that day, the final home edition headlined DE-TECTIVE CALLS ARONOW KILLING GANG-STYLE 'HIT'.

"The killing of Don Aronow is being described by one [unnamed] police detective as being characteristic of a gangland-style murder, but friends of the offshore powerboat magnate say they are baffled about any possible motive."

Since Aronow had built and sold Cigarette-style fast boats that smugglers used, as well as Blue Thunder catamarans for U.S. Customs to catch those Cigarettes, the *News* asked whether the U.S. Attorney was investigating Aronow or whether he had been an informant for any government agency.

Ana Barnett said he hadn't been under investigation, nor was he an informant, as far as she knew. Clifton Stallings, a U.S. Customs spokesman, answered a firm no to both questions. Barnett said that when Customs contracted for drug interdiction boats, they would have been very reluctant to deal with anyone under that kind of suspicion.

It was a quirk that just two hours before the shooting, *Miami News* reporter Jim Steinberg had talked to Aronow briefly by telephone for an upcoming business section article about the local boating industry, in advance of the forty-sixth annual Miami International Boat Show.

Steinberg was quoted in the main story that Aronow had given him no indication he knew his life was in danger. He was "jovial and ebullient," and talked about building new styles of boats and getting back into racing.

Steinberg also wrote a sidebar story illustrated by a posed shot of Aronow taken the previous Friday afternoon for the business section. He stood on N.E. 188th Street, arms folded; the frame also revealed the spot in the distance where, in a few days, he would be murdered.

"Just hours before offshore powerboat-racing champion and boat designer Don Aronow was gunned down, he answered his last questions from a reporter.

"Asked by *The Miami News* about 2 P.M. yesterday

whether drug smugglers had ever tried to buy one of his famous high-speed boats, Aronow replied, 'I suppose they have. It's hard to tell . . . you can have your suspicions . . . My business is with law enforcement.' "

Aronow said that of the twenty $150,000 Blue Thunders he had sold the previous year, U.S. Customs had bought thirteen. "He then quipped, 'So they could catch smugglers using boats my other companies have made.'

"Aronow planned to come back into competition this summer, [boat-racing promoter and former Aronow public relations man John] Crouse said, and enter the grueling 362-mile Miami-Nassau-Miami Searace when a contract prohibiting competition with Cigarette expired.

"Time and again over the past twenty years, Aronow would found a company, develop a racing boat, build the company's reputation by winning races, and then sell the company.

" 'Finally they (the buyers) got smart and started putting non-compete clauses in the purchase contracts,' Crouse said.

"[F.M. "Ted"] Theodoli [owner of Magnum Marine] said Aronow's macho style made him 'a lot of friends and a lot of people who didn't particularly care for him.

" 'I found him to be a difficult person to deal with,' Theodoli said.

"Aronow had told several people that he would buy Magnum back from Theodoli at 'ten cents on the dollar,' Theodoli said, adding that Aronow seemed to resent the company's success since he sold it."

6:25 A.M.
Miami Beach Police Department

Officer John Murphy, working the midnight shift, got an anonymous 911 call from someone who lived in an apartment on Collins Avenue in south Miami Beach and said that Don Aronow had been having an affair with Ilene Taylor, who was married to a Miami criminal defense attorney named Skip Taylor. The caller said Mr. Taylor had found out about the affair only within the last couple of weeks, and it had prompted a confrontation between him and Aronow at either Calder or Hialeah race track. An hour and a half later, Murphy called Metro-Dade Police homicide and told this to Greg Smith.

7:30 A.M.
Metro-Dade Police Homicide Unit

First thing in the morning, Sergeant Mike Diaz asked Greg Smith to contact John Valor, a sketch artist for City of Miami Police, who could sit with the witnesses and draw composites of the suspect. Diaz wanted him to meet with Mike Britton, and also Patty Lezaca and Jerry Engelman, on the assumption that ''Jerry Jacoby'' and the murderer were the same man.

9 A.M.

Smith picked up John Valor at the Miami Police Department and took him to Mike Britton's workplace in Pembroke Park, which was just across the county line in Broward County.

MORNING
Dade County Medical Examiner's Office

With Mike DeCora present, Assistant Dade County Medical Examiner Dr. Charles Wetli did the autopsy and classified Aronow's death as a homicide.

Afterward, DeCora called the Metro-Dade Police aviation unit and asked them to fly a helicopter over the general area of the crime scene to see if they could spot the dark Lincoln. The results were negative.

11:50 A.M.
USA Racing Team

After Valor had finished working with Britton, Smith took him to the USA Racing Team office on N.E. 188th Street to meet Lezaca and Engelman. Valor worked separately with each, nor did he allow them to see the sketches he had already made.

12 NOON
N.E. 188th Street

BOBBY SACCENTI

A number of detectives were assigned to canvass the businesses on N.E. 188th Street.

Danny Borrego interviewed Bobby Saccenti, the owner of Apache Performance Boats. Saccenti said he had known Aronow since 1968, and, further, Aronow had gotten him started in the boat business. They had since stayed close friends.

Saccenti had been severely injured in a boating accident within the previous six months, and since then Aronow had usually visited him once a week in the afternoon. On Tuesday afternoon, about five minutes after he, Aronow, George Bacher, and Mike Britton had finished talking, someone told him there had been a shooting. He ran into the street and helped those who were giving Aronow CPR until fire rescue arrived. He wasn't a witness to the shooting, he said, and couldn't provide any investigative leads.

ANTHONY ROBERTS

Detective Jerry Crawford spoke to Anthony Roberts, owner of Mer-Cougar Marine. He hadn't witnessed the shooting, but he had an opinion on why it happened; it wasn't over a drug deal, he said.

True, the drug trade was moving into the boat industry, but Aronow had been upset over the bad image it projected. Aronow was a self-made millionaire, successful at everything he did, and didn't need to make money from drugs.

There must have been a business angle involved, he said. Whenever Aronow would sell one of his businesses, he always held back the mortgage. He was a very stern businessman; no matter what would occur, he would hold you to the original terms agreed upon even if it ruined you financially. It was nothing personal with Aronow; that was just the way he did business. Roberts then added that his dealings with Aronow had been mutually beneficial.

TED THEODOLI

Filippo "Ted" Theodoli, owner of Magnum Marine, told Detective Rex Remley that he had gotten a call from a customer in Bahrain telling him that someone at Cigarette said Aronow had just been shot. The caller wanted Theodoli to find out more.

Theodoli knew that Aronow had upset a number of people because of the shrewd way he did business, but he had never heard of any of those disagreements turning physical, nor did he think Aronow had any involvement in the drug trade.

PATTY LEZACA

Detective Archie Moore's assignment was to interview Patty Lezaca, Aronow's personal secretary and office manager.

Lezaca was still upset from the day before. First she gave Moore a brief history of Aronow's boatbuilding holdings. Before she came to work for him, in 1971, he had created and then sold Formula, Donzi, and Magnum, all well-known names in the boating industry. In 1971, he had owned Cigarette Racing Team, and in 1973 he repurchased Magnum, then sold it again in 1974 to Ted Theodoli.

Aronow kept Cigarette until 1978, when he sold it to

Halter Marine. Lezaca stayed with Cigarette and worked for Halter until 1981, when Aronow bought it back. Then, in 1982, he sold Cigarette again, this time to a New York investment group.

In 1983, Aronow started two new companies. He kept Squadron XII for only a few months, then sold it. Next he started USA Racing Team, which built catamarans—twin-hulled racing boats. In 1985, he won a contract to build thirteen 39-foot catamarans for U.S. Customs, which they named "Blue Thunder," at a cost of $142,000 apiece. He built one boat in 1985, then twelve in 1986 at the rate of two per month.

But by then, she said, Aronow wanted to get out of the catamaran business. The public wasn't interested in cats; aside from fulfilling the Customs contract, Aronow had sold only a few. So he sold USA Racing Team to Jack and Ben Kramer, who owned Fort Apache Marina.

When the Kramers took over USA Racing, Lezaca stayed and worked for them. But only a few months later, the Kramers sold it back to Aronow; once Customs had learned that the Kramers owned the company, they threatened to back out of their contract.

Lezaca said Kramer and Aronow were not close friends and were, in fact, competitors.

Aronow didn't spend much time at the office, she said. Sometimes he would be away for two or three days at a time. He spent most of his time at Calder or at the new house he was refurbishing. When he was at the office, he didn't keep a rigid schedule; he usually arrived at ten or eleven in the morning, and left by two.

When Moore asked Lezaca if she had any idea why someone would murder Aronow, she answered that some people might have disliked him because he was shrewd in business, but she couldn't think of anyone specifically who would want to kill him. Nor did he have any disgruntled employees, past or present. When Moore asked if Aronow was involved in the illegal drug business, she professed that he wasn't, to the best she knew. He was very much against drugs and didn't let any of his employees use or possess them on the premises.

BOBBY RALPH

Canvassing Cigarette Racing Team, Detective David Kosloske found Bobby Ralph, aged thirty-six, a Cigarette employee. He said he had first noticed a dark blue Lincoln Town Car with tinted windows and chromed doors at about three o'clock the day before, in the area of Biscayne Boulevard and 203rd Street, while he was driving the company truck back to the plant. At one point, when both vehicles had stopped at a traffic light, the driver's window of the Lincoln was partially down, and Ralph observed the driver.

He was in his late thirties to early forties with somewhat of a salt-and-pepper moustache that extended out from the corners of his mouth, he said. His hair was lighter in color, salt-and-pepper or grayish, combed back and neatly trimmed.

Turning off Biscayne Boulevard, then winding through the back roads on to 188th Street, Ralph noticed that the Lincoln was still behind him. When he turned into the Cigarette parking lot, then the Lincoln continued east.

Several minutes later, Ralph walked south across 188th Street and saw the Lincoln parked about 100 to 150 feet west, on the north side of the street. Then, when Ralph walked back just moments later, he saw that the Lincoln had changed spots; now it was parked on the south side of the street, facing east.

1:30 P.M.
5800 N. Bay Road
Miami Beach

Fifty-eight hundred N. Bay Road, the house that Aronow had planned to move into, was one of the most glittering pieces of real estate on Millionaire's Row, the best street in Miami Beach.

Detective Steve Parr wanted to know whether there had been any problems with the workmen or subcontractors. When he arrived, he found Wendel Reis, in charge of the remodeling. He said there hadn't been.

Reis said Aronow was at the house at 10:30 the morning before. The phone had rung, and Reis answered it; it was Norman Moffett asking to speak to Aronow. Aronow took the call and didn't seem upset.

Later, between 3:15 and 3:30, Reis said Aronow called and told him he would be at the house by about five o'clock.

Calder Race Track

Next, Parr headed for Calder race track to look for Moffett, one of Aronow's horse trainers. Parr couldn't find him, but he did talk to Bobby Garrard, another trainer who worked for Aronow. Garrard said he didn't know anything about Aronow's personal life outside of the track. He had last seen him Sunday, at Calder, and he hadn't mentioned any problems.

AFTERNOON
Metro-Dade Police Substation
South Dade

Two men who wanted to stay anonymous had come to the Metro-Dade Police substation in Cutler Ridge, in the south part of the county, volunteering information about the murder. Officers there called the homicide unit, and the informants waited for Mike DeCora to arrive from downtown Miami.

DeCora thought they looked like Lenny and Squiggy, the pair of not-so-tough greasers from the TV show *Laverne and Shirley*. They told him they knew five people believed to be involved in drugs who might have had a connection to Aronow.

First they named "John," whom they described as: white, about thirty-five or forty, six-feet-two-inches with a muscular but slender build, deeply tanned, wavy-to-curly dirty blond hair combed straight back, which almost reached to his shirt collar and revealed a high forehead. In addition, he normally wore one to two day's growth of beard.

That was very close to the descriptions of the suspect that witnesses had given police the day before.

The men also described the other four in the organization the best they could. There was a woman who they believed had partied on Aronow's boat in April 1986, during an offshore powerboat race in the Florida Keys, and three other men they described.

The sources told DeCora they didn't think Aronow had been hands-on in the drug business, but they thought he might have laundered money or customized boats for smugglers. Since police had seized a lot of drug shipments lately, they suggested that the group might have blamed Aronow for their losses.

Also, they said that "John" and one of the others had had a conversation about Aronow on the Friday or Saturday before the murder. They had seen "John" last on the morning of the murder.

When the interview ended, DeCora watched "Lenny and Squiggy" leave so he could copy down their license plate. But instead, they left on foot. They had told DeCora that "John" lived near an intersection in South Dade, but when DeCora went there, he couldn't find the house.

(Later, when DeCora ran criminal checks on all the names, he found that "John" had a record in Dade County, but he couldn't find anything on the others.)

PRESS CONFERENCE

Late that afternoon, Metro-Dade Police held a press conference to ask the public for help. They passed out Mike Britton's police sketch of the killer and asked all local media to highlight it.

That evening, WSVN Channel 7 aired the picture and a clip of the press conference.

Police spokesman Commander Bill Johnson: "Based on Mr. Aronow's prominence and the number of business contacts that he has, and the fact that they stretch literally around the world, the potential is for a very complicated investigation.''

''While police scramble for clues, Aronow's friends struggle to cope today with the sudden loss of a man they saw as larger than life,'' reported Michael Williams.

''What Aronow's stunned friends cannot imagine is that the man they loved also had an enemy, or enemies, who, at least at this early stage of the police investigation, are proving to be an elusive quarry.''

3

___

Thursday morning, *The Miami Herald* began their lead local page story WHO KILLED BOAT RACER DON ARONOW?

A reporter had asked Commander Bill Johnson at the press conference whether police thought Aronow knew the driver of the Lincoln.

"It's possible that he did and possible that he didn't, and right now, we have a lot more questions than answers," Johnson replied.

"On Northeast 188th Street, friends say, it was entirely in character for [Aronow] to stop his car in response to a signal from another driver—assuming it was someone he had met once, or an old friend in an unfamiliar car, possibly a stranger asking directions.

"Not someone who was about to murder him."

The *Hollywood Sun-Tattler* quoted Johnson further: "We will start with the simplest solution first. That there is some local person in the boatyard who became involved in an argument with him and shot him."

Johnson said certain details of the murder investigation would be kept away from the public, including the type of weapon used, the number of shots fired, and the number of times Aronow was hit.

Also that morning, the story made *The New York Times*. They reported that a spokesman for the Miami office of the U.S. Drug Enforcement Administration described the murder as a " 'typical hit' carried out by 'Colombian drug traffickers.' "

The spokesman, Billy Yout, said, "In ninety percent of similar killings, Colombian drug dealers were found to be involved."

However, the Fort Lauderdale *Sun-Sentinel*'s story rebutted that. They quoted Aronow's friend John Crouse: "Don would never sell to anybody he knew to be involved in drugs."

The *Sun-Sentinel* also reported that Aronow's family received condolences from King Juan Carlos of Spain and King Hussein of Jordan, as well as Vice President George Bush.

While the rest of the reporters in town filled their stories with the press conference, reporters for the afternoon *Miami News* searched Dade County courthouse public records and found three cases concerning Aronow that had been filed in the previous year.

The first, in June 1986, was Frances Wolfson's allegation that Aronow had conspired with her ex-husband, Elton Cary, to defraud General Insurance Corporation, which she had financed.

Then, on July 9, Cigarette Racing Team sued him for helping design a boat for Hollywood-based Apache Powerboats—owned by Jack Kramer. That was allegedly in violation of the five-year non-compete agreement Aronow had signed when he sold Cigarette in 1982, for $5.05 million.

That was odd; Patty Lezaca had said Aronow and Apache were competitors, but Cigarette's suit called them collaborators—against Cigarette.

Attached to the suit was a copy of an advertisement for a $250,000 Apache boat, "a race breed descendant from the legendary stables of Don Aronow, the industry's trendsetter for the past twenty years," it read.

However, the suit had been settled December 1, just

two months before the murder. Records didn't specify for how much, and reporters were unable to contact the attorneys for either side.

In a third case, Aronow was the plaintiff. On December 9, he had sued Prudential-Bache Securities for $180,000 in a dispute over $1 million of investment bonds.

Digging further, the reporters found that Aronow had divorced his first wife, Shirley, in 1978, then married Lillian Crawford in January 1979. He was also an officer in eight firms when he died, including General Insurance Co., Financialfed Services, Aronow Stables, and USA Racing Team, Inc.

LILLIAN AND MICHAEL ARONOW

Lillian hired the Miami private detective firm of Riley & Black, which encouraged her to offer a $100,000 reward for information leading to the arrest of a suspect. Claimants to the reward were to call Crimestoppers or the Metro-Dade homicide bureau. The private detectives also advised that she hire bodyguards for herself and Michael, concerned that they also might be murder targets.

Homicide Bureau

In the morning, crime lab reports were ready. They were mostly bad news; no fingerprints could be developed from any of the evidence submitted by the crime scene technicians.

The firearms section at least had something. Every weapon leaves its individual "fingerprint" on bullets fired from it; those marks are called "lands" and "grooves". In this case, the crime lab didn't have the gun, but they did have six bullets, which were in fact .45 caliber, removed from either Aronow or the Mercedes. With both gun and bullets, they would have tried to match them; however, even with just the bullets, they could still determine that it was either a Star, Llama, or

Astra—all considered off-brands—.45-caliber semiautomatic pistol that had fired them. If it was a standard model, it held six rounds, plus one in the chamber.

Greg Smith called around to find out which rental car agencies used green bumper stickers on their cars. He came up with three: National, Snappy, and Enterprise. He then learned that Snappy agencies from Miami to Fort Lauderdale rented only Lincoln Town Cars that were pastel-colored. Enterprise didn't rent Lincoln Town Cars at all.

That left National. Smith asked a representative there to research the contracts of all their black or dark blue Town Cars unaccounted for on February 3. The representative offered to compile a list of all those cars rented between Miami and Orlando, two hundred miles north.

In addition, David Kosloske called Ford Motor Company in Detroit to get ownership lists of all the four-door Lincoln Town Cars sold in south Florida during the model years 1985 through 1987.

As a result of police's request for assistance through the media for assistance from the public, and Lillian's offer of a huge reward, detectives were deluged with promising leads, vague dead ends, and even some nuttiness.

First, Metro-Dade organized-crime detectives Bill Bailey and Wayne Adams called Mike DeCora. In the '70s, they had investigated gambling and knew that Aronow had been suspected of being an on-track bettor with various bookmakers. In 1974, he had been seen with an on-track bookie; further, in 1976, Aronow had testified to a state grand jury investigating on-track bookmaking.

They also knew that Aronow had testified to another grand jury, in Virginia, just eighteen months before his murder.

DeCora followed up: an investigator for the Virginia State Police confirmed Aronow's appearance before a federal grand jury and told DeCora that it was a drug-dealing case concerning a man named Jerry Kilpatrick. Aronow's testimony had been limited to a land purchase

Kilpatrick had made from Aronow. Kilpatrick was later convicted and sentenced to eighteen years. The investigator believed that Aronow and Kilpatrick had had a good relationship before his testimony, and Kilpatrick held no grudge after. Kilpatrick was currently in federal prison in Danbury, Connecticut, he said.

Next was an anonymous call to Crimestoppers: a woman said her thirty-five-year-old ex-boyfriend looked like the composite drawing released to the press. He was six-feet-two-inches, 200 pounds, with dark, wavy, almost curly hair, and he usually had two to three days' worth of beard, and a moustache. He drove a 1979 gray-over-black Lincoln. She also said he was bad tempered, dealt drugs, and owned a government-issue .45. She hadn't seen him in a week.

Paul Miller, spokesman for the Miami office of the FBI, also called DeCora: the FBI's office in Lansdale, Pennsylvania, had received an anonymous call saying that a man named "Cowboy" had admitted to killing Aronow. According to the caller, Cowboy lived north of Philadelphia and dealt in weapons and drugs.

DeCora checked Metro-Dade records and found nothing for him. (The next day, Miller called back with Cowboy's FBI number and full name.)

After taking those three leads himself, DeCora delegated Danny Borrego and two other detectives to log and follow up on any other leads that might come in.

11:30 A.M.

DETECTIVE ARCHIE MOORE

Moore returned to USA Racing to ask more questions and look at business records. Patty Lezaca let him take whatever he wanted, including lists of Aronow's customers going back to the early 1970s, and his telephone book.

Mike DeCora wanted Moore to ask Lezaca if Aronow had attended the most recent New York boat show, around Christmas, and whether he had planned to attend the big Miami boat show that would open a week from the next Saturday. DeCora had heard that Aronow might have had a problem with someone at the New York show.

That couldn't have been, Lezaca said. Aronow didn't go to the New York show, nor did he display any boats there. Nor had she heard of Aronow having any problems at previous boat shows. The last time USA Racing had displayed a boat at a show was 1986 in Fort Lauderdale, but Aronow hadn't attended there, either.

Moore then asked about any civil lawsuits that might have caused Aronow problems. Lezaca said he had been involved in several minor ones, but none so angry that could have led to his murder. She said that in 1986 [actually 1985], Aronow had taken a government agent on one of his speed boats for a test ride, and the agent had fallen and broken his leg. The agent then sued Aronow's insurance company.

There was also a breach-of-contract suit filed against him in the late '70s, she said; however, she couldn't remember many details. It had gone to court, concerned someone's refusal to pay Aronow, and Aronow had countersued.

Lezaca made no mention of the suit Cigarette had filed against him in 1986, also alleging breach of contract.

Lezaca then asked Moore whether the police had developed any suspects. Moore said no; then Lezaca suggested they look closely at Ben Kramer.

She repeated that Aronow and Kramer were competitors and didn't get along. She also thought there were problems surrounding two salesmen who had worked for Aronow and Kramer.

When Aronow had sold USA Racing to the Kramers, USA salesman and boat designer Mark McManus went to work for the Kramers. Then, when Aronow bought USA back, McManus split his time between USA and Kramer's Hollywood plant, Apache Powerboats.

Later, Lezaca guessed that McManus had been leaking trade secrets both ways between Aronow and Kramer, and it had caused a lot of friction between them.

Then, when McManus found out two months ago that Aronow had hired Mike Peters as a salesman, McManus quit and began working exclusively for Kramer. McManus and Peters both had worked for Halter Marine in New Orleans and hadn't gotten along.

She said Ben Kramer was very jealous that Aronow was selling more boats, and of better quality, than he.

Kramer had a hot temper. Once she overheard him say that Aronow had ''screwed'' him over a deal, although she didn't know his exact reference. She also said she had overheard Kramer threatening Aronow at about the time of the USA Racing sale; however, she didn't know the exact circumstance, nor whether Aronow had ever taken it seriously. She said she had never seen Kramer overtly violent.

Moore asked whether she knew if her boss had had any extramarital affairs that could have led to murder.

It was true, Lezaca answered, that Aronow was known as a ladies' man and that he had had several extramarital relationships over the years. His current girlfriend, she believed, had been Ilene Taylor, whose name had already surfaced in a call to the Miami Beach Police.

Lezaca described Taylor as quite attractive. She was in her late twenties, five-feet-six-inches, a slender 110 pounds, with blond hair and blue eyes. She would visit Aronow at the office two or three afternoons a week, parking her red Mercedes [the same year and model as Aronow's white Mercedes] in the back. She owned horses at Calder, and they had started going together after they met there, a year and a half before. She was married to Skip Taylor, an attorney, but she had filed for divorce two months ago [actually, July 1986]. Despite that, Aronow said he wasn't going to leave Lillian.

Ilene had called on the afternoon of the murder between 4:00 and 4:30. Lezaca told her that Don had been shot and was in critical condition. Ilene got hysterical and hung up the phone, and Lezaca hadn't heard from her since. She said Ilene had told Don that her husband was very jealous and might try to kill him if he found out about their affair.

Lezaca also talked about a former steady of Aronow's, Missy Allen.

Aronow had dated her while he was still married to Shirley, but they broke up just before his divorce and subsequent marriage to Lillian. They did start again while he was married to Lillian, she said, but they had ended it two and a half years ago.

While talking to Lezaca, Moore also spoke to the shop foreman, Ralph Johnson, who had worked for Aronow for ten years, going back to when he had owned Cigarette. When Johnson saw the composite drawing in the newspaper, he thought it looked like a bodyguard for an organized crime figure who had met with Aronow the day before his murder.

11:30 A.M.

JERRY CRAWFORD

Detective Jerry Crawford ran down an anonymous lead that a vehicle matching the description had been parked behind Sunset Pharmacy in South Miami.

Crawford met with the pharmacy owner, Herbert Margolis. He didn't know anything about the car, but he did know Aronow and his family; for many years, they had had an account at the store, which was still used by his first wife and children.

12 NOON

LEADS

Danny Borrego assigned Rex Remley to follow up on an anonymous call saying that the owner of a house in South Miami had a racing boat and might also have a Lincoln matching the one used in the homicide.

Remley went to the address. The elderly renter of the property said there wasn't any car there that fit the one police were looking for, and referred Remley to the landlord, at a nearby business address.

Remley went there and spoke to the landlord, Omar Elesgaray. He said he was owner of the Captain America Racing Team and had met Aronow twice through the American Power Boat Association (APBA), but he knew nothing about his personal life.

At the same address was a limousine service. While Remley interviewed Elesgaray, Jerry Crawford looked for the limousine business owner. The door was open, but no one was inside. Instead, Crawford wrote down descriptions and tag numbers of the ten cars parked in front of the address. None were Lincolns.

From there, Crawford wandered all over Dade County to check out five addresses received by Crimestoppers where the Lincoln might be. Out of the five stops, he found one Lincoln; it was registered to a sixty-seven-year-old woman, and the car didn't match the description.

SWORN STATEMENTS TAKEN AT CIGARETTE RACING TEAM

1:13 P.M.

BOBBY RALPH

Ralph told detectives David Kosloske and Greg Smith that when he was driving back to Cigarette, he noticed that the driver of a "mint condition" blue Lincoln Continental by his side kept staring at his truck. "I noticed him when I was driving and when I stopped at the stoplight," he said. The Lincoln had dark-tinted windows, too dark to see through.

"Were you able to see inside the car at any time?" Kosloske asked.

"At one point, the window was down not quite halfway, and that's when I had a glimpse of the face. The only thing I could describe is he had salt-and-pepperish hair, combed back like mine, and a thick, long moustache, salt-and-pepperish, and a tan face. That's about all I could see. I guess he would have been in his late thirties, early forties.'' That added a bit to his previous description.

''Could you observe anybody else in the car?''

''I didn't see anybody else in the car, but it seemed like he was talking to somebody, but I don't know. His head was turning back and forth.''

Ralph said motorists often stared at him while he drove the Cigarette Racing Team truck. He liked to kid around with them when they did it.

''I always give them a few cuss words to the window, which I don't say; I just move my lips. Then, I thought, 'Oh, God, the guy is following me.' That's why I noticed it.''

1:30 P.M.

DAVID PEÑA

Peña didn't have much more to tell Greg Smith than what he said on the day of the murder. He did add that when he walked across the street with Mike Harrison, he saw a white Mercedes pass before he heard the five shots. And although he didn't get a good look at the Lincoln's license plate, he noticed it was a Florida tag.

1:39 P.M.

MICHAEL HARRISON

On the day of the murder, Harrison had told Officer Oscar Plasencia that he had been in his vehicle traveling west when he heard the shooting, and described the suspect as dark-complected, with dark hair and a light beard; but two hours later, he had told Greg Smith he was crossing the street with David Peña when he heard it, and therefore he didn't see the shooter.

Smith took his sworn statement. Harrison repeated the version that he was walking across the street, north to south. He saw the two cars, stationary, side by side; the Mercedes was facing west, the Town Car facing east.

Harrison had also been inconsistent in describing the color and model of the Lincoln. On the day of the murder, he had told Plasencia it was a black Lincoln Continental; then he told Smith it was a black or dark blue Lincoln Town Car. In his sworn statement, he described the Lincoln as a blue Town Car, adding for the first time that it had stock hubcaps. He couldn't add to his descriptions of the license plate or the green bumper sticker.

He said he heard a shot, then turned his head quickly and heard four more shots.

"I observed the car pulling away from the Mercedes. I observed it turn around in the grass nice and slow. It didn't spin out or anything. It got back on the street, and you could see a little bit of exhaust come out, like he gave it some gas, and it took off not exactly at a high rate of speed, but, you know."

"After the Town Car left the scene, did you do anything?" Smith asked.

"I started to run down to the car, and the guy who was with me, David, said it was a drug hit and not to go next to it. He said he thought the Mercedes was a drug dealer that keeps a boat over at Apache Marina. He said, 'Don't even go to help him. It's a drug dealer, and you might get in trouble.' So I just went over to the truck and put the tools away."

3 P.M.
Miami Beach

SHIRLEY ARONOW PARKER

The funeral was that afternoon. An hour before it, detectives Steve Parr and Andres Falcon met with Aronow's close friend, Dr. Bob Magoon, at his house. Also there was Aronow's first wife, Shirley Parker, now remarried, who earlier in the day had flown from New York to Miami for the service.

They spoke ten minutes; Parr asked if she could think

of any possible motive for the murder. No, she answered. She had been out of his life for too long to know anything about his business or new friends. However, she did mention that while he was married to her, he had kept a girlfriend, Missy Allen. But she didn't think the murder was a result of anything in his past.

3:30 P.M.

DETECTIVE DANNY BORREGO

All day, Danny Borrego's leads had gone nowhere.

A Metro-Dade detective assigned to the warrants bureau had thought the composite looked like a drug dealer he knew of. A Fort Lauderdale pawn shop owner thought it looked like someone who had pawned $100 of jewelry and drove a late '70s Lincoln Town Car. An anonymous caller said the sketch matched a man in South Dade who drove a dark blue Lincoln Town Car. Borrego had checked out that one himself. He found the car, but it was light blue.

The most far-out lead came from a man who did, in fact, give his name. He said the sketch was similar to a man he had worked with in the CIA in 1967, who since had become chief of police in a city in South Carolina.

But at 3:30, something promising came in at last: Crimestoppers had transferred a call from a barmaid at the El Elegante Club, which was in a lower–middle class neighborhood west of downtown Miami. On the night a few hours after Aronow was killed, she was working between five and six in the morning, cleaning up the club, when a man named Lazaro came in to speak with the club's owner, Cheka.

She said she had overheard their conversation: Lazaro said he had killed Aronow because his father had told him to do it. Lazaro looked pale and extremely frightened.

Borrego already knew the name Lazaro. He and Remley had interviewed his father during the homicide investigation of a victim named Orlando Rivera.

Borrego couldn't get the woman to give her name, but she promised to call back the next day.

4 P.M.
Riverside Memorial Chapel
Miami Beach

Dr. Bob Magoon delivered a brief eulogy to the two hundred mourners that rainy day:

"Don died as he would have wished, with his boots on and front-page headlines. Those of us who knew and loved him know that he could never tolerate growing old and being sickly.

"He lived his life to the fullest and would not have any regrets.

"He will be sorely missed. He would not wish anyone to shed a tear, but to be happy and to live life to the fullest and to remember him for his joy and vitality."

The Miami News reported (the next day) that Mike Aronow appeared to be the only family member greeting mourners. They also noted the following attendees: Bill Wishnick, racer and chairman of Witco Corporation, which sold Kendall motor oil; Don Soffer, developer of Turnberry Isle; Shirley Aronow and her husband, Alfred Browning Parker, a noted architect; Bob Saccenti; prominent boat racer Jim Wynne; Hal Halter, the New Orleans shipbuilder who had once bought Cigarette from Aronow; and Jay Smith, president of American Power Boat Association.

The *Associated Press* added the name James Kimberly, aged seventy-eight, heir to the Kimberly-Clark corporation, which manufactured Kleenex. Kimberly said Aronow was one of his closest friends, and that he had introduced Aronow to King Hussein.

"He was a diamond in the rough," said Wynne. "His language was a little rough at times, but coming from Don, no one could take offense."

"He was very outspoken, didn't give a damn about

anything," said Wishnick. "Everything he did, he did with enthusiasm. He was never blasé."

The body was cremated.

That evening, WCIX Channel 6 interviewed John Crouse: "People don't sit around shedding tears for Don; we loved the guy, but we know he lived every minute of it. It was kind of like racing—you pay your nickel and you have your fun. That's what he did. He was best at everything he did. And there won't ever be another one like him."

WSVN Channel 7 reported that Aronow's murder might be linked with the 1983 murder of another powerboat builder and racer; Tom Adams was "gunned down in a similar manner," and the case was still unsolved.

NBC Nightly News also covered the funeral. Reporter Peter Kent: "There were lawmen and, quite possibly, lawbreakers in attendance. Aronow was remembered as a strong man and a fierce competitor. As a boat-designing genius, and a champion driver and salesman.

"Above all, despite his brutal murder, Aronow was remembered as a meticulously honest man."

(John Crouse, interviewed by Kent:) "Don had no illegal goings-on that would cause somebody to want to shoot him."

Kent's report showed video footage of the 1984 offshore world champion boat that Don Aronow had helped to design—an Apache, raced by Ben Kramer. "They were popular with rock stars, kings, and vice presidents. But Aronow also knew many of his boats were bought by drug smugglers."

Kent said George Bush owned an Aronow boat, and that Aronow had been thoroughly investigated before he got the lucrative U.S. Customs contract to build Blue Thunder drug interdiction boats.

8:30 P.M.

Borrego and Remley went to the home of Lazaro's father, who lived not far from the El Elegante.

Without telling him the real reason they had come, the detectives asked where his son was. He said he hadn't seen him in more than a month; he thought he had gone north with his girlfriend. When the detectives told him that his son had been arrested two weeks prior, he said he wasn't aware of it.

4

FRIDAY, FEBRUARY 6
8:15 A.M.

At National Car Rental at Miami International Airport, Greg Smith picked up computer printouts of all black or dark blue Lincolns the company had rented from Orlando south to Miami that were out on February 3. However, for the rentals outside of Miami, they could offer only the contract number; Smith would have to call each regional office to find out the name of the renter. Later, Smith called National's offices in Boca Raton, Fort Myers, Orlando, and at the Fort Lauderdale and West Palm Beach airports.

AFTERNOON

When the anonymous barmaid called back, she gave her name and address, on Miami Beach. She was Mary Shirley Abdel-Hadi, seventeen years old. Danny Borrego went to visit her.

She said she had come to Miami from Puerto Rico eight months before and had worked for the El Elegante Club since. Lazaro was a steady customer at the club. Since she usually saw him spending a lot of money there, she pegged him as a narcotics dealer.

She offered more detail of what she had seen in the

early morning hours after the murder. The bar was closed, she and two other employees were cleaning up the kitchen, and Lazaro knocked on the door. She unlocked it to let him in, then led him to a table where Cheka—one of the owners—joined him.

Lazaro was wearing a light-colored T-shirt and blue jeans. When she asked him what he wanted to drink, he looked pale, nervous, and agitated. He asked for water, which was unusual; in the past, he had always asked for beer or liquor.

When she came back with the water, she overheard their conversation:

Lazaro was explaining how he had killed Don Aronow—the "old guy boat designer"—in his white Mercedes. He said his father had made him do it. At the time she heard it, Abdel-Hadi didn't know who Aronow was, or that he'd been murdered, and it seemed that Cheka didn't, either.

She said the two men talked for about half an hour, during which time she tried to listen as much as she could. Finally, her work finished, she left. Borrego asked if she had seen Lazaro's car. No, she said; the parking lot was in the back, and she had left by the front door and was picked up by a cab.

Abdel-Hadi said she thought Lazaro's father was also in the drug business, and she thought it was credible that he had forced his son into killing someone.

Earlier that afternoon, Abdel-Hadi had gone to the club to get her paycheck and quit her job—out of fear because she had overheard too much. Cheka asked her if she was quitting because of what she heard. She said no, but he didn't believe her. Cheka threatened her not to say anything and refused to pay her.

Borrego showed her a picture of Lazaro. She positively identified it.

Another anonymous caller to Crimestoppers suggested that a former owner of Signature Boats had killed Aronow. The man had gone to jail on drug charges as a result of Aronow's setting him up, the caller said; however, he was now out on probation. Crimestoppers then repeated this to DeCora.

Also, "Lenny and Squiggy" called DeCora. They wanted to know when and where they could pick up their reward money.

Later, Joe McSorley, the chief assistant U.S. attorney in Miami, called DeCora; he said Joe Weichselbaum, whom the office had just convicted and who was awaiting sentencing, knew Aronow and might have information about the murder.

McSorley suggested that DeCora call Weichselbaum's prosecutor, assistant U.S. attorney Dan Cassidy. Cassidy told DeCora that he didn't know if Weichselbaum would talk, but he would ask.

1:45 P.M.

FERNANDO GANDON

Rex Remley took an anonymous call from a man who said that the newspaper composite looked like Andrew Gandon, a former police officer in North Bay Village, a north Dade County waterfront suburb. [Actually, Gandon's given name was Fernando.] He said Gandon's wife had worked for Cigarette, and the couple had had marital problems.

Gandon's name was well known among local cops. In February 1986, FBI agent Dan Kingston had posed as a coke dealer and negotiated with Gandon and three other North Bay Village cops for "protection" so he could unload his cocaine from speedboats onto the dock of a North Bay Village hotel. [Another North Bay Village officer indicted in the case was named Andrew; perhaps the caller had confused the names. A third indicted officer had taught a drug prevention course in North Bay Village's elementary school.]

Gandon had pled guilty a month later, and, with his cooperation, the remaining codefendants were convicted in December. On January 21, Gandon was sentenced to seven years in federal prison. Because his wife was expecting a child on February 17, he had been granted two additional months before he had to report to prison.

Remley called the two assistant U.S. attorneys who had prosecuted the case. They told him that Gandon's wife had left him. Once, Fernando had gotten into a fight at a party sponsored by Cigarette because he suspected his wife was having an affair with someone in the company. He thought somebody at Cigarette had fathered the child.

The prosecutors referred Remley to FBI agent Kingston and Gandon's probation officer, Wayne Custis.

Kingston said Gandon had been brought into the drug deal because the other officers needed somebody who wouldn't have hesitated to shoot, had the deal gone bad. Gandon kept a .45 handgun, Kingston said.

Custis said Gandon had gotten extremely upset when they had discussed his wife's pregnancy and their separation. But he knew nothing about Gandon driving a dark Lincoln.

3 P.M.

DR. WESLEY KING

Borrego called Dr. Wesley King, who had begun CPR on Aronow before fire rescue arrived. He had come to the street to see his patient and close friend Bobby Saccenti.

King calculated that he had gotten to Aronow about forty-five seconds after he was shot. But even before that, a man named Ralph [Johnson?] had already started giving assistance. However, King said he hadn't seen the shooting himself, nor as he arrived in his Buick Riviera had he seen any car leaving the area.

[N.E. 188th Street does not intersect Biscayne Boulevard, although it begins only about a half mile east of it, then dead-ends into the Intracoastal Waterway. There are only three ways to get there; from Biscayne Boulevard, turn east at either N.E. 187th Street, N.E. 191st Street, or the Loehmann's Plaza shopping center entrance between them; from there, go north or south onto N.E. 29th Avenue, then east on N.E. 188th.]

King said he drove onto N.E. 188th Street from Biscayne Boulevard and N.E. 187th Street—the southern entrance. For the getaway car to leave either of the other ways implied that it was either going north, toward Broward County, or it was going to park in the shopping center lot.

4:30 P.M.

David Kosloske met with Elton Cary again to see if he had heard anything new. He said he hadn't.

5

The Miami News continued to do the best journalism in town. Their Saturday story began: "Don Aronow's murder has shocked the boating industry, but Aronow is not the first offshore powerboat manufacturer to be slain in South Florida."

The *News* was referring to the two unsolved murders of Signature Boats's former partners: Thomas Fitzgerald Adams, shot and killed in April 1983 on I-95 in Hollywood, and Eugene Otis Hicks, stabbed to death with a butcher knife at his Hallandale home, nearby, two months later. Channel 7 had mentioned Adams briefly Thursday evening. The *News* reported that Hollywood police had called the Aronow investigators Friday to suggest there might be a link.

Signature, like Aronow, had built boats on N.E. 188th Street. But Adams had sold Signature in 1980, and by 1987, the company no longer existed.

Adams had been driving southbound on I-95 in his 1983 Chevy pickup at about eleven o'clock on a weekday morning when someone in another car began shooting at him. Seven bullets from a .30-caliber carbine rifle hit his truck. He weaved in and out of busy traffic at high speed until one shot got him in the head; then the truck crossed the median into the northbound lane, hitting a Pontiac and causing it to spin and then stop in the middle of the interstate, creating other accidents. Adams was found facedown on the floor on the passenger side. Everyone else survived.

Two weeks before, in the middle of the night, someone had pumped fourteen shots from a high-powered rifle into Adams's $800,000 waterfront home. And two weeks even earlier than that, someone had thrown a Molotov cocktail onto his roof.

Adams had been suspected by the DEA and the Broward Sheriff's Office organized-crime division as a financier of a large marijuana and cocaine smuggling ring. However, he had never been charged.

Gene Hicks, though, had been indicted in federal court in 1977, then convicted, as part of a big smuggling operation that used boats, planes, and trucks to get dope from Central America and the Caribbean to Florida. Earlier in 1977, two gunmen had broken into Hicks's home and demanded money, then tied him up with a telephone cord and shot and killed his companion. In 1981, armed robbers broke in again, handcuffed Hicks, and stole $40,000.

Hicks's conviction was later overturned, but he lost his retrial in 1980. He was weeks away from beginning a four-year sentence when he was murdered, despite the security at his luxury subdivision; there was only one road in, and it was blocked by a twenty-four-hour security guard and cameras.

Both Adams and Hicks were boat racers, too. Adams was the 1974 United States national champion in the production boat class, driving an Aronow-built Magnum named *Miss America.*

However, there were signs that Adams was not well liked. That year, at a dinner the night before a race in Miami, Adams put a $24,000 marker in a "Calcutta" betting pool between racers, to be paid to the top finishers. Adams lost the race, but when it was time to collect, he welshed, said John Crouse. Months later, after a competing racer threatened to protest to the racing association that Adams had unfairly doctored his engines, Adams confessed that he had.

The *News* asked Metro-Dade homicide sergeant Mike Diaz if they were investigating whether either case had a connection to Aronow's murder. Diaz said they knew about them, but he played down their importance.

Crouse, asked by the *News*, had more to say: Aronow knew both men, but they had no business connection. "I don't believe there's any link in their deaths. Adams and Hicks were sleazy operators. Don Aronow was a classy man."

Then Crouse added that Adams and Hicks were not the only recently murdered boat racers with apparent drug connections. "At one time, half of these racing people were involved in drugs."

That trend had begun in the late '70s and early '80s, he said. "Don was a multimillionaire with a very conservative political point of view and had nothing to do with these people. [He] was into boat racing when it was a sport."

9 A.M.

HOMICIDE BUREAU

The *Miami News* story set the tone for the day. Mike DeCora asked Greg Smith to follow up on an anonymous call received two days before, suggesting they look into the 1985 murder of Sam Glogger in North Miami. The same caller had also mentioned Adams's murder and suggested that the motive for all three murders was that the victims had all been federal informants.

Meanwhile, Rex Remley prepared flyers asking the public for assistance in identifying the killer.

HAL HALTER

David Kosloske's assignment was to reach New Orleans boatbuilder Hal Halter. Halter told him he had bought Cigarette Racing Team from Aronow in 1978, but he sold it back in two transactions between 1980 and 1982. They had stayed friends; although he hadn't seen

Aronow since a dinner in October, they had talked two to three times a week by telephone.

In fact, Aronow had called him the morning of the murder, he said. The Nigerian government had commissioned Halter to build two 78-foot patrol boats, but after they were completed, the deal fell through and Halter got stuck with them. In November 1985, Aronow bought them for $700,000–800,000, well under their real value. (Mike Aronow had referred to the deal.) Aronow's last call to Halter was to ask him to call the Panamanian government to see if they would buy them.

JOHN CROUSE

DeCora called John Crouse to follow up on his comments to the *News*. Although police hadn't made public the "Jerry Jacoby" episode that foreshadowed Aronow's murder, Crouse had heard about it and volunteered that he had a suspicion of who it was: someone who owned a racing team in North Miami.

Crouse said the man knew Ben Kramer, and he himself had seen him at Fort Apache Marina several times. Crouse gave DeCora an address and business phone for him in North Miami, but when DeCora went there, he found it was a residential neighborhood.

11:50 A.M.

SAM GLOGGER

Smith and Kosloske went to City of North Miami Police to speak with detective Margie Dellerson, who had promised to pull the Glogger case by the time they arrived. As it turned out there was no file; it was a City of Miami Police case, Dellerson remembered.

From North Miami, Smith called Miami Police homicide detective Jon Spear. Spear said Glogger, his wife, and a friend had been shot and killed at his home with a .22-caliber semiautomatic pistol on March 19, 1982. No one had ever been arrested, but he believed that the murder was narcotics related.

Glogger had built boats on the Little River in Miami under the name Bandit Boat Company, and he owned a black thirty-six-foot Cigarette named *Bandit*. Spear gave Smith a list of people he had learned were associated with Glogger, but none of them matched names in the Aronow investigation.

After he hung up with Spear, Dellerson told Smith she was currently investigating a drug-related murder from around New Year's Day of a man named Douglas Everette; his father had bought a Cigarette from Aronow in the past five years. Police had found cocaine and a large amount of cash at the scene, but the similarities ended there.

1:50 P.M.

Following up on Thursday's lead regarding the thirty-five-year-old ex-boyfriend who matched the killer's composite, who drove a dark-colored Lincoln, owned a .45, and dealt drugs, Rex Remley and Danny Borrego went to the address in North Miami they had for him. However, the address turned out to be a business. Checking another address, they found a home that had a brown 1972 Pontiac parked outside that was registered to him, but the detectives didn't knock on the residence door.

3:30 P.M.

Remley asked Keith Lindholm, a Metro-Dade detective working in the pawn shop unit, to check whether any .45-caliber handguns had been sold in pawn shops in the north end of the county since January 1, or if any had been pawned in the days since the murder.

4 P.M.

TOMMY ADAMS

Smith and Kosloske arrived at the Hollywood Police Department to ask about Tommy Adams's murder. Hollywood Police opened the file; they had a list of suspects, but again, no names matched.

10 P.M.

MISSY ALLEN

Steve Parr and Andres Falcon met with Missy Allen—mentioned by both Patty Lezaca and Shirley Aronow Parker as one of Aronow's paramours—at the Metro-Dade Police substation near the crime scene. [Mike Aronow had called her Missy Holiday.]

Missy, a tall, thin blonde, lived in an apartment in Turnberry Isle. She said she had met Aronow in 1969 or 1970, and admitted that she was his girlfriend for the next five or six years. When the relationship ended, she had married someone else, then divorced him at about the same time Aronow married Lillian. Missy said she had never gotten back with Aronow [contradicting Patty Lezaca] and hadn't talked with him much since.

But in March 1986, when she had a skin problem that needed treatment, she said her girlfriend asked Aronow to help her pay for it. He did. But save for an occasional phone call, that was the last time she had spoken to him. She had no idea why he was killed.

6

Five days after the murder, *The Miami Herald* relegated its coverage to Outdoors editor Jim Hardie. He wrote:

"Talk to a dozen people who knew offshore power-boat builder/racer Don Aronow and you hear a lot of the same comments. ' . . . fiercely competitive . . . honest . . . always laughing . . . excellent businessman . . . full of life . . . practical joker . . . energetic, enthusiastic.'

"When Aronow, 59, was gunned down in midafternoon in North Miami last Tuesday word of his murder surged through the boating community like a tidal wave. And behind the initial shocked reaction came the predictable question, 'Why would anyone want to kill Don Aronow?' "

In a Sunday feature, *The Washington Post* wrote that 188th Street "from this week on, will forever be associated with the fast life and violent death of Don Aronow, a prototype of the American dream.

"The motive for Aronow's murder remains unclear, according to police. The possibilities seem as varied as his life, which friends portray as a constant quest for excitement in the form of women, money, success, and, above all, speed."

The *Post* quoted people close to him, after the funeral.

Bill Wishnick: "Every day was an adventure for Don. He was a fierce friend. He would behave as if he didn't give a damn about anybody."

Jim Wynne: "He was a great *bon vivant*. His language could be crude occasionally, but it fitted his personality."

Ted Theodoli: "He was a hard-nosed guy. Some people loved and adored him. Others did not. If he didn't like you, he could find a way to abuse you."

Days before, a U.S. Customs spokesman had firmly denied to *The Miami News* that Aronow had been an informant for the agency, but the *Post* got a different answer: "Customs officials described the boatbuilder as 'cooperative' when approached for information about a client."

However, the *Post* then proceeded to critique the idea that his murder had anything to do with drug smuggling—although DEA and U.S. attorney's office spokesmen had suggested earlier in the week that it probably did.

"The problem with this theory is that Aronow's murder doesn't resemble a professional hit job. The gunman drove his own getaway car. He had attracted the attention of passersby by hanging around [188th Street] for some time before the murder. His escape could easily have been foiled if someone had managed to block the street's only exit."

John Crouse: "It looks to me like a crime of passion. Here in Miami, you can get into a killing fight in a restaurant or at a stoplight. It's quite possible that someone had a personal grudge against Don. He was an opinionated guy. If you got him riled, he would come at you."

Ted Theodoli: "The symbolism of Don Aronow getting killed in this street is so obvious that it's stupid. You have to look elsewhere. If I had wanted to kill him, I would have done it in New York."

MONDAY, FEBRUARY 9

ILENE TAYLOR

Since Ilene and Skip Taylor's divorce had been less than amicable so far, and guessing that Skip would make something of her friendship with Aronow, Ilene insisted that Steve Parr's interview of her take place at her attorney's office.

Ilene said she knew Aronow from the track, since they both owned and trained horses. But she didn't say that she had been seeing him.

However, she did volunteer the name Ben Kramer. She said that in late 1985 or early 1986, Kramer had bought USA Racing from Aronow, then Aronow bought it back. Then only just recently, they were talking about it again. In fact, they were supposed to have had a meeting about it the day before the murder, but she didn't know if it had happened or not.

Parr asked if she had a theory of who killed Aronow. No, she said. She played down the possibility that her husband, Skip, killed him. Skip knew Aronow, she said, but not well.

9:30 A.M.

U.S. Customs had a confidential informant (CI) who said he had information about the murder. Sergeant Diaz assigned Greg Smith to contact customs agent Wayne Roberts, who said a meeting had been set up for later that morning at a Holiday Inn near downtown Miami.

At the Holiday Inn: the CI was cloak-and-dagger. He didn't want Smith to know his name and said he had only learned of Aronow's murder in the news, but he recognized the composite as a former owner of Signature Boats, who had been released from federal prison within the last year. The CI was also interested in the reward.

[Apparently the CI was the same person who anonymously had called Crimestoppers the Friday before.]

The CI said he had heard that Aronow and the Signature owner had had some sort of dispute five years earlier over a hull design, and that Signature Marine, once owned by Tom Adams, was involved. [Adams and this man had been racing partners in a boat named *Signature*.] Perhaps Aronow had stolen Signature's design.

JOE WEICHSELBAUM

Mike DeCora followed up on the Joe Weichselbaum lead by calling DEA agent Roger Edwards, who since had talked to Weichselbaum.

Weichselbaum had told Edwards he thought that Aronow had been involved in drugs beginning in the mid-'70s. He leased his boats to smugglers on a short-term basis and let them off-load on the canal behind his business on 188th Street, charging $500,000 to $1 million per night. If for any reason the smugglers' drugs were delayed, Aronow still kept the money; if they wanted to use the site again, they'd have to pay again. One of those deals a few years back had prompted Aronow's murder, he said.

This was not the first time Mike DeCora heard that Aronow had rented out his location for off-loading.

Weichselbaum also said Aronow was close with New York Mafia figure Frankie Viserto, currently serving time on gun charges. Aronow had visited Viserto in federal prison, in Otisville, New York, a few times.

And by the way, Weichselbaum was interested in the reward.

JERRY JACOBY

Because all bases needed to be touched, David Kosloske called the boat racer Jerry Jacoby, who lived in New York City. Jacoby, aged fifty, had been part-owner of Cigarette in 1981, but he said he no longer was associated with the company.

Jacoby said that on the day of the murder, he had been in Orlando doing business; then he flew to Miami at

8:00 or 8:30 that night and went from the airport to see his mother. He stayed overnight at Turnberry Isle Resort and Club.

He said that Aronow had been famous throughout his career as the pioneer designer of "deep-vee" hulls for speedboats—boats whose bottoms were V-shaped instead of flat or round, which cut the water more efficiently. But in 1982, after Aronow foreclosed on Cigarette, then resold it, the new owners had made him agree not to compete in the deep-vee business for five years. In that time, Aronow had built only catamarans—which weren't big sellers. But the five years were just about up, and Jacoby said he had heard that Aronow was planning to start building deep-vees again, which, he added, might have made some competitors unhappy.

3:50 P.M.

TOMMY ADAMS

When Greg Smith and David Kosloske had visited Hollywood Police the previous Saturday, neither co–lead investigator on the Adams case had been on duty. Monday afternoon, Hollywood detective Jack Hoffman called Smith to chat.

Hoffman said that not only hadn't he been able to develop any strong suspects in Adams's case, he hadn't settled on a motive. Adams, he said, had many enemies from his boat business years, as well as from the construction business he had begun afterward.

TUESDAY, FEBRUARY 10
8 A.M.

FRANK VISERTO

At the morning briefing, DeCora assigned Greg Smith to find out more about Frank Viserto. Within two hours, Smith had located him in the Federal Correctional Institute in Otisville, New York, where Weichselbaum said he was.

Smith called the prison to ask for a search of the visitors' log. Again Weichselbaum was right: on August 6, 1984, Aronow had visited Viserto with Frank's father-in-law Carmine Saglimbene from Fort Lee, New Jersey; then on May 9, 1985, Aronow visited again, alone.

[Later, detectives learned from prison visitors' logs that Aronow also had visited Viserto at Leavenworth Prison in 1986. Lillian confirmed that Don and Viserto had been friends for a very long time, and in addition to visiting him, Don had helped out his family while he was in prison.]

1:30 P.M.

JACK KRAMER

Looking for both Ben and Jack Kramer, Archie Moore went to Fort Apache Marina but found only Jack.

Jack said he hadn't seen the shooting. However, he did see Aronow about ten minutes before, in his car in front of Apache Boats. He figured he had come to visit Bob Saccenti.

At the moment of the shooting, Jack said he and Ben were on the patio bar at Fort Apache Marina, drinking. He didn't hear the shots, but his office manager, Edythe Vollender, ran out to tell them what had happened. Then he and Ben went to the street in time to see Dr. King run over and begin assistance. A few minutes later, Jack watched police and paramedics arrive.

Jack said he had known Aronow a long time and had great respect for him and for how he had built up the powerboating business on the street, which Jack called "Gasoline Alley." He said Aronow had bought all the land on 188th Street from the Clyde Beatty Circus.

However, he added, Aronow was a shrewd businessman who may have had a number of enemies. He continued, he and Ben had had a deal with Aronow to buy USA Racing, which had the contract to build Blue Thunder police boats for U.S. Customs. However, the whole deal fell through when the government decided they would pull the contract if the Kramers owned the company.

Jack said he wasn't aware if Aronow had been threatened before his death, nor did he have any ideas who killed him.

2:30 P.M.

ROADBLOCK

Since it had been a week exactly since the murder, detectives had an idea to roadblock N.E. 188th Street again to look for witnesses they might have missed in the chaos the week before or who might have seen something earlier in the afternoon but left before police arrived. So this time, they began the roadblock an hour earlier.

For two hours, six detectives worked the crowd, interviewing 127 people, mostly factory workers. Out of that, only Greg Smith got anything worthwhile. First, a Cigarette employee, Aracelio Rodriguez, said he had seen a black Lincoln Continental in the area during the afternoon the day *before* the murder. Its driver was a white man in his mid-sixties, with salt-and-pepper hair.

Then Smith found brothers Levon and David Tindall, who both said they had seen a black or dark blue Lincoln Town Car on the street the afternoon of the murder.

Both brothers were eighteen-year employees of the Atlantic Foundation Company, located about forty yards west of the murder site and across the street from Fort Apache Marina. Although David said he didn't see the Lincoln's driver, Levon described him as white and middle-aged, with sandy-colored hair and what appeared to be a small goatee. Levon was also more specific about where he had seen him: parked in Atlantic Foundation's driveway. At one point, he said, he watched the man get out of the Lincoln and put on a one-piece racing coverall, dark gray with red stripes on the sleeves. Smith arranged to interview him later at more length.

WEDNESDAY, FEBRUARY 11, 1987

The Miami News reported that Aronow's will was worth "in excess of $1 million in stocks, bonds, and real estate" and that he had directed his businesses to be liquidated. He left larger shares of his estate to his two youngest sons, by Lillian—six-year-old Gavin and six-month-old Wylie—than to his grown children. He did so, he said in the will, "not because of any lesser love and affection. All my children are dear to me, but it is merely recognition that the children born of my first marriage were provided for by me during my lifetime and all have reached majority."

In addition, he left his Miami Beach home, condominium in New York City, and vacation home in Southampton, New York, to his "beloved wife" Lillian. He left nothing to his first wife, Shirley.

PHOTO LINEUP

With so many leads going in so many directions, Mike DeCora and Greg Smith decided to gather photos of six possible suspects and place them in a collage with twelve placebo pictures to show to the witnesses.

The six included: Fernando Gandon, the crooked North Bay Village cop, who allegedly was jealous of his wife because he thought she had had an affair with someone at Cigarette; "John" and another man identified by "Lenny and Squiggy," who said they were part of a drug organization affiliated with Aronow; the former owner of Signature Boats, who an anonymous caller suggested had killed Aronow because he set him up on drug charges five years before; and Sheldon "Skip" Taylor, who was divorcing Ilene Taylor, said to be Aronow's girlfriend.

12:10 P.M.

MIKE BRITTON

Smith and DeCora went to Mike Britton's workplace to show him the collage. After looking at all eighteen pictures, he picked out Fernando Gandon. He thought he looked similar to the man he saw in the Lincoln; however, his facial hair and scalp hair were different. Britton emphasized the word "similar."

While the detectives were there, Britton gave them two new leads:

A friend who had a business near Biscayne Boulevard and 151st Street had said that someone in his neighborhood had told him that on the day before the murder, one of three white men in a light-colored Lincoln Town Car had asked for directions to "Gasoline Alley." The man answered that it was five miles away. Then the man in the Lincoln replied that he had just come a thousand miles, so five more wouldn't make a difference. Britton said he was trying to find the man who had offered the directions.

Britton also said there was another witness to the Lincoln leaving the scene of the crime. He was a hatch maker who worked for Aronow, and the Lincoln had sprayed him with gravel as it left. Britton didn't know his name either, but said he would find out and tell them.

[However, Britton never did come forward with anything more on either lead.]

AFTERNOON

Two more anonymous leads came in to DeCora in the afternoon. First, Fort Lauderdale Police said they had gotten an anonymous call saying the composite printed in the newspapers resembled a Customs informant who had been convicted of tax evasion but was free on bond until he had to report to federal prison. The Customs informant, the Fort Lauderdale detective said, was five-feet-ten-inches tall and weighed two hundred forty pounds. DeCora checked and found that he also had a record with Metro-Dade, but when Fort Lauderdale Police later mailed him a picture, DeCora determined that he didn't fit the description.

Another anonymous source called DeCora directly and said that a Miami attorney resembled the composite. DeCora checked his driver's license picture and information but determined that he didn't match the description, either.

THURSDAY, FEBRUARY 12

In a story naming its 1987 Boater of the Year, *The Miami Herald* recalled that Don Aronow had received the honor five years before.

"Don Aronow was never one to do things halfway.

"The most common description of Aronow among people who knew him was 'larger than life,' a phrase that cropped up continually about this big, powerful, ruggedly handsome man.

"It was the way he lived, and the way he died. His epitaph won't be words on a stone, but the thunder of high-performance racing engines and the brutally beautiful sight of his boat's daughters carrying on the search for speed at any price."

11 A.M.

Mike Aronow called Steve Parr. He said someone at USA Racing had gotten an anonymous call that they had seen a black Lincoln Continental with tinted windows, Florida license tag 170-ZKE, in the area of the murder— after it happened.

DeCora had Greg Smith run a check on the number. It was a 1985 Lincoln four-door, registered to Pershing Auto Leasing on Miami Beach.

Smith immediately called Pershing and spoke to the general manager, Hill Silver, who said that the car had been rented before February 3 and was still in the same person's possession. Silver said he could offer more details, but not over the phone.

11:45 A.M.

PERSHING AUTO LEASING

Within thirty minutes, Smith arrived at Pershing. There Silver showed him the contract; on October 10, 1986, he had leased the Lincoln for $1,500 a month to Jeffrey D. Brody, who lived in Turnberry Isle's south tower [the same building as Missy Allen].

Silver also said he had leased Brody another car, a black 1983 Porsche Targa 911 SC, contracted in August 1984 for $906 a month. What was very interesting was that he had put it under his business's name, Squadron Marine Company.

[One of Aronow's boat companies was called Squadron XII. He had begun it in the late '70s after he sold Cigarette to Hal Halter; in 1981, when he repurchased Cigarette, he merged the companies.]

Salesman Sergio Scalerandi described Brody to Smith: he was in his forties, five-feet-nine-inches tall, 170 pounds, with blondish brown hair, and clean shaven.

12:30 P.M.

JEFFREY DONALD BRODY

Back at the homicide bureau, Smith ran an NCIC (FBI National Crime Information Computer) check on Brody. In 1982, he had been convicted of grand larceny in New York state court, and sentenced to one year. Another check showed that he didn't have any firearms registered to him.

Archie Moore had been spending the day at USA Racing again, looking through records and talking to Patty

Lezaca. DeCora called and asked him to inquire around about Jeffrey Brody.

The name struck pay dirt. Brody had borrowed $50,000 from Aronow in 1983, using a boat that a man named Wayne Boich had bought from Aronow as collateral.

5:30 P.M.

During the evening briefing, DeCora asked Smith to check on Wayne Boich. Boich had no criminal record in Dade County, but he had a traffic ticket. At the time, he had shown an Ohio driver's license, but the address on the citation was another Turnberry Isle building: the north tower.

FRIDAY, FEBRUARY 13
1:50 P.M.

Smith and Parr reinterviewed Anthony Roberts, owner of Mer-Cougar Marine, who told them something he hadn't mentioned to the detective questioning him before: he had seen a dark-colored Lincoln Town Car with tinted windows in the area for several afternoons prior to the murder. However, he hadn't noticed whose car it was.

Also, Archie Moore briefly interviewed Ben Kramer at Fort Apache. He would have done so sooner, but Kramer had previously scheduled a trip to Europe that began the day after the murder—something detectives checked out. He was in the process of preparing a new boat to challenge the speed record across the Atlantic.

Kramer praised Aronow for helping put him in the boat business. Moore asked if Aronow somehow was in the drug business, and Kramer answered no, but he did build boats for both dopers and the U.S. government.

That conflict, Kramer suggested, may have been why he was killed.

SATURDAY, FEBRUARY 14

Saturday was opening day to the public for the Miami International Boat Show at the Miami Beach Convention Center. DeCora and four detectives went to pass out flyers asking witnesses to come forward, and to see who they could find to interview.

Snooping around, the detectives got to see the gleaming boats that the companies on N.E. 188th Street, including Cigarette and Apache, had built.

At USA Racing's display, Greg Smith found Mike Peters. Although Aronow's last day was only Peters's second day working for him, he said he had known him for years.

Peters said it was rumored that Aronow had been threatened within the last several months, and he had joked about it. He had told someone he might not make it to the show, but if he lived that long, he'd see him there.

SUNDAY, FEBRUARY 15
NOON

The same five detectives attended the offshore powerboat races and a party afterward at a restaurant called Sundays on the Bay, on the Intracoastal Waterway at Haulover Park, to pass out more flyers. They also looked for racers wearing dark gray coveralls with red stripes, like the man Levon Tindall had described getting out of the Lincoln. They saw none.

7

WEEK THREE
TUESDAY, FEBRUARY 17

Roads seemed to be leading to Jeffrey Brody. On Tuesday, DeCora got a call from Captain Steve Foster of the Warsaw, Indiana, Police. He said he had a friend in the boat business who had gone to Miami about a year and a half ago to buy two boat molds from Brody. During that time, Brody and another man drove him around town in a blue Lincoln Continental.

Foster's friend had said that Brody was legit, and he bought the molds. But he had suggested that the other man might have been involved in Aronow's murder. He described him as six to six-foot-three-inches tall, rugged-looking, and very tense.

DeCora did a check on him. He was thirty-seven years old and lived in North Miami, but he had no criminal record.

WEDNESDAY, FEBRUARY 18
4:20 P.M.

JEFFREY BRODY

DeCora arranged to interview Jeffrey Brody at the Steak and Ale restaurant on Biscayne Boulevard, just south of N.E. 188th Street, but at the last minute they changed it to the Metro-Dade Police northeast substation. Greg Smith came also.

Brody, aged forty-five, said he had met Aronow at the New York boat show in either 1978 or 1979, when he bought a Cigarette from one of his salesmen, either Mark McManus or Byng Goode. He moved to Miami in 1980. When Aronow disbanded Squadron XII, Aronow sold him Squadron's twenty-four-foot and twenty-seven-foot boat molds. Then, with Aronow's permission, Brody set up a business using the name Squadron XII.

But Brody made no money selling boats. In either 1984 or 1985, he sold the molds to someone in Indiana, then sold a thirty-four-foot mold to his friend.

Brody admitted that he had made $2 million in a "phony billing" scheme in New York, but then he got arrested for it and convicted of grand theft. He spent ninety days in jail and had to pay restitution. Aronow lent him $50,000 toward that end; another friend, Wayne Boich, let Brody use his boat as collateral toward the loan. Brody said the loan was repaid June 1, 1984.

Brody said he hadn't seen Aronow for a year and thought he was out of the business of selling boats to the public. He commented that Aronow's clientele was "very diverse," then added that the boat business was "just a toy" to him. When DeCora asked why he thought Aronow had been killed, Brody suggested the jealous husband theory.

Brody said that on the afternoon of the murder, he had planned to test a boat at Mer-Cougar Marine, on 188th Street. However, because he was having his apartment's wooden floors refinished by a company called A Cut Above, he instead stayed home with his wife, his housekeeper, and the workmen.

DeCora asked if he had ever lent his car to anyone. No, he said. But since his building had a valet parking service, they had his keys. However, he said, they wouldn't use the car because they knew he asked for it at irregular times.

During the interview, DeCora had crime scene investigators photograph Brody's Lincoln, which he had driven to the police station. In fact, it was a Town Car. It was clean and in excellent condition, and was black, not dark blue. It had dark-tinted side windows; a chrome strip along the bottom third of the sides; a light brown pinstripe along the top of the sides; hubcaps with brass-colored spokes curving inward, like a bowl; and a beige leather interior, and the rear half of the top was covered in black imitation leather.

At the end of the interview, DeCora asked Brody to sign a consent to search his car. He agreed. However, when the detectives went through it, they found nothing of evidentiary use.

Later, DeCora called A Cut Above. They confirmed that they had been at Brody's on February 3, and that Brody had supervised them until at least four o'clock, which was after the time of the murder.

Also, when DeCora and Smith checked the security logs at Brody's building, they showed that vehicles from A Cut Above had signed in, destination Brody's apartment

THURSDAY, FEBRUARY 19
10:25 A.M.

HERMAN GOLDSMITH

When Archie Moore had asked people at USA Racing about Jeffrey Brody, he learned the name Herman Goldsmith. DeCora had asked Brody about Goldsmith, and he answered that they were friends from New York, but they hadn't done business together. Brody told DeCora he could find Goldsmith on his yacht, *Dani*, berthed in slip D-6 at the Ocean Reef Club in Key Largo—an exclusive development on the northernmost of the Florida Keys.

DeCora and Smith went there. Goldsmith, aged thirty-four, said he had bought a Cigarette from Aronow at the 1980 New York boat show, sold it, then bought a cata-maran from USA Racing—one of the few cats Aronow had sold to the public.

In July 1986, a fire in Montauk, New York, severely

damaged Goldsmith's cat. In November, Goldsmith arranged with Aronow to transport it to Miami so he could repair it, but work had never begun. Goldsmith said the last time he talked to Aronow was two or three weeks before the murder.

Goldsmith said he had known Brody for ten years but hadn't seen him for more than a year. He knew that Aronow had lent him money, which was repaid when the boat that Aronow had kept as collateral was sold.

Asked if he thought Aronow could have been involved in something illegal, Goldsmith answered, "Absolutely not." But he did know that Aronow had had a girlfriend, Missy Allen, whom he had named a boat after—*The Mistress*.

2:30 P.M.

SKIP TAYLOR

Speaking of alleged mistresses, DeCora and Smith's next stop was the downtown Miami legal office of Sheldon "Skip" Taylor, husband of Ilene. The detectives knew that attorneys, when they were in trouble personally, usually hired other attorneys to sit in on interviews like this. Taylor hadn't. On the other hand, the first thing they noticed was that Taylor's hands began to shake. They decided not to mention talk that Ilene and Aronow had been lovers.

Taylor, aged thirty-five and heavyset, said he met Aronow in 1981 or 1982 when Aronow had bought a horse from him after a claiming race. However, they never socialized. He said Aronow owned between forty and eighty horses and spent more than a million dollars a year on them.

Aronow was successful with horses, he said, as well as very lucky. His strategy was to buy cheap horses, then race them against horses of even lower class. The purses were small, but he won more often. He was well known in Florida racing circles, but he was virtually unknown out of state.

[Taylor himself was successful with horses. In 1985, a horse he had bought for $65,000, Important Business, won more than $250,000, including the Illinois Derby. He entered it in that year's Belmont Stakes, and it ran fifth to winner Creme Fraiche.

In a 1985 *Miami Herald* business section feature story, Taylor had bluntly said that most of his legal clientele were drug dealers, because in Miami criminal law, that's where the money was. He explained that although other local criminal lawyers hired bodyguards or carried guns to protect themselves, he relied on the expensive, highly trained German shepherds he kept on each side of his desk when he met with volatile clients.]

Taylor said he had last seen Aronow about six or eight months before, at the new house he was fixing up. Aronow was usually a loner; when Taylor saw him at the track, he was either alone or with Lillian at the Turf Club.

DeCora asked him about Aronow's relationship with Ilene. Skip said that he knew they spent a lot of time together at the track, since they both loved horses, but they were only good friends. Then DeCora asked if he thought Aronow was a factor in his divorce, and he replied, "Not at all."

Taylor said he couldn't remember where he was at the time of the murder. When DeCora asked him what his take on the motive was, he suggested it might have had something to do with on-track bookies who had lost so much money to him because he was so lucky. He said he himself had no motive and would be at the bottom of his list of suspects—if he had made a list at all.

FRIDAY, FEBRUARY 20
8 A.M.

DeCora and Smith went to USA Racing to check on Herman Goldsmith's catamaran. Goldsmith had said repairs hadn't begun, but in fact they had.

11:45 A.M.

MARK MCMANUS

Mark McManus worked for Apache Powerboats—the Kramers' shop in Hollywood—about ten miles north of 188th Street. But for a time, he had split his days working for both the Kramers and Aronow. He said they all got along.

McManus said he had met Aronow in 1978 when his New Orleans employer, Hal Halter, bought Cigarette. Then, when Aronow repurchased Cigarette a few years later, McManus went with Aronow.

McManus said he wasn't aware of any problems Aronow had had with people in business. He was very generous to his employees and was fast to fix customers' problems with their boats, even if they weren't his fault.

But then McManus recalled one incident: in 1986, while Aronow was building Blue Thunder boats for U.S. Customs, Aronow told him he was concerned that some nut might blow up the factory, kidnap his wife, or hurt him. It was the only time he had ever seen Aronow worried about anything like that.

He also claimed that Ilene Taylor had been Aronow's girlfriend for about two years. However—Aronow told McManus—he had said to Ilene that he wouldn't leave Lillian.

3 P.M.

FERNANDO GANDON

Fernando Gandon had refused to be personally interviewed, so the two detectives went to see Wayne Custis, the U.S. probation officer assigned to write Gandon's presentencing investigation.

Custis said Gandon's wife, Lynn, had been marketing director for Cigarette from September 1984 to April 1986. However, after Fernando was arrested, Cigarette asked her to resign. The party at which Fernando had gotten into a fight was her going-away party, on April 4,

1986. He had crashed it, was asked to leave, then had to be thrown out.

Gandon's upcoming surrender date was March 2. Custis said Lynn had consented to be interviewed, but not before then, because she was afraid of him.

[Custis made arrangements for an interview, but Lynn returned to her family in England before it could happen.]

TUESDAY, FEBRUARY 24
3:30 P.M.

LEVON TINDALL

Levon Tindall was the single worthwhile discovery detectives had made during their week-after roadblock of 188th Street. There hadn't been time to do a relaxed interview then, so Smith had promised to return later.

Tindall repeated that he had seen a black or dark blue Lincoln Town Car several times on the day of the murder. The first time was about two o'clock, at the eastern end of 188th Street (closer to USA Racing than to Apache Boats), parked on the north swale, facing west. That's also when he saw the driver get out and put on the silver/gray racing coveralls with the red stripe.

He described the man: white; six feet to six feet, two inches, tall; in his fifties, fluffy and curly hair; and a salt-and-pepper goatee. He said he had never seen him before; however, he thought he had seen the car before.

At 2:30, Tindall saw the car again, this time parked on the grassy area in front of Apache Boats—about where the murder took place. He said he couldn't tell if anyone was in the car at the time.

He described the car as a 1986 or 1987 model, and very dirty. The front wheels had bare black rims—no hubcaps. He didn't get a license plate number.

DeCora and Smith showed Tindall their photo lineup, which had swelled to twenty-one pictures. Tindall didn't think any of them was the man he had seen, but one looked similar: "John," who "Lenny and Squiggy" had said was part of a drug organization that associated with Aronow.

LEVON TINDALL
SWORN STATEMENT

The next morning, Smith and DeCora had Tindall give a recorded sworn statement at the Metro-Dade Police northeast substation.

Tindall said he had first noticed the Town Car because it was new, but so filthy, and it didn't have hubcaps. Although Miami hadn't seen snow for ten years, it appeared to him the car might have gotten that soiled from going through snow and road salt.

This time Tindall described the person he saw as six feet tall. He said his face was clean-shaven, no sideburns, but he had a goatee beard that was part gray and sandy.

"About how old did he look?" Smith asked.

"He's middle-aged. He must have been forty-five or fifty. He wasn't no young guy." He said his build was medium, and he had curly hair the same color as his beard.

Tindall explained that his employer, Atlantic Foundation Company, had two buildings on N.E. 188th Street: one across from Fort Apache, the other at the east end of the block. He first saw the Lincoln at two o'clock at the east end, where the man had changed clothes. Then, twenty-five minutes later, when Tindall drove back to Atlantic's west building, he saw the same car driving slowly, also going west.

Smith asked if Tindall had ever before seen gray-and-red coveralls like the ones he had described. Yes, he said, racers for Cigarette wore them.

At about 3:15 or 3:20, Tindall returned to Atlantic's east building, and he saw the Lincoln once again, the same man sitting at the wheel. He was parked about twenty-five feet from Apache Boats, backed in, facing the road. The murder happened just minutes later.

THURSDAY, FEBRUARY 26

DON SOFFER

Don Soffer, the developer of Turnberry Isle, had been close friends with Aronow. DeCora gave Detective Paul Ohanesian a list of names to ask him about.

Soffer told Ohanesian he had no idea why anyone would kill Aronow, but shortly after it happened, he got an anonymous call from a man who said, "Don Aronow got his, and you're next."

Ohanesian went down his list.

- Jerry Jacoby: Soffer knew he had bought Cigarette from Aronow, then lost it back. He knew of no bad feelings between them.
- Missy Allen: Not only was she Aronow's girlfriend, but boat racers Joey Ippolito and Bob Rautbord had also dated her at the same time. He said Aronow had been very good to her, and there weren't any problems between them.
- Joey Ippolito: He raced for Bernie Little's racing team, and did business with Aronow. Again, he knew of no bad feelings among the three.

[Joey Ippolito, Jr., winner of five offshore races between 1977 and 1980, had been arrested and indicted with his brother, Louis, in federal court in New York in 1979 for trafficking in 22,000 pounds of marijuana. Louis allegedly bragged to a Florida undercover agent that he had 300,000 pounds of marijuana in Colombia. Louis was convicted and sentenced to eight years, but Joey was acquitted, then arrested again in 1981 with thirty others for unloading part of 30,000 pounds of marijuana on a beach in East Hampton, New York. He was convicted on that charge and sentenced to eight years.

He and Louis were the sons of Joseph Ippolito, a reputed New Jersey mafioso. Police documented the brothers themselves as members of an organized crime family, and in three weeks, Louis would be charged with forty-eight others in a conspiracy to manufacture 70 percent of the United States' counterfeit quaaludes in Quebec and sell them in Fort Lauderdale. He would be convicted in 1988.

Bernie Little was a Florida beer distributor who owned the *Miss Budweiser* racing team, which he began in the early '60s. John Crouse described Little as a "high roller" as well as the most successful owner in boat racing history. In 1977, Little put Ippolito in a thirty-five-foot Cigarette called *Anheuser-Busch Natural Light*, and in 1978, *Michelob Light*. Little dropped Ippolito after his smuggling conviction.

Bobby Rautbord was a director of the American Photocopy Corporation, to which Aronow had sold Magnum Boats in 1968; later, Aronow bought it back from them at terms favorable to Aronow. Rautbord won seven races in his career; in 1972, he was powerboating's world champion, winning five races in Europe and South America.]

• Joey Weichselbaum: Soffer said he was involved in helicopters and had been sentenced to prison, but he had no motive to kill Aronow. [Weichselbaum was also a racer, winning two production-class races in 1974, driving a twenty-eight-foot Aronow-built Cigarette called *Mighty Mouse*.]
• Jeff Brody: He had also served prison time, about three or four months, for white-collar crime. He and Aronow had no business relationship and were friends.

Soffer said he himself never did any business with Aronow because it might have hindered their friendship. The last time he saw him was at a bar mitzvah in December 1986.

MARCH 11, 1987

A month after the murder, the investigation was dying. In talking with the media, police tried to put the best face on it they could.

The Miami News reported:

"Five weeks after millionaire powerboat racer and builder Donald Aronow was shot to death on the Dade street where he earned an international reputation, police still have no motive and few leads."

The composite sketch had produced no solid suspects. The dark Lincoln hadn't been found, nor had they found the person who some witnesses said had tried to follow the getaway car.

"But [Metro-Dade homicide Sergeant Mike] Diaz is not discouraged. Investigators have not exhausted their leads, he said. 'I'm not optimistic or pessimistic. We're just continuing,' he said. 'As time passes, more and more is being accomplished. It's a very complex investigation. There's just a lot of people to talk to.'

"Some areas of inquiry now look less promising than others, he said, but nothing has been eliminated. Among the theories nearly discarded is that the shooting was prompted by a traffic entanglement with a stranger.

"As for narrowing the investigation down to one area, it's still too early, he said.

"Asked if police believe Aronow was the target of a 'hit' or assassination, Diaz said, 'At this point, we can't even say that.'

"Five detectives are on the case, Diaz said, but they have to work other cases at the same time.

"Aronow knew and had business with hundreds of people, Diaz said, adding, 'You're not dealing with just a few people to interview. We're dealing with a large volume of people and it just takes time to complete the interviewing process."

The *News* also interviewed John Crouse. " 'I think they've got some leads,' he said. 'They don't tell me that, but I think they have some idea what they're looking at, if not who.' "

MARCH 23, 1987

EDNA BUCHANAN

The Miami Herald's Pulitzer Prize–winning police reporter Edna Buchanan had the lead story on page 1:

"Ocean-racing superstar Don Aronow loved it when writers called him a living legend. His life of adventure is well known. It is his death that baffles police.

"He was afraid of nothing, no one. In his final hour, when a stranger spoke to him in riddles and talked about killing, Aronow laughed. He felt no fear, until he lowered the window of his white Mercedes and looked death in the face. And then it was too late.

" 'What we're looking for is a motive,' " said Metro-Dade homicide detective Michael DeCora, lead investigator on the toughest case of his career. " 'There are endless possibilities.' "

Buchanan had interviewed Patty Lezaca and reported the dialogue between her and "Jerry Jacoby" as such:

" 'You're not Jerry Jacoby,' [Lezaca] said.

" 'Nahh,' the man said, 'he's a lot taller than me.'

" 'No,' she said, 'he's shorter.'

" 'You mean the Jerry Jacoby from Palm Beach,' he said.

" 'No, he's from New York.' "

When "Jacoby" next mentioned that he owed everything to his boss, and would even kill for him, Lezaca told Buchanan:

" 'I just ignored it, and so did Mr. Aronow,' she said. 'It was just stupid. Why would anybody say something like that?'

" 'He wasn't just some nut. He was here for a reason,' Lezaca said.

Buchanan reported that Aronow's gold Rolex Presidential watch was missing, slipped off his wrist as he lay dying. Rolex had presented it to him for winning the offshore powerboat championship in the '60s.

She also wrote that police said there was no evidence that Aronow, "who sold boats to lawmakers and lawbreakers alike," was involved in the drug trade.

She quoted Michael Aronow: "The family doesn't get it. We just don't get it. That's what is so sickening.

"He dealt with every kind of person in the world, the best and the worst. He came from Brooklyn, and he wined and dined with royalty. It was such a cowardly goddamn act.

"It wasn't played by any of the rules he always played by. He was a sportsman."

MARCH 30, 1987

PEOPLE MAGAZINE

People magazine added little to the facts of the story, but a great deal to creating a legend out of Aronow and his murder. It was cleverly titled DON ARONOW'S MURDER LEAVES MIAMI WONDERING: WERE "CIGARETTES" HAZARDOUS TO HIS HEALTH?

"It was the kind of crime for which Dade County has become notorious, a brazen, daylight hit carried out before a dozen onlookers. 'Aronow's murder fits the profile of 90 percent of the Colombian, drug-related assassinations we see in southern Florida,' says DEA spokesman Billy Yout. 'They like dramatic killings, and they usually don't care who witnesses them.'

"Why Don Aronow? That was anyone's guess, but everyone knew that the high-speed boatbuilding business attracted plenty of cocaine-smuggling clients. Customers on 188th Street were said to pay for their Cigarettes or Magnums with suitcases stuffed with $150,000 in cash, and there were reputedly frequent requests for speedboats customized with secret compartments or hollowed-out hulls.

"In the offshore cat-and-mouse game between cocaine smugglers and federal lawmen, Don Aronow was known as a merchant who dealt with both sides. He had just fulfilled a $2.5 million contract to deliver 13 high-speed catamarans to the U.S. Customs Service, even as he continued to sell to the druggies. 'If you came in and announced flat out that you were a drug dealer, Don wouldn't have anything to do with you,' says Mike Kandrovicz of USA Racing Team. 'But if you (said nothing) and had the money, he'd gladly sell you a boat.'

"The rewards of dealing with drug runners could be practically limitless. 'I had druggies promise that I'd never have to work again if I brought a coke-laden boat in from Costa Rica,' says Knocky House, a mechanic and former offshore racer who once teamed with Aronow. 'The business is rife with easy money.'

"But Aronow didn't need it. Associates swore he would never have risked his reputation by getting directly involved with drug traffickers. 'If Don found out a man who worked for him was dealing in drugs, (that man) didn't have a job. I know that for a fact,' says a friend."

People re-quoted Aronow from a 1979 *Sports Illustrated* story: " 'We in the ocean-racing fraternity are flattered that the dope runners prefer our kind of boat, but when they get caught we don't like it. We have torn emotions. A kid who works for me was offered $100,000 to run out to sea one night and resupply fuel for a dope boat. He refused, but it must have been a terrible temptation. Heck, lately, we've been getting letters from jailbirds, asking for complete specs and prices on our Cigarettes.'

"As the investigation of Aronow's murder continued, some speculated that he could have been killed as a suspected informer. 'Don was a very astute guy. He loved to keep tabs on his colleagues—he knew everything that happened on 188th Street,' says John Crouse. 'It's possible he had learned something incriminating and was killed for that.' Some Miamians theorize that the great racer may have run afoul of the law of the jungle. 'Don Aronow could have been shot for something as stupid as delivering a bad boat to a drug smuggler,' says Art Nehrbass of the Metro-Dade Police. 'We've got emotions in this community that you just don't find anywhere else in America.' "

April 4, 1987
2:15 p.m.

ROBERT SCOTT

Detective Andres Falcon got an anonymous call from a man who said that a month prior to the murder, he had been traveling around Miami Beach in a black Lincoln Town Car with a man named Robert (Bob) Scott who said he had been offered $30,000 to kill a man in the Miami Beach area; however, Scott wasn't more specific.

The caller knew that Scott carried a .45 handgun, and that a man known as "Ski" leased the Lincoln he drove. He described Scott as forty years old, white, six-feet-two-inches tall, strong build, short beard, rough-looking with a rough voice. He said "Ski" owned a crane business somewhere north of Fort Lauderdale, possibly in Boynton Beach [in south Palm Beach County].

Scott had also told him that he had killed fourteen other people, worked for Colombians, and had traveled to Colombia often. Scott used other names, but the caller had seen his driver's license, and it was under the name Robert Scott.

The caller offered lengthy directions to both Scott's house and the crane business, but they were vague. When DeCora and Steve Parr tried to follow them, they had no success.

May 2, 1987

NEWS FROM AMERICA

Three months after the murder, the news reached the other side of the pond. The London *Daily Mail* headlined: MIAMI VICE MURDER AT THE MARINA; DRUG MOBSTERS' HIT-MEN KILL MILLIONAIRE IN HIS MERCEDES. Under a photo ran the caption "Donald Aronow . . . he defied Miami's drug bosses".

The text: "[Unnamed] Detectives believe that Don Aronow, 59, had rejected mobsters' invitations to use his boatbuilding yards as a cover for cocaine rackets and his racing skills on smuggling runs.

" 'Those guys had him pinpointed. They did a good job for their bosses,' said one detective.

"Police are convinced that Aronow was a victim of the ruthless drug barons often portrayed in the BBC TV series *Miami Vice.*

"A drug enforcement official said: 'Obviously in his line of work, particularly in this part of the country, it would have been difficult for him not to come into contact with the big boys of crime.' "

MAY 7, 1987

In a story about the annual Fort Lauderdale Spring Boat and Sport Show, the *Sun-Sentinel* wrote that the largest boat in the show was a seventy-four-foot motoryacht co-designed by Hal Halter and the late Don Aronow.

MAY 14, 1987

Although Florida law normally seals probate records, at least initially, Aronow's was cracked open to the public because the Florida Department of Revenue had filed a $12,451 claim against his estate for unpaid 1985 intangible personal property taxes.

The Miami News reported that the state based its claim on Aronow's own evaluation of his estate, which he gave to Prudential-Bache at the end of 1985; he said it was worth at least $7 million. He valued Aronow Stables at $1 million; $604,000 for USA Racing; $74,306 in money market assets; and $5,385,583 in bonds, plus an unspecified amount of Florida municipal bonds.

MAY 27, 1987

More on probate: Aronow had written that he wanted all his businesses liquidated within a year of his death, but lawyers for his widow, Lillian, convinced Dade Circuit judge Moie Tendrich to nullify that proviso because it would have led to a "fire sale" of the assets.

Miami Herald columnist Fred Tasker asked the attorneys why Aronow would have put that proviso in his will, but they declined to answer.

JUNE 11, 1987

WSVN Channel 7 investigative reporter Robert Gilmartin broadcast that Lillian Aronow's private investigator had hired a mobile billboard to travel around Dade County.

It read: "Tell us who shot Don Aronow. $100,000 reward leading to arrest. Murderer appx. 6', white, sandy hair, driving Lincoln Town Car/blue or black. Call Aronow Tip Line, 823-2569."

The reverse side was in Spanish. The line would be answered by the PI.

"The billboard idea is not the only thing private investigators have tried," Gilmartin reported. "They've been talking to people who fear police contact. They've entered the world of fast boats—the favorite mode of transport of drugs entering the country.

"There could be many motives for the Aronow murder. No one has confirmed that he was scheduled as a witness before a federal grand jury."

8

DON ARONOW

Don Aronow was born wealthy in 1927. It didn't last.

He once said his first memory was riding home to Brooklyn in his Russian immigrant parents' limo, listening to his father, Herman, tell his mother, Gertrude, that he had lost his taxicab company. Days later, they let the maid and cook go. "All of the sudden, we were very poor," he recalled.

Instead of having the pampered life his parents had intended for him, when he got old enough he sold newspapers and worked at his father's gas station and new small taxi operation. As a young teenager in the early '40s, he bought used cars, fixed them up, then resold them.

Aronow's life could be viewed as a series of anecdotes, many of them advanced by John Crouse, Aronow's longtime public relations man. All are wonderful; most of them need to be taken with a whole shaker full of salt. One of the earliest and best was how he had bought a surplus Army tractor in the Bronx for $350 and gotten it running, but then had to figure a way to get it home to Brooklyn. He spotted an army surplus store, bought a set of fatigues and a helmet for $1.50, then began driving at eight miles per hour through Manhattan, then across the Manhattan Bridge to Brooklyn. Not only did the police not stop him, but they gave him an impromptu escort through intersections. He made it home in ten hours.

Although he was a loner, Aronow wanted to be noticed. When he got an usher's job at a movie theater, he made sure his uniform always looked neat, and he made head usher within a year. In 1944, at age seventeen, he took the money he had saved and bought a 1934 Cadillac convertible from a railroad president. People noticed. In 1945, he joined the Merchant Marine Academy and signed up for hazardous duty, to earn the extra five dollars a day. Crouse wrote that he lied about his age, then got assigned to a ship making the Murmansk run, ducking German submarines. Crouse marveled that Aronow had returned home without any visible scars—but this story might be the most apocryphal one of all.

Home in 1947, he attended Brooklyn College on the G.I. Bill and lettered in football, wrestling, and track. In the summers, he was a lifeguard at Coney Island. His son Mike, in his 1992 vanity-published bio of his dad, _Don Aronow: King of Thunderboat Row_, wrote that he made 700 rescues. He was also offered an audition to be cast as the next Tarzan, but he turned it down. Definitely not an apocryphal story was that he met Shirley Goldin, "the prettiest girl on the beach," Mike wrote, and married her on July 4, 1948.

Aronow became a junior high school phys-ed teacher in Brooklyn after graduating in 1950. Later, he recalled, "I remembered how sharp the gym teachers looked back in high school. They wore snow-white T-shirts and tight, gray flannel slacks." Soon he felt the job was a dead end, and began working weekends for Shirley's dad and brothers in their New Jersey construction business, building homes.

"I needed excitement. And the construction business was a lot more interesting than teaching gym class," he said.

In-law personalities clashed, and in 1953, Don went independent as a contractor, using his car as his office. Mike Aronow says that through 1961, he built a thousand homes, plus shopping centers, apartment buildings and industrial parks. Crouse wrote that the union once sent a thug to warn him there would be trouble if he didn't play ball with them. Aronow then broke the man's legs with a two-by-four.

In 1961, Aronow "retired" at age thirty-four from the construction business with his first million and came to Miami. Later he said he did it because "I was bored." Mike wrote that he came because of "the long hours, cold winters, exhaustion, and serious stomach ulcers." But persistent rumors had him running from the Mafia, at first hiding out in hotels in Bal Harbour and the Caribbean. Aronow said that during those first months away from New Jersey, "I carried on a lot and did a lot of gambling."

Aronow had grown up near shipyards and yacht berths. In New Jersey, he had kept a forty-foot sport fisherman boat, *Tainted Lady*, and he brought it south. He kept it on the Miami River, just west of downtown. That's where Aronow first heard about the annual 184-mile Miami-Nassau-Miami powerboat race across the open ocean. He said later, "Friends talked me into it, and I was ready to be hustled."

Forest Johnson of the Prowler Boat Company had won some powerboat races, and introduced Aronow to racer/mechanic Dave Stirrat, who brought him to boatbuilder Howard Abbey. Aronow asked Abbey to build him a boat capable of winning the race in 1962.

Powerboat building and racing were just beginning to be revolutionized. In 1960, elsewhere in Miami, Dick Bertram had built a wooden boat with a deep-vee hull and raced it for the first time in that year's Miami-Nassau race. On a day when the seas were so rough that "the fainthearted [were] advised to stay home," Bertram's deep-vee won, taking eight hours but breaking the course record by four minutes. Another deep-vee finished second. To show what a quantum leap in technology they were, everyone else who finished did so the next day.

Then, in 1961, Bertram designed a fiberglass deep-vee and won that year's race in calmer seas, breaking his previous record by *three hours and forty minutes*.

Dick Bertram had all the pedigrees and boating credentials that Aronow lacked. Bertram had won his first sailing race in New Jersey at age eight. During the depths of the Great Depression, he was enrolled at Cornell University and became the first commodore of the school's Corinthian Yacht Club. He competed for the America's Cup and owned a yacht brokerage that became the Bertram Yacht Company, which suddenly at that moment in 1961 was the hottest small boatbuilder in the world. His official racing team shirt was a short-sleeve button-down, sky blue with white polka dots.

V-bottoms had been around before, but what was new about them in the '60s was that the entire hull was now V-shaped, not just the fore. They cut the water with less drag than boats with round or flat rear bottoms. A deep-vee was a "V" with a sharper angle. It seemed paradoxical at first, but they were more stable in rough water; the down side was that deep-vees needed more horsepower, and tended to be wet—that is, its drivers tended to stay less dry.

For the 1962 race, Abbey built a semi-V hulled wooden boat that Aronow named *Claudia*, after his nine-year-old daughter. In trials, *Claudia* approached sixty miles per hour, but days before the race, they switched engines and lost speed. Still, with just ten miles left in the race, Don driving, Stirrat as codriver/mechanic, and Abbey navigating, they led. Then an engine blew a clutch. Dick Bertram and a driver in still another Bertram passed him. *Claudia* finished, but fourth. The winning time was thirty-eight minutes faster than the year before.

"What a race!" Mike wrote. "My father was hooked. The thrill of competition and the aphrodisiac that only winning could bring were a combination that he couldn't resist."

Yet it was not Bertram whose name would come to be most associated with deep-vee hulls; it would be Don Aronow.

Back to the drawing board for the 1963 race, Aronow hired Jim Wynne and Walt Walters to build two prototype deep-vee fiberglass boats, one twenty-three feet, the other twenty-seven feet, both named *Formula*—like the Formula race cars. Aronow took the bigger boat and finished third, although he beat the 1962 winning time by three minutes. Once again, a Bertram triumphed.

In an interview explaining why he didn't win races in those early years, he said, "I had no regard for the equipment. I'd get into the lead and then blow up the boat. The only reason I started to use my head was because I wasn't winning. I'll do anything to win."

"In the beginning, he was all guts and no sense," said Wynne.

Trying to make a business out of his hobby, Aronow bought land on N.E. 188th Street for a factory to construct Formula boats to sell to other racers as well as the public—which would get more luxurious versions, including teak decks and trim, and sleeping quarters. The street, built on undeveloped swampland, had canals on both sides, leading into Biscayne Bay.

Aronow knew from Bertram's success that the best way to promote his boats was to win races in them. Two months later, a Formula won its first race, from Miami Beach to Bimini and back, with Jim Wynne driving.

At the November 1963 race from Miami to Key West, in ten- to fifteen-foot seas and a thirty-knot wind—one of the roughest offshore races ever run—Aronow finished second to a forty-footer. Although Dick Bertram and seven other of the nineteen starters didn't finish, all four Formulas that entered did—even though one of the pilots, Miami seafood restaurateur Mike Gordon, was knocked unconscious.

Especially considering that he owned the boat, *Fish Peddler*, Gordon had a tough day. Racer Allan Brown recalled the craziness of a race of that era, as printed in John Crouse's book *Searace*, his compendium of powerboat-racing:

"The first Miami–Key West offshore powerboat race crowd was a tough bunch. Hairy chests, bulging muscles, beer drinking, tobacco spitting, swearing, brawling . . . and that was just the women."

Brown described Gordon's throttleman, Sam Sarra, as a savage competitor who "was not at all hampered by sanity." Gordon was the driver, but because he had trouble keeping behind the wheel, Sarra and navigator Pres Coulter strapped him into the rear of the craft with a window washer's belt. Communication on deck was largely unnecessary, "since Mike couldn't see and Sam didn't care." Navigation, too, was barebones, "requiring only that you keep America to the right."

After a while, Gordon flipped upside down in the harness. With each wave, his head pounded into the deck.

Two miles from the finish line, in the lead, a battery cracked and the port engine quit. *Fish Peddler* was reduced to making counterclockwise circles. The eventual winner passed them at forty-three miles per hour, tittering; then came Aronow.

In 1964, Aronow won his first race, "Around Nassau". That day, Formulas also finished second, third, fifth, and sixth.

"We were a little wild," he said. "When we needed a navigator, we'd hold up a stalk of bananas and anybody who would jump in, we'd take. We needed a gorilla."

When the Beatles came to Miami Beach in 1964, Aronow took them out for a spin in the Atlantic. He even let Ringo hold the wheel. Mike reported that when the Fab Four returned an hour later, they were "white as ghosts and almost speechless."

Just as Formula was taking off, Aronow sold the twenty-seven-footer to Marlin Boats, and the twenty-three-footer and the name Formula to Thunderbird Boats. He said those companies could mass-produce the vessels for the public, and his factory couldn't.

"It was like building tract housing," Aronow said later. "I was more interested in developing new models than in production. Then I'd say, 'Why did I do that? Maybe I should have just taken a vacation instead.'"

Aronow had more property on N.E. 188th Street, and that same year he began Donzi Marine—named after his own nickname. He kept his design team, which came up with a sixteen-footer he called *Sweet Sixteen*.

Aronow named his Donzi race boat *007*, a stolen reference to James Bond. In this tiny craft, in 1965, Aronow finally overtook his rival Dick Bertram, beating him in the Miami-Nassau race that Bertram had dominated for the previous five years. That year, Donzis won four races in all—two with Aronow at the helm—and Formulas won three. In one rough-water race off Miami, twenty-three boats started, but only eleven finished; eight of those remaining were Formulas or Donzis. In a Donzi, Bill Wishnick had to stop at a referee boat to drop off his older brother, Jack, who was injured when the boat had slammed head-on into a wave. The officials airlifted him to a hospital in Miami; then Bill went on to win the race.

In another race, off Palm Beach, Aronow made a move on the leader, Jim Wynne. With just a mile to go, a prop blade flew off Aronow's boat, leaving him and Dave Stirrat with a decision: give up, or juice every last bit of momentum the boat had. For Don Aronow, it was no decision at all. They left the throttles full open; the vibration was awful, and the shaft and drive broke under the exertion, causing the boat to sink. Still, Wynne won by only five hundred yards. Onshore, the crowd saw Stirrat's bashed face and Aronow's bloody hands dashed with brine.

Mike wrote of the time a kid asked Don to test ride his expensive new jet boat. After ten minutes' ride in the bay, Don reentered the canal behind his business at full speed, intending to spin the boat in a circle. He cut the power, which, without his realizing it, cut off the power steering. While the kid watched, the eight-foot-wide-boat tried to squeeze through a five-foot opening in the pier. Don called over to the dock, "It runs like a piece of shit!" Everyone laughed except the kid. Don paid to repair the boat.

Donzi got orders from all over the world. The Israeli army bought some to use as remote-control bombers on driverless suicide missions. Many were used during the Six-Day War in 1967.

It also carried a jet-set image. Abercrombie and Fitch bought two for its Fifth Avenue window display. The Secret Service bought one to tail President Lyndon Johnson while he fished on his favorite Texas lake. Mike wrote that when LBJ found out the Donzi was faster than his boat, he commandeered it. The Secret Service returned to ask Aronow to build them two more "only faster, but the President can't ever know."

Then, later in 1965, Aronow did it again: he sold his company, Donzi, at its height, and created a new label—Magnum, a name inspired by a bottle of champagne.

Aronow was the maddest racer of a mad bunch. Rough conditions stopped no one. In the 1966 Houston Channel Derby, Aronow warned other drivers that he had steering trouble. When two boats crowded him on a turn anyway, "I had to make a decision whether to pull back on the throttles and lose hundreds of yards, or wipe them out. I decided to wipe them out." His boat leaped fifty feet in the air, then landed nearly on top of them. He won the race.

In 1967, Aronow decided he wanted to win the Union of International Motorboating (UIM) world championship. All over the globe that year, he raced his twenty-eight-foot Maltese Magnum. When school let out, he had Mike travel with him to England, Italy, Sweden, and France.

The 1967 Bahamas 500 offered a $50,000 purse, but the seas that day were up to fifteen feet, and the winds reached thirty-five miles per hour. Three-quarters of the boats dropped out; three had no choice: two sank and one burned. Eight of the seventeen finishers took more than twenty-four hours, some drivers taking shelter for the night at checkpoints.

Mike called the race a "massacre." As night fell, he and his mother nervously stayed in the wire room at the Kings Inn, listening to muddled radio reports. But when the next boat crossed the finish line, "It was Dad. Here he came, with his little outboard. It was unbelievable." Don, Knocky House, and their navigator, David Albury, had taken horrible lumps; Albury couldn't stand up or rotate his neck.

The next day, Mike wrote, Aronow told reporters: "As dusk set in, we went through Current Cut and were only minutes behind the third-place boat. Then the seas began picking up again. We pushed hard, wide open, and took a terrific beating. We used our legs as shock absorbers and believe me, mine had had it. Then I felt something against my legs and tried kicking it aside, thinking it was a loose cushion. It wasn't. It was Knocky, and he was unconscious. I grabbed him by the back of his life preserver, lifted him up and in sheer desperation slapped him across the face three or four times. He opened his eyes and said, 'Get it on, Don, I'm OK.' That's part of what wins races."

In the 1967 West Palm Beach Gateway Marathon, Aronow had trouble with his fuel system. In an attempt to flush out leaking gasoline from the tank, they began the race slowly, with the engine hatches open. But that was no way to run a race, as far as Aronow was concerned. Impatient, he ordered Knocky to slam down the hatches at the moment he'd hit the throttles. When they did so, the engine hatches exploded into the air, sending debris close enough almost to down a private plane overhead, and throwing Don and Knocky into the drink. They were rescued, but the boat and engines were total losses.

During a trial for the 1967 Miami-Nassau, Don hit a seawall, almost killing his crew. The next day, in a replacement boat, he finished eleventh. In the Long Beach-San Francisco race, his boat hurtled fifteen feet into the air over a wave and collided with a hovering press helicopter.

Don and Knocky got so terrified, they couldn't speak. As Knocky tells the story, "Finally Don broke the silence. He looked at me and said, 'What are ya gonna do when we get to Morro Bay?' I said, 'The first thing I'm gonna do is get in the shower. I just shit in my pants.' Don answered, 'I get the shower first; I own the boat.' "

Mike recalled his father hobbling around the house in

his bathrobe after those rough races, "looking like he'd just gone fifteen rounds with Ali or Liston."

The punishment was rewarded with both the 1967 World Championship and United States Championship. That year, Aronow-designed Formulas, Donzis and Magnums won nine of the twenty-five races run.

Then, almost predictably, in 1968 he sold Magnum.

Aronow wanted to repeat as World Champion in 1968, but in a practice run for the Bahamas 500, he tripped his boat doing sixty. As Don flew out of the boat, Knocky caught him by the belt and kept him in. Don cracked his sternum and tore his chest muscles, and Knocky dislocated his shoulder—it was the worst mishap either had had. Nor was either wearing a helmet. They flew on to the race anyway, but Don was in so much pain that he had to fly back to a Miami hospital.

The injury set him back from winning the 1968 World Championship, but not the United States Championship.

It seemed that every race had its own story. In the 1968 Miami-Nassau race, Don and Knocky were leading with just three miles left when their boat started burning. Both men went overboard, then struggled to climb into the life raft, which was itself burning. That fire they managed to put out with an extinguisher. The boat was about to explode, so they tried to get as far away from it as possible, but the boat kept following them until they realized that boat and raft were connected with a line. In the struggle, Knocky cut himself. Aronow ordered him, "Stop bleeding, Knocky, will you? You'll attract sharks."

Nineteen sixty-nine was Don Aronow's year. Magnum's new owners specified that Aronow could not compete against them by setting up yet another new boat company, but Aronow got around that. Under the aegis of his friend Elton Cary, he built a thirty-two-foot boat he called *The Cigarette*, named after a Prohibition-era pirate ship—legendary around Sheepshead Bay—that hijacked bootleg liquor from rumrunners, then scooted away faster than anyone could catch it. *The Washington Post* had written that "the idea of bad guys outracing other bad guys and seizing their fortune appealed to Aronow.''

Magnum sued him. Aronow settled, then opened his most famous company: Cigarette Racing Team. The name Cigarette would become synonymous with go-fast boats.

Just before *The Cigarette*'s first race, from Long Beach, California, to Ensenada, Mexico, Aronow bet Long Beach mayor Edwin Wade that his boat would beat Wade's car to the finish line. He even spotted Wade an hour head start. Seas were six to eight feet, so when the mayor got to the Ensenada docks, he was very surprised to see Aronow waiting for him. *The Cigarette* had won the race, with an average speed of 67.3 miles per hour. It would have been the fastest average speed ever had a Bertram not done 71.4 six days earlier.

At seventy miles per hour, racers absorb a G-force as great as twenty-five Gs. In comparison, astronauts on takeoff endure about ten Gs.

Mike's comparison of his father to Muhammad Ali was apt. Both men's secret to winning was to take more punches than anyone else. ''It's sort of like a street fight,'' Don said. ''Once you get hit in a street fight you don't feel the punch, the pain, or think about the danger involved. You're not only racing against other drivers, you're trying to outdo the seas.

''The sea is going to win, by the way.''

He won the Gateway Marathon in May, and showed his bloody hands to the press afterward. ''We took the worst beating ever,'' he said. ''We have never run such a long distance at those speeds in such a rough sea before.'' But as long as the boat could hold up, so could he.

In June, Aronow and *The Cigarette* won the Bahamas 500 although he was sick with a high temperature. He had intended to let Knocky drive after the halfway mark, but the race was so close, he never let go. At the finish line, they beat a Bertram by only a boat length.

In July, Aronow won a race off Viareggio, Italy, in a new world record of 74.7 miles per hour. After, he said,

"The speeds that we are running now are almost unbelievable. If we don't stop trying to break offshore records, someone's going to get killed."

Rival driver Doug Silvera noted Don's arrogance toward the waters. "We'd be racing in rough seas, taking a terrible pounding, and I'd be almost beaten down to my knees when Don would come alongside and grin from ear to ear, then take off.

"God, he was so demoralizing."

Although he never topped seventy miles per hour again, Aronow won three races in August: the French Dauphin D'Or, the Long Beach Hennessy Cup, and the English Cowes-Torquay race. Then, in October, he won Miami-Nassau, followed by two more Cigarettes finishing in second and third.

There were onshore anecdotes, too. Before the Italian race, Knocky House told him that a dockworker had refused to lower his boat into the water without a bribe. Aronow ran to the dock, asked Knocky if this was the guy, and delivered a punch that dropped him into the drink. Aronow then lowered the boat himself.

At a bar one night, Aronow and three friends anted up $100 each, to be paid to whoever picked up a local girl first. The other three found pretty girls and bought them drinks; then Aronow picked out the ugliest woman in the bar and sat down next to her. Five minutes later, he whispered something in her ear, and they left before the rest of the others had finished their first drink.

In total, Aronow won eight of eleven races in 1969—something no one else had ever done. With them, he won his second World Championship and third straight United States Championship.

They would also be the last races he would ever enter.

By then, Don's wife, Shirley, was frantic, trying to stop her forty-three-year-old husband from racing again in 1970. Finally he agreed—or at least, that's what he said. But he sobered up for good in the summer of 1970 when nineteen-year-old Mike and his friend went to pick up dates at college and blew a tire at 100 miles per hour, then crashed. Mike damaged his spinal cord, permanently paralyzing his legs. The other boy was killed.

"All those years, I never took my kids in a raceboat with me," Aronow said, years later. "I was afraid they'd get hurt during a race and I'd have to slow down. Then Michael gets badly injured in a car wreck."

Don spent much of the next year helping Mike recover. In part so that he could share something with Mike, Don began buying horses to race, and in 1972, he established Aronow Stables. Gradually, Don got more and more interested in horses than boats.

From 1970 to 1971, Cigarettes won twenty-six straight races in which they competed. But in March 1972, two Australian brothers, Val and Paul Carr, were killed racing the very same Cigarette that Aronow had won his World Championships in. They were the sport's first fatalities. Ironically, the boat was undamaged and won the same race the next year.

In 1974, Aronow launched a thirty-five-foot deep-vee that even today remains the industry standard. He called it the "Mistress", and his target market was wealthy men in midlife crises. If you didn't have a mistress, for $90,000, Aronow's "penis boat" would attract you one.

"You can sneer all you want," someone told a *Sports Illustrated* reporter, "but the guys in those boats always end up with the good-looking women."

Another selling point was that the production Cigarettes were custom-made by the same workers who built the racing Cigarettes. And before every boat left the factory, Don Aronow personally tested it.

Aronow sold Mistresses to Spanish King Juan Carlos, Jordanian King Hussein, Princess Caroline of Monaco, Richard Nixon, Robert Vesco, Haitian dictator "Baby Doc" Duvalier, the Shah of Iran, and banker Charles Keating.

[In 1978, Aronow succumbed to his own midlife crisis. He divorced Shirley, his life-partner of thirty years, then married and began a second family with Lillian Crawford, a Palm Beach socialite-heiress-fashion model. King Hussein, who had dated her, introduced them. She knew who Aronow was; when she was sixteen, her dad had bought her a Donzi Sweet Sixteen.]

Average men were turning into powerboating champions. After Miami Beach eye surgeon Bob Magoon won the United States Championship in 1973, Aronow said, "With these boats I'm building, the crews I'm getting these guys, and with the new engines, I could strap a monkey into the cockpit and make him a champion."

In 1975, out of thirty-seven sanctioned races throughout the world, Cigarettes won twenty-three. Meanwhile, Aronow's former companies got left in the wake; Magnums and Formulas won just once each. In 1976, Aronow repurchased Magnum, added two boats to its line, then eight months later sold it to Ted and Katrin Theodoli for what Mike described as "a quick and sizeable profit."

Then, in 1978, Aronow sold Cigarette, too, for $5 million. The buyer, Halter Marine of New Orleans, obliged Aronow to produce no more than twelve boats a year in competition. That was the birth of Squadron XII. In 1981, Halter asked Aronow to buy Cigarette back, for $3 million; he said he couldn't make the company profitable, although its annual sales were $5.5 million. Aronow merged Cigarette with Squadron XII, raised sales to $8 million within a year, then turned it around for $5 million again. This time he sold to an investor group headed by a man whose name would figure later: Jerry Jacoby. Jacoby had just won the World Championship in a Cigarette.

Cigarette's new owners insisted that Aronow could not build any V-bottomed boat under sixty feet until May 1987.

Aronow's way around that was to build catamarans.

By mid-1983, he had a thirty-foot cat ready for sale, and yet another new company to sell it: USA Racing Team, a name fit for the flag-waving '80s. On straightaways, standard V-hulls had broken 120 miles per hour; Aronow's new cat topped 150 miles per hour and gave a smoother ride.

Next he built a deep-vee cat. Taking his Cigarette thirty-six-foot design, he added three feet, then split it in half and attached the halves with a four-foot-long tunnel. Now he had both a fast boat and a boat for rough conditions.

By the late 1970s, the go-fast boat business had changed dramatically. Pot smugglers had discovered 188th Street.

Asked by *Sports Illustrated* in 1979, Aronow suggested how a smuggler's boat should be equipped.

''I would estimate that for $65,000—or maybe less— you could put together a top drug-running racing boat, a 35- to 40-footer fully equipped with twin 454-cubic-inch MerCruiser engines, outsized 350- to 400-gallon fuel tanks, sophisticated navigation and radio gear, the works.''

Sports Illustrated reported that smugglers liked their hulls stripped—no bunks, no head, no galley. Thanks to trash compactors, 3,000 pounds of pot, bundled in waterproof plastic, could now fit in a forty-foot boat.

Among the boats of choice, the magazine wrote: Donzis, Magnums, Signatures—all built on 188th Street.

Law enforcement admitted being caught flat-footed. ''There's no way that we can run with the offshore racing boats,'' said a Coast Guard lieutenant.

''Rumors circulate along Fleet Street (N.E. 188th Street): trucks backing in and out of certain docks all night; offers from shady characters of $25,000 to leave a factory's gates open and its electric hoist switched on.''

Days before Aronow sold Cigarette in 1982, *The Wall Street Journal* did a page-1 feature on him. In it, he did nothing to dispel rumors that his boats and druggies were intertwined.

''When you hear of boats caught in smuggling—which our boats are very famous for—it's often a Cigarette.

''We don't mind the publicity, but we do have torn emotions when one of our boats gets caught in a high-speed chase. I always hope that ours was caught running out of gas or something. Anyhow, it usually takes a Cigarette to catch a Cigarette.''

In fact, U.S. Customs had twenty of them, all confiscated during drug busts.

In 1984, another longtime client helped Aronow again: Vice President George Bush.

Bush had bought his first fast boat from Aronow in 1964; then in 1974, he bought a twenty-eight-foot Cigarette that he kept at Kennebunkport, Maine, which Aronow repowered for him in 1981. "The last time I talked with him, he said he really wanted to buy a new boat from me, but he told me he just couldn't afford it," Aronow said in 1982, laughing.

By then, Bush was head of the President's Joint Task Force on Crime, which was concentrating its efforts to stop smuggling off Florida's coastline. When U.S. Customs decided they needed to keep up with the technology to catch the smugglers, Aronow—with Bush's influence?—got the contract.

Customs eventually ordered fourteen 39-foot cats, which they called Blue Thunder. In February 1985, _The Miami Herald_ shilled:

"The man who designed the roaring Cigarette speedboats, favorite vehicle of oceangoing drug smugglers, has built a better boat, one that will snuff the Cigarettes.

"Watch out, dopers. A crack of Blue Thunder, faster than a shiver, stable as a platform, is about to become the state of the salt-watery art on the side of the law."

If the dopers shuddered for even a moment, they shouldn't have bothered. Blue Thunder was a marvelous name for a boat that didn't deliver as promised. It turned out to be steady but slow, and required too much maintenance. Customs got more public relations mileage out of them than anything else. It acquired the nickname "Blue Blunder."

Cigarette wasn't happy with Aronow, either. In 1983, they sued him, claiming he had breached the noncompete provision of their contract by consulting to Apache Powerboats, the company owned by Ben and Jack Kramer. In addition, they alleged that, months in advance of the sale, Aronow improperly had given the

Kramers a Cigarette mold, although Cigarette was supposed to keep them all.

Further, Cigarette claimed Aronow had cooked the books to show that the company was more profitable than it really was. They also complained that Aronow had bad-mouthed the new owners as "unethical" and "doomed to failure," to its customers and even to their own employees. His motive was to make the company fail so he could buy it back for a profit, as he had done before. Angrily, they asked a court to rescind the sale. Then, in 1984, they sold out to a Cleveland group for a $2 million loss.

In 1986, the newest owners of Cigarette sued Aronow once more, claiming that he was jumping the gun by preparing a new forty-five-foot deep-vee to market just as soon as the five-year non-compete was up—which would have been just six weeks after he was murdered. In fact, Aronow had already contacted many of his old friends to help him launch it. John Crouse, who was promoting the upcoming Miami-Nassau race in June, said Aronow himself was going to leave racing retirement to pilot it.

However, as the '80s progressed, Aronow in fact was trying to stay out of the boat business.

In 1983, *The Miami Herald* named him Boater of the Year, but when he posed for its photographer, he stood in front of a framed picture of a horse race; the newspaper caption read, "I don't even own a boat right now." The reporter observed that Aronow's dozens of silver cups, racing trophies, plaques, and bowls "nestled four and five deep" were dusty and tarnishing, and were "obviously receiving no care whatsoever."

He told an interviewer in 1985 that "horses are my main business. Boats are secondary."

Aronow spoke of the differences between winning boat races and horse races:

"I could always sleep comfortably the night before a big boat race. I'd just get in the boat and feel good and go. But it's so different with the horses. Before a race, I can feel my heart palpitating. I'm not light enough to ride, and it kills me. I guess it's because I'm in a situation where I don't have complete control.''

In 1983, Aronow took a longshot horse, My Mac, to the Kentucky Derby, the year Sunny's Halo won. By 1985, he owned eighty horses, and his stable was the top winner at Gulfstream Park—which was so close to 188th Street that you could almost hear the cheering during races.

As Mike told police on the night of the murder, Don was a betting man. He took a *Sun-Sentinel* magazine writer to the track in early 1985 on a day that one of his horses ran. ''Aronow's pockets are stuffed with fifties and hundreds. He has just cashed in six figures' worth of winning tickets—a very healthy six figures,'' the reporter wrote.

Should anyone think Aronow had lost his recklessness just because he had gotten older, he described how he had banged himself up on a motorcycle in 1982.

''Lillian decides she wants to ride one. So I say, 'Well, I'd better test it before you get on it.' So I get on and ride around near the house, and by about the third time around I'm getting pretty cocky again and going faster. Then: Wham. Down I go on some sand.'' He needed fifty stitches near his eye, thirty more elsewhere.

Most murder investigations lead in a single direction, but not this one. Was the killer . . .

The jealous husband of his current girlfriend, who got hysterical when she found out he had been shot? Or some other woman's jealous husband?

Any one of a number of businessmen whom Aronow had beaten?

Related to the horse track, where he was a prolific and reportedly fabulously lucky customer of bookies?

Associated with the underworld, as his daughter, Claudia, had suggested to police?

Connected with stories that Aronow had rented his docks in the middle of the night so drugs could be unloaded?

A direct or indirect smuggling partner, angry because

he was building enforcement boats for the Feds?

Or could Aronow have been killed for his inheritance? Had Don really been able to keep secret for so long his philandering ways?

9

AUGUST 26–28, 1987

BEN KRAMER

One of the suspects, Ben Kramer, was about to begin a bad time. A federal grand jury in the Southern District of Illinois indicted him August 26 for running a "continuing criminal enterprise" that smuggled more than a half million pounds of marijuana into the United States between 1980 and 1987. It was the result of an eighteen-month multiagency federal investigation.

Kramer was called the "organizer, supervisor, and manager" of the ring. Federal agents arrested him the next day as he was about to leave his Miami apartment for a powerboat race in Bay City, Michigan. When IRS agents searched the apartment, they found a loaded .357 Magnum, a videotape showing a test-firing of an automatic machine gun on a farm in Colombia, and an underlined photocopy of an explanation of the federal Continuing Criminal Enterprise statute.

The indictment also charged that Kramer had used his illegal profits to purchase assets, and an arrest warrant said that agents had learned that Kramer had planned to sell everything he could in advance of a seizure.

At five o'clock on Friday, August 28, about forty DEA and FBI agents swarmed onto 188th Street and into Fort Apache Marina, seizing it and sealing it off so they could separate Kramer's boats from among the two hundred stored there. It ruined the weekend plans of innocent boat owners, not to mention the plans of some most-likely suspicious persons who never showed up at all to claim their boats; the government took those as abandoned property. At the same time, other agents seized Kramer's boatbuilding plant in Hollywood, Apache Powerboats. Agents in Michigan had orders to grab Kramer's champion race boat, *Apache*, but apparently someone there got word to hide it before the Feds arrived. [It was seized a month later, in Fort Lauderdale.]

The charges against Kramer carried a mandatory penalty of life in prison without parole, if convicted.

The Miami Herald collected reactions: "We consider him to be an extreme risk of flight," said assistant U.S. attorney Dan Cassidy. "We consider him to be an extreme danger to the community."

An attorney for Kramer, David Bogenschutz, told the *Herald* he had received no indication that he was involved in the Aronow case. (Another paper, the *Hollywood Sun-Tattler*, quoted DEA spokesman Jack Hook saying that the Kramer investigation had nothing to do with the Aronow murder.)

Kramer's father, Jack, thought the Feds indicted Ben so as to put the squeeze on him against someone else.

"This is from something that happened back in 1978 and 1979," Jack said. "I don't know why they've done this."

AUGUST 31, 1987

At a hearing in front of a federal magistrate in Miami, Kramer was denied bond. Robert Dueker, an FBI agent from Carbondale, Illinois, testified that in October 1985 Kramer and his smuggling partner, Randy Lanier, had ordered the murder of a man named Tommy Felts, who himself had murdered one of Kramer and Lanier's cocaine customers. Dueker said witnesses had told him they heard Lanier discussing the murder.

In August 1984, Ted Richards, a convicted smuggler

and "computer whiz" who Dueker said had bought co-caine from Kramer and Lanier, was found murdered at his home in an elegant section of Fort Lauderdale. Dueker said witnesses told him that Kramer and Lanier paid $50,000 to "the Colombians" to have the killer, Felts, tracked down and himself killed. On Sunday after-noon, October 7, 1985, Felts was shot and killed as he drove his 1983 Ford pickup truck on Stirling Road in Hollywood.

In addition, Dueker said he also had a witness who said Kramer had sent four people to threaten him after he didn't pay for six thousand pounds of marijuana.

Kramer had been on parole for smuggling until 1986, but that hadn't stopped him from often flying to Colom-bia in a private jet, Dueker said. Nor was his lifestyle consistent with his income tax reports.

NOVEMBER 24–25, 1987

Three months later came a second indictment against Kramer, this time for racketeering, money-laundering, and income tax violations. Among his codefendants were his father, Jack, and his attorney, Melvyn Kessler.

The indictment, in Fort Lauderdale federal court, said $14 million of Kramer's marijuana smuggling profits were laundered through a number of offshore bank ac-counts, then used to buy a poker casino in southern Cal-ifornia and his marina and boat factory, and to finance the Apache offshore racing team.

Kramer was charged for a second time under the Con-tinuing Criminal Enterprise law, which could again give him life without parole. The other defendants faced se-rious but lesser charges. At a bond hearing the same day, twenty-four well-known members of the Miami criminal defense bar came to testify to Kessler's good character. They said he had known of the impending indictment for at least a year and hadn't fled. A magistrate gave Kessler a $2.5 million bond, and Jack Kramer a $250,000 bond. Ben Kramer already had been denied bond before.

BENJAMIN BARRY KRAMER

In the world of powerboat-racing, Ben Kramer and Don Aronow were opposites. Aronow was of the hell-bent-for-sea-spray old-timers, in it for sport and to sell some boats, and Kramer came from the new generation to whom racing was something you did with your boats when you weren't smuggling.

Powerboat-racing fans practically worshipped Aronow, but they often despised Kramer and feared his attitude and short fuse. However, the two men may have been much closer than the public ever knew.

Kramer idolized Don Aronow, everyone on 188th Street agrees. Even *The New York Times*, in their story reporting the second set of indictments, wrote that he was known "as a protégé of Don Aronow." That Aronow accepted his adulation, or for how long, there is no consensus.

Yet the two men seemed to be made out of much the same cloth. Both were bad boys who hadn't grown up—although only Aronow was lovable for it.

Ben Kramer was close in age to Don's eldest son, Mike, who, paralyzed from the waist down, would never be able to surpass his father's achievements. David Aronow, his younger son, was never in the running; Don and David weren't as close as Don and Mike. Kramer, however, was the brash, risk-taking, achieving son who Aronow could be proud of—with qualities that Aronow himself reeked of.

In 1985, Aronow executed a contract with the Kramers to sell them USA Racing, whose thin grip on solvency was the pending Blue Thunder government contract. Even with Aronow's name on the boats, the public wasn't buying catamarans.

But wasn't it a no-brainer that Customs never would have accepted drug interdiction boats built by a convicted marijuana smuggler who was back in business? There is little doubt that Aronow knew what Ben Kramer's trade really was. And even though Aronow tried to keep the sale quiet, did he really think Customs wouldn't find out?

Legal papers still had to be filed in official records at the county courthouse. Perhaps Aronow's relationship with Ben clouded his thoughts.

And, in fact it, took Customs only a few weeks to discover the news. They met with Aronow and threatened to pull the contract unless he took the company back.

So followed some sticky business. Some people have eccentricities, and one of Aronow's was that he liked to buy his companies back for less than what he sold them for. That seemed to be his formula for making money in a business that was unprofitable for most of his competitors. But did it happen? Did Aronow steal from his "son"?

Mike Aronow was the first to mention (to police) that Kramer had paid Don a million dollars under the table—in addition to the contract price—in cash that stank of marijuana, and that "hard feelings over money had followed." He added, in his self-published biography of his father, a boast that Don had made "a nice profit during the exchange."

As time went on, the buzz on 188th Street was that Kramer had ordered Aronow's murder so he could become the new king of "Thunderboat Row." If he did, you could argue that it was a patricide.

Where was Jack Kramer through all of this? Jack took no offense to Ben's adoption of Aronow. But Jack and Ben's roles as father and son had reversed long before.

Ben Kramer was born in Hollywood, Florida, in 1954. Then, when he was five, his father, Jack, moved the family back to his native Philadelphia so he could work at an insurance agency with his father and brothers. Later, when a friend hired him to run a small lighting business, Jack improved revenue a thousandfold. In 1966, Jack returned to Florida and eventually took over a lighting business as his own.

The family bought a lakefront house in the oldest and best part of Hollywood, with a view of the Intracoastal and the coast road, A1A. From the front windows, you could hear splashing up onto the waterline each time a boat made a wake in the distance. It wasn't a big, showy house, but it had a quiet, dignified elegance about it. And it came with room for its own dock.

Ben, however, had liked Philadelphia and didn't want to move. By age sixteen he was hanging out with the wrong crowd, smoking pot at Hollywood Beach.

At that time, Ben and Jack fought. Ben wore a pony-tail, and Jack considered long hair "dirty." By then, Ben was selling marijuana by the ounce; later, by the pound. When Jack first caught wind that Ben was taking LSD and dealing dope, he gave him an Archie Bunker ulti-matum: quit it, or hit the door. Ben chose the door and dropped out of school. Father and son didn't talk for a year.

When they reconciled, Jack said, Ben explained that he understood why his father had wanted him out and, in retrospect, agreed with him.

A pot-smoking acquaintance of Kramer from his South Broward High class remembers him well, hanging out at Hollywood Beach around 1970 and 1971. The beach divided into three subgroups: surfers, freaks, and dopers. Kramer was a doper; the acquaintance was a freak and smoked the marijuana he bought from the dopers.

"Benjy was into being obnoxious," he remembered. "Most people disliked him very, very much. I was one of those who was a little afraid of him."

The acquaintance requested that his name not be used—not because he doesn't want people to know he smoked marijuana, but because he doesn't want Kramer to know who's speaking.

He remembered that Kramer hated people smoking to-bacco cigarettes. Once, at a Grand Funk Railroad concert at the Hollywood Sportatorium, he went around pulling cigarettes out of peoples' mouths, then informed them, "You're a fucking asshole."

And if you'd let him, he'd dab your eye with window-pane LSD, which, with the music, produced a wild sight-and-sound sensory combination. Of course, hardly anyone did.

* * *

At about this time, Ben was arrested as a juvenile for marijuana possession and placed in an alternative school, a state marine academy for boys. Ironically, this gave Ben his first exposure to powerboating.

And it may have been that same year that Kramer first met Aronow while hanging around 188th Street, admiring him and his boats. In 1971, when he needed a boat to smuggle marijuana from offshore, he coveted a Cigarette and bought—though not from Aronow—a used, canary-colored one he named *Mellow Yellow*.

As his father was raising annual revenues in his businesses, Ben was, too. On July 18, 1974, at age nineteen, he was arrested as an adult for the first time. Using a confidential informant's tip, Broward County sheriff's deputy G. Schoppe set up a sting. He bought a pound sample of marijuana from Kramer's minion, then said he had $30,000 more to spend. The next night, Schoppe was introduced to Kramer. In the parking lot, Kramer told him, "If there is any trouble, I will kill someone," Schoppe wrote. He then pointed and said, "My man in the blue Corvette has a gun and will shoot anyone that starts trouble if I am not out of here by a certain time."

Inside, the men made a deal for forty-one pounds of marijuana, in two large green bags, for $10,250. While Kramer counted the cash, Schoppe and three other officers arrested him and three others. When they searched bodies, they found that Kramer was concealing a .38 revolver and the man in the Corvette was carrying a .380 semiautomatic pistol.

Kramer pled guilty in January 1975 and got four years' probation. But within six months, he was in trouble again.

In the early morning hours of June 14, 1975, a security guard at a waterfront community in Delray Beach, Florida, spotted what looked to him like two fast boats dropping off drugs on the shoreline. He called local police, who followed and caught up to a pickup truck that apparently had received the contraband. The occupants then ditched the truck and fled in different directions, eluding the officer.

A Palm Beach County sheriff's deputy on the scene spotted fourteen burlap bags in the abandoned truck, which was then seized. Inside was 1,415 pounds of marijuana.

At 4 A.M., a deputy spotted a disheveled young man on the beach near where the bags had been off-loaded. He said he had helped chuck the bales onto the pickup truck, owned by Ben Kramer.

According to a DEA report, the man, Jeff Krader, aged twenty-two, said, "If I talk, these people will kill me."

But later that morning, he did talk. He said he had come from Philadelphia with $9,000 to buy marijuana from Ben Kramer to sell back home. Kramer had been his source in the past.

Krader said Kramer had approached him six months before to help him buy a Cigarette boat so Kramer could smuggle large quantities of marijuana into the country. They had bought it a month later.

Later that day, Palm Beach deputies rang the doorbell at the Kramer house. Jack Kramer said his son was somewhere in the Florida Keys. A mile away, at the address of a second suspect, Leroy Wisser, deputies found both the men they were looking for, trying to escape by the back door, and arrested them. They also found a second truck containing nine similar burlap bags, holding 927 pounds of marijuana. Kramer admitted the truck was his.

Kramer then told the two arresting officers that he knew they didn't make much money. According to the DEA report, "Kramer asked, 'How would $100,000 look to you if you let us walk?' Kramer stated then that they were stupid to be working for what they got when they could make a lot of money." The suggestion was declined.

Kramer later said the dope was owned by two Italians he had met just days before. They had promised to pay him $15,000 for a day's work driving a Magnum loaded full of pot. When the Italians' drop-off point looked dicey, he brought the dope onshore at a backup spot he had arranged.

Kramer bonded out for $100,000 but skipped his court appearance in Palm Beach County in September 1975. So did Jeff Krader and Wisser. The DEA then made out federal fugitive warrants for all three. Since Kramer was now also in violation of his Broward County probation, a state probation officer visited the Kramer house. Again, Jack said his son was in the Florida Keys, but he expected him back that day. The next day, the probation officer returned and spoke to Kramer's mother, Maxine. Ben wasn't back, she said, and she didn't know where he was except that he might be with his girlfriend. She'd have him surrender next time she saw him.

With Kramer still a fugitive a year later, Metro-Dade police offered Broward a lead that Kramer was living at a Hollywood address with two men, dealing narcotics. It didn't check out, but police finally caught him on the afternoon of June 14, 1977.

A Hollywood Police marine officer tried to stop a white thirty-five-foot Cigarette traveling northbound on the Intracoastal Waterway, just a few blocks north of the Kramer home. Instead of stopping, the driver "made an obscene gesture" and accelerated "full throttle at an estimated speed of eighty to ninety miles per hour" through a no-wake zone.

The Hollywood officer radioed Florida Marine Patrol (FMP), which spotted him minutes later near Port Everglades. The FMP boat switched on its blue flasher.

Kramer glanced at the officer, then turned east out of the Intracoastal, into the Atlantic, and south toward Dade County. FMP asked for assistance from a Fort Lauderdale Police airplane, which caught up overhead. Just across the Dade County line, Kramer beached his boat in the exclusive town of Golden Beach, fled on foot, and was captured by a Metro-Dade Police officer. This time he was denied bond.

Kramer pled guilty in November 1977 in federal court to one count importation of marijuana and was sentenced to four years plus five years of parole, then pled guilty to violating state probation and was sentenced to four years, concurrent with the federal time.

His attorney on the federal charges was Melvyn Kessler.

While at Memphis federal prison, Kramer wrote to the court *pro se* in the third person that he had been a fugitive for two years because "threats had been placed against his life. Therefore, it was necessary for petitioner to run and hide to protect his life."

Living on the run, Ben had gotten his girlfriend, Chris, pregnant, and his first son was born in 1977, three weeks after Ben was captured by the police. After that, Ben's parents took in Chris and the baby to live with them for more than a year; then they bought them a house.

After Kramer was released from prison in 1980, he made two separate partnerships—one aboveboard, one below.

Below board, Kramer approached his high school bud Randy Lanier to get back into the drug business, said Michael Carr, assistant U.S. attorney for the Southern District of Illinois. At the time, Lanier had capital and an organization in place—of which Kramer had neither, but Kramer had sources for marijuana. After they partnered, Kramer got Mel Kessler to fraudulently write to his parole officer that Kramer was working for him as a boat captain for $2,000 a month. That gave him a legitimate cover to show some income.

Aboveboard, looking for advice on how to get into the boatbuilding business, Kramer went to Aronow, who suggested that he partner with Bobby Saccenti. Saccenti had worked for Aronow as a rigger at Cigarette, then left in the late '70s under good terms to begin Apache Boats because he wanted to race. Saccenti allowed Ben to invest in his shop.

Since Aronow liked both young men, he decided to help them out. He made them a sweet deal on a deep-vee Cigarette mold to modify: no money up front, $5,000 royalty on each boat sold, up to eight boats. It got a grateful Apache afloat; the boat became *Warpath*, which eventually won Kramer a world championship. But that was the same transaction Cigarette sued Aronow over, failing to see his magnanimity.

In 1981, Apache sold an exclusive distributorship to a New York company, which placed a $1.5 million order, but payable only on delivery. It was sometime later, Jack said, that his son called and said, "Pop, you gotta come out and take over the business."

Jack did. He closed the lighting business that had made him his fortune, and went to work full-time for his son, selling boats and straightening out the books. Apache needed his help; they had $300,000 in payables, and just $20,000 in receivables. Jack got on the phone with their creditors, promised them a payment schedule, then met it.

"Once I got there, I saw that Ben had the ability to manufacture money," Jack said. He knew that the cash, in large amounts, was drug proceeds, but he said he never confronted Ben about it. Quite a change for the man who, a few years before, had Archie Bunker's tolerance for the counterculture.

Jack said he ran Apache while Ben "kept us away from it—myself, his mother, his brother." That seems to have been true regarding the smuggling end of Ben's business, but for Jack, certainly not the money-laundering end.

Sometime toward the end of 1981, Saccenti and the Kramers split financially. They agreed that the Kramers would build larger boats at a new plant in Hollywood called Apache Powerboats, and Saccenti would build noncompeting smaller boats at a plant called Apache Performance Boats. Saccenti would remain part of Kramer's Apache racing team.

To illustrate the aboveboard, below-board natures of Ben's partners, Dade County's official records reveal the story of one telling day in November 1981, when Aronow completed two sales of a total seven and a half acres of land on 188th Street adjacent to Cigarette. He sold one parcel to Saccenti and another to two men named Michael Wurth and Jerry Kilpatrick.

Jerry Kilpatrick was a rookie racer in 1981, winning the Michelob Light Grand Bahama 200 on April 18, 1981, in a thirty-nine-foot Squadron XII—an Aronow boat—called *Apache*. That day, as on others that year, his throttleman was Bobby Saccenti.

On November 14, 1981, Kilpatrick and Saccenti lost the UIM World Championship at Key West to Jerry Jacoby by just twenty-eight seconds. Two days later, Kilpatrick and Wurth bought Aronow's land, yet sold it less than two months later, on January 7, 1982, to "Lawrence Berrin Trustee." Berrin was a Miami attorney.

Who Berrin was trustee for became apparent on August 29, 1984, when the property was conveyed to Los Angeles financier Sam Gilbert. In 1985, the Kramers built Fort Apache Marina on the site—with proceeds of drug money, according to the 1987 Fort Lauderdale federal indictment that charged Gilbert, his son Michael Gilbert, Ben and Jack Kramer, and Mel Kessler with laundering.

Sixteen years later, Saccenti still has his land. It is hard to believe Aronow did not know that when he sold to Kilpatrick and Wurth he was really helping to wash Kramer's money. In 1985, both Kilpatrick and Wurth were indicted in federal court in Virginia for conspiracy to import more than a thousand pounds of marijuana. Kilpatrick was convicted that year; Wurth became a fugitive and was not caught and sentenced until 1994. According to what a Virginia State Police investigator had told Mike DeCora, Aronow was subpoenaed to appear at their grand jury to testify about land sales, and did.

Ben Kramer watched the 1983 World Championship at Key West from a helicopter with his father. "Next year I'm going to get into it, Pop," he told Jack. His first race, in 1984, was the New Jersey Offshore Grand Prix, a 160-mile race in a dense fog. In *Warpath*, he and Saccenti finished second by just fifteen seconds.

Ben was hooked. At Key West in 1984 he won the

Open class World Championship, averaging seventy-three miles per hour.

Aronow was proud that Ben had won the same honor he had, Jack said. "That's when he told us that now that we had won a World Championship, it was time to promote the hell out of it. That was how he built up his boat companies."

Part of Apache's promotion were two races Kramer hosted in 1985 and 1986: the Fort Apache Challenge and the Apache Offshore Grand Prix. At the latter, John Crouse said it looked like he had spent $500,000 on the party, which included music by the rock band Santana. It was cosponsored by the Miami Beach tourist authority.

Sun-Sentinel sportswriter Craig Davis remembered both parties. "Everybody suspected where the money came from for those," he said.

Once, in Kramer's boatyard, Davis thought he had walked into the television show *Miami Vice*. "It looked like a lot of extras were working there. A lot of punks." He labeled Kramer a punk, too.

In December 1982, the *Sun-Sentinel* had done a page-one story on how a significant number of powerboat racers had been arrested for smuggling drugs. Further, the association that governed the rules of powerboat-racing had none prohibiting even convicts from competing.

"During the day, we're asked to patrol their race course during events for emergency rescues," the paper quoted an unnamed United States Coast Guard official. "But at night, we're chasing many of the same guys for smuggling. That used to be a joke. Now it's reality."

The paper listed thirteen racers who had been arrested. Most of them had been convicted as well and were serving prison time, and some had organized-crime ties.

In 1983, Kramer's friend George Morales, a thirty-four-year-old United States citizen born in Colombia, won the APBA Superboat World Championship, then—in March 1984—got indicted by the Feds as a "drug kingpin" for smuggling and income tax evasion. Between 1980 and 1981, he said, he earned $37,000; the

IRS said he earned $2.2 million. John Crouse wrote in *Searace* that by 1983 Morales was "endowed with a seemingly bottomless money pit for state-of-the-art racing boats." Free on $2 million bond pending trial, Morales won three races, including the World Championship in the Superboat class again.

In 1985, Bobby Saccenti mentioned out loud that he and Kramer were thinking of trying to break the eleven-year-old speed record between Miami and New York—then considered the most elusive mark in boating, set by Bob Magoon in 1974. Racer Al Copeland overheard the remark and suggested they make a race out of it. Before long, five racers, including Morales, had anted up $100,000 each for a winner-take-all 1,257-mile race in July.

A month before the race, Harrah's, the casino giant, added its name as a sponsor of Team Apache. Actor James Caan was to come along as backup driver for Ben. Jack Kramer said Ben and Morales had an agreement to repay the other their $100,000 entry fee if either of them won.

Racing at top speed through pitch darkness was a scary proposition. "When you're doing that, the thing you can't help but think about is hoping you make it through the night," Saccenti told *The Miami News.* "All that has to happen to knock us out of the race is for us to run into a log with nearly full fuel tanks. Then there is always the possibility of having some yokel running a speedboat without lights across our path. We could go right over the top of them." A speedboat without lights sounded like a reference to a smuggler.

Morales confidently showed up at the starting line off the tip of south Miami Beach wearing a black jumpsuit with the words "Miami–New York Champion" stitched on it. Both *Miami Vice* stars Philip Michael Thomas and Don Johnson (later a world champion himself) were present—in fact, the most notable absentees were Kramer and Saccenti. One of their three 700-horsepower Lamborghini engines had burst into flames in the canal behind 188th Street because a thirty-dollar fuel pump had leaked. Only

Morales and Copeland finished the race. Morales won, shattering the old record by more than three hours, but Copeland broke the old record, too.

In August 1985—the same month as the USA Racing sale—Aronow was quoted in a *Miami News* story talking about Kramer's idea to race across the Atlantic, to England—that is, after he tried to break Morales's new record between Miami and New York.

"I designed and built the molds for a sixty-footer for them," he said. "I'm thinking about riding with Ben during the transatlantic crossing, but it is still about a year away."

Obviously, at least through then, they were still friends.

Just a week before Aronow's murder, Morales pled guilty to his federal charges, admitting that he smuggled marijuana and quaaludes from Colombia to south Florida in 1980 and 1981, and also conspired to bring in more than a ton of cocaine in January 1986. It turned out that the cocaine deal was being brokered by a DEA informant. Morales was sentenced to sixteen years.

But Morales said that soon after his arrest in June 1986, he had told his Miami prosecutors a stunning tale, one that they either didn't believe or didn't want to pursue. Then later, beginning in November 1986, he told it to CBS News, which broadcast it on their magazine show *West 57th* in April 1987:

Weeks after he was arrested in 1984, he was approached at his office at Opa-Locka airport by a Nicaraguan contra who said he was a CIA operative. He promised that "high-level Washington people" would see that his legal problems would vanish if Morales would donate money and use his fleet of small planes and pilots to help them. Specifically, the operative said he had talked directly about his situation with George Bush.

Morales had his own friends with CIA connections, and he checked out the offer, apparently to his satisfaction. So, for the next year and a half, until his 1986 arrest, Morales said he flew weapons for the contras from small airports in Fort Lauderdale and Miami to Costa Rica and El Salvador, countries near Nicaragua. That was the only way the CIA could think of to supply the contras with weapons after Congress passed the Boland Amendment, prohibiting direct military aid to them.

But return flights were something else. At least nine, he said, were loaded with cocaine and marijuana, the eventual proceeds to be used to buy more weapons for the contras. At U.S. airports, he landed and unloaded in plain sight of DEA and United States Customs agents, who were in on it, he said. Customs, while not admitting involvement, did later confirm to *The Boston Globe* that the CIA had arranged between fifty and one hundred flights that had taken off or landed at United States airports without undergoing inspection—that is, hands off everything.

In retrospect, Morales gave a quote to a *Sports Illustrated* reporter in November 1984, just after winning his second world championship, that sounded like he believed his indictment would bring him no trouble.

"Look," he explained, "if those charges were true, would the judge let me go around free like this on just my *signature* on a bond?" In fact, under indictment for the federal government's most serious drug charges, Morales got permission to fly all over the Caribbean and Central America, and was even cleared for regular trips to Cuba, according to his attorney, John Mattes.

In 1987 and 1988, Morales testified as a star witness to congressional Iran-contra investigation committees. The CIA denied involvement. So did George Bush.

Meanwhile, auto racing had problems with drugs, too.

Randy Lanier had taken up car racing, and he won twice in 1984—the L.A. Times/Nissan six-hour and the Nissan/Red Lobster 100. With fellow Fort Lauderdale resident Bill Whittington, he shared a team ironically (as it became later) named Blue Thunder Racing, which won the 1984 International Motor Sports Association (IMSA) championship. Whittington and his brother Don were best known for winning the twenty-four Hours of Le Mans race in 1979.

But in March 1986, Bill and Don Whittington were charged in federal court with earning $73 million from a marijuana smuggling ring, quelling years of racetrack rumors.

Guessing that the Whittingtons' illegal proceeds might have been invested in Blue Thunder Racing, the _Sun-Sentinel_ asked Lanier about it a week after the indictment. Lanier answered, "If it was, I didn't see it."

Boats, for Kramer like anyone else, were a hole into which you pour money. Smuggling marijuana, financially, was just the reverse.

Kramer and Lanier had begun their partnership in December 1981, smuggling the way everybody else was doing it then: loading a fast boat with up to 20,000 pounds of marijuana at a time, eluding slower patrol pursuit boats if necessary, then dropping their bales on some dark beach or inland waterway. They liked Melbourne, Florida, east of Orlando.

Then they made an innovative quantum leap. In April 1983, they jammed the ballast of an oceangoing barge in Colombia with 130,000 pounds of marijuana, covered its deck with a legitimate shipment of Venezuelan cement, then sent it to no less than New York harbor, where it was unloaded in plain sight and trucked away by customers who came up to the dock. Flush with their success, Kramer and Lanier later brought barges with up to 165,000 pounds of marijuana into San Francisco and New Orleans harbors.

When the Feds eventually counted all the marijuana the ring had sold, the grand total came to 326.6 tons. They calculated its gross as a staggering $305 million.

The Miami Herald later called Kramer "a bold risk-taker of particular vision." They quoted IRS criminal investigation agent Roger Edwards, who admired Kramer's business acumen: "Kramer did it right. You do it big, you do it brazen, you bring it right into one of the busiest ports, and you only do it one time a year so you cut your risk."

When the Feds discovered the kind of cash that Kramer and Lanier were earning, they safely assumed that some sort of parallel money-laundering operation was occurring. After the United States passed new banking laws to fight drug trafficking in the '80s, that kind of cash became impossible to negotiate lawfully without attracting attention. As an assistant United States attorney said later, if not for laundering, Ben Kramer would have been cash-wealthy and driving an old Chevy.

In fact, by 1986, a separate, far-flung investigation offshore had found their money-laundering scheme and wondered the reverse of the proposition.

That investigation began with a most unusual event. At 6:40 A.M. Saturday, November 26, 1983, six hooded men burst into a Brinks-Mat security depot near Heathrow Airport in London, handcuffed six guards, then doused one with kerosene and threatened to set him on fire unless they opened the vault.

Inside were 6,800 gold bars—three tons of gold worth twenty-five million English pounds ($38.7 million)— owned by a subsidiary of American Express. By comparison, Britain's famed "Great Train Robbers" in 1963 had gotten about 2.5 million pounds.

It was considered an inside job. The warehouse had a formidable array of security devices for overnights, but the day staff had arrived just ten minutes before the robbers and had turned them off.

The London papers called them "The Gang That Got Too Much"; Brinks-Mat usually didn't keep that much gold there. Then a detective was murdered on a stakeout, and New Scotland Yard resolved to spare no effort unraveling the case. Following the money, they uncovered a laundering ring on the Isle of Man, a banking haven offshore from England in the Irish Sea.

From there, the trail led to a baby-faced, twenty-seven-year-old Fort Lauderdale drug smuggler named Scott Errico, arrested in September 1985, also at Heathrow Airport.

Errico talked; he fingered another man, who then fingered a young accountant named Shaun Murphy, in Tortola, British Virgin Islands. On April 7, 1986, Scotland Yard arrested him, and he quickly decided to cooperate.

Investigators searched Murphy's files and found a letter of instruction for a Liechtenstein bank officer. It was signed by Jack Kramer. The story was, Mel Kessler's secretary was supposed to have mailed it to Liechtenstein but had sent it mistakenly to Tortola. Murphy filed it instead of tossing it.

The Brits called the Yanks. The evidence matched some information Hollywood Police and Kramer's federal parole officer had gathered in November 1983, when they had surveilled the Kramers meeting with financier Sam Gilbert in Los Angeles. From a wastebasket in the Kramers' Beverly Hills hotel room, they had seized a note written in Gilbert's hand, roughing out what was later realized to be the middle of the laundering scheme: checks were to be deposited in a trust account in Liechtenstein, then wire-transferred to Tortola—both, bank secrecy havens.

When Kramer had needed a money-laundering scheme, he turned to a longtime family friend, attorney Mel Kessler, who made his living representing drug dealers. With thinning hair and a graying moustache, he looked and dressed establishment. But he had offshore connections, and he himself dealt in cash. In 1985 he told _The Washington Post_ he had flown to Colombia more than a hundred times, and that his clients always paid him in cash. "I've got more cash than Burger King," he quipped.

Investigators later filled out the details: Kramer's cash was flown from Miami to Los Angeles crammed into suitcases and once even an Igloo portable water cooler, then either deposited with a friendly banker who wouldn't file the IRS form showing cash deposits of $10,000 or more, or given to coin dealers to buy Krugerrands. Either way, the money next became cashier's checks sent back to Jack Kramer in Miami.

But that was only the first step; that money was still too easy to trace.

Smugglers had discovered that a few small countries and island nations in the British Commonwealth still enforced bank secrecy laws, so they wired their money there. The object then was to send it back and forth around the globe until at last they could pop it into an untraceable "clean" hole in a United States account, and use it.

In practice, Jack Kramer took his cashier's checks to Kessler's Miami office, where they were mailed to their trust account in Liechtenstein. Next, they went to a shell account in Tortola, set up by Shaun Murphy, which would send it to Los Angeles. It was brilliant. Investigators who might find the smuggling money could trace it no further than Liechtenstein; anyone tracing the L.A. money backward would get no further than Tortola.

Next, Sam Gilbert invested the money to build Fort Apache Marina and a California card casino called the Bell Gardens Bicycle Club. He also bought numerous toys for Ben, such as a corporate jet and a ninety-six-foot yacht. But none of the assets had Kramer's name on them.

Money for both big projects began flowing in January 1984. The Bicycle Club opened in November 1984 and was immensely profitable immediately, growing in value from its $22 million investment to about $150 million.

But for all the elaborate schemes designed to fool Uncle Sam, none succeeded very long. Was it bad luck— or maybe bad karma?

At almost the same time the Feds found Shaun Murphy, they broke through the smuggling ring. Even though Customs never suspected bales in the ballast, federal prosecutors in the Southern District of Illinois built a case beginning with the marijuana-smuggling conviction of a local man named Billy Barrow.

To reduce his sentence, Barrow led FBI agents in Carbondale, Illinois, to another man in southern Illinois, who, when he agreed to plead guilty and cooperate, led them to one of Randy Lanier's New Orleans distributors, Conrad Ingold. Threatened with a long prison sentence, he, too, agreed to sing, and prosecutors put him in witness protection.

With the Feds closing in on both the smuggling and the money-laundering enterprises, the candle was now burning at both ends.

With Shaun Murphy's arrest, things went downhill quickly.

Mel Kessler got a federal subpoena for his records, which he was able to quash. But the Kramers' problems weren't strictly with the government. Once the Bicycle Club had started making big money, Sam Gilbert decided to remove them from their financial interest. Since the whole scheme had been designed to keep the Kramers' names off all official records, it wasn't impossible. In April 1986, with Fort Apache ready to open in two months, Gilbert was trying to do it again.

[Sam Gilbert died of an illness just three days before he was indicted in November 1987.]

Late in April, Jack Kramer and others met at a Miami hotel to discuss how to recover his $11 million investment in the marina. Jack later testified that he got a check for $9.5 million, which he deposited in Switzerland. In December 1986, he flew to Los Angeles to try to get the remaining $1.5 million, to no avail.

Also in December 1986, a grand jury convened in Miami and heard subpoenaed testimony from the scheme's friendly L.A. banker. The indictment followed in November 1987.

It would be fair to say that most of 1986 and the beginning of 1987 was a pretty nervous time for Ben Kramer and Randy Lanier.

Both men were in the sports limelight. In May, Lanier finished tenth in the Indianapolis 500, with an average speed of 209.964 miles per hour, then the fastest Indy time ever for a rookie. The next day, he was named the race's Rookie of the Year.

Meanwhile, Kramer won two races: the Nissan Offshore 150, at Fort Myers, Florida, on May 17, 1986, then the Northport 200 in Michigan, on August 24.

Yet perhaps more indicative of what their faces belied, both men had crashes racing that summer. On August 2, Lanier broke his leg in a collision with the concrete wall at the Michigan 500 and had to be pried from the wreckage.

On September 10, at the Coca-Cola Offshore at Sodus Point, New York, Kramer and Saccenti "shot off a wave crest, leaped half a boat length, then submarined," wrote John Crouse in *Searace*. A year before, two racers had died in the same sort of accident.

The boat stayed under for a minute. When Kramer got to the surface, he got out of the cockpit and began looking for Saccenti. He was still in his seat, unconscious and bleeding from his mouth and ears. He had a skull fracture. Kramer lifted his buddy's head out of the water and got him breathing. Saccenti spent the next two days in intensive care.

"I thought I was dead," Kramer told the *Sun-Sentinel* a day later. "When that water came down on top of me I thought I was definitely gone this time."

Kramer kept racing. Two weeks later was his host event, the Apache Offshore Grand Prix, and he was still within range to win the 1986 APBA United States Championship in the Open class.

In a story a few days before the event, *Sun-Sentinel* reporter Craig Davis wrote how powerboating had cleaned up its act, as proven by U.S. Coast Guard and City of Miami Beach cooperation with the race.

"To its credit, the offshore racing establishment has battled back bold and determined from the wave of drug scandals that swept over the sport four years ago . . . The core of honest sportsmen has made significant strides in restoring credibility."

Since Kramer's boat was wrecked in the New York crash, he accepted an offer from friendly competitor Sal Magluta to use his boat. Davis saluted the offer as part of racing's new "good guy image."

[Years later, Magluta and his racing partner, Willie Falcón, were indicted in federal court in Miami for smuggling seventy-five tons of cocaine between 1978 and 1991, worth $2.1 billion—seven times what Kramer and Lanier grossed. Prosecutors monickered them the "Kings of Cocaine," the biggest-volume smugglers in the history of the country. At a five-month trial ending in 1996, they conceded trafficking drugs until 1981, when they had pled no contest to state charges but denied doing so afterward. In the years leading to the latter trial, prosecutors associated them with the intimidation, attempted murder, and murder of some witnesses. A jury acquitted them of all charges, stunning prosecutors, defense attorneys, and even the defendants. A day later, it came out that previous to trial, they had volunteered to forfeit $40 million and 2,000 kilos of cocaine in exchange for a light sentence, but the Feds had turned it down.]

"Good to see the white hats outnumbering the black these days in powerboat-racing," Davis wrote.

Kramer finished second in the race, good enough to clinch the championship. The water had been rough, and Kramer, normally good for a banal sporting quote, told the _Sun-Sentinel_, "The first lap I was scared to death. I was sweating bullets."

Lanier was indicted first, on October 15, 1986, charged in Fort Lauderdale federal court with laundering money from marijuana smuggling—a result of the Isle of Man investigation. He was arrested by the FBI on his pleasure boat in Antigua but bonded out for $100,000. Also charged two months later was attorney Lawrence Berrin, involved as trustee in the 1981 sale of land on 188th Street between Aronow and Kramer. One of his shell companies was called G. Reedy Holdings—greedy. [In May 1987, Berrin pled guilty to laundering $50 million in drug profits from three separate smuggling rings and agreed to cooperate with the government.]

Then, on January 28, 1987, Lanier was indicted again in the Southern District of Illinois for smuggling. Under the then-new federal Continuing Criminal Enterprise law, this charge was much more serious. Now, because he could be considered a "drug kingpin," he faced a mandatory life sentence without parole if convicted. It was a harsh penalty compared to the days before the Drug War had accelerated, when marijuana smugglers faced only a few years, like Kramer had gotten in 1977.

There were other events in the month before Aronow's murder that probably unnerved Kramer and Lanier:

On January 5, Bill and Don Whittington were sentenced according to their negotiated plea agreements for smuggling $73 million worth of marijuana. Bill got five years; Don got eighteen months. Those light sentences implied that they were now helping the Feds with information.

On January 10, West Palm Beach race car driver John Paul was sentenced to twenty years for trying to murder a federal witness in his case. Paul and his son, John Paul Jr., also a race car driver, still faced charges of conspiracy to smuggle cocaine.

On January 23, boatbuilder Byng Goode—who Don Aronow had once hired to sweep the floor at Cigarette and later became company president—pled guilty to laundering $500,000 of drug profits through his new firm, Midnight Express Boats. Goode was also caught as part of the Isle of Man investigation.

And on January 26, George Morales pled guilty to smuggling cocaine and marijuana.

10

The Miami Herald's year-after-the-murder story suggested there were "enough hypotheses to fill a shelf of pulp suspense novels." Whoever shot him "killed one legend and created another—bestowing upon Don Aronow even more intrigue in death than he had in life."

And in the same paragraph, the *Herald* established a false speculation as fact: that Aronow had been shot in the groin. For years after, would-be sleuths on 188th Street would remember that detail.

Homicide detectives were still stumped as one lead after another self-destructed—a thousand in total, the *Herald* wrote. George Bush's office and King Hussein had called to ask how things were progressing, or to help. Still, Mike DeCora said there was a list of people they hadn't eliminated as suspects yet—less than a dozen.

"I don't think we ever even scratched the surface of the world he moved in. We still don't have a solid motive. And without a motive, we can't focus on one person," he said.

"Everybody has a story," said Dr. Bob Magoon, Aronow's friend. "That's the problem with this thing—the further the cops got into it, the more rumors they'd hear. You've got fifty thousand stories, and still, every lead has led no place."

Theories included:

- "The Angry Husband Theory"—"A high-
performance ladies' man, Aronow reportedly once
leaned over at a large dinner party and whispered to a
friend: 'I've had every woman at this table.' " DeCora
said he had kept a suspicion that one jealous husband
might have ordered the hit; he may have been referring
to Skip Taylor—but beyond a gut feeling, DeCora had
nothing on him.

  Lillian had told DeCora that her husband was faithful
to her. "And I think she really believes that," he said,
"but his first wife, Shirley, told me: 'I used to think
he was true blue, too, when I was married to him. Only
later did I find out that that wasn't the case.' "

  Lillian hadn't said a word to the press until the *Herald* asked her for an interview for this story.

  "It was the happiest time of his life. We were moving into a wonderful phase, with the new house, the
new baby. The horses were winning. Everything was
just wonderful. It was really a total fantasy."

  Patrick May, the *Herald* reporter, asked her to speculate whether Don could have had a girlfriend.

  "The man was home at six o'clock every night for
dinner. He was reaching into the refrigerator and I'd
say, 'Honey, you have to wait.' He was so *Father
Knows Best*, you wouldn't believe it."

  DeCora: "There were allegations, rumors that he had
extramarital affairs. Three women were named. We
talked to them and they all vehemently denied it, said
they were just friends of Aronow's."

  Magoon: "He may have had girls here and there, but
that's not the reason he was killed."

  Don Soffer, developer of Turnberry Isle: "Had there
been another woman involved, people would have
known about it. Don was not the kind of guy to sneak
around corners."

- "The Mob Hit Theory"—relating to New Jersey mobsters in the construction business who Aronow may
have dealt with thirty years before. Rumor had it, he
came to Florida in 1961 to flee them. Another rumor
had him continuing to work for the mob while in the

boat biz.

The *Herald* quoted "a man who calls himself an 'old friend' of Aronow's": "I heard it was a mob-type deal and they'd been trailing him for seventeen days to do it in some bizarre place. That two guys were involved.

"The second car was a crash car, someone acting like an innocent bystander who would run into whatever car tried to give chase. The story about his retiring from New Jersey was bull. He was in the mob up there—he wasn't a builder. He grabbed his wife and kids and blew down here, stayed six months in a hotel. And he had tremendous mob ties down here," to include Meyer Lansky.

DeCora: "We checked out the mob theory. He had friends in New Jersey—quote mobsters unquote—and we talked to them and to authorities, and he didn't owe anybody anything. He really was a self-made man."

Mike Aronow flatly denied the mob story. Magoon: "So what? I knew Meyer. He was a patient of mine. I'd see him once a year."

• "The Kramer Theory"—DeCora said Ben Kramer had been one of the more promising suspects early on—and was still on the list—because of his links to Aronow and his smuggling charges going back to the '70s.

DeCora said it appeared that Kramer had lost out when he purchased USA Racing from Aronow, which might have created animosity.

Mike Aronow: "Kramer has nothing to do with nothing."

Lillian: "I've never even met the Kramers. That's just nonsense."

• "The IRS/Drug Theory"—"Aronow was selling fast boats to drug dealers for cash. Federal authorities, unable to beat the smugglers at their high-speed offshore game, decide instead to go after the profits.

"As a straight-up, everything-by-the-book businessman, Aronow not only talked to the Feds—he talked too much, some people think.

" 'The IRS was trying to catch them like they caught

Capone,' says an [unnamed] Aronow associate, 'and Don was the only guy who could testify that yes, I sold so-and-so ten boats for a million in cash.'

"Soffer: 'That's my theory. Don was an honest businessman and reported all his stuff. Now we know these drug guys are all crazy and don't care if a life can save them ten minutes. Someone was afraid Don would testify for the government against some guy who doesn't even have a green card and is buying a $150,000 boat with cash.' "

But DeCora tended to discount that theory, the *Herald* wrote.

Mike Aronow: "No one knows what happened. But it's not related to Kramer or drugs in any way. That's the biggest joke of all. That's stupid. That's number one in stupidity. My father was the cleanest guy in the world. He had nothing to do with those idiots. He owned the street."

Now that it had been a year since the murder, Mike said, "I treat it like he's away on vacation and I'm just waiting for him to come back."

APRIL 19, 1988

A federal grand jury in Oklahoma City indicted Robert Young, Robert Vann Wilson, Skip Walton, David McCallister, and Colombian national Rodrigo Chegwin-Vergara in a Colombia-to-United States drug conspiracy, after a three-year investigation. The FBI said the men had begun to distribute 1,500 kilos of cocaine—worth $50 million wholesale—into the Oklahoma/Arkansas area, starting November 1986. They had gone there because detection in Florida had grown too hot.

APRIL 28, 1988

Tommy Teagle, a cooperating witness in one of the Isle of Man cases, volunteered to a DEA agent in Fort Lauderdale that he knew who had killed Aronow. The agent called Mike DeCora in the morning, and by 9 A.M., DeCora was in Broward to meet him.

In custody but wearing regular clothing, Teagle first asked about the $100,000 reward. DeCora told him it was contingent on an arrest.

Then Teagle began his story. He said he knew the killer's name was Bobby Campbell—or that's what his friend Rick Fidlin had told him. Campbell had told Fidlin that he was paid about $45,000 for it, and he was alone when he did it. Teagle didn't know who had contracted for the murder, but Campbell had been desperate for money to finance a load of marijuana from Jamaica.

Campbell was forty-two years old, about five feet, ten inches, or five feet, eleven inches tall, skinny, and had blondish hair cut very short and a short gray beard, Teagle said.

Teagle recalled that the murder was around the time of the 1987 Miami Grand Prix. That day, Campbell called Fidlin, asking to be picked up at the Omni Mall, near downtown Miami. Fidlin went; Campbell had gotten a haircut and shave there, and had bought a new shirt. He was carrying his old shirt, which had blood on it, and had wrapped it around a .45 handgun.

[The 1987 Miami Grand Prix, however, had been run in the first week of March, a month later than Aronow's murder.]

Although all of that came secondhand from Fidlin, Teagle said he knew firsthand that Campbell lived in Jupiter, Florida, and used his house to shelter mercenaries and store weapons such as C-4 explosives, grenades, handguns, and rifles. He always carried two pistols, including a .357 Magnum revolver.

Teagle also said Campbell had told him directly that he had shot two other people: a Colombian in Colombia, for which he was arrested, then freed; then, only two months before, someone at a marina near I-95 and State Road 84 in Fort Lauderdale.

Teagle offered the names of two people Campbell associated with. One was Paul Silverman, who had once been a lawyer and who Campbell used for legal advice. He lived on Hollywood Beach, and Campbell's wife, Kathy, was friendly with Silverman's wife, Tammy. Teagle also knew of a man name Wayne, from North Carolina. Although he couldn't remember Wayne's last name, he offered two local phone numbers from an address book for him, and one for his mother in North Carolina.

MAY 17, 1988

A second federal prisoner came forward with information about Aronow's murder. FBI agent John Hershley, in Oklahoma City, sent a message to DeCora that David McCallister wanted to talk to Miami detectives.

On the telephone, Hershley told DeCora that McCallister had made a plea agreement in his narcotics case and was now cooperating. His codefendant was Robert Jason Scott—real name Robert Samuel Young—and McCallister said that Young had killed Aronow.

Robert Scott was the same name an anonymous caller had mentioned to detectives a year before. At that time, the caller said Scott had been offered $30,000 to kill someone in the Miami Beach area, and that he drove a black Lincoln Town Car.

MAY 27, 1988

A police SWAT team found Robert Young, a.k.a. Scott, (a.k.a. Campbell?) and his wife, Kathleen Kunzig, at their five-acre home in Palm Beach County and arrested them both. Young was a fugitive on three charges: the Oklahoma City drug conspiracy, a murder in Miami, and bond jumping on an attempted murder in Fort Lauderdale—the one Teagle had referred to. Kunzig, too, had been charged in the murder and the attempted murder.

In addition, the Oklahoma City federal indictment had documented that Young was in Miami for a meeting four days before Aronow was killed.

JUNE 15, 1988
8 A.M.

Just as Mike DeCora went on leave from work to have surgery, a torrent of new information gushed in.

First, FBI agent John Hershley called again from Oklahoma City. Detective Archie Moore—part of DeCora's team—picked up the phone.

As Hershley detailed it, McCallister's information matched what the anonymous caller had said about Robert Scott: Scott (a.k.a. Young) had been contracted to kill Aronow for $30,000; he owned a .45 handgun and had been seen driving a black Lincoln leased by Skip Walton.

[And, in fact, McCallister later admitted that he was the anonymous caller. When Detective Falcon had taken the call in April 1987, he wrote down that the person who had leased the car was named "Ski." Since then, Skip Walton had been indicted twice: with Young, in Oklahoma; and, separately, for murder on the high seas, in federal court in Fort Lauderdale, where he was being held pending trial.]

Hershley said McCallister told him that Scott had bragged about shooting people in crowded areas and figured that people wouldn't be able to identify him because of the element of surprise.

Hershley told Moore that McCallister had worked as a pilot for Scott's drug ring, bringing cocaine into the United States from Colombia and Jamaica. He was now serving time in federal prison in Texas, but the FBI had brought him to Oklahoma City to talk. If Metro-Dade wanted to see him personally, Hershley could arrange for him to stay longer.

11:30 A.M.

Just hours later, there was another new lead. FBI agent John Thompson, in Miami, called and spoke to Moore about Frank Meade, who the federal Bureau of Alcohol, Tobacco and Firearms (BATF) had arrested with an AR-

15 rifle in Palm Beach County. He had been an enforcer for Bobby Young (whom he knew as Scott) and had turned informant, and his information had set up Young's arrest.

Meade also said Young had admitted to him that he had killed Aronow; Young and his drug ring wanted him dead because he was playing both sides of the street, building speedboats for the government as well as for smugglers. Thompson said Meade could also provide at least four other witnesses who were part of the ring but were now willing to testify.

JUNE 16, 1988

FBI agent Hershley called again. He told Moore he could come see McCallister at a county jail just outside Oklahoma City, and that Robert Vann Wilson, another codefendant of Young who had made a plea agreement, might also talk.

JUNE 21, 1988

DAVID McCALLISTER

Moore flew to Oklahoma City to meet with David McCallister.

McCallister said the FBI had arrested him in June 1987 for conspiracy to traffic cocaine. He was now serving a sentence of eighteen months for it.

He said he had first met Bobby Scott in Miami during the fall of 1986 through a man named Wayne, whose last name he didn't know. At the time, McCallister, a pilot, was flying drugs from Jamaica to Miami. He later saw Scott in Fort Lauderdale in December 1986, and again in January 1987 at North Perry Airport, a commuter field between Miami and Fort Lauderdale. At both times, he saw him carrying a .45 semiautomatic, which Scott had bought at a local gun show.

He described Scott as a white male in his forties, with

a thin salt-and-pepper beard and somewhat long, brownish gray hair, grown over his ears. He wore red-and-white baseball caps bearing the name of his boat charter business, multicolored shirts, and sneakers. He drove a black four-door 1986 or 1987 Lincoln, which Skip Walton had leased. He and Walton both had portable phones, but McCallister couldn't recall the numbers. Walton carried semiautomatic pistols as well.

McCallister said Scott had once told him that he had killed at least fourteen people, which helped McCallister form his opinion that Scott was very dangerous and unpredictable. Also, in late October or early November 1986, Scott had mentioned to him that someone wanted him to do a hit for $30,000, but he didn't want to do it.

McCallister said that when he read about Aronow's murder in a months-old edition of _Time_ magazine, he suspected that Scott was responsible, in part based on its circumstances and the car that was used. That was when he had called Metro-Dade Police, anonymously.

McCallister also said he had once visited 188th Street—he called it "Gasoline Alley"—in early 1986 with Walton and a man who kept his thirty-foot Cigarette at Fort Apache Marina, a place McCallister believed was owned by someone named Kramer.

JUNE 29, 1988

The Miami Herald reported that earlier that month, Lillian Aronow had sold the mansion at 5800 N. Bay Road in Miami Beach that she and Don had planned to move into. The price was $3.1 million, the second highest price ever paid for a residence in Dade County. The record was $3.2 million, paid for a house a block north.

JULY 1–July 22, 1988
Southern District of Illinois
Benton, Illinois

TESTIMONY OF CHARLES VICTOR PODESTA
FEDERAL SMUGGLING TRIAL OF KRAMER,
LANIER, GENE FISCHER AND OTHERS

The star prosecution witness at Kramer and Lanier's smuggling trial was Chuck Podesta, who had known them both from high school days, selling pot on Hollywood Beach, and had risen to become Lanier's bookkeeper and paymaster. At trial, he dressed more like an accountant than a pothead. But there was some truth to his appearance; he had once been an executive in his family's food brokerage business.

Podesta detailed the inner workings of the ring. Beyond his duties as bookkeeper, he had rented secluded homes to use as stash houses, had steel doors installed in them to guard certain rooms, and bought digital scales to weigh marijuana and rubber inflatable Zodiac boats to shuttle bales in shallow water between the beach and Kramer's fishing trawler.

He described their first smuggling adventure, in April 1982: the night was "pitch-black," and the plan was for the trawler to stay a mile offshore of Melbourne, Florida, so it was just "a small, blinking light in the distance." Leroy Wisser, the trawler's captain, held his position based on a strobe light placed on the beach.

[Wisser, a.k.a. "Slick," was the same man arrested with Kramer in Hollywood back in 1975 for importing marijuana. He had jumped bond a few months later—as had Kramer—but Wisser had managed not to get caught until 1987, when the FBI had pursued him on this case.]

From the beach, Kramer talked to Wisser by walkie-talkie. When the Zodiac boats, loaded with bales, came onshore, a human chain was formed to chuck the bales onto a sand dune, to be loaded later onto vans.

Lanier was stationed at a stash house. He and others stripped the burlap from the bales and inventoried them. All of the pot was distributed within a week; Lanier decided when customers would come, how much pot they would get, and what they would have to pay. Prices were about $300 a pound.

The idea to bring marijuana into the United States in the ballast tanks of barges was George (Tommy) Brock's, Podesta said. Where Kramer had always been in charge of buying the pot, and Lanier of distributing it, now they cut in Brock and his friend Gene Fischer (together to share one-third of the profits), who took charge of shipping the pot from Colombia to the United States.

(Although Brock faced the same charges as the others, he was not present at trial, still a fugitive.)

Podesta testified that the ring knew by the middle of 1986 that the Feds' noose was tightening around them.

In November 1986, while they still could, they slipped one last big load into San Francisco harbor. They had planned it for New Orleans, but once they realized that one of their Louisiana customers, Conrad Ingold, had been arrested and was probably working undercover for the Feds, they shifted the location.

From December 1986 to January 1987, Podesta received payments of more than $31 million for it. From that, he paid $12.5 million to Kramer, $10.2 million to be split between Fischer and Brock, and the remaining $8 million-plus to Lanier. Kramer got the most because he had to pay the Colombians out of his share.

In late December, anticipating a need for mad money in the near future, Podesta flew to Geneva with $1.5 million cash to give to a local attorney to deposit in Lanier's account.

Podesta and Lanier were both indicted January 28, 1987. Lanier knew about a week before that it was coming, Podesta said. That week, he met Lanier at his Miami high-rise apartment; Lanier was making arrangements to leave in the next few days, and he instructed Podesta on how the remaining $7 million in marijuana receivables were to be shared.

Podesta said he then saw Lanier once more, the day after the indictment, in a Fort Lauderdale parking lot.

Understandably, Lanier was in a hurry, and Podesta gave him a hundred grand in cash.

Podesta was arrested the next day, January 30. He had gone to a driver's license bureau in Pompano Beach to get new identification with a false birth certificate he had purchased from a smuggling customer. But a clerk became suspicious of it, called police, and then asked him into a back room—where, "petrified," he stumbled over a question about his mother's name and place of birth. He was arrested, his car was searched, and police found his black briefcase containing $18,000 cash and a small spiral notebook—his master ledger of Lanier's transactions and customers' addresses.

"Oh, no, not the book," Podesta quoted Lanier as saying at the time.

[Lanier, however, remained a fugitive when, a week later, on the morning of February 3, 1987, the *Sun-Sentinel* ran a two-inch story that he was expected to turn himself in the next day, in Fort Lauderdale. That afternoon, Don Aronow was murdered. The next morning, Lanier didn't show.

Lanier wasn't arrested until eight months later, stepping off an airplane in Puerto Rico with Leroy Wisser.]

At first, Podesta had faced a maximum penalty of fifteen years and was able to bond out for $100,000. But to pressure him to flip, the government later reindicted him (and other lesser coconspirators) on the same charges as Lanier—so now Podesta faced life without parole as well. On August 25, 1987, he capitulated and signed a deal to testify in exchange for a promise from prosecutors that they recommend a sentence between ten and twenty-two years. He apparently then testified to a grand jury, which returned an indictment against Kramer the next day.

Apparently as well, Podesta was FBI agent Robert Dueker's source of information that Kramer and Lanier had avenged the killing of Ted Richards, allegedly one of their drug customers. Podesta didn't name Richards at trial, but he did testify that Lanier had to move out of his house because one of their customers had been "murdered in a drug rip-off."

In cross-examination, Podesta acknowledged that he had written a letter to Kramer, also in jail, that Podesta was sitting in a "dungeon" while the FBI "harassed" his wife. They'd be better off in Russia, he lamented.

But Podesta explained that he wrote the letter to encourage Kramer to plead guilty to lesser charges and not "make the mistake of playing hardball." He overdramatized his letter, he said, because Kramer is a "rather thickheaded individual."

AUGUST 24, 1988

Miami Review, a daily business newspaper, reported that Lillian Aronow had closed on a new home in Coconut Grove for $930,000. It had half the square footage of the house she had sold, but the same number of bedrooms— eleven.

SEPTEMBER 2, 1988

To compare notes, Mike DeCora asked Archie Moore to meet with the two other local detectives who had pending cases involving Bobby Young, a.k.a. Robert Jason Scott. Miami Police detective Nelson Andreu had a homicide, and Fort Lauderdale Police detective Steve Robitaille had an attempted murder.

ROBERT SAMUEL YOUNG

Bobby Young, six feet tall, 180 pounds, blond hair, blue eyes, born in East St. Louis, Illinois, and about to turn forty years old, had made national news before 1988. In July 1981, he was among four men who were arrested by Cuban authorities and whose boat was seized, allegedly for straying into Cuban waters, but not before a gunfight. The men claimed they were on a scuba trip and had lost their way; the Cubans charged that they had 300 pounds of marijuana aboard their vessel. They were convicted of smuggling and sentenced to sixteen years in a Cuban jail.

But in June 1984, an angel for Young appeared in the person of the Reverend Jesse Jackson, then running for president. After successfully negotiating for the release from Syria of a captured American pilot, Jackson turned his attention to American prisoners held by Fidel Castro. After a few days' visit, he convinced Castro to release twenty-two of the twenty-six Americans he was holding, mostly for drug offenses.

When Young arrived in the United States, he was detained by the United States Marshals Service for violating parole, which he had received in 1980. He had been sentenced to nine years for using interstate commerce to promote a "floating prostitution enterprise" in St. Louis; Columbia, South Carolina; Wheeling, West Virginia; and Las Vegas. Young spent the next few months in a federal prison.

But on closer examination, there was another compelling name on the list of prisoners released from Cuba, arrested on the same boat as Young: Jerry Lee Jacoby.

It was *not* the same Jerry Jacoby as the boat-racer friend of Don Aronow. In fact, *The Miami Herald* had printed a large front-page photo of this Jacoby and Jesse Jackson embracing on the day after Castro had decided to let the twenty-two men leave. A *New York Times* photo of racer Jacoby proved they were different people.

Jacoby told the *Herald* he had been working as a diesel mechanic on the Miami River when he met Young, a boat captain. Young invited him on a scuba and fishing trip. They had engine trouble near Jamaica, then hit a storm and drifted near the Cuban coast.

Was this the answer to the mysterious reference to "Jerry Jacoby" at USA Racing on the afternoon Aronow was killed?

The City of Miami homicide case against Young involved the shooting and dumping of the body of John E.

Panzavecchia, aged thirty-nine, whose nickname, "Big Red," reflected his six-foot, one-inch size, red beard, and red hair that was actually a wig covering his bald head.

Panzavecchia apparently also had a connection of some sort to Ben Kramer. Two months earlier, when Chuck Podesta had testified, he said in an aside that he remembered a man on board a tugboat helping them smuggle drugs who had bright red hair and a bright red beard, whom he knew as "Red." Podesta recalled that that had been in 1984 or 1985.

That sounded like Panzavecchia, unless it was 1985. That's because on Saturday morning, December 29, 1984, a fisherman and his son found him floating in an Everglades canal west of Fort Lauderdale. He was wearing a gold and diamond ring shaped like a panther, with the word "Red" engraved inside it. There were also four .25-caliber bullets in his head. The Broward County medical examiner said he had been in the water less than a day.

Broward County detectives found Panzavecchia's common-law wife, Mary Hilda "Candy" Schuck. She said she had witnessed her husband's murder, the day before, at a house in north Miami.

Schuck told Detective Nelson Andreu that early on Friday morning, she and Panzavecchia had gone to meet Bobby Young, whom she described as an associate of his. While she was off in a side room with Young's girlfriend [later wife] Kathleen Kunzig and another woman, she heard at least two gunshots.

When Schuck came into the Florida room, she saw Panzavecchia motionless on the floor, bleeding. She said Young immediately confronted her and said he had killed him to protect her; then Young assured her that he wouldn't harm her.

Young and two other men then divvied up Panzavecchia's jewelry, including his bracelets and Rolex Presidential model watch. They wrapped his body, took it to the garage, and talked about how to dispose of it.

Andreu got a search warrant for the house the next

day, and found traces of blood that later tested positive as Panzavecchia's.

The third woman, Siobhan Fernandez, told Andreu in July 1985 that she had seen Young and Panzavecchia arguing. Young asked her to make him a sandwich, and while in the kitchen, Fernandez heard gunshots. She said she ran back and saw Young holding a gun and standing over Panzavecchia, who was still moving convulsively. Young said, "He's still breathing"; then she watched Young put his gun to Panzavecchia's head and fire a final shot.

Fernandez also saw Young and the two other men wrap the body, carry it into the garage, and then heard them drive away.

In September 1985, Dade County indicted Young, Kunzig, and one other for first-degree murder. A month later, the state attorney gave Kunzig immunity in return for a statement.

Kunzig, who had prior arrests for prostitution and giving false information, said she first met Panzavecchia on the evening of the murder. He and Young were at a 7-Eleven and were planning a dope deal. Young, she said, had just gotten out of prison.

On their way to the house, Panzavecchia took a shot at the car that she and Young were driving, shattering their driver's-side mirror.

At the house, Kunzig said Candy Schuck showed her a number of old bruises around her vagina. She told Kunzig, "Please don't tell John, but John beat me."

After the shooting, Kunzig said she overheard the words "It had to be done because he would have killed us. He was a crazy bastard." At first she said she didn't know who had spoken that, but later she added, "Bobby told me that he had to shoot John because John was crazy and that he had a gun and he was going to shoot at him, something to the effect that 'He had a gun, he was going to kill us, so I shot him.' "

Kunzig also said Young used her rental car to dump the body.

Later, *The Miami Herald* reported that Panzavecchia

was a member of the "Dixie Mafia." The newspaper said he ran guns and kept newspaper clippings about unsolved murders in his house—at least one of which that he had committed.

Also, the *Herald* wrote, when the medical examiner had found him, Panzavecchia was wearing underwear with the words "Be My Baby."

The Fort Lauderdale case began in the summer of 1986. Young—a fugitive on the Panzavecchia indictment and perhaps for that reason now using the name Robert Jason Scott—was introduced to a Fort Lauderdale man named Craig Marshall, who agreed to lend him $8,000 so he could repair his charter sailboat, *Cat Dancer*. [That was also Kathleen's nickname, she being an exotic dancer, but Marshall had no idea because he knew her as Mary Ann Nixon, an alias.] Young agreed to repay Marshall $30,000 in two months, and signed a lien against the boat to Marshall.

But a year later, August 1987, Young hadn't paid up. Under his legal rights, Marshall had *Cat Dancer* repossessed and moved from its berth at a Fort Lauderdale marina. The next evening, Young came looking for Marshall at his home, and found him as he pulled into his driveway.

According to Marshall, Young told him, "I want my Goddamn boat," pointed a .25-caliber Beretta pistol at him through his windshield, then opened the car door. "Where's my Goddamn boat?"

"I don't know, Bob," Marshall answered. Then, almost instantaneously, Young fired a shot into Marshall's leg, from a distance he described as not more than two inches away.

"Craig, I hoped you weren't gonna have that attitude. I'm gonna ask you one more time, and the next one will be in the face. Where is my Goddamn boat?"

"Bob, I don't know what marina it's in," Marshall pled. Then, as Young's hand rose up, Marshall turned his head, heard another shot, and felt it enter his back.

Young pushed Marshall to the passenger side of the

car, got in, then put the gun to the side of his head.

"I ought to blow your fuckin' brains out now. You don't do shit like this to me," Young said. Then Skip Walton—present along with Kathleen and Robert Vann Wilson—tried to mediate.

"Calm down, calm down, we're gonna get the boat, calm down," Walton said.

Hurt and scared, Marshall led Young and the others on a tour of marinas around I-95 and State Road 84 in Fort Lauderdale where his repossessor might have taken the boat. At the first one, Young threatened, "If I don't find that boat, you're dead meat. You're gonna be history." But when they checked the second one, they did find it.

"Well, what are we gonna do with him?" Young asked, after they drove to an abandoned gas station nearby.

"We gotta waste him. We gotta waste him," Kunzig urged.

"Well," said Young.

"Now, wait a minute," Walton interrupted. "Look at the guy; I think he's had enough. If you're willing to pay him off, I don't think he's gonna say a thing."

Young opened the car door and suggested an arrangement to Marshall, now woozy, four hours after being shot: "What do you say, if I pay you off, cover your hospital bills, you forget about this whole thing?"

Marshall agreed he would invent a story about being mugged if they would take him to a hospital. They did. Marshall made up something to tell doctors but changed it later when he spoke to detectives, then consented to take a polygraph.

While Marshall was at Broward General Hospital, Young and Kunzig called at least twice, once while Detective Robitaille happened to be present. They offered to pay Marshall $60,000 within two months if he would immediately release the lien on the boat.

Young offered to set up a meeting with Marshall's private investigator at a Fort Lauderdale McDonald's. The meeting took place on September 3, and Fort Lauderdale police arrested Young and Kunzig.

Young waived his Miranda rights and made a taped statement to Robitaille. He admitted shooting Marshall twice but said he hadn't intended to:

"Uh, I walked up to the car and I had a .25 automatic with me. And, uh, I asked him where the boat was. We started wrestling. Uh, it accidentally went off. I didn't mean to shoot the man. Accidentally went off and shot him in the leg as he was going over the seat to the other side.

"I said, 'Well, I'll drive, I want to see where my boat's at.' He said, 'Well, I'll take you to your boat.' And as he was going over the console—it's a four-speed car— the gun went off accidentally again.''

Young [as Scott] and Kunzig [as Mary Ann Nixon] were charged with kidnapping and aggravated battery, bonded out, then failed to appear in court for trial.

When the police SWAT team arrested Young and Kunzig in May 1988 and placed them in sheriff's cars, Robitaille asked Young if he remembered him.

"Goddamn, Steve, is that you? How did you find me?'' Young asked.

Robitaille couldn't reveal how but said he did know who Young/Scott really was, to which Young replied:

"Just remember, Steve, I never did anyone who didn't deserve it.''

Young asked what else they had on him. Robitaille answered, the Miami case and the federal charge out of Oklahoma City.

"What thing out of Oklahoma City?'' Young said.

"You know, that thing with Skip Walton.''

"Goddamn, do you know where Skip Walton is now?''

"He's at MCC [Metropolitan Correctional Center, a federal prison] in Dade County for murder on the high seas.''

Young asked if Fort Lauderdale was going to charge Walton in the Marshall kidnapping case. Yes, Robitaille said.

"Damn, Skip was the one who drove the guy to the hospital."

"Yeah, I know, that's not like him," said Robitaille.

"Yeah, it's not like me, either," said Young.

SEPTEMBER 7, 1988

At a meeting at the Miami office of the FBI, Agent Nikki Deary told Archie Moore she had heard that Skip Walton was looking to make a deal on his federal charges of murder on the high seas and cooperate on the Aronow case. According to Deary's informant, Tommy Teagle, Walton said he could describe the weapon that Bobby Scott had used to kill Aronow and tell where it might be now. In addition, he could testify that he supplied Scott with the Lincoln he had used.

SEPTEMBER 30, 1988

Kathleen Kunzig, charged and brought to trial as Mary Ann Nixon, was convicted by a Fort Lauderdale jury of armed kidnapping in the Craig Marshall case. She was sentenced to six years.

OCTOBER 4, 1988
Benton, Illinois

After fifteen weeks of trial and two days of deliberation, all the defendants were found guilty on charges of engaging in a continuing criminal enterprise and conspiring to distribute more than 1,000 pounds of marijuana between 1982 and 1986. The same day, the jury found that Kramer and Lanier should forfeit $150 million.

Outside the courtroom, Lanier's attorney, Robert Ritchie, from Knoxville, Tennessee, told a reporter for the *Southern Illinoisan* that Lanier had made mistakes and was willing to pay for them.

But "life without parole for a marijuana offense is not fair and is not just. We have a drug problem in this country. It should—indeed it must—be addressed. But life without parole is a product of drug hysteria, certainly as it applies to marijuana."

NOVEMBER 1988

Miami Herald Pulitzer Prize–winning reporter Edna Buchanan, writing in *Fame* magazine, said stumped cops now believed that Aronow had been shadowed for days, possibly weeks. Because he was killed in such a public way on the street that he had built, they deduced that "somebody sent a message."

"He pissed somebody off," Buchanan quoted a detective she didn't name. "He was a tough businessman. If you made a deal with him, he stuck by it. If you faltered, that was your problem. If you were going hungry, your children were in the street, it was sad, but you made the deal, tough shit—which of course made enemies. We haven't talked to anybody who ever bested him in a business transaction. Don Aronow was always one up on everybody."

Buchanan rehashed all the other theories mentioned in the *Miami Herald*'s January 1988 one-year story. Regarding the theory that Aronow had volunteered information to the IRS about drug dealers who bought boats—again attributing to unnamed detectives—she wrote that Aronow had not been expected to testify in any such cases.

NOVEMBER 17, 1988

Frank Meade brought his friend Billy Schaab to the homicide office to meet detectives. But instead of talking there, Archie Moore took them to the Dade County Metro Justice Center to see assistant state attorneys Gary Rosenberg and Abe Laeser.

Schaab, a self-employed painter in West Palm Beach, said he had known Bobby Scott for a few months because they lived in the same neighborhood. When Scott wanted to buy a Rottweiler puppy, Schaab introduced him to Meade, since Meade bred the dogs.

However, Schaab knew that Scott was "very crazy and extremely dangerous." He also knew he carried a .45 pistol and was involved in the drug business.

Twice, Schaab said he kept packages at his house for Scott; he suspected that they contained large amounts of either money or narcotics. One of those times, an evening around the time when Aronow was murdered, Scott told him that the package contained about $100,000. He asked Schaab to hold onto it for a day or so; then he would return to pick it up.

Two evenings later, Scott did. The next morning, Scott came by again and asked if he had read the newspaper. While Scott stood nearby, Schaab picked up the paper and read the lead story about Aronow's murder. He then turned to Scott, then Scott nodded his head and smiled. That made him believe Schaab was involved.

DECEMBER 5, 1988

U.S. District Court judge James Foreman sentenced Ben Kramer and Gene Fischer to life in prison without parole.

One of Kramer's attorneys, Kate Bonner of Miami, told the judge that as a citizen, she found the new federal rules that forced codefendants like Podesta into becoming government witnesses—because it was the only way to get a fair sentence—"reprehensible."

The judge then asked her how she would propose fighting the country's drug problem. Bonner said she didn't have an answer.

Foreman told Kramer, "What really brought down the house on the three of you" was that they had transported that last barge of marijuana after they knew they were under investigation. Had they refrained, all of their criminal actions would have taken place before the new Continuing Criminal Enterprise bill became law, and they wouldn't have gotten mandatory life sentences.

DECEMBER 9, 1988

Archie Moore and Steve Parr compiled new photo line-ups to show to witnesses. One six-picture lineup had Bobby Young, and the second had Wayne Shehan—the "Wayne" that McCallister as well as Teagle knew.

First they brought them to Mike Britton. He couldn't pick out anyone.

Next they showed them to Patty Lezaca. She didn't identify anyone in Young's deck, but when they showed her Shehan's deck, she thought Shehan "resembled" the person who said he was Jerry Jacoby. However, she wouldn't make a positive ID.

DECEMBER 12, 1988

In the morning, FBI agent Nikki Deary called Moore with addresses for Wayne Shehan in Georgia and North Carolina.

In the afternoon, Moore took the lineups to Levon Tindall, but he couldn't ID anyone, either.

DECEMBER 21, 1988

Randy Lanier also got life without parole for smuggling.

"You have before you, Judge, one of the richest men in the United States because of his dealings in drugs," said assistant U.S. attorney Mike Carr.

Lanier, who hadn't taken the stand at trial, spoke at sentencing: "A person should not have to spend the rest of his life in prison for marijuana." Afterward, his attorney, Robert Ritchie, said Lanier's tone had sounded hostile because he was trying to keep from crying.

11

BOBBY YOUNG

Bobby Young, from the Broward County Jail, wrote a letter to Skip Walton, at MCC Miami.

Regarding his Broward County case, "The only problem with this one is if I lose they are going to try to give me 2 life sentences, and if I take a plea, I'll get between 12-17, and at the most do around another three to four, tops! I am trying to get them down to 12 with a 3 mandatory."

Regarding his federal case: "Those fuckers told them anything they wanted to hear and they were the ones who were doing everything themselves. Jesus Christ, what 'Scumbag' Low Life Mothers! I know they can't look themselves in the mirror in the morning, that's for sure! I even helped David [McCallister?] with money for his father's cancer operation. But no one knew that, did they, and he does this to me! I really can't write straight I'm so hot just thinking about it! Burns my ass, man!

"Seems everyone is trying to talk their way out of jail but us! Least I smile in the mirror every day!!! When I got the wire that you thought I was turning, well, yes, I was, but on myself and no one else.

"Skipper, we don't have any major problem with the Feds, just relax, I'll do everything I can to help you. I am your friend, Skip, I would never ever hurt you for anything! Big Smile! And I would never disrespect myself that way, besides, my mom would disown me, my father was in the rackets, he would roll over in his grave, believe me! So give me a big smile, kiddo!''

JANUARY 22, 1989

WAYNE SHEHAN

Detectives had heard that Wayne Shehan was dead, so they were a little surprised to find that credit cards for him had been recently used in the vicinity of Tryon, North Carolina, a small town on the hilly South Carolina border, about forty miles between both Asheville, North Carolina, and Greenville, South Carolina. Metro-Dade had called local police, who confirmed that Shehan was alive and well and living with kin there.

In fact, the fugitive warrants bureau of the Palm Beach County Sheriff's Office had already found him. A year before, he had skipped a felony trial date; however, North Carolina had refused to extradite him.

In July 1987, two men told Palm Beach County police they had just bought lunch at a Winn-Dixie grocery when they passed a woman at a pay phone. After ending her conversation, she entered a red Chevy Blazer. The two men heard her quarter drop back into the coin return and tried to get her attention. As they approached the Blazer, they saw a man making faces at them. Then the man opened his driver's-side door, pointed a chrome .357 Magnum at one of the Good Samaritans and said, "I'll blow your fucking head off. That's my old lady." Later that afternoon, police stopped a 1979 Blazer with Wisconsin tags, and the victims identified Shehan. He was charged with aggravated assault with a firearm.

So Mike DeCora, back on the job but working midnights, was pleased to hear back from Tryon Police that they had just arrested both Wayne Shehan and his wife, Cynthia, during a traffic stop and charged them with possession of suspected heroin and drug paraphernalia—a syringe.

JANUARY 24, 1989

Shehan hadn't been able to make his $75,000 bond, so with a bond reduction hearing pending in a day, DeCora flew north to see if he would speak to him from inside the Polk County Jail.

When DeCora identified himself as a Dade County homicide detective, Shehan got fidgety and evasive, but he did agree to talk briefly, without an attorney present.

Shehan, aged forty-two, was six feet, three inches tall, 195 pounds, with blond hair and blue eyes. He admitted that he and Young (whom he knew as Bobby Scott) had been colleagues for years, and that he had been together with Young early on the day of the murder. He remembered that Young had been driving a rented black Town Car with tinted windows, and that at sometime during the day, Young had told him to watch the six o'clock news. That was the first time he knew anything about the murder, he said.

DeCora asked Shehan where he had been at the time of the shooting. He said Toys "R" Us, with his wife, buying things for their children. But when DeCora pressed for the store location, he couldn't remember.

That answer failed to endear him to DeCora.

Speaking about his arrest for aggravated assault, Shehan said that the .357 revolver he was carrying belonged to Young. Young had asked him to hold it.

Near the end of the talk, Shehan said he was afraid that Young might try to kill him—he wouldn't say why. But that fear had caused him to take his family and flee south Florida for North Carolina, where he was born and raised.

In the afternoon, DeCora found Cynthia Shehan, Wayne's wife. She volunteered that Young was crazy, and she wouldn't be surprised if he was involved in the murder. Then DeCora asked if she remembered where Wayne was at the time of the murder. She said she didn't.

JANUARY 25, 1989

The next morning, DeCora attended the bond reduction hearing. After it was over, deputy sheriff James Carter, who had escorted Shehan from the jail to the courthouse, came forward to DeCora and told him that Shehan had just blurted out that he had been with Young when Aronow was murdered.

However, Carter then explained that Shehan immediately tried to take back what he had just said. What he really had meant to say, Shehan had said next, was merely that he knew Young had killed Aronow.

JANUARY 26, 1989

Shehan consented to one more interview with DeCora. This time, with his attorney present, he went into more detail.

Shehan said he had known Young for a year and a half prior to the murder; Young had liked Shehan's two children and wanted to make sure they had food on the table and a place to stay. However, Shehan explained that he had to leave Florida the day before his trial was to begin in December 1987 because Young was supposed to be a witness for him, and Young had just been arrested by Fort Lauderdale police for attempted murder. Before he fled, he had someone tell Young that he had died of an overdose, so Young wouldn't go looking for him.

Shehan said Young often bought firearms and ammunition at a gun store near his attorney's office in Fort Lauderdale. Right after Aronow's murder, Shehan recalled that Young traded in his .45 semiautomatic pistol for a new nine-millimeter pistol.

Shehan held to his story that at the time of the murder, he and his wife were at a Toys" R" Us, the location of which he still couldn't remember. He said Young had beeped him, and when he called back, Young said he needed him "right now." Shehan replied that he couldn't make it; then Young said he would get someone else and told him to watch the six o'clock news—at which time he learned about the murder.

There was more. That evening, Shehan saw Young again. They and a man named Carl (whom he had met through Skip Walton) rode in the same Town Car to a phone booth on the corner so Young could make a pay-phone call. Carl drove, Shehan was in the passenger seat, and Young sat in back. Shehan described the Lincoln as a "limited edition" with chrome on the sides. He also remembered bags of clothing on the back seat that he believed belonged to Carl, who was then moving in with Young. Carl, he said, resembled the composite picture of the killer that the newspapers had published.

Later that evening, Young described Aronow's murder to him: he pulled up next to Aronow's car, driver's door to driver's door, and shot him five times. Falling limp, Aronow "mashed down" his accelerator, racing the engine as Young made a U-turn around him, then sped off toward Biscayne Boulevard.

After that night, Shehan never saw the Lincoln again.

Shehan also told DeCora that someone whom he couldn't remember had told him that Young was paid $60,000 for the murder. Afterward, Young got arrested in South America, and he used that money to pay bribes to get free.

And one last thing: Shehan knew who might be responsible for having hired Young. Shehan didn't know his name, but he owned Apache Boats. He and Young were friends, and they had once smuggled drugs together.

JANUARY 30, 1989

Detective Parr talked further with Billy Schaab, who gave him telephone numbers for Bobby Young's pager and cell phone. Detectives then subpoenaed the phone records and found that the cell phone number was registered to a Miami man named James J. Fidlin from December 6, 1986, until he terminated the service at 4:29 P.M. on February 3, 1987—almost exactly one hour after Aronow's murder.

JANUARY 31, 1989

Bobby Young pled guilty to one count of armed kidnapping in the Craig Marshall case and was sentenced to seventeen years, Florida State Prison.

FEBRUARY 1, 1989
9 P.M.

DeCora and Moore visited the home of James Fidlin, and his son of the same name. The younger James, aged twenty-two, said his uncle Richard Fidlin [a name Tommy Teagle mentioned] had asked him in November 1986 to buy a cell phone, get service in James's name, and give the phone to Richard. But Richard never paid the bill, and finally, in February, James called the cell phone company and canceled the service. James didn't know who was using the phone, or why Richard wanted to go through that ruse, since Richard had two other cell phones installed in his cars.

FEBRUARY 2, 1989
8 A.M.

Moore and Parr knocked on Richard Fidlin's door in Fort Lauderdale but got no response. Later in the day they spoke to his wife and left a message.

FEBRUARY 3, 1989

PAUL SILVERMAN

On a day that was exactly two years after the murder, Mike DeCora and Steve Parr found an address on Hollywood Beach for Paul Silverman, who Tommy Teagle had said was a friend of Bobby Young's.

The detectives arrived unannounced with Miami FBI agent Joe Ciccarelli, who was familiar with Silverman. The FBI agent introduced the detectives, then left.

Silverman, aged fifty-four, had problems of his own but was willing to talk. First, he was suffering from heart disease. He was also awaiting trial on federal narcotics charges.

On October 12, 1988, Silverman—disbarred as an attorney in Georgia after a previous drug case—was in the process of completing a marijuana deal near Nashville when his contact told him he was working undercover for the FBI. Silverman was arrested; then, days later, his New York partner got stung, too, holding $229,800 of cash meant to buy 350 pounds of marijuana.

The third man indicted with them was Richard Fidlin. Unlike Silverman, he was in jail.

But by February, Silverman and Fidlin were in the process of negotiating plea deals for lighter sentences, trading information about other drug dealers in south Florida, deals they would consummate in two months.

Silverman told the detectives he had first met Bobby Young, in December 1986, under less-than-desirable circumstances. Young was about to extort money from him until Young's wife, Kathy, recognized Silverman from Atlanta. Young then dropped his demands and instead befriended Silverman. Then it turned out that they had even more in common: Richard Fidlin had sent Young to collect the money, and Silverman had once been partners with Fidlin.

In the next few weeks, Young bought a Rottweiler puppy from Silverman; then, on the Sunday about ten days before Aronow's murder, Young brought Kathy, the dog, and two teenagers to visit Silverman's townhouse.

At the house that day, Young asked Silverman if he knew how to get to an address—the Cigarette boat company on "Gasoline Alley." He said he did, and Young asked Silverman to show him. It was only about fifteen minutes away, so they drove there.

Afterward, they went to Apache Bar and Grill, on the same block, for coffee. There, Young told him that Fort Apache Marina was built without a bank loan, and that its owner was having some sort of problem with Don Aronow.

The problem, Young said, revolved around another problem in New Orleans and possible testimony by Aronow. Young then intimated that he was going to kill Aronow because of it, for $25,000, but he offered no further clue as to who was paying him, how he would do it, or when.

Silverman said he learned of the murder while reading the newspaper.

After the murder, drinking at Young's ranch, Silverman said Young admitted killing Aronow. He said he was alone and in a big black car, which he never got out of.

Silverman said he knew that Richard Fidlin was frightened of Young. He also knew that Fidlin had lent a cell phone to someone—he thought to Young.

Silverman had cell phone and beeper numbers for Young; they were the same numbers Billy Schaab had given police. Later, when detectives looked at the cell phone bill they had subpoenaed, they found Silverman's home phone number had been called twice on February 3, 1987, the day of the murder: 12:20 P.M., for one minute; 2:51 P.M., for one minute.

FEBRUARY 7, 1989

SKIP WALTON

William George (Skip) Walton had been waiting to see if he'd have to play his Aronow card. It was all dependent on whether he could win his murder on the high seas case.

After all, he had beaten a murder rap once before.

In 1974, Walton, a crane operators' union organizer and eighth-grade dropout, had been accused in Broward of murdering a man who allegedly was his accomplice in other union-related murders and industrial sabotage. The victim's wife testified that Walton had told her he was going to kill him because he was talking too much; then Walton called a few hours after the murder to tell her that it had been done. Still, the jury acquitted.

The murder on the high seas was from 1982. Witnesses testified that Walton was smuggling hundreds of pounds of marijuana from Jamaica and agreed to take on a woman whose transportation for her own pot had fallen through.

But the woman had gotten drunk in port, fought with Walton, and then made a scene on the docks that she wanted her *ganja* off Walton's boat. Witnesses testified that once at sea, Walton beat her to death with a baton and then tied her body to an anchor and dumped it. One of the witnesses was a codefendant, first mate William Pryor, who had made a deal with the government in November 1987 to plead guilty and testify. Walton was indicted and arrested immediately afterward.

Once again, that sounded like enough to convict. But not Skip Walton. His attorney, Don Ferguson, successfully argued the only hole in the prosecutors' case: the lack of a body.

The *Sun-Sentinel* reported that Walton seemed stunned when the verdict came down in his favor. A *Palm Beach Post* reporter asked the jury foreman why someone would plead guilty to a murder that never occurred, and he answered, "That threw us off a little."

FEBRUARY 9, 1989

WILLIAM PRYOR

DeCora met at FBI Miami headquarters with Agent Nikki Deary to discuss what to do now about Skip Walton. While there, they spoke to William Pryor.

Pryor said Walton had told him that he had an "ace" in his back pocket, since he knew that Young and Carl Davis had killed Aronow. However, Walton had not elaborated beyond that, he said.

[Wayne Shehan had described Carl as the driver of Bobby Young's Lincoln, but hadn't offered a surname for him.]

Pryor also said that Young might have told a man named William Bud Leroy about the murder. Leroy was Davis's friend and might have sold guns to Davis and Young. Pryor thought that Leroy was in federal custody for narcotics.

FEBRUARY 13, 1989

CARL DAVIS

DeCora checked the state criminal database and found a 1987 aggravated assault charge against a Carl Davis in Palm Beach County. He sent Archie Moore to West Palm Beach to look up the police report.

At 5:15 A.M. on May 4, 1987 (three months after Aronow's murder), a Palm Beach County sheriff's officer had responded to a bar on A1A—the ocean road—in Lake Park to find two men holding it hostage by gunpoint, sitting in a maroon-and-white 1987 Lincoln Continental. They had threatened to shoot anyone who left the bar.

The two men were father and son. The father was Carl Davis, aged forty-six, five feet, eleven inches tall, 240 pounds.

At first, Davis cooperated with the deputy, who noted that Davis was badly slurring his words, his eyes were bloodshot and glassy, and he had a strong odor. Then he turned extremely hostile and started running toward the officer, poised to attack with a clenched fist, yelling obscenities: "I'm going to beat your ass" and "What do the fuck do you want, motherfucker?"

Backup arrived, and they tried to arrest him. Davis resisted, swinging at them wildly; then one officer struck him with his police baton. Once forced inside the police cruiser, Davis kicked out a rear window and continued shrieking at them.

Inside the Lincoln—a leased car, indicated by the letters on the license plate—police found a fully loaded Ruger .357 Magnum concealed between the two front seats. Talking with Davis's son, police learned that Davis was upset because he had found his girlfriend in the bar with another man.

Then, when Davis was booked at county jail, he threatened, "As soon as I get out I'm going to kill you, motherfucker. I have a lot of friends I can hire to kill you. Do you know how easy it is to buy a bomb around here?"

MARCH 1, 1989

TOMMY TEAGLE

Tommy Teagle, now out on the street, wanted to talk more. Mike DeCora set up a meeting at Bennigan's restaurant in North Miami Beach, and sent Archie Moore and Steve Parr.

Teagle said that he, Skip Walton, and Bobby Young (whom Teagle knew as Bobby Campbell) were all associates, but his source that Young and Carl Davis had killed Aronow was Walton, who told him while they were together at MCC Miami.

Walton had detailed that Davis drove the black Lincoln to 188th Street, then sat in the car while Young went inside Aronow's business for a half hour to talk to him about buying a boat. Then, back in the Lincoln, Young told Davis to drive to Apache Boats, where Young went inside and again pretended to be a potential buyer.

Later, back together in the Lincoln, Young and Davis spotted Aronow inside his car, parked in front of Apache Boats. Davis drove up to Aronow's car, and Aronow rolled down his window. Then Young leaned across Davis and shot him.

Teagle said Walton owned the .45 that Young used, and that later someone tossed it into a nearby freshwater lake—possibly Maule Lake, a few blocks south of the murder scene, off Biscayne Boulevard. He also said that the Lincoln was Walton's, but that Davis drove it frequently. He thought the car might have been registered in Walton's girlfriend's name, and that they had stored it somewhere since the murder.

A Colombian named Wimpy, he said, hired Young to kill Aronow on behalf of a Colombian drug cartel; the price was $250,000.

[That was different from what Teagle had told detectives the first time, reporting what he said was Richard Fidlin's information. Then, the price was $45,000. He also said Fidlin told him that Young was alone when he did it.]

Teagle offered Moore six car telephone and beeper numbers that Richard Fidlin used, which included the same numbers that Schaab and Silverman had said were Bobby Young's. Pretty well convinced now that the mobile phone number was, in fact, Bobby Young's, detectives were able to see four calls from Young to Fidlin on the day of the murder: 11:26 A.M., to Fidlin's beeper, one minute, his first call of the morning; 3:05 P.M., to Fidlin's car phone, 2 minutes; 3:07 P.M., to Fidlin's car phone, 2 minutes; 3:33 P.M., just minutes after the murder, to Fidlin's car phone, 3 minutes.

MARCH 13, 1989

Tommy Teagle called DeCora again to say that Skip Walton now wanted to talk personally to detectives about the murder. DeCora set up a meeting, at MCC Miami, for that evening. Although Walton had won his murder on the high seas case, he hadn't won his freedom; he still faced narcotics charges in Oklahoma City.

The meeting lasted ten minutes, long enough for Walton to make a pitch: if someone could help him with his Oklahoma City indictment, he would tie up the Aronow case. He could provide an eyewitness to the murder, the location of the vehicle, the location of the murder weapon and the motive, and could implicate the "Colombian."

Besides, he said, he wasn't really involved in the Oklahoma case; all he had done was speak about renting airplanes to David McCallister.

MARCH 14, 1989

The lead FBI agent in the Oklahoma City case was Floyd Zimms, who in 1995 would become lead agent in the investigation of the Oklahoma City Federal Building bombing. In the oft-repeated video clip showing Timothy McVeigh when he was first arrested, Zimms is the gray-bearded, balding agent next to him.

DeCora called Zimms to see what the FBI's position would be regarding Walton's offer. Zimms said the Aronow murder was more important than Walton's narcotics case, and that the FBI would cooperate as much as possible.

MARCH 16, 1989

Two days later, Miami-based FBI agent Nikki Deary called DeCora. She said Skip Walton's attorney, Don Ferguson, had contacted her to say that Walton was ready to cooperate on the Aronow case. She told Ferguson to call Metro-Dade detectives. [However, he never did.]

MARCH 23, 1989

The Miami Herald reported that television producer Stephen Cannell was developing a series pilot for ABC loosely based on Don Aronow's world of fast boats. After spending a research week in Miami talking to cops and boatbuilders, Cannell dubbed it *Thunder Boat Row*— one of 188th Street's nicknames.

It sounded like *Miami Vice* on water. In true Hollywood-TV-style, the show concept began with something real and original but then degenerated into well-trodden cliché. A strike force of local cops would fight all sorts of crime, from smuggling to pornography to spies selling secrets to the Russians.

APRIL 5, 1989

When Skip Walton was charged with murder on the high seas, he was also indicted for conspiracy to import 1,400 pounds of marijuana during the same 1982 voyage. That charge, he pled guilty to, in advance of the murder trial. Perhaps because he had won the murder case, the government argued that he should get the maximum penalty for the dope charge, and U.S. District Court judge Norman Roettger agreed. He sentenced Walton to nine years—one year short of the maximum.

APRIL 17, 1989

Stephen Cannell was trying to make art imitate life. Ben Kramer tried to make life imitate art.

Kramer was less successful—unless drama counts.

Transferred in December after his smuggling conviction in Illinois to MCC Miami to await his money-laundering trial, Kramer ripped a page from the movies. He arranged for a helicopter to land in the prison exercise yard—the size of a basketball court—at about 10 A.M., then quickly climbed in. Astounded guards and inmates froze.

With Kramer inside, the helicopter rose, spinning erratically, underpowered to carry his lately acquired 250-pound bulk. Then its tail rotor snagged an edge of the fourteen-foot-high wire fence. The bird sputtered, flopped back toward the yard, then slammed to the ground and dumped Kramer five yards across pavement. The pilot got pinned in the wreckage and had to be pulled out; all the while, the fuel tank was leaking.

"Had it not hit the fence, he would have escaped," said warden John Clark.

"He was no Charles Bronson," critiqued U.S. marshal Dan Horgan.

Kramer badly broke his left ankle. The pilot, Charles Clayton Stevens, was hurt in the head, neck, and back, and broke both legs. Belatedly, both men got their helicopter rides—they were airlifted downtown to Miami's Jackson Memorial Hospital.

Stevens, aged thirty-four, from Gold Beach, Oregon, was charged with assisting an escape, conspiracy, and destruction of government property (the fence). He had bought the helicopter the previous December—the same month Kramer had been sentenced—for $35,000 cash.

Stevens had a student's pilot license. Later in the day, pilots at nearby Tamiami Airport recognized him and knew that he had taken off from there twenty-five minutes before he landed at MCC. They described him as a "squirrelly" flier and wondered why he chose a thirty-seven-year-old helicopter that, they said, was slow and generally used for light-duty observation.

Actually, Kramer's inspiration may have come from a previous helicopter escape attempt in the mid-'80s at MCC Miami. Gary Betzner, a former drug-smuggling pilot for Kramer's friend George Morales, had arranged for a chopper to drop from the air onto a prison flower bed to pick him up. Unfortunately for him, that didn't work, either. Federal agents had learned about it in advance and were actually on board when it landed.

The Miami Herald asked homicide sergeant Mike Diaz for a reaction: "We haven't tied [Kramer] in to Aronow yet. He remains one of many suspects; he has neither been eliminated nor confirmed."

MAY 16, 1989

Skip Walton had been transferred to a prison in Oklahoma City, and DeCora flew there to meet with him. But first, he sat down with FBI agents and assistant U.S. attorney Seth Mydans. They would offer Walton a deal: if he would plead guilty to one of their counts and cooperate fully in both the Aronow investigation as well as their narcotics case, they would drop the other count. Then the agents, the prosecutor, and DeCora all met with Walton to pitch him.

Walton seemed a little disappointed. He wanted something better than that.

Late that evening, Walton's court-appointed attorney, Tony Lacy, spoke to Carl Davis on the telephone, then called FBI agent John Hershley. Lacy said that Davis had agreed to come to Oklahoma—on the government's tab—to talk.

May 19, 1989

Two days later, Davis came to town. The next morning, he, Walton, the Feds and DeCora all met. When the prosecutor agreed to improve Walton's deal—the count he'd have to plead guilty to would be reduced—he and Davis both agreed to cooperate.

Walton said he wouldn't give up any details until his deal was signed. However, he did repeat his promise of what he and Davis would talk about: the triggerman, the murder weapon, the getaway car, who hired the killer, and the motive. Plus, Davis would testify that he was an eyewitness.

June 1989

Soundings, a boating industry newspaper, printed an interview with Mike DeCora and others about the two-year-old murder mystery. Although it seemed that police were on the verge of a breakthrough, DeCora was poker-faced about it:

"No motive. No suspects. No idea why. Everybody I spoke to said money wasn't the issue with Aronow. It was winning the game. Business, boating, racing, horses. It didn't matter."

John Crouse: "Aronow could have been killed for a hundred reasons. He'd make sharp deals with guys and then laugh at them as he cut them up. He knew what he wanted, and he knew how to get it—money, women, boats."

The Aronow estate had since sold USA Racing to a company that renamed it Aronow Powerboats. The newspaper quoted Gary Garbrecht, its president: "I never ran into anyone who ever got screwed by Aronow who didn't deserve it."

[Funny how close that line was to what Bobby Young had told Detective Steve Robitaille, that he never did anyone who hadn't deserved it.]

DeCora said he had heard stories that Aronow was tied to the Mafia.

"I heard he was paying Meyer Lansky and that when Lansky died, he told his widow, 'That's it. I ain't paying no more,' and that's why the mob killed him.

"So we ran that down with our organized-crime folks and came up negative. They were friends, but there was no indication that Lansky was his godfather keeping him alive, nor that Aronow was paying him."

DeCora also dismissed a rumor that Aronow had sold a boat to a druggie and equipped it with a secret transponder, for the government's benefit. "It just isn't feasible," he said.

Kramer, he confirmed, was at one time a suspect. Because of the USA Racing sale that fell through, "There was bad blood between them."

At this point, detectives hadn't yet made the Jerry Jacoby connection to Jesse Jackson and Bobby Young. "We just can't get a handle on why the man used the name Jerry Jacoby when everybody knew Jerry Jacoby," he said.

"Will police ever solve the murder?" the newspaper asked.

"Down here?" Aronow friend Knocky House answered with another question. "Who knows? We're in a very rough area."

JUNE 6, 1989

DeCora compiled new photo lineups that included pictures of Paul Silverman, Carl Davis, and Richard Fidlin, then took them to show Mike Britton, who had seen the man in the Lincoln.

Again, Britton couldn't positively identify anyone as the man he had seen. But he did point to Richard Fidlin's picture; he said his face was the right shape—but the person he had seen had more hair.

A half hour later, DeCora showed the same pictures to Patty Lezaca. None of them looked to her like the person who had claimed to be Jerry Jacoby.

JUNE 13, 1989

SKIP WALTON

Despite Britton's failure to pick out Carl Davis's photo from the lineup, DeCora and assistant state's attorney Gary Rosenberg kept their date in Oklahoma City to interview Skip Walton once his federal deal was finalized. Next was the matter of his Florida state deal for immunity. That afternoon, Rosenberg, Walton, and Walton's attorney hashed that out. Then, in the evening, finally, Walton talked.

Walton said he had met Bobby Young and Kathy Kunzig in 1985. However, he had known Carl Davis for twenty years, since both were union brothers in the Teamsters local run by Walton's brother. Wayne Shehan had done electrical work for him, but he didn't know Richard Fidlin.

In 1986, Young introduced Walton to a Colombian he called Wimpy. Wimpy had emeralds for sale, but Walton later learned that he was a middleman for Colombians shipping narcotics to the United States. Walton believed that Wimpy worked for the Ochoa family—the Medellin cartel.

Young had been smuggling cocaine but had problems "losing" portions of his load. That put Young in debt to the Colombians, and they were pressuring him to pay.

In December 1986, Young approached Walton for help. He said the Colombians had given him a list of people they wanted dead, and although Young didn't show Walton the actual list, he said there were two people on it in the federal witness protection program: one lived in Georgia, the other in Louisiana.

Walton agreed to help. Walton, a pilot, flew Young both places to plan the murders, but Walton didn't know if they ever went down.

Then Young told Walton that Don Aronow was on the same list. Walton believed the price on his head was $250,000. That's when Walton said he backed away; it would be too hot afterward, he told Young.

However, Walton suggested that Young use Carl Davis—"a good, reliable man" who worked for him and needed the money. Further, Walton helped plan the hit by mapping out 188th Street and suggesting the best escape routes and the best time of day to do it.

Walton was at work on the day of the murder. Young called him between 4:00 and 4:30, nervous but excited. "It went down," Young said. He asked Walton if he'd be home later, and Walton said yes; Young said he'd come by. Walton took that to mean that both Young and Davis would come by.

[In fact, the telephone record reflected calls throughout the day of the murder from Young's car phone to Skip Walton's business phone number in Pompano Beach, Expert Crane Services: 11:38 A.M., for two minutes; 2:33 P.M., for two minutes; 2:41 P.M., for one minute; 2:45 P.M., for one minute; 4:35 P.M., for one minute; 4:40 P.M., for one minute; 4:52 P.M., for one minute.]

Shortly after Walton got home, he said, Young and Davis did arrive, driving the black Lincoln Town Car that Walton had rented for Davis at Budget Rent-A-Car by Fort Lauderdale Airport.

Walton described Young as wearing a pullover shirt, blue jeans, and a beard that he shaved off right after the murder, although he kept his moustache.

The three men sat in Walton's den while Young described how he had just killed Aronow. When they arrived at Gasoline Alley, he went into USA Racing and spoke with office workers and Aronow. When he left, he was upset with himself that he hadn't killed Aronow when he had had the chance.

Back in the Lincoln, Young driving, he began to leave, then impulsively made a U-turn and parked alongside the road. Young and Davis then switched places so that Davis was in the driver's seat. Young told Davis to drive back toward USA Racing, but before they could leave the side of the road, Young spotted Aronow in his white Mercedes.

Young told Davis to pull up to the Mercedes. Young waved out of the driver's window to get Aronow's attention, and the Lincoln pulled up, driver's door to driver's door with the Mercedes.

Then Young reached across Davis and shot Aronow several times.

To escape, Davis drove around Aronow's Mercedes and back west toward Biscayne Boulevard. From there, they went south, but for only a few blocks, to a shopping center at Biscayne and N.E. 183rd Street. They sat there for a while to watch what was happening around them. It was also from there that Young called Walton and said, "It went down."

There was another car behind Aronow's, Young had told him, but it wasn't involved with them.

During the entire conversation in his den, Walton said, Davis never denied nor confirmed Young's story.

Because Young had used Walton's Lincoln, which could be traced back to him, Young gave him $5,000. Then the three men decided to return the Lincoln to Budget and get a new car, a white Town Car.

While unloading the black Lincoln, a Budget employee found a .45 casing in the front seat. The employee asked him if they wanted the casing, and Young grabbed it.

The trunk also held several garbage bags full of Davis's clothes, as well as explosives that were supposed to be taken to Louisiana.

Walton had promised to tell where the murder weapon was, but on that he came up short. He said Young had had the .45 semiautomatic when he came to Walton's house, but he later dumped it somewhere. Walton didn't know where.

The interview had taken about five hours, ending around 11 P.M. Still, DeCora had the feeling Walton was holding back.

JUNE 16, 1989

DeCora sent Archie Moore to serve two subpoenas on Budget Rent-A-Car at Fort Lauderdale Airport: one to see all vehicles rented to Skip Walton from November 1986 to February 1987, and another to learn the names of all employees on the job there February 3, 1987.

With Moore present, Budget's supervisor found that Walton had rented a black four-door Lincoln Town Car on January 8, 1987, and returned it on February 3, 1987, at 5:59 P.M.

However, they no longer had the car. The supervisor could tell that it had been sold twice since then to auto auctions, most recently to one in Columbus, Ohio.

JUNE 29, 1989

On this day, Skip Walton was reinterviewed twice: first in a sworn taped statement taken at the United States attorney's office in Oklahoma City by Dade County assistant state's attorney Gary Rosenberg, with DeCora, Archie Moore, and Walton's own attorney, Tony Lacy, present; then, later, by FBI polygraph examiner Bill Brown.

Walton made a few additions and changes to his story in the sworn statement. He said Young—"Crazy Bob"—first came to him in November 1986 (not December 1986) with a plan to kill Aronow. Young told him that Aronow had "double-dealed" the Ochoas, so they wanted him dead. Young also said that Wimpy, the Ochoas' middle-man, had already paid him a deposit of either $20,000 or $25,000 by November, and between then and February, the Colombians were pushing him to get it done.

He also added that it was Young's idea that Walton rent cars for him—including the black Lincoln. But he denied knowing in advance that one of them would be used for Aronow's murder.

Walton had been vague before on the number of times Young said he shot Aronow, but this time Walton said it was either three or four times. Also, this time he said Young drove to Loehmann's Plaza shopping center after he shot Aronow, to see if anyone was following him. Before, he had said that Young went to a shopping center five blocks south on Biscayne Boulevard. Loehmann's Plaza was only about a block from the murder scene, directly west of N.E. 188th Street.

Walton also described for the first time the .45 murder weapon in some detail: it was new, a late-model military weapon, model 1911.

Polygraphers ask "relevant" questions as well as innocuous ones in order to get comparative scores. The relevant questions that Brown asked that evening, and Walton's answers, were:

* Did you kill Don Aronow? No.
* Were you on-site when Don Aronow was killed? No.
* Are you deliberately concealing from me anything Carl Davis told you about that murder? No.
* Was your gun used in the murder of Aronow? No.
* Did you ever take possession of the gun used after the murder? No.

The bad news was, Brown's opinion was that Walton's answers were "indicative of deception" to all five.

Upset, Walton gave Brown a few more details after the test: he knew that Bobby Young had made several attempts to kill Aronow, and that Carl Davis had gotten $30,000 for his help. But Davis had recently told him that he wasn't in the car at the time of the murder, although Walton said he disbelieved his denial.

Walton evaded Brown's further questions about Davis's involvement, saying it would be up to him to make his own deal with the state in exchange for testimony.

Afterward, DeCora talked to Walton about his test results. He said he couldn't understand how he had failed it because he was telling the truth. DeCora said he would have to pass a polygraph, or else his deal would be off.

JULY 5, 1989

Regardless, Walton's federal deal on the Oklahoma drug case went through. He pled guilty to one count of aiding and abetting the conspiracy, and was sentenced to three and a half years.

JULY 18, 1989

Archie Moore spent the day on the phone, tracing the black Lincoln Town Car that Walton had rented. From the Columbus, Ohio, auto auction, it went to a Lincoln-Mercury dealer in Lima, Ohio, who sold it in November 1987 to a woman in Lima.

JULY 19, 1989

VANCE WATSON

Moore also found the young man who had helped unload the Lincoln that Walton returned to Budget on the day of the murder. He was Vance Watson, and he was still working for Budget, now in Tampa. He had told Moore he was coming to south Florida in the next few days anyway, and volunteered to meet him at Metro-Dade Police headquarters.

Watson remembered the incident well; Budget had just hired him a few weeks before, after he had turned eighteen, and the car's passenger had given him a $20 tip to help unload all the clothes strewn about in the trunk and place them in two brown garbage bags. Underneath some of the clothes he found a dark blue large-caliber revolver, which he called to the passenger's attention.

Watson described the passenger as thirty to forty years old, a little taller and heavier than Watson's five feet, seven inches and 160 pounds, average tan for Florida, with a neatly trimmed salt-and-pepper moustache and beard. Although his head was balding, he had a medium amount of light brown hair combed straight back. He wore a short-sleeved, bright red, flowery Hawaiian shirt, unbuttoned, revealing a hairy chest. A second man, the car's driver, had gone into Budget's rental office, so he couldn't remember him at all.

Later, when Watson pulled the car away to the gas pumps, he found four or five large-caliber empty shell casings lying on the passenger seat. He returned to the rental office and handed those back to the passenger, too.

JULY 24, 1989

DeCora and crime scene technician Tommy Stoker flew to Lima, Ohio, to photograph and process the Town Car. The owners, who met them at Lima Lincoln-Mercury, said they hadn't changed the appearance of the car since they bought it.

DeCora thought the car matched what the witnesses described. He looked at the windows; they had been factory-tinted, and although the developed photographs didn't reflect how dark they were, DeCora was satisfied that at certain angles, you couldn't see through them.

AUGUST 30, 1989

At a jury trial, James Marren, one of Ben Kramer's co-defendants in the escape attempt, was found guilty. Charles Clayton Stevens, the helicopter pilot, had turned government witness in a plea deal and testified against

Marren. Later, Stevens was sentenced to thirty months in prison.

Had his helicopter cleared the prison fence, Stevens testified, he would have flown back to nearby Tamiami Airport and put Kramer in a twin-engine plane headed for central Florida. From there, Kramer would have left the country, headed for either Honduras or South America.

Also pleading guilty earlier in the week was Ben's younger brother, Marc Kramer, a law student in California, but he didn't testify. Stevens said that Marc had solicited him to fly the helicopter. Marc, however, had never been implicated in any of his brother's smuggling or laundering activities, nor had he ever been in trouble before.

SEPTEMBER 15, 1989

Because there were so many more leads to pursue and the investigation was stagnating, three more senior detectives were assigned to help DeCora: Greg Smith, John LeClaire, and Bill Saladrigas.

To refamiliarize them, DeCora returned with them to the scene of the crime. After that, he gave them their first assignment: find Carl Davis's girlfriend at the time of the murder, Tina Palmer.

Saladrigas found that Palmer had moved to Los Angeles in mid-1987, then to Syracuse, New York.

Saladrigas also learned that Richard Fidlin was currently at a federal prison camp at Eglin Air Force Base, Florida, serving a year on drug charges.

SEPTEMBER 19, 1989

Greg Smith had learned that after Tina Palmer broke up with Carl Davis, she dated a man named John Kiefer. Saladrigas found him at his home, and not a moment too soon; he said he was about to surrender at five o'clock that day for violating his community control. He was to serve four months.

Kiefer said Tina had dated both him and Davis. He hadn't seen her in about a year, but he had just seen Davis four days before. Through Davis, he had met Bobby Young.

Kiefer said neither Tina nor Davis had ever mentioned anything to him about a murder. But just before Saladrigas left, Kiefer asked him what kind of police protection he would get if he did know something about Davis, and if he told the police.

Saladrigas told him whatever protection was necessary.

"You'll be hearing from me," Kiefer promised.

SEPTEMBER 20, 1989

DeCora and Smith flew to Eglin in a single-engine police plane to see if Richard Fidlin would talk. He said yes, but only after he contacted his attorney.

That afternoon, Saladrigas spoke to Metro-Dade organized-crime detective Jerry Todd. He said that two years before, a man named Stanley Diamond, who had known ties to New York organized crime, had spoken to his division about the Aronow murder. In fact, Diamond was a minor player in Nicholas Pileggi's 1985 book _Wise Guy_, about Mafia snitch Henry Hill.

Saladrigas told that to DeCora, who remembered that homicide detective Rex Remley had also interviewed Diamond at the time. Diamond had said that he knew Ben and Jack Kramer and offered to infiltrate their "organization" to get information about the killing. However, to do it, he wanted $5,000 from the police and was turned down. Regardless, DeCora asked Saladrigas to see if Diamond had anything new to say.

SEPTEMBER 21, 1989

Diamond had a condo in Aventura, about fifteen blocks from the site of the murder. Saladrigas and LeClaire went there in the morning, got no response, and left a card.

Also that morning, DeCora got a call from FBI agent Joe Ciccarelli, who was handling Paul Silverman's case. Three days before, Silverman had been sentenced to three years for narcotics, but he had a month to surrender. Ciccarelli said Silverman told him that if he was subpoenaed to a grand jury investigating Aronow's murder, he would tell the truth.

DeCora also got a call from a lieutenant at MCC Miami who said he had an inmate, Thomas Caldwell, who had information about the murder. DeCora and Smith went there immediately.

Caldwell said Jesus Haim, a former Apache employee who had witnessed the Lincoln leaving the crime scene, was in his cell block. Caldwell had the impression that Haim hadn't told police everything he knew; Haim had actually watched the killer shoot Aronow—plus, he had seen him before on 188th Street.

That afternoon, Stanley Diamond called Saladrigas and agreed to meet him the next evening at 6:30 at Aventura Mall's food court.

SEPTEMBER 22, 1989

Checking with the DEA, DeCora learned that they had investigated a number of Bobby Young's associates for drugs and, in fact, had surveillance photos of Kathy Kunzig, Tommy Teagle, Frank Meade, and Wayne Shehan.

At 6:30, Saladrigas met Diamond, who said that his wife had been very close to Ben Kramer's mother back in 1987, and through her, he had gotten friendly with Ben and Jack Kramer.

He also said that Ben had ripped off $30 million from a group of Colombians, whom he was running from when he got arrested. Jack, he said, was now paranoid, thinking everyone was coming after his money. At Saladrigas's suggestion, Diamond said he would try to renew his relationship with Jack but added that it would be difficult. The subject of payment didn't come up.

SEPTEMBER 26, 1989

Greg Smith, who had interviewed Jesus Haim on the day of the murder, now spoke to him again, at MCC. Haim denied telling Caldwell that he had actually seen the person commit the murder.

Following the FBI agent's prompting, DeCora had a subpoena drawn up for Paul Silverman to give a sworn statement to the state attorney. At four o'clock, DeCora sent Saladrigas to Silverman's townhouse on Hollywood Beach to serve him with it. When he got there an hour later, he found chaos; police and emergency vehicles were all over the place.

Saladrigas asked the Hollywood Police lieutenant in charge if he could just go serve the subpoena to the person he was supposed to, then get out of there.

"Yeah. Who do you have to serve?" the lieutenant asked.

"Paul Silverman."

"Silverman? Sorry, he's the guy that got blown up."

It turned out that Silverman and his girlfriend, Deborah Walls, had arrived home in his jeep-style Suzuki at 4:09 but were still inside the car when the bomb detonated under the driver's seat.

Silverman's legs were seriously hurt, and his pants were torn into bloody rags. Flying metal debris from the Suzuki broke the window of a nearby van. His girlfriend, however, had only minor injuries. Both were taken to Hollywood Memorial Hospital.

Saladrigas got there at 5:45. In the emergency room,

with Hollywood detectives also present, Saladrigas asked Silverman if he thought the bomb had anything to do with his talking to the police about Aronow. In extreme pain, Silverman answered that he had told only two people about his cooperation: his attorney and Miami FBI agent Joe Ciccarelli.

Saladrigas then asked who he thought was behind it. In between groans, Silverman repeated "Tennessee. Tennessee." He said Ciccarelli had called him from New York the previous day and asked him about his health. Seconds later, Silverman was wheeled out of the room, leaving Saladrigas to ponder why a Miami FBI agent had called him from New York to ask that.

At seven o'clock, Agent Ciccarelli came to the hospital, and Saladrigas confronted him. Ciccarelli answered that Silverman was talking about Bart Anthony Chicarelli, his codefendant in the Nashville federal narcotics case, labeled a "drug kingpin" in the Nashville press. Silverman had told the FBI that they had done numerous bulk drug deals together. Earlier that day in New York, Chicarelli had pled guilty to conspiracy to distribute marijuana.

SEPTEMBER 27, 1989

Smith and DeCora flew to Syracuse, New York, to interview Tina Palmer.

In the afternoon, they found her at home. She said she had been involved with Carl Davis only for about two months, and because she was constantly using cocaine during that time, she couldn't recall things very well. She did remember him driving a black Lincoln, then later a white Lincoln. Carl was also a heavy cocaine user, she said, and had been arrested at least twice for possession.

She knew Bobby Young—"Colombian Bobby"—as well as Wimpy. They and Davis were probably in the drug business together, she said.

She said she didn't know anything about Aronow's

murder, then added that it wouldn't surprise her if any of the three were suspected in a killing.

OCTOBER 2, 1989

DeCora and Smith visited Patty Lezaca to show her a photo lineup with Bobby Young's picture in it.

And, in fact, Lezaca picked out Young's picture from the six; she said it could have been "Jerry Jacoby." But, she added, she couldn't be positive.

Next, DeCora and Smith showed the lineup to Levon Tindall. He, too, said Young's picture looked like the person he had seen driving the black Lincoln. But like Lezaca, Tindall offered the same caveat: because of the passage of time, he wasn't absolutely sure it was the same man.

Mike Britton was last on the list. He didn't pick out any of the photos.

OCTOBER 3, 1989

Saladrigas had never been able to serve the subpoena on Paul Silverman, so Smith, DeCora, and assistant state's attorney Gary Rosenberg went to Hollywood Memorial Hospital to do so and, while there, talk to him.

They found that he was still in intensive care, after a week, and that the Hollywood Police had kept up a twenty-four-hour guard by the room's entrance. Silverman, in traction and under medication, said Bobby Young was responsible for Aronow's murder, but he was in too much pain to go into details, nor did he want to get involved anymore.

OCTOBER 12, 1989

Jerry Engelman, for his own reasons, had grown more and more distant from detectives. In order to get him to look at photo lineups, they had to subpoena him to come to Gary Rosenberg's office, where DeCora and Smith met him.

They showed him pictures of Bobby Young, Carl Davis, Wayne Shehan, Paul Silverman, and Kathy Kunzig—none of whom Engelman said he recognized as "Jerry Jacoby."

OCTOBER 13, 1989

It had been three weeks since Smith and DeCora met with Richard Fidlin at Eglin Air Force Base, so they flew up again. Fidlin told them he still hadn't reached his attorney to consult him about whether it would be okay to talk, and suggested it would be easier to reach him if he could get a prison transfer to Miami.

OCTOBER 16, 1989

One of the most persistent side rumors about the murder concerned what had happened to Don Aronow's gold Rolex Presidential wristwatch, which Rolex had awarded him after he won the world's offshore powerboating championship. Had the killer taken it as a trophy? It was gone by the time Aronow got to the hospital.

Detectives had heard the names Doug and Tony as possible witnesses to the shooting, but didn't have last names. A few days before, Greg Smith had visited Bobby Saccenti, who identified them as brothers Doug and Anthony Palmisano, who had worked in Apache's laminate shop that day. Neither of them had been interviewed by police.

DeCora and Saladrigas found Tony Palmisano at his home in Miami. He admitted that he had heard the shots, was one of the first to run to Aronow's side, and had even seen the Town Car speed past him—although he said its windows were too dark to see inside.

Then, when he looked down on the street near the

driver's door of the Mercedes, he saw the Rolex, with the wristband broken. He put it in his pocket, then turned off the car ignition and left.

For the next ten days he tried to sell the watch, but because it belonged to Aronow, no one would take it. Eventually, he said, he melted it down and sold the metal for $600.

OCTOBER 25, 1989

DeCora and Smith returned to Eglin Air Force Base with a writ to transport Richard Fidlin to the Dade County Jail.

NOVEMBER 1, 1989

Compiling background on Carl Davis, detectives Le-Claire and Saladrigas talked to FBI agent Gunnar Askeland, in West Palm Beach. He said the FBI had kept tabs on Davis a few years before as part of a larger drug-trafficking investigation in Palm Beach County. Davis, he said, had collected drug debts.

Askeland suggested that the detectives speak to Raymond Leroy [apparently the same person who Skip Walton's codefendant, William Pryor, had referred to in February as William Bud Leroy] and Howard Lawson, who both knew Davis; and Keith Pinder, who was a confidant of Ben Kramer. All three men were at MCC Miami and were cooperating with authorities.

NOVEMBER 3, 1989

LeClaire and Saladrigas interviewed Raymond Leroy, who had been in prison since June 1987 on narcotics and counterfeiting charges. He said he met Carl Davis in 1980 when they shared a semiprivate hospital room, at which time they proposed their first dope deal together.

Sometime in 1986, Davis introduced him to Bobby Young, whom he knew as "Crazy Bob" or "Colombian Bob," but he and Young never became close.

When Leroy heard about Aronow's murder on the radio, he said Davis told him, "Things like that happen." The way Davis said it, Leroy thought it meant that he knew something about it.

Later, he said, Skip Walton told him about the murder and that Davis had used his rental car. Also, William "Poco" Pryor told him as well that Davis had been the driver.

[And if Raymond Leroy was the same as William Bud Leroy, could he have been the same as Bud F. Leroy? Bobby Young's phone bill showed a two-minute call the evening before the murder to Bud F. Leroy, president of a swimming pool maintenance service in West Palm Beach. Later, Frank Meade described Bud Leroy as a pool builder who was a friend of another of Young's associates.]

NOVEMBER 6, 1989

LeClaire and Smith interviewed Howard Lawson, then Milton Keith Pinder.

MCC was abuzz with rumors about the Aronow murder, Lawson said, and he had heard that Carl Davis was somehow involved in it.

Pinder, later, said the same thing. He had met Carl Davis in the late '70s when they were competing drug dealers in Palm Beach County. At some point, they realized they could do better if they merged.

Pinder also volunteered a story that he had been in an interview room at MCC with Young and his attorney, Mel Kessler. When Young spoke, he denied that he was involved in Aronow's murder, but at the same time, he gestured with his hands and face that he did, in fact, commit the murder. "Without a doubt," Pinder concluded.

NOVEMBER 14, 1989

Tommy Teagle, back in jail at MCC for violating his parole, called Greg Smith. He said he had a cellmate named Julian Bearden who knew both Ben Kramer and Bobby Young, and might be willing to talk.

NOVEMBER 15, 1989

Gary Rosenberg had subpoenaed Kathy Kunzig to give a statement at the State Attorney's Office, and when she showed up, she asked for more time so she could first consult with an attorney.

She gave a phone number where she could be reached: her mother's number in Fort Lauderdale.

When detectives compared the number to their car phone bill for Young, they found a call on the day of the murder at 5:14 P.M., for one minute.

That provided perhaps the strongest single corroboration of all that the car phone was in fact used by Young.

NOVEMBER 17, 1989

Greg Smith had just found out from the Feds in Oklahoma City that when Teagle testified to their grand jury investigating Bobby Young's narcotics ring, Teagle added to his story from what he had told Metro-Dade detectives. Teagle told the grand jury that Young had directly admitted to him that he murdered Aronow. Previously, he had said his information had come only from others.

Since Smith and Saladrigas were at MCC to see Bearden, they sat down first with Teagle to ask about the discrepancy. Teagle explained that Young *had* admitted the murder to him, but he hadn't told detectives that because he didn't want be in the position where he had to testify to it. But at the grand jury, under oath, they asked him directly whether Young had personally admitted the murder to him, and he answered truthfully, he said.

[However, when Teagle first talked to detectives, he did say that Young had admitted to him having shot two other people.]

Teagle said that Young's admission about Aronow was months after the murder. He and Young were at Young's ranch, discussing problems about a marijuana deal; then they went to Teagle's home. A man named Eddie had kidnapped Teagle, and Young volunteered that he would kill anyone—and he would kill Eddie "as he had killed Aronow."

In addition, Teagle remembered that Young said Richard Fidlin had telephone bills that could tie him into the murder, and it was imperative that he get them.

An hour later, the detectives met Teagle's cellmate, Julian Louis Bearden, who was serving an Alabama state drug sentence but was "on loan" to the federal system in Miami because he had volunteered to give information.

Bearden was very nervous during the talk. He said he had owned a diesel mechanic shop in Miami and, through it, met a number of narcotics traffickers. He got involved as well with some of them—including Ben Kramer and Bobby Young. In 1986, he serviced the engines of Young's catamaran *Cat Dancer*.

Young was introduced to him as a "hit man." That was in 1980, before his arrest off Cuba, when he was definitely transporting marijuana—3,500 pounds from Jamaica, he said. The word on the street, he learned later, was that Young was responsible for a number of murders, and he would kill anybody for a price.

Bearden also named two people who he said were associates of Kramer's: Joe "Jockey" Marino and John Flynn. He thought either of them might have been involved in Aronow's murder or might know something about it. Flynn, he said, was the closer of the two to Kramer.

[John Flynn's name had come up before. Chuck Podesta had testified in the smuggling trial that John Flynn had worked for Kramer as a manual laborer on the beach, humping bales of marijuana.]

Bearden remembered the morning that Aronow was killed: Marino, Flynn, and two others were hanging around his business in a rented dark blue Pontiac Trans Am; then, at eleven o'clock, they said they were going to Kramer's place, and left.

When Bearden got home at five to his ranch in Homestead, south of Miami, he found Marino there with a woman. Marino told him he might be in some trouble; could he stay there for a few days? Bearden said sure and thought nothing of it at the time.

Then, sometime in the next two hours, Flynn showed up, too, in an old pickup truck. Bearden overheard Marino telling Flynn that he had to leave town because of the "Aronow thing." It wasn't until the next day that Bearden found out about the murder.

NOVEMBER 21, 1989

Robert Ralph had since moved to Scarborough, Ontario, near Toronto. He was the witness who had driven the Cigarette Racing Team truck on the afternoon of the murder and had looked inside a black Lincoln that was headed, like him, toward 188th Street.

DeCora sent LeClaire and Saladrigas to show him the most recent photo lineups to see if he could pick anyone out. Included were pictures of Bobby Young, Skip Walton, Carl Davis, Richard Fidlin, Wayne Shehan, Paul Silverman, and Kathy Kunzig.

Ralph picked out Carl Davis but didn't say he was the man inside the Lincoln; instead, he said he might have seen him around 188th Street previous to the murder. But if he ever did see the man inside the Lincoln again, he said, he thought he would still be able to make a positive ID.

NOVEMBER 30, 1989

It had been two months, and Richard Fidlin had never been able to reach his attorney, so at long last, one was appointed for him. After two days of discussion, an immunity deal for him was agreed to and signed. His attorney, Tony Vitale, proffered that Fidlin was not present during the murder and wasn't involved.

DECEMBER 1, 1989

RICHARD FIDLIN

Finally, Richard Fidlin's interview began. He was a big man but not muscular, about six feet, three inches tall, 200 pounds, blond hair, bad teeth, thirty-six years old. He also stuttered when he spoke.

First he told Greg Smith and Gary Rosenberg his home telephone number. It matched a call on Bobby Young's phone list on the day of the murder: a one-minute call at 12:05 P.M.

Fidlin said he met Young—whom he knew as Bobby Scott—in 1984 while Fidlin was the owner (with Tommy Teagle) of a luxury car dealership in Fort Lauderdale. Young came in to buy a diesel motor for a VW Rabbit that he said a friend in Jamaica owned. Soon after, the three men teamed up to sell cocaine.

Fidlin said his main responsibility was supplying vehicles to Young. After their drug deals were consummated, Young always promised to pay him in full but rarely gave him much. He described Young as an intimidating person who usually got his way.

Young and his wife bought a catamaran and set up a company called Basic Charter Service, but it was a front to smuggle a large cocaine shipment from Colombia. It sailed to South America, then returned to Miami three or four months later with 280 kilos of coke. Young unloaded it from the vessel's cross-beams at a canal in Eastern Shores, in north Dade, next to a residence Paul Silverman owned.

Fidlin eventually realized that part of the load was missing. He heard that Young had told the Colombians that some of it had gotten wet by accident. But the Colombians didn't buy that, and Young had to return there for several weeks to settle things.

Fidlin said the .45 that Young used to kill Aronow was in fact Fidlin's. He had kept it in a zippered pouch in his car, but Young had taken it. Fidlin remembered the name of the man who had sold it to him, and that the make was an off-brand, but he couldn't remember which one. Smith wrote down some names, and without hesitation, Fidlin picked out "Star".

Young had called him several times the night before the murder, telling Fidlin he needed him to pick him up the next day. Young gave him a time—which he could no longer remember—and a location somewhere near U.S. 1 [Biscayne Boulevard in north Dade] and the Dade-Broward county line. Fidlin thought Young was going to do a drug deal.

Fidlin remembered that Young had called him on his mobile phone several times to make sure he was en route. But once he got there, Young called again to say he didn't need him anymore. Still thinking Young had scored on a drug deal, Fidlin insisted on meeting him someplace. He suggested the Dry Dock Restaurant, on U.S. 1 in Hollywood, which was about five miles north of 188th Street. Young agreed.

[Phone bills corroborated four calls between Young's car phone and Fidlin's car phone from 3:05 to 3:48 that afternoon.]

When Fidlin got to the restaurant parking lot, he saw a dark Lincoln Town Car with a rental tag. Young was alone inside the lounge, talking to a barmaid, visibly nervous, his hands shaking. He told Fidlin he had done something really big, and he would hear about it.

Then he asked Fidlin to smell his hands; they had the odor of lacquer or paint thinner. Once before, Young had told Fidlin that by spraying his hands with whatever it was, he could fire a gun and the police wouldn't be able to detect the residue on his hands that a gun would normally leave.

When Fidlin realized that the gun Young was talking about might be his .45, he immediately asked for it back. Young told him to forget about it; he had splashed it.

That night, when Fidlin watched the eleven o'clock news and saw that Aronow had been murdered, he figured that Young had done it.

Only much later did Young admit the murder, he said.

He and Young were together at Silverman's townhouse in Hollywood, and Silverman came into the room wearing a white Cigarette Racing Team jacket. Young made a shooting motion toward Silverman, then laughed.

A little later that day, Young talked about the murder. He described how he had called Aronow's attention over to his car as if to ask him for directions, then shot him. Young also said that as he pulled the trigger, he (Young) was on the phone with the person who wanted Aronow dead.

Fidlin didn't say who that was. [The murder was sometime around 3:25, and the phone bill showed a one-minute incoming call (the bill doesn't say from where) at 3:23, then a three-minute outgoing call starting at 3:33—to Fidlin.]

Police could now put together a chronology of what appeared to be Bobby Young's phone activity on the day of the murder.

In addition to the information witnesses had given them, police discovered that one of the numbers dialed on Young's car phone was that of a public phone booth at Loehmann's Plaza, about a tenth of a mile away from the murder site. Greg Smith found the phone, which was close to the southeast corner of the mall, the side nearest to the shooting. The logical conclusion was that the killer(s) had some backup waiting for them there—perhaps even a change of getaway cars, if needed.

Cellular telephone bills are more detailed than regular telephone bills. All outgoing calls, even local calls, are billed with the number dialed. Incoming calls are billed as well, but without a listing of their originating phone numbers. Only in one instance had police been able to tell where an incoming call had come from:

- 11:26 A.M., to Richard Fidlin's beeper, one minute
- 11:38 A.M., to Skip Walton's business, two minutes
- 11:40 A.M., an incoming call, three minutes
- 11:58 A.M., an incoming call, three minutes
- 12:05 P.M., to Richard Fidlin's home, one minute
- 12:11 P.M., to whoever was wearing Bobby Young's pager, one minute
- 12:20 P.M., to Paul Silverman, one minute
- 1:51 P.M., to the phone booth at Loehmann's Plaza, three minutes
- 2:26 P.M., a wrong number, off by one digit, similar to the Loehmann's Plaza phone booth number, one minute
- 2:27 P.M., to the phone booth at Loehmann's Plaza, five minutes
- 2:33 P.M., to Skip Walton's business, two minutes
- 2:39 P.M., an incoming call, one minute
- 2:41 P.M., to Skip Walton's business, one minute
- 2:43 P.M., an incoming call, one minute
- 2:45 P.M., to Skip Walton's business, one minute
- 2:51 P.M., to an unknown Fort Lauderdale number, most likely a beeper, one minute
- 2:51 P.M., to Paul Silverman, one minute
- 2:57 P.M., an incoming call, two minutes
- 3:02 P.M., an incoming call, two minutes
- 3:05 P.M., to Richard Fidlin's car phone, two minutes
- 3:07 P.M., to Richard Fidlin's car phone, two minutes
- 3:13 P.M., to Tango Yacht Charters, in Fort Lauderdale, two minutes
- 3:23 P.M., an incoming call, one minute

[The murder occurred at approximately 3:25 P.M.]

- 3:33 P.M., to Richard Fidlin's car phone, three minutes
- 3:48 P.M., an incoming call from Fidlin's car phone, two minutes
- 4:29 P.M., to an unknown Fort Lauderdale number, most likely a beeper, one minute
- 4:35 P.M., to Skip Walton's business, one minute

- 4:37 P.M., an incoming call, one minute
- 4:38 P.M., an incoming call, two minutes
- 4:40 P.M., to Skip Walton's business, one minute
- 4:40 P.M., an incoming call, two minutes
- 4:52 P.M., to Skip Walton's business, one minute.
- 5:14 P.M., to Kathy Kunzig's mother's, one minute.

[Wayne Shehan had told Mike DeCora that he was with Young later in the evening when Young asked Carl to drive him to a phone booth on the corner to make a call. After using his cell phone all day, why would Young suddenly decide he needed the untraceability of a public phone? Perhaps the consistent answer was that James Fidlin had terminated the cell phone service that same afternoon.]

DECEMBER 4, 1989

Smith reinterviewed Fidlin to see if he would be consistent or could add more details. There was one difference: this time, he was no longer certain whether Young had admitted at either the Dry Dock or at Silverman's that he killed Aronow. However, he remained certain that the conversation had occurred somewhere.

DECEMBER 5, 1989

Part of Fidlin's agreement was that he had to pass a polygraph. Smith checked him out of the Dade County Jail and took him to Metro-Dade Police headquarters, where polygraph examiner Robert Gately tested him.

Gately asked five relevant questions:

1. Did you lie to Detective Smith about the details of this case?
2. Did you help plan the shooting of Donald Aronow?
3. On February 3, 1987, did you shoot Donald Aronow?
4. Did you have prior knowledge that Donald Aronow was going to be shot and killed on February 3, 1987?

5. Were you present on N.E. 188th Street when Donald
   Aronow was shot and killed?

Fidlin answered no to all five.

Bad news again. Gately concluded there were "significant reactions indicative of deception" regarding Fidlin's answers to whether he had lied to Smith, had prior knowledge of the shooting, and was present when Aronow was killed.

DECEMBER 6, 1989

The next day, Gately tried again, with exactly the same results, although Fidlin insisted he was telling the truth. Smith was surprised, too; he also had thought Fidlin was being candid.

DECEMBER 8, 1989

Fidlin, upset after bombing both tests, called a private investigator to reinterview him. The PI, Bill Venturi, called Smith and suggested that Fidlin and his family would pay for a private polygrapher to do a retest. Smith called Gary Rosenberg, who agreed.

DECEMBER 11, 1989

Venturi's choice was Warren Holmes, dean of polygraphers in Miami. Three officers and Gary Rosenberg ushered Fidlin to Holmes's office.

Before the test began, Fidlin admitted to Holmes that he had minimized some of the details he had known:

It _was_ at the Dry Dock Restaurant that Young said he had just hit a guy and described rolling down his window as if he were asking for directions, which got Aronow to roll down his window, too. It was also at the Dry Dock that Young admitted he had been on the phone with the person who wanted Aronow dead when he shot him, and he was to get either $50,000 or a "big favor" from the man.

The admisssion at Paul Silverman's house took place also, about a month later. While Young and Fidlin were walking on the beach, Young talked about the murder then as well.

Young had taken Fidlin's gun, which he used to kill Aronow, only about a week before the murder. Fidlin said he had gotten the gun from a friend.

Holmes asked these relevant questions:

- Did you know, in advance, that Bobby was going to shoot anybody on February 3, 1987?
- Did you have any discussions with Bobby prior to February 3, 1987, about killing Aronow?
- When you gave Bobby the .45-caliber handgun, did you know he was going to kill anyone?
- Did you see Bobby shoot Aronow?
- Did you shoot Aronow?
- Did you know that Bobby had shot anybody before you met him at the Dry Dock lounge?
- Are you now deliberately withholding any information regarding the Aronow murder?

Fidlin answered no to all the questions. In Holmes's opinion, he was deceptive in *all* his answers, except for whether he shot Aronow.

"It is possible that Mr. Fidlin lied to one or more of the pertinent test questions, which affected his entire test results," Holmes wrote.

Confronted with the results, Fidlin once again insisted he was telling the truth.

DECEMBER 19, 1989

In Fort Lauderdale, DeCora and Smith found Charles Egan, the man who Fidlin said had sold him the .45.

Egan vaguely remembered Fidlin and the sale, which had been about three years before. He went to look for the receipt for when he had originally bought it at a gun store, and found it. It was a Star P.D. .45 semiautomatic, blue in color, and the serial number was written on the slip.

[Two days after the murder, the police ballistics lab had determined that a Star .45 semiautomatic was one of three makes that could have fired the bullets removed from Aronow's body.]

The detectives also asked Egan if he had kept any casings that had been used in the gun—hoping to match them up in the ballistics lab with empty casings taken at the murder scene. No luck there.

Back at headquarters, Greg Smith put a trace on the serial number through the FBI and BATF's databases. There was no information on it to indicate that it had been stolen or previously used in a crime.

DECEMBER 21, 1989

DeCora and Smith talked to Ira Rosenblum, the Fort Lauderdale gun store owner who had sold the gun to Egan. Rosenblum found receipts that showed he had sold the gun to Egan two weeks after he bought it in November 1985 from Jack Goodrich.

DECEMBER 22, 1989

Bobby Young pled guilty to a reduced charge of second-degree murder in the Panzavecchia case. He was sentenced to seventeen years, concurrent with his seventeen-year sentence in the Craig Marshall case.

DECEMBER 26, 1989

DeCora found Jack Goodrich in Boca Raton. He said he had bought the gun at a gun show in Phoenix, Arizona, in 1984. He had not kept any casings.

12

TAMMY SILVERMAN

Once detectives found Tammy Silverman—estranged wife of Paul Silverman—in San Francisco, Mike DeCora and Greg Smith went there to interview her.

Tammy said they had separated in August 1988, a year before the bombing. But Paul had called and written since, telling her that "Bobby did it," which she took to mean Bobby Young.

Young, along with Kathleen Kunzig [Young], Richard Fidlin, a Colombian named Wimpy, and a man named Frank [Meade?], frequently visited her house and discussed drug deals together. They had trusted Tammy enough to speak in front of her until she got angry at Paul for having an obvious extramarital affair. She demanded that he give her a divorce; then, when he refused, she threatened to tell police about the drug ring.

Tammy admitted that she had been heavily abusing cocaine and alcohol at the time. Once she made the threat, she said, Paul and Bobby terrorized her. Then, to keep her quiet, they gave her more and more cocaine.

She said she didn't know anything about the murder, or even the name Aronow. She did confirm that her husband owned a Cigarette Racing Team jacket, which she thought Bobby Young gave him.

JANUARY 24, 1990

KATHLEEN KUNZIG YOUNG
SWORN STATEMENT

Because the Fifth Amendment says that witnesses cannot be compelled to incriminate themselves, when someone gets a subpoena—which forces them to testify—he or she receives immunity against prosecution for whatever they say or whatever investigators can derive from what they say. The only exception is that when witnesses are found to be untruthful, they can be prosecuted for perjury. Given all that, Kathleen Young was still a very reluctant witness.

It had taken two months to get her to answer Gary Rosenberg's questions, and when she did, with her attorney, Billy Thomas, present, she didn't volunteer much: She had married Bobby Young in June 1985, she knew he had taken some trips to Colombia, and she knew Carl Davis. She remembered reading about Don Aronow's murder in the news, but nobody ever told her they murdered him, nor could she remember if Bobby had ever driven a black Lincoln.

JANUARY 30, 1990
Madison, Wisconsin

WAYNE SHEHAN
SWORN STATEMENT

Within the previous year, Wayne Shehan had been indicted and convicted of federal marijuana charges in Madison, Wisconsin. Before the prison system sent him off to Lewisburg Penitentiary in Pennsylvania to serve his sentence of a year and a day, they stuck him in the local Dane County Jail in Wisconsin.

Without telling him in advance, DeCora, Smith, Rosenberg, FBI agent Joe Ciccarelli, and a stenographer showed up to the jail to take a sworn statement from him.

Again, Rosenberg asked the questions. Shehan said he had met Bobby Young (whom he knew as Bobby Scott) in August 1986 in Jamaica. Three months later, back in south Florida, Shehan called him again. By the first of the new year, 1987, he began doing maintenance for Young on his catamaran.

Shehan knew that Young was in the cocaine business and that he always carried guns, including .45s. But he didn't know in advance that he was plotting to kill Aronow.

On what had happened the day of the murder, Shehan changed his story a bit from what he had told DeCora a year before. At that time, he said he had been with Young early that day—Young was driving a rented black Town Car, and later, Young beeped him, saying he might need him.

This time, Shehan said Young's beep in the afternoon was his first contact of the day with him.

Shehan repeated that he had been at Toys "R" Us with his wife, Cynthia. When he called Young back, Shehan told him he was too far away to help. That's when Young said to watch the six o'clock evening news.

After shopping, he and Cynthia returned to their duplex in Deerfield Beach, in north Broward. They watched the local news, which led with Aronow's murder.

After the news report, he said Bobby called and told him to come to his house in Boynton Beach, not far away. Shehan said he went, with Cynthia and his nephew. Bobby, Kathleen, and Carl Davis were already there, although Shehan didn't know Carl's last name.

Everyone sat down in Bobby's living room, and Bobby told them he had just shot Don Aronow five times with a .45; Aronow was in a white Mercedes sports car, Bobby was in his black Lincoln. The cars were facing in opposite directions. [A year before, Shehan hadn't said where Young had told him this.]

"I think he mentioned one bullet went through the door. He slumped over, and the gas went wide open."

Shehan repeated that Young got $60,000 for the murder. A year before, he had made a reference that the owner of Apache Boats had paid it. Now Shehan added to that: "There was a mention that Apache Boats would be a million dollars richer, and be the number-one boat.''

Shehan also repeated that he, Bobby, and Carl Davis had driven to a pay phone. Bobby told Carl to check the car to make sure there wasn't an empty casing left in it.

[There were a couple of additional conflicts in Shehan's statement.

First, Skip Walton had described an après-murder meeting at Young's house as well. Although both mentioned that Carl Davis was present, Walton didn't mention Shehan or his wife and nephew being there. Shehan didn't mention Walton. Both men said the black Lincoln was present, and Shehan said he even rode in it with Young to a pay-phone booth. Shehan also saw bags of Davis's clothing.

But Walton said they returned the black Lincoln to Budget Rent-A-Car at Fort Lauderdale airport (to exchange it for a white Lincoln), and the Budget receipt showed that the black car had been returned at 5:59 P.M. that day. In addition, Budget employee Vance Watson had described a man very much like Bobby Young—and the clothing bags.

Yet Shehan said that he watched the news at home in Deerfield Beach, Young called him to come to his house in Boynton Beach (about fifteen miles north), and once Shehan was there, Young detailed the murder. Even if Shehan had watched the earliest south Florida TV newscast—at five o'clock, not six—there still wouldn't have been enough time for all that—plus driving in rush-hour traffic about thirty miles, from Boynton Beach (in southern Palm Beach County) south to Fort Lauderdale Airport, and arriving by 5:59—to happen.

Another problem was Shehan's beeper. Although Young's phone bill had three calls to likely beeper numbers on the day of the murder, none were to the number Shehan had told DeCora was his.]

JANUARY 31, 1990
Federal Medical Center, Rochester, Minnesota

PAUL SILVERMAN
SWORN STATEMENT

While up north, the same investigators swept through Rochester, Minnesota, to see Paul Silverman. The Feds in Nashville had decided that as soon as Silverman could travel, he should begin his sentence, for his own protection. They placed him in a prison system hospital.

Silverman was now able to move around, but with difficulty. He again described the time a few days before the murder, when Young showed him an address for the Cigarette boat company, and Silverman volunteered to drive him there. While they were drinking at the bar next to Fort Apache, Young said the owner of Apache had had a run-in with Don Aronow.

"I got the impression that it wasn't a standard business problem. And that they were going to—I don't know— eliminate him, I guess, is my word. But I really didn't give much thought to it because I just thought it was bragging. You know, just bar talk."

Then, he again described the cookout at Young's ranch after the murder, when Young admitted killing Aronow.

"He never used—never said killed or murdered. He didn't speak that way. Maybe 'whacked' or 'hit.' "

Silverman said that every once in a while afterward, Young would raise the subject of "the boat man."

"When he would talk about this, would it be to you like almost bragging about what he had done?" Rosenberg asked.

"Yeah, like braggadocio. I guess maybe what brought it up—I never thought about it until you mentioned it now, but one of my favorite jackets that I used to wear was a Cigarette jacket, you know. And he used to see that and maybe get on it. I don't know."

[Silverman's reference to his Cigarette jacket—which Richard Fidlin had mentioned initially—was the only thing different Silverman said that he hadn't told Mike

DeCora almost a year before. In every other way, his sworn statement was consistent with his first talk.]

FEBRUARY 12, 1990

Tommy Teagle, from MCC Miami, called Greg Smith in a panic. Over the weekend, he said, he was in a common area of the prison when he felt a finger pressing against his head. He looked up and saw next to him none other than Bobby Young, holding his finger as if it were a gun.

"Bang, bang, you're dead," said Young.

Teagle said he admitted to Young that he was talking to investigators, but pled that he wasn't really giving them much.

Smith called the prison and verified that Young had been at MCC that weekend. He was in transit from the Dade County Jail to a federal prison in El Reno, Oklahoma, to face his narcotics charges there. But a transportation glitch had occurred, and the Bureau of Prisons had stuck him in general population at MCC Miami for the weekend.

FEBRUARY 15, 1990

Chasing their rainy-day list, DeCora and Smith interviewed Robert Dana Johnson, who had been arrested by the Cubans in 1981, along with Bobby Young and Jerry Jacoby. Johnson said he hadn't seen Young since their release in 1984, but he did offer some leads on how to find Jerry Jacoby.

FEBRUARY 21, 1990

JERRY JACOBY

The Jerry Jacoby who had been arrested with Young was now living in Citra, Florida, a few miles north of Ocala, in the middle of the state. DeCora and Smith went there and met him, but he didn't have much to tell them; he hadn't seen Young since their release, either. He did say that Young had had a visitor in Cuba, a woman possibly named Kathy, who he said was his sister.

FEBRUARY 28, 1990

CYNTHIA SHEHAN

DeCora and Smith, back on the road with Gary Rosenberg, returned to Tryon, North Carolina, to talk again to Wayne Shehan's wife, Cynthia. They found her at work at a factory that made floral-smelling potpourri. From a photo lineup, she identified pictures of Bobby Young, Kathleen Kunzig, and Frank Meade, but not Skip Walton, Wimpy, or Carl Davis.

When DeCora had asked a year before, Cynthia said she couldn't remember where Wayne was on the day of the murder. But now she gave the same answer Wayne offered: they were shopping at a Toys "R" Us when Young beeped him.

After Wayne called Bobby back and told him he was too far away to be of any help, Young told him to watch the local evening news. When they did, Wayne said something like "My God, that son of a bitch did it. He's crazy."

[Cynthia said nothing about being at Young's house later that evening, as Wayne had told investigators a month before.]

Detectives also found Rick Shehan, Wayne's twenty-five-year-old nephew, who Wayne had also said he brought along with Cynthia that night. Rick and Cynthia now lived in the same house and worked at the same potpourri factory.

Rick said he had worked for Bobby and Kathy Young, taking care of the animals at their ranch and maintaining their catamaran. He got along with Kathy but tried to keep his distance from Bobby. When he left Florida in

1987, he said it was because he wanted to get away from him.

Rick remembered that around the time of the murder, Young drove a black Town Car. When DeCora showed him the same photo lineups, he identified Carl Davis, as well as Bobby and Kathy Young, and Frank Meade. He didn't know Richard Fidlin, Wimpy, or Skip Walton.

MARCH 9, 1990

CARL DAVIS
SWORN STATEMENT

Gary Rosenberg subpoenaed Carl Davis to come to his downtown office and give a statement. Davis appeared without a lawyer present.

He said Skip Walton introduced him to Bobby Young at the end of 1986. Not only did Young tell him in advance about Aronow's murder, but he wanted Davis to do the hit for him.

"He wanted me to check out the Cigarette boat company," he said, "wanted me to check out the canal behind Aronow's place." Davis said he had a hard time finding it because the area had changed so much since he had last been there.

He also admitted that when he went to scout the area, he drove a dark blue Lincoln Town Car, which Skip Walton had rented. Afterward, he gave Young directions for getting there. But he denied being there on the day Aronow was murdered.

He said Young did admit the murder to him, but not later that day.

"He said he whacked him."

" 'Whacked,' is that the word he used?" Rosenberg asked.

"Yep."

Rosenberg asked for details. Davis said Young told him that he drove into the parking lot of either Cigarette or USA Racing and then turned around.

"Did Bobby talk about this murder in your presence more than one time?"

"He tried to."

"And what would your response be?"

" 'I don't want to hear it.' "

MARCH 13, 1990

RICHARD FIDLIN
SWORN STATEMENT

Fidlin went into a bit more detail regarding the afternoon of the murder, when, he said, Bobby Young had had him come to north Dade to pick him up if need be.

Fidlin said he was driving south on Biscayne Boulevard, and around the 190 block, he pulled into a parking lot of an abandoned office building and made a U-turn.

"My phone rang as soon as I pulled in," he said. It was Young, who didn't need Fidlin to pick him up, but asked where he was. Fidlin told him.

"Then he said, 'Did you hear anything?' I said no."

After Fidlin asked Young to meet him at the Dry Dock lounge on U.S. 1 in Hollywood, Fidlin said he called Young back on his car phone, to make sure he was still coming. Young answered that he was almost there. [The phone bill showed a 3:33 P.M. call from Young's car phone to Fidlin's car phone. On Fidlin's car phone bill, there was a two-minute call to Young's car phone at 3:48.]

Everything else was consistent with what he had told Greg Smith four months before.

MARCH 15, 1990

BOBBY YOUNG

Since Smith and DeCora had come to Oklahoma City to see John Flynn, they thought, why not take a run at Bobby Young, too, and see if he would say anything?

They found him in the Oklahoma County Jail, in

Aronow family Christmas card photo with Don, Lillian, and son Gavin.

(Photo courtesy Newcomb and Fran Green)

Lillian and Don after winning the Tampa Bay Downs.

(Photo courtesy Newcomb and Fran Green)

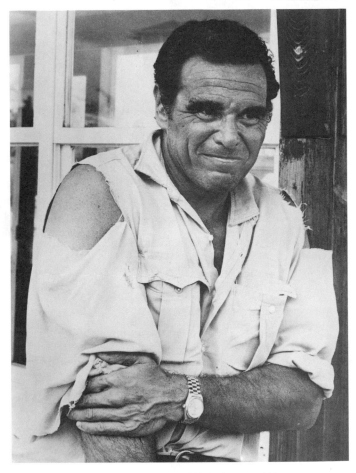

Don Aronow after winning the 1969 Bahamas 500.

(Photo courtesy John Crouse)

At the 1983 Kentucky Derby, Aronow (wearing the white Cigarette Racing Team jacket) talks with Howard Cosell.

(Photo courtesy Newcomb and Fran Green)

In 1984, George Bush flew to Miami to see Aronow's prototype for what would be the Blue Thunder model. *From left:* Willie Meyers, Bush (driving in ski goggles), two Secret Service men, and Aronow.

(Photo courtesy John Crouse)

Helicopter shot of the crime scene. On left is boat storage facility of Fort Apache Marina; behind that is Apache Performance Boats.

(Photo courtesy Metro-Dade Police)

Don Aronow's Mercedes-Benz at the scene of the shooting, in front of Apache Performance Boats.

(Photo courtesy Metro-Dade Police)

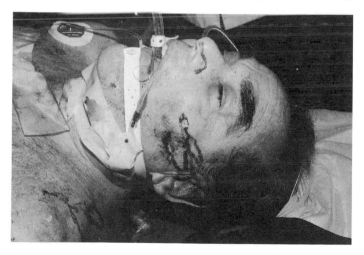

The last photograph of Don Aronow. He had expired a half hour previously.

(Photo courtesy Metro-Dade Police)

From left: Willie Falcón, Sal Magluta, Keith Eickert, Bobby Saccenti, and Ben Kramer.

(Photo courtesy John Crouse)

1990 police lineup includes Robert Young (*second from left*).

(Photo courtesy Metro-Dade Police)

Ben Kramer and Bobby Saccenti piloting World Championship boat *Warpath*.

(Photo courtesy John Crouse)

Ben Kramer, 1993.

(Photo courtesy Metro-Dade Police)

Oklahoma City, still awaiting trial on his federal narcotics charges.

Young agreed to talk, but tried to set the ground rules first: the discussion had to be "off the record," he wouldn't sign a waiver of rights, nor would he say anything at all if the detectives read him his Miranda warning.

The detectives hadn't heard that one before. Okay, DeCora said.

To begin with, Young denied that he was involved in Aronow's murder. But he also knew that Skip Walton, Richard Fidlin, and Tommy Teagle all said he was and planned to testify against him. All of them were lying, he said, and the case had become political.

[Young also made reference to "Wayne," who he said was dead. Wayne Shehan had told detectives he had gotten word to Young that he had overdosed, so Young wouldn't chase him.]

The detectives asked Young how he knew about the witnesses. He wouldn't say, but seemed proud that he knew what track the police were on. Nor would he explain what he meant by "political."

Smith confirmed to him that he was a suspect in the murder, then suggested that if he had any information that could clear himself, now was the time to offer it. No, Young declined, the truth would come out at trial. Asked where he was on the day of the murder, he demurred again; he would give an alibi at trial.

But Young did want to talk about drug smuggling, and he bragged about his contacts. He personally knew Ochoa, Escobar, and Gacha, the heads of the Medellin cartel. He was a smuggler of both marijuana and cocaine—but not a hit man, he said. He also admitted that he *was* smuggling marijuana when he was caught by the Cubans.

He then spoke about his two most recent convictions: the Panzavecchia murder and the Craig Marshall attempted murder.

Young admitted that he killed Panzavecchia, but he felt justified because Panzavecchia had tried to shoot him the day before. Young said he had warned him to stay away, but instead Panzavecchia came to Young's home, looking for him.

In the Marshall instance, he said Marshall had locked himself in his car in his driveway, then finally opened the door to let him in. During a confrontation, Young shot him three times. Then Young insisted Skip Walton take him to the hospital. [That was different from what he had told Fort Lauderdale detective Steve Robitaille. Young had insisted then that the shots were accidental.]

Smith asked if Young knew Ben Kramer. Yes, he said; Kramer had off-loaded marijuana for him in the '70s. Further, Kramer had dated Kathleen years before she married Young.

JOHN FLYNN

Later that day, Smith and DeCora met John Flynn at El Reno federal prison, outside of Oklahoma City. Julian Bearden had mentioned that Flynn and Joe Marino were Ben Kramer's associates.

At first, Flynn refused to talk at all, explaining that he feared retribution against his family if he did. Then he said he'd answer just a few questions: He didn't know who was responsible for Aronow's murder, and although he was very close to Kramer, it was his understanding that he wasn't involved.

MARCH 28, 1990

Mike DeCora testified to a Dade County grand jury; later in the day, it indicted Bobby Young for the first-degree murder of Don Aronow. However, the indictment would stay sealed for more than two months.

MARCH 29, 1990

Ben Kramer; his father, Jack Kramer; and attorney Melvyn Kessler were convicted on all counts of money-laundering and racketeering in Fort Lauderdale federal court. Michael Gilbert was found guilty on four counts and acquitted on seven counts.

APRIL 4, 1990

DeCora and Smith went to Lisle, Illinois, to interview Joe Marino. He admitted that he had worked "off and on" for Ben Kramer and knew Julian Bearden, but he said he didn't know who was involved in Aronow's murder, either.

APRIL 6, 1990

When a jury determined that the Kramers had to forfeit their interest in the Bell Gardens Bicycle Club, a legal poker casino in southern California, a federal judge ordered that the U.S. government could seize it.

Dexter Lehtinen, U.S. attorney for the Southern District of Florida, called it "the single most valuable asset ever forfeited to the United States," worth $150 million. The year before, it had grossed $100 million. The club would continue to operate as before, now under government ownership, he said.

APRIL 13, 1990

Ben Kramer was sentenced to ten years and a $100,000 fine for attempted escape—that, on top of his life without parole for smuggling, plus whatever he would get for the money-laundering conviction. Kramer limped out of federal court on a wooden crutch.

Kramer's brother, Marc, was sentenced to ninety months in prison.

APRIL 16, 1990

Properly unaware that a grand jury had already returned a sealed indictment charging Robert Young with murdering Don Aronow, *Miami Herald* writer Sydney Freedberg penned a lengthy page-one story wondering whether the case would ever get resolved.

However, Freedberg did at least know the direction in which the investigation was going: Young and Kramer.

"The murder of Aronow, shot to death three years ago, seems to be unraveling as one of the most sensational chapters in the nation's drug story.

"A double-dealing mob tale, it might out-Godfather *The Godfather*—if, of course, it's not fiction.

"Says Michael Aronow, the slain racer's son: 'The way my father lived, it [the murder] could have been as casual as a handshake . . . It could have been international. It could have had to do with the CIA.'

"Or it could have had something to do with Ben Kramer, he says."

[In early 1988, the last time the *Herald* had quoted Mike, he had insisted, "Kramer has nothing to do with nothing. It's not related to Kramer or drugs in any way. That's the biggest joke of all. That's stupid. My father was the cleanest guy in the world."]

Mike explained to Freedberg that his father had sold USA Racing to Kramer, but the story that Kramer had paid for it at least in part with under-the-table money was "hearsay."

[What the *Herald* also didn't know at the time was that the cash-under-the-table story was "hearsay" descended from none other than Mike Aronow, who told it to police on the night his father was killed.]

Freedberg mentioned street talk that Don Aronow had kept Kramer's under-the-table money after he took the company back. She quoted Dr. Bob Magoon, Aronow's friend: "They didn't like each other in the end. They were having trouble with a deal."

Freedberg asked one of Bobby Young's attorneys, Fred Haddad, to describe him: a "soldier of fortune type," he said.

MAY 11, 1990

FBI agent Joe Ciccarelli offered Greg Smith a new lead: an inmate at MCC Miami, Ronald Phipps, had just called and said he had been talking at the prison with Ben Kramer about Aronow.

MAY 14, 1990

Greg Smith went to MCC to see Phipps, an armed bank robbery convict who had served ten of his eighteen years.

Phipps said he had talked with Kramer several times, beginning in the end of March. Kramer told him that he had been in business with Don Aronow, and that Kramer had laundered some of his drug profits through him. However, when Aronow realized it, he stopped doing business with him.

Since Kramer had such a large investment in the company, he decided he had to kill Aronow. He hired two men for the job, and they did it while Aronow sat in his car.

Afterward, Kramer told his partner that the two hired killers were going to rip him off, and the partner had Aronow's killers killed.

MAY 15, 1990

Just a month after Bill Saladrigas talked to him, Stanley Diamond was arrested for dealing three kilos of cocaine, while armed, by a Broward County Sheriff's street narcotics unit. He bonded out of county jail, but then the

Feds took custody of him on violation of his federal parole and dropped him off at MCC Miami—the current domicile of Ben Kramer.

By the time Diamond called Saladrigas with this news, he was back at the Broward County Jail; he had promised the Aronow detectives inside information, and now it would come from Kramer's own mouth.

Saladrigas went to see him again. At MCC, Diamond said Kramer had arranged for the two men to talk several times by getting his attorney, named Forman, to call them both out to the visiting room. Then Forman would step away so they could be alone.

During those talks, Kramer talked about Bobby Young, who he said could "destroy [me] if he wanted to" and "put me in the electric chair" if he flipped and testified for the government. Kramer asked Diamond for advice and eventually solicited him to arrange to kill Young—using his organized-crime contacts—once he got released from prison.

Diamond said he had tried to stall Kramer so he could tell this all to the state and work out a deal for himself on the fifteen-year minimum sentence he was facing. If he didn't have to serve any of that time, he offered to tell everything Kramer had said to him, wear a wire the next time they talked, and testify in court about it.

JUNE 7, 1990

Bobby Young pled guilty to his federal narcotics charges in Oklahoma City and was sentenced to ten years. That was on top of his concurrent seventeen-year Florida state sentences for the Marshall and Panzavecchia cases.

JUNE 11, 1990

Young arrived at the Dade County Jail from Oklahoma.

JUNE 12, 1990

11:45 A.M.: At the U.S. Marshal's office at the federal courthouse in downtown Miami, Greg Smith and Mike DeCora transported Young in handcuffs and shackles to the Metro-Dade Police homicide office in order to charge him with the murder of Don Aronow.

12 NOON: Secure inside the police interview room, detectives removed Young's shackles and cuffs, gave him coffee, and let him smoke.

12:10 P.M.: Smith and DeCora entered the room and asked Young some questions about himself. Young said he was born in East St. Louis, Illinois, finished two years of college at Southern Illinois University, then at age eighteen, in 1966, moved to south Florida. Asked to state his profession, he said, "drug smuggler."

When the detectives began to read Young his Miranda rights, he gave them the same spiel as last time: he was aware of them and wouldn't waive them. If his rights were read to him, he would stop talking. However, he would continue speaking if his rights were not read to him.

Once again, given the circumstances, DeCora and Smith went along and deliberately did not read him his rights.

Again Young denied that he had anything to do with the murder, but wouldn't offer anything to prove it.

He did consent to answer questions about others who police considered his associates:

- *Ben Kramer*. Young said he had never spoken to him nor had any relationship with him, but in 1972, Kramer did off-load marijuana from boats for him as part of his crew.

  Everyone else, Young admitted knowing from after the time he was released from Cuba:
- *Paul Silverman*. Young met him through his wife, who had known him since she was seventeen. Silverman

owned one of his dogs. [Silverman had said Young bought one of *his* puppies.]

- *Richard Fidlin.* Fidlin was a liar. The story he had given police about the murder directly conflicted with what actually happened.
- *Skip Walton.* Skip, too, was a liar. Young also knew that he had failed a polygraph in Oklahoma.
- *Carl Davis.* Davis had a severe cocaine habit and was always under the influence.
- *Wimpy* (Rodrigo Chegwin-Vergara). Wimpy was one of his drug connections, currently serving a federal prison sentence.

Young volunteered that he had murdered someone in Colombia in 1987. As a result of a drug deal gone bad, a child had been abducted, and Young had to kill the kidnapper. Young was arrested there for the murder but was freed shortly afterward. He said charges were dropped and hinted that it was because a bribe had been paid.

2:10 P.M.: Archie Moore and Smith walked Young to the ID section, where he was fingerprinted.

2:50 P.M.: Back at the interview room, Smith and DeCora gave Young a standard Miranda warning form and asked him to read it aloud. He did, then initialed it. He repeated that he wasn't willing to waive his rights or give a statement without an attorney present, indicated that on the form, then signed it.

3:10 P.M.: Smith and DeCora walked him to the Dade County Jail, then booked and charged him with first-degree murder.

JUNE 13, 1990

The Miami Herald asked Gary Rosenberg if anyone else would be charged with the crime.

''Not today,'' he answered.

Beyond the statement of Young's arrest, police released no details to the press. However, the *Herald* noted that Young did not look like the composite picture made by witnesses after the murder, nor had any of the witnesses positively identified Young's picture. Young was a blue-eyed blond, and the witnesses said the man had wavy brown hair and a tanned complexion.

Could fear have altered their ability to identify anyone? the *Herald* suggested.

"Everyone was terrified," answered John Crouse.

When the papers first quoted Crouse after the murder, he vigorously denied that Aronow had had anything to do with drug smugglers. But with three years gone by, he had changed his mind.

"Don mingled with all sorts of people. He sold boats to mobsters. He was a high roller, and in the fast world of fast boats, Rolexes and Porsches are strange bedfellows. You couldn't be an offshore racer and not have an association with somebody involved in drugs," he told the *Herald*.

Later in the day, police and prosecutors went to every length to keep Young under wraps. They had scheduled witnesses to come in the next day to view a live lineup, and to keep that from being prejudiced, they didn't want Young's picture in the press in advance.

That prompted a cat-and-mouse game. Reporters anticipated a routine, brief bond hearing early in the day, at which time they could get their photographs. That was canceled; then prosecutors snuck Young into another judge's court at two o'clock.

A *Herald* reporter found out about it and showed up. Gary Rosenberg then asked the judge to order Young to stand facing a wall, in case a photographer arrived. A cameraman did come, but by that time, it was too late. Young was gone.

JUNE 14, 1990

The Miami Herald: "As long ago as last fall, frightened witnesses in the Don Aronow murder case were told by investigators not to be afraid: Two suspects were already in custody.''

One, evidently, was Bobby Young. No one would say who the second suspect was.

Smith and DeCora spent the afternoon searching police headquarters for five employees who looked as much like Bobby Young as possible, to stand in a lineup with him. They found them, all white and clean-shaven, and about the same age, build, and hair color.

At 5:30, the five plus Young were assembled in a room in the building. All of them were dressed in bright red Dade County Jail short-sleeved jumpsuits and were barefoot. Also present were DeCora, Gary Rosenberg, and Edith Georgi, a senior public defender.

Young was placed in position number two. Both Young and Georgi were asked if they wanted him to take a different position. They declined.

6:10 P.M.: From the other side of the one-way glass, Levon Tindall was the first witness to see them. One by one, each man stepped forward, turned ninety degrees four times, then stepped back.

As the man he had seen in the Lincoln, Tindall picked out the person in position number one.

[In fact, number one was very close in appearance to Young. He was one year older and exactly the same height. His main variations were that his complexion was slightly darker and his eyes were brighter blue.]

6:15 P.M.: Mike Britton couldn't pick out anyone.

6:25 P.M.: "Do you recognize anyone?" Gary Rosenberg asked Patty Lezaca.

"Possibly, yes."

"Which number is that?"

"Number two," she said.

"From where do you possibly recognize that person?"

"Down at Aronow's office."

"Did you see that person on the day of Mr. Aronow's death—or possibly?"

"Possibly," she repeated.

"Do you remember what name he used?"

"Jerry Jacoby."

Edith Georgi spoke up. "Let the record reflect there is a minute delay between your question and her saying 'Possibly.' "

"The record can reflect a delay between her answer. I didn't time it because it wasn't delayed," Rosenberg held his ground.

"I said 'possibly,' " Lezaca repeated again.

After detectives walked Lezaca away from the glass, she mentioned that she would have liked to have seen number two wearing shorts, because the man in the office had been wearing shorts, and his legs were very hairy.

6:35 P.M.: "Possibly," Jerry Engelman answered the same question.

"What number?" Rosenberg asked.

"Four."

"From where could you possibly have recognized this person?"

"He looks a little like somebody I was shown a picture of."

At 7:15, Smith put Young in an interview room, then asked him what he thought. Once again, Young set the same ground rules: he'd talk off the record, but wouldn't waive his constitutional rights.

Young asked the first question to Smith: was he disappointed by what had just happened? Smith sighed; he had expected this, given the amount of time that had passed.

Commiserating, Young volunteered his opinion. He shouldn't have been able to see through the one-way glass, but he said he had.

He knew that the woman was the same woman in Aronow's office on the day of the murder. He was surprised that she didn't positively identify him because she had seen him for the longest period of time.

JUNE 16, 1990

Miami Herald headline: WITNESSES STUMBLE IN ARONOW LINEUP.

JUNE 22, 1990

A Broward Sheriff's Office homicide sergeant had gotten
a letter in the mail, dated June 12, from a Broward
County detention center inmate who claimed he had information about the Aronow case. The Broward sergeant
called DeCora, and he sent Archie Moore to get the letter
and meet with the inmate, Scott Deering.

The letter read:

> *To whom it may concern in regards to the shooting
> of Don Aronow in January '88 [February 1987],
> I, Scott Deering, formerly in the employ of Fort
> Apache Marina, did see and make eye contact with
> the driver of a blue over black Mark IV Lincoln
> Continental. Having seen the suspect at a range of
> between thirty-five to 50 yards, I believe I might be
> of some help in your line-up. Be advised, however,
> I would only agree to complete and total anonymity
> for fear of mine and my daughter's lives. At your
> service, Scott A. Deering, PL900112, North Bro-
> ward Detention Complex.*

[In fact, Scott Deering had been interviewed on the
afternoon of the murder by WCIX Channel 6. He had
kinky brown hair and a full curly beard. He had said, "I
heard a bunch of shots that I thought at the time were
firecrackers."]

Moore met Deering at the detention center, in Pompano Beach. He had been charged the previous January
for selling cocaine. He said he sent the letter after hearing
that an arrest for the murder had been made.

At the time of the killing, Deering said he was Fort
Apache Marina's assistant dock master. He was working
near the boat storage facilities when a dark-colored car
driving slowly on 188th Street caught his attention because it went back and forth five or six times. He saw
only one man inside it, whom he described as about

thirty-five to fifty, with a "square face," clean-shaven, and possibly wearing a light blue shirt.

Deering said he walked away to the rear of the marina; then, two minutes later, he heard what sounded like four to six firecrackers. A bit later, he learned that Don Aronow had been shot.

Deering also said that a coworker whom he couldn't remember told him that Aronow had been at Fort Apache earlier that day. Further, he and Ben Kramer had gotten into an argument then. Deering said he wasn't close to Ben, but he was to Jack Kramer, who had hired him.

Moore showed Deering photo lineups that included Bobby Young, Carl Davis, Richard Fidlin, and Skip Walton, but he couldn't pick anyone out.

Tommy Williams, a Dade County Jail cellmate of Bobby Young, called Gary Rosenberg and said he needed to talk. Rosenberg called DeCora and arranged for Williams to be transported to the state attorney's office.

Williams, a twenty-year-old black man whose arrest record included theft, escape, and impersonating a judge, said he and Young had struck up a friendship, and they had discussed his case.

Williams said Young bragged about being a hired hit man. If the money was right, he said, he would kill his own mother. He also claimed to be a master of disguise; he would wear glasses, a beard, anything to change his appearance during a murder.

Young boasted that the eyewitnesses in the case couldn't identify him at the lineup because he wasn't wearing a beard. He called the female witness a "dumb fuck." He added that the cops didn't have the murder weapon, nor would they ever have it because his partner had it. Young didn't identify his partner, but Williams said Young called him frequently from the jail, long distance, and Young said they had a legitimate business out of the country.

Young said someone was with him in the area at the

time of the murder, but Williams didn't think the person was in the car with him.

JUNE 30, 1990

Jack Kramer, convicted in March for money-laundering, was sentenced to nineteen years and fined $200,000. Michael Gilbert got four years and a $350,000 fine.

JULY 2, 1990

Williams called Rosenberg again, and later that day, Rosenberg arranged for him to be transported to his office.

Williams said that over the weekend, he overheard Young on the telephone telling someone that he needed to find a crucial state witness—Young didn't say who.

After Williams returned to the jail, Rosenberg and Smith decided they should ask a judge for a wiretap on Young's phone.

JULY 3, 1990

Bobby Young was absent at his arraignment, but his attorney Billy Thomas (who had represented Young's wife, Kathleen, at her subpoena earlier in the year), entered a written plea of not guilty for him. Thomas said that Young didn't want to appear in person because, as an escape risk, they would have brought him in shackles. He was being kept in isolation, under tight surveillance.

The Miami Herald wrote the next day, "Investigators have hinted that somebody else is on the verge of formal accusation, but they will not say who."

JULY 6, 1990

The wiretap on Young's phone began. Detectives logged every call Young made for about the next month, but it produced no information relevant to the case, nor did they ever discover the name of the witness Williams had referred to.

August 1990

In a story reporting Young's indictment, *Motor Boating & Sailing* magazine interviewed Gary Garbrecht, CEO of Aronow Powerboats—the successor to USA Racing. Garbrecht disbelieved the Kramer theory and its accompanying scenario about money under the table that wasn't repaid.

"They had done deals together after the USA Racing Team deal," he said. "Both had hot tempers and were hands-on types of guys. I think if Ben felt he had a problem with Don, he'd walk over and take him on."

Garbrecht speculated that the murder might have been related to Blue Thunder. "The boats were having a big success in drug interdiction. Maybe a disgruntled shipper wanted Don out of the way."

August 29, 1990

Ben Kramer was sentenced to forty-three years in prison for the money-laundering case (in addition to his life without parole for smuggling) and fined $460,000.

September 28, 1990

Fifty-five-year-old Melvyn Kessler, also convicted for laundering, was sentenced to thirty years in prison and fined $176,000. However, United States district judge Norman Roettger allowed him to post $1 million bond and surrender voluntarily in six weeks, so he could have abdominal surgery and spend time with his family.

NOVEMBER 23, 1990

BLUE THUNDER

"A new book about the murder of speedboat designer Don Aronow is in pretty shallow water," wrote Sydney Freedberg in *The Miami Herald.*

It was called *Blue Thunder* and subtitled "How the Mafia owned and finally murdered Cigarette boat king Donald Aronow," published by Simon & Schuster. To say the least, that theory surprised a number of people familiar with the case.

Author Thomas Burdick began the story: "Don Aronow knew he was going to be murdered." It ended with Bobby Young's arraignment, which Burdick believed was a blind to cover the real solution to the murder.

Aronow had Mafia connections from when he owned a construction company in New Jersey; then, in Miami in the early '60s, he made ties to Meyer Lansky, Burdick wrote. Aronow got involved in a Lansky-organization drug-smuggling ring, but when Lansky died in 1983, so went Aronow's protection. The Mafia murdered him because he knew too much, and he was about to be subpoenaed by a grand jury.

The 1990 arrest of Bobby Young as Aronow's killer—and the expectation that police would eventually implicate Ben Kramer as having hired Young—came late in Burdick's book, long after he had set down his Mafia theory.

But Young didn't kill Aronow, and Kramer was a fall guy, too, Burdick said. Instead, he named two Chicago hoods as the real killers and even printed their photos—one that Burdick took himself. He met with Metro-Dade police and the U.S. attorney's office to make the case against them, but neither wanted to listen—because the Mob controlled them, he said. The real truth, he said, would have damaged George Bush, who was running for president in 1988.

But Freedberg quickly found problems throughout the text. "Many people quoted in the book say it fabricated statements, took things out of context and sealed rumors into facts to fit a giant Mob-conspiracy theory,'' she wrote.

Ironically, Freedberg's story was a sidebar to the main Aronow story of the day: the release of hundreds of pages of Metro-Dade Police reports into the public record, information that Burdick had gone to press without waiting for.

''The book should be under the category of fiction,'' Freedberg quoted Gary Rosenberg, the lead prosecutor. ''It's all unsubstantiated theories checked out by the Metro-Dade Police Department years ago.''

''Smarmy, unethical journalism,'' said _Herald_ reporter Edna Buchanan, who Burdick quoted and thanked in his preface. Buchanan also said Burdick introduced himself with a different name, ''Tom Mitchell.''

Freedberg tried to contact Burdick through his publicist and his beeper, but he didn't respond. A spokesman for Simon & Schuster said they stood by the book.

[A later _Herald_ book review called it ''runaway conjecture.''

''The book is actually more a sucker's game than a carnival, a paranoid fantasy trip for the kind of people who want to believe that the Trilateral Commission killed JFK. The mystery of the moment is not who killed Aronow, but how _Blue Thunder_ found its way into print.'']

NOVEMBER 26, 1990

With the publication of _Blue Thunder_ and Sydney Freedberg's story about the release of the police reports, Skip Taylor angrily motioned the civil court to end his alimony payments to Ilene—since married to Elton Cary— and for her to return all the money he had already paid.

''It has now become clear that the former wife [Ilene] was having long-standing sexual affairs with both Aronow and Cary during the course of the marriage [to Skip].

"As details of the Aronow investigation have become public, it is clear that [Ilene] divorced [Skip] in an effort to culminate one of those affairs into a marriage, which would occur immediately after [Ilene] could get what she could from [Skip], by improperly using the process and powers of the Court.

"[Ilene's] shocking conduct during the course of the marriage, which has become public as a result of the investigation into the Aronow murder, has caused the respondent to be a murder suspect, whose business and reputation, nationally and in this community, have, as a result, been greatly diminished.

"[Ilene's] plot to marry Aronow fell apart shortly after she filed for divorce, with the death of Aronow.

"[Ilene] then took up residence with Cary, all the while alleging that she needed support and alimony from [Skip]. Yet during this time, she was planning the marriage to Cary, which occurred only a short time after the divorce became final.

"[Ilene] is wealthy as a result of her marriage to Cary, some 35 years her senior. He is the CEO of a bank, and they have a small baby. Her plan has worked."

Skip then served Elton Cary and former USA Racing employees Jerry Engelman and Randy Riggs with subpoenas for deposition. Ilene countered with motions to the court to quash those subpoenas, and to seal the divorce file.

Skip responded: "Under the circumstances, it is easy to understand why Elton Cary would like to avoid answering any questions, especially since he is no stranger to allegations of fraud in a domestic setting. In fact, in what may not be entirely coincidental, Cary and the deceased, Don Aronow, were sued by Cary's ex-wife, Frances Wolfson, for defrauding her. The scope of [Ilene's] dishonesty, fraud, and efforts at concealment . . . extends at least as far as [Ilene's] denial to Metro[-Dade] homicide investigators that she even had an affair with Aronow."

A judge denied both of Ilene's motions. However, she

offered to settle the matter—terms confidential—before anyone had to give testimony.

DECEMBER 1, 1990

Although *The Miami Herald* had panned *Blue Thunder*, reviewers around the country believed the book, and Simon & Schuster bought a half-page ad in the *Herald* to publicize what they had said.

Kirkus Reviews wrote that the book was "A suspenseful investigation into one of the most sensational scandals in America's current drug war . . . Admirably dogged crime reporting . . . and a piercing look at the long, strong arms of the Mob."

Nick Taylor, author of *Sins of the Father,* called it "an awesome piece of investigative work that leaves the 'official' story of Don Aronow's death without a shred of credibility."

And John Katzenbach, in *The New York Times Book Review,* wrote that it was "Likely to have many prominent folks, particularly in Miami, squirming uncomfortably in their seats."

DECEMBER 19, 1990

Prosecutor Gary Rosenberg got a letter, full of grammatical errors, from a federal prisoner in Leavenworth named Samuel Cooper.

Dear Mr. Rosenberg:

Before you disregard this letter as trash, I fervently hope you'd consider its facts and content carefully.

Cooper wrote that from February to July of 1990, he had been housed at MCC Miami to help the Feds prosecute members of the Yahwehs, a black religious cult suspected of multiple murders in Miami. But that's not what he told inmates at MCC; instead, he said his own case was back on appeal, and that Metro-Dade was investigating him for four murders. That, plus the fact that he had come from Marion (Illinois) Penitentiary, the highest-level-security prison in the federal system, made him somewhat of a celebrity.

During this time, I was befriended by a guy name Ben Barry Kramer and I became his most trusted confidant in the prison.

Ben, it seems, is like a kid fascinated with toys but he prefer[s] tough guys presence around him— and this I offer freely. He would tell me these stories that I found hard to believe and thought he was just trying to impress me, being that I was from Marion.

But the stories persisted and even got more unbelievable and during one of these occasion[s] that I mention[ed] to Ben Kramer that if I'm charged with the (phony) 4 murders I could get the chair. Then he shocked me with the reply, "I could get the chair if they ever found out the truth."

Cooper said he cut Kramer off right there, but weeks later, Kramer, depressed, told him that Metro-Dade was

bringing some guy from Oklahoma that could ty him into the Aronow murder. And he was hoping the guy wouldn't break and he wanted to know if I knew anybody in dade-county jail that would kill this guy for 10,000 if it was possible.

I related that I would check into it, meanwhile he (Ben) related to me how he had paid almost $250,000 to this guy from Oklahoma and an old italian friend who has been a hit man for years to murder this Aronow guy. He (Ben) went even further to tell me how this italian friend (hit-man) of his had killed everyone that was involved with a case with him (hit-man) and when it was time for the case to be tried it was thrown-out because *everyone was dead except his italian (hit-man) friend.*

He (Ben) told me that the reason Aronow was killed is because he had been paid millions in cash to have drugs delivered at his boat shop and [if] the drugs didn't show as designated, he would charge the price again for the anticipated shipment. Ben claims Aronow did this numerous times without compensation and the last straw was when he (Aronow) threaten[ed] to dissociate himself from Ben Kramer and the drug business.

Sometime later after Ben told me this story, he came to me very delighted and told me he had heard the best news he had heard in a long time (the guy from Oklahoma was not identified in a physical line-up) and jokingly stated "looks like you will be going to death-row by yourself—but hold me a cell just in case."

Me and Ben became so close, he would even have his lawyers to pull us (me and him) out on interviews so we could discuss escapes, murder plots, etc together for hours.

Respectfully,
Samuel Cooper

13

MARCH 31, 1991

Did Blue Thunder (the boat) really make much difference in the war on smuggling? The *Sun-Sentinel* had a reporter hitch a ride with the Customs Service on one:

"The strategy for catching drug smugglers is almost embarrassingly simple: choose a spot of ocean—virtually at random—go there and wait. If a boat comes from the east moving toward south Florida, board it and look for drugs. After spending a few hours in one spot, move on to another.

"The strategy has paid off three times in the past three months—an unusually high rate of success. In December, [U.S. Customs officer John] Farrell intercepted two shipments of cocaine totaling 1,600 pounds. In February, he seized another 1,500 pounds from one boat.

"Despite these results, the jury is still out on the effectiveness of operations like those involving the Blue Thunder. Critics claim that offshore patrols are ineffective at stopping the flow of drugs into South Florida. Farrell cites government estimates that the various law enforcement agencies intercept less than 10 percent of all drugs headed for South Florida."

April 4, 1991

MELVYN KESSLER

Melvyn Kessler, six months earlier sentenced to thirty years, had since flipped to the government's side and thus extended his November 1990 surrender date. He volunteered to testify against the Kramers' money-laundering partners and others who claimed an interest in their southern California poker casino, which had cost $12 million in ill-gotten money to build but had quickly risen to a value of about $150 million when the government seized it a year before.

The government made no deal in writing, but Kessler understood that in order to reduce his sentence—or stay out of prison entirely, he hoped—he'd also have to cooperate "freely and truthfully" with Metro-Dade police investigating Aronow's murder.

Roger Edwards, the IRS agent who had investigated Kessler and the Kramers, called the lieutenant in charge of homicide at Metro-Dade and said that Kessler wanted to discuss what he knew about Ben Kramer's role in the murder, but he didn't want to meet directly with the lead detective just yet. However, he would feel comfortable talking with Al Singleton, whom he had known for years as a detective and sergeant.

Sometime after Young's indictment, Mike DeCora had wanted out of the homicide bureau, and Greg Smith became the case's new lead detective. Smith didn't like Kessler's terms but agreed to send Singleton to do the interview. His assignment was to convince Kessler to meet with Smith.

At the meeting, at the Fort Lauderdale federal courthouse office of Robert Bondi—the assistant U.S. attorney who had prosecuted the money-laundering case—Kessler proffered a summary of what he knew:

Ben Kramer hired Bobby Young to kill Aronow and paid him $100,000 for it. However, Kramer and Young had never met; Kramer set it up through a middleman, possibly Steve Romano, who was married to Kramer's wife's sister. Romano was in federal prison in Terre Haute, Indiana.

[According to Charles Podesta's testimony at the smuggling trial, Romano had worked for Kramer, chucking bales of pot onto the beach.]

Further, Kramer tried to have Paul Thompson kill Young while both were in the Dade County Jail. Meanwhile, Young was currently upset that his legal fees had not been paid.

[Few people had a reputation for more violence than "Big Paul" Thompson. In January 1980, he had been arrested and charged with two others for the murders of four apparent undercover drug informants whose bound, beaten, strangled, and stabbed bodies had been left in a burning car beside I-95 in north Dade just before dawn earlier that month. Two of the bodies were covered with blood and wrapped in blankets. But by faking mental illness, Thompson had managed to avoid a prison cell for ten years; a codefendant would be executed for the crime in 1995.

And even before that, Thompson, a member of two drug gangs in the '70s, had a 1975 conviction for the murder and dynamiting of a fellow gang member; however, he served only two years. In 1977, he was indicted in federal court for conspiring to bomb witnesses who were to testify against him in the 1975 case.]

APRIL 15, 1991

SAMUEL COOPER

Gary Rosenberg hadn't responded to Samuel Cooper, so this time he mailed a letter to Greg Smith, who had visited him at Marion Penitentiary in 1989 regarding other Miami murder cases Cooper said he had information about.

He and Kramer had a mutual acquaintance, he wrote— none other than John "Big Red" Panzavecchia. Cooper met him while doing time at Florida State Prison at Starke, the highest-security prison in the state.

Ben ask me had i ever heard what happen to Red Panzavecchia. I replied that i lost all contact with him once i left Stark. He said that he had 'Red' killed because Red was taking from him like he was nothing but a sissy.

[Later, Kramer told him that] the guy he had to kill "Red" will be brought to Miami on a murder for a line-up. And if the guy is picked and break[s] he could put him (Ben) on death row for sure.

Then several days later Ben tell me that the guy beat the line-up. But that he was still somewhat worried about the guy standing-up.

One day after all of the events was over, Ben ask me did my mother like the roses he sent her for Mother-day. And i replied yes and then he wanted to know my birthdate. I told him it was February 4th and he looked at me strange and said, that's the day the guy i had killed was to appear at the grand-jury. He says he had the guy killed a day before the 4th and his reasons was that the guy owe him several hundred thousands and was jerking him around about paying. And when he heard that the guy was going before the grand jury, he knew that the guy (Aronow) would tell things on him (Ben) to put him in prison thus never paying the debt.

P.S. I've got a photo here that Ben gave me and it has him and the guy on it, that he claims set the "hit" up. The guy names is Saccenti.

> *Sincerely,*
> *Samuel Cooper*

On the back of the photo was handwritten:

Flick
Three Florida crackers
Best Homies you got
Friends for life
Ben

["Flick" was Cooper's nickname. The photo was taken inside MCC Miami, but neither of the other two in the picture with Kramer was Bobby Saccenti. They were Florida drug convicts Ricky Cravero and Ronnie Chandler.]

MAY 2, 1991

MELVYN KESSLER

Mel Kessler finally consented to meeting Greg Smith, and an interview was set up at the U.S. attorney's office in Miami.

With his attorney, Bruce Zimet, present, Kessler told Smith that he had known Ben Kramer for many years, through his father, Jack. Although he had represented Ben in a criminal case when he was a teenager, their attorney-client relationship had ended, and therefore no privilege existed for what Ben had since told him.

Kessler repeated that, to his knowledge, Ben had never met Bobby Young. But Kramer did know Bobby Young's wife, Kathy, through an escort service she had worked for.

Kessler, however, knew Young very well. Kramer had directed him to represent Young on his Fort Lauderdale attempted-murder case and his Oklahoma City federal drug case. At first, Kessler had trouble finding Young in the Broward County Jail because he had told police his name was Bobby Scott.

Kramer was concerned that Young might flip, so he wanted Kessler to keep an eye on him. But initially, Kramer didn't let on that what really concerned him was that Young knew about Aronow's murder.

When Kessler first met Young at the Broward County Jail, he told him, "Ben sent me to represent you." Young apparently knew why; he apprised Kessler that he was involved in Aronow's murder. But Kramer shouldn't worry, he added. As long as he paid Young's legal fees, Young would go "balls to the wall"—that is, he'd keep his mouth shut to the prosecution. He also realized that

Kessler would relay everything he said back to Kramer.

A week or two later, Kessler said he met Kramer at a Texaco station just east of I-95 at 79th Street in Miami and told him what Young had said. Kramer then enlightened Kessler that he had paid Young $100,000 for the murder and that Steve Romano had made the payment for him.

[There was a timing problem in the story, however. Young was arrested by Fort Lauderdale police for the attempted murder of Craig Marshall on September 3, 1987. Kramer had been taken into federal custody on August 27, 1987—so Kramer couldn't have made any meeting at a Texaco station around then. But Kessler may have been confused. He later said he had met with Kramer at that Texaco "four or five times over the period of years."]

Despite Young's "balls to the wall" assertion, Kramer remained extremely fearful of him. He mentioned more than once that Young could put him in the electric chair.

In 1990, after Young was returned to Miami from Oklahoma City and indicted for Aronow's murder, Kessler met Kramer in the visiting room at MCC Miami. Kramer then gave Kessler a letter and asked him to deliver it in person to Paul Thompson in the Dade County Jail.

Kessler did what he was asked; he was afraid of Kramer and didn't want to upset him, he said. The letter asked Thompson to arrange for Young to be "hit" in the jail. Thompson told Kessler he wouldn't do it, but that he should tell Kramer he would "see what he could do."

That Kramer should try to kill a snitch who planned to testify against him was not out of character, Kessler said. Kramer had tried to kill a snitch in his smuggling case: Conrad Ingold. Ironically, he had sent Young to do it. It wasn't successful.

Kramer had also discovered that Skip Walton was cooperating with investigators. Don Ferguson—originally Walton's attorney, now Kramer's—told him.

But after a while, Kramer told Kessler that he was no longer worried about Skip. He knew that Skip said that the Colombians had drawn a list of people they wanted killed, Skip had seen it, and Aronow's name was on it. He also knew that Skip had flunked his polygraph.

[Later, Kessler related that Kramer told him he met with Walton a few times in the attorneys' visiting area at MCC Miami. Ferguson would call out both men so they could talk together.]

JUNE 1991

"THE MAN WHO HAD DON ARONOW KILLED" *MOTOR BOATING & SAILING,* JULY 1991

The author of *Blue Thunder,* as it turned out, had told more than one source that his name was something other than what he put on the book cover. But the writer of "The Man Who Had Don Aronow Killed" didn't even use a byline. The title page described him as a "critical" witness in the case who had given the state inside information, but who for his own protection, wanted to stay anonymous.

The story offered another beginning-to-end coherent narrative of the players and the motive for the murder. However, this time readers and observers on 188th Street were convinced by its wealth of details. But on closer examination, many of those alluring details could be proved false—or just could never be proved at all.

After the story was published, the author's name became public record: Charles Kelvin Smith—at the time a federal prisoner in Danbury, Connecticut. In 1982, he was convicted in Louisiana of transporting a stolen aircraft, sentenced to thirty years, and paroled in 1992.

Charles Smith wrote that he had met with Detective Greg Smith and prosecutor Gary Rosenberg on October 26, 1990—seven months after Young's indictment. But since then, he said, rivalries between state and federal law enforcement agencies had jeopardized the investigation—and for talking, his own safety was now at risk. Smith said his inside connection was that he had worked for Kramer's ring as a bale-chucker; that's how he knew Randy Lanier. Then, when Lanier turned up at his prison, Lanier spoke freely about the murder. Later, when Kramer needed to find a helicopter pilot for his attempted escape, Lanier put Smith directly in touch with Kramer—by a three-way phone connection set up through the office of one of Kramer's Miami attorneys. During those conversations, Kramer directly admitted he was involved in the murder, Smith said.

Smith fingered Bobby Young as Aronow's hitman, adding that Young and Kramer were longtime associates, and this was Young's third hit for Kramer. The driver of Young's getaway car was not Carl Davis but, instead, Robert Vann Wilson, whom Smith described as a small-time street dealer known by several aliases, including "Wimpy."

Kramer and Lanier had succeeded in misdirecting detectives to investigate Carl Davis as the driver, he wrote. When Kramer and Lanier learned from a Miami attorney that Wilson was about to turn state's witness, they induced Tommy Teagle and Skip Walton to volunteer that Young was the shooter, but had Teagle introduce Carl Davis's name as the driver to help discount any information Wilson might offer.

That sounded clever, but readers couldn't have known then that Wayne Shehan and William Pryor had already told police a month before Teagle that Davis was the driver of the Lincoln.

Smith said Kramer's motive for the murder flowed from his obsession to replace Aronow as the King of Thunderboat Row.

Smith said he knew from personal observation in the early '80s that Colombian smugglers did business with both Aronow and Kramer. However, the Colombians trusted Kramer more than Aronow, and in 1982, they financed Kramer's boatbuilding business. Then, in January 1983, Kramer bought Aronow's company.

Although Aronow was well known for getting the better of any business deal, this time, Kramer stole Aronow blind, according to Smith. Buried in fine print was a clause that gave Kramer possession of Aronow's forty-one-foot championship catamaran mold and his helicopter. That generated a feud that eventually led to the hit. Years later, Kramer won the U.S. Open class championship with a boat he made from that mold, he wrote.

After Aronow ridiculed Kramer in public at a boat race, Kramer decided to convince the Colombians that Aronow needed to be whacked.

Knowing Aronow's connections to George Bush, the cartel decided they couldn't kill him. Instead, they suggested Kramer use their money to buy USA Racing from Aronow. That way, the Colombians would be in charge of the Blue Thunder contract, Aronow would see who was in control, and Kramer could perceive himself as the new King of Thunderboat Row.

Aronow agreed to a $3 million sale on the condition that $2.4 million of it be cash under the table, with half the cash paid upon signing.

But this time, Aronow screwed Kramer, to get even, Smith said. Aronow slipped a "standard" ninety-day escape clause into the contract, reading that either party could rescind the sale within that time for any reason. Two weeks later, Aronow invoked it and sent a $600,000 certified check to Kramer's attorney, canceling the deal.

Kramer and Lanier immediately demanded that Aronow hand back the $1.2 million cash. According to Smith, Aronow just laughed.

When the Colombians asked Kramer for their money back, he told them he'd personally repay it if they'd let him kill Aronow. Kramer even suggested the man to do it: Bobby Young, who owed Kramer and the Colombians for losing eighty-two kilos of coke during a shipment.

Young was hired after New Year's Day 1986—not to kill Aronow, but to dun him into paying. Over the next several months, he and Wilson visited Aronow at his office late at night, threatening him and his family. Although Aronow eventually paid $700,000, he refused to pay the balance.

By late 1986, Young and Wilson were harassing Aronow constantly. They called him at home at all hours of the night and hung up, and followed him everywhere, staying in his obvious sight.

Smith said that Kramer convinced the Colombians to fund the hit by faking evidence that led the Colombians to believe Aronow was a confidential police informant. Supposedly, Kramer solicited a Metro-Dade narcotics officer to create a bogus file showing that Aronow had hidden transmitters in boats he had built for the Colombians, so the DEA could trail them.

Next, Kramer planted a transmitter on one of those boats. After showing the bogus file and hidden transmitter to the Colombians, they became convinced that Aronow had to be taken out. They authorized Young to do it for a fee of $100,000 cash, plus forgiveness of his debts to the Colombians and 1,400 to 2,000 kilos of coke to begin a distribution network in Arkansas and Oklahoma.

February 2 was supposed to be the murder date. Young had someone call USA Racing claiming to represent a wealthy man who wanted to buy a boat. Actually, the caller just wanted to know if Aronow was in. He wasn't, but would be next morning.

On February 3, Young and Wilson lay in wait for Aronow on 188th Street, inside their midnight blue Lincoln Town Car. After Aronow passed them and went inside to his office, Wilson—not Young—followed him in. He pretended to inquire about a boat but was actually demanding payment one final time. After Aronow spurned him, Wilson warned that his time was out, and left.

Back at the Lincoln, Wilson got in behind the wheel, Young concealed himself behind the driver's seat, and they watched as Aronow drove his Mercedes to Bobby Saccenti's shop. When he came back to his car, Wilson started the Lincoln and waved at Aronow from the opposite direction. They stopped, driver's window to driver's window. As Wilson ducked, Young sprang up and fired five shots before Aronow knew what was happening.

* * *

It was true that Detective Greg Smith and prosecutor Gary Rosenberg had gone to Danbury, Connecticut, in 1990 to meet with Charles Kelvin Smith. But when Smith tried to check out his story, he got nowhere.

"I did not believe him. Nothing he told me was verifiable, including being at a federal institution with (Randy Lanier)."

Detective Smith and Rosenberg concluded, soon after their meeting, that Charles Smith's account was fictionalized on the back of already-published information on the murder, which included Charles Smith's collection of *Miami Herald* stories. Then, a month after the meeting, *Blue Thunder* was released. Greg Smith read Charles Smith's printed story and compared it to what he had told the lawmen earlier: "History got better," Detective Smith reported.

Therefore, the first problem in the story was that Charles Smith wasn't a critical witness in the case. In fact, he wasn't going to be a witness at all, nor was the state planning to argue his thesis that Kramer had convinced his Colombian bosses to kill Aronow.

Perhaps the biggest verifiable flaw in the story was that Dade County official records showed no business transactions between Kramer and Aronow in 1983. However, the 1983 sale as Smith described it did sound like the aborted 1985 sale of USA Racing, which included Aronow's catamaran molds.

Regarding the forty-one-foot catamaran mold which Smith wrote that Kramer stole from Aronow in 1983, then built a world-championship-winning boat from: "He's wrong," said John Crouse. Kramer's cat was built by Mike Peters in Sarasota, he said. "It had nothing to do with Aronow. Aronow's cat was a monster—a V-bottom cut in half and attached. Kramer's was small, a low-profile cat. It was a different animal whatsoever."

JUNE 14, 1991

ROBERT VANN WILSON

One of Greg Smith's first steps to check out the *Motor Boating & Sailing* story was to interview Robert Vann Wilson. He was at the federal prison camp at Eglin Air Force Base, Florida.

Wilson denied being with Young at the time of the murder. In fact, he said he never even met Young until after the murder. However, at a party at Young's house during Easter 1987, Young did tell him that he knew about the murder and knew how much was paid for it. Beyond that, however, he didn't elaborate.

Skip Walton and Carl Davis were at the same party, he said. Later, after he, Walton, and Young were arrested in the Oklahoma drug case, Walton told him that Young had shot Aronow and that Davis had driven the car. After the murder, Skip cleaned the vehicle, then returned it to the rental agency. Skip also mentioned that the price for the shooting was $250,000.

Wilson also said he met Rodrigo Chegwin-Vergara—whom he knew as "Wimpy"—at Walton's business. Greg Smith then asked Wilson if he had ever been known as "Wimpy," as Charles Smith had written. No, he answered.

[Perhaps that was an example of how Charles Smith had borrowed from previously published material. In a *Motor Boating & Sailing* story printed almost a year before, writer Joanne A. Fishman had referred to an affidavit in the Oklahoma case that said one of Wilson's aliases was "Wimpy." Smith made exactly the same mistake.]

JUNE 18, 1991

MELVYN KESSLER
(CONTINUED INTERVIEW
WITH GREG SMITH)

Kessler said Kramer asked him to travel to Oxford, Wisconsin, where Randy Lanier was imprisoned, to hit him up for money to pay for Young's defense. Kessler made two trips, and each time he swung by the Marion County, Illinois, Jail to visit Kramer as well. When Kessler returned, bags containing $30,000 to $40,000 cash were delivered to his office.

[Later, Kessler said Lanier was unhappy that Kramer wanted him to pay the bulk of Young's legal fees.]

JULY 18, 1991

MELVYN KESSLER
(CONTINUED INTERVIEW)

Kessler said Kramer paid $5,000 to attorney Billy Thomas to defend Young; Thomas told him that himself.

However, Thomas didn't get the money directly from Kramer; an accountant named Max Forman paid him with a check drawn on a corporation called "Robteri," or some similar name. Later, Kessler learned from both Kramer and Thomas that Kramer had paid Thomas a total of about $35,000 to defend Young.

In both verbal messages intended for Kessler to pass on to Kramer, as well as two letters he wrote (one each to Kessler and Kramer), Bobby Young demanded that Kramer pay for his defense—or else he'd talk. Kramer was livid at the threat, as well as upset that Young was sending letters that might implicate him if they were seen.

JULY 21, 1991

In a sidebar story, *Miami Herald* reporter Sydney Freedberg wrote that Mel Kessler had testified for the Feds in the Kramers' criminal forfeiture trial.

She also reported: "Police hope he can tell them something about the daylight assassination of Donald Aronow, the Cigarette boat king."

JULY 22, 1991

Jack Kramer had also decided to testify for the government in the criminal forfeiture trial, in hope of reducing his nineteen-year sentence. In a final order, U.S. district court judge Norman Roettger found that both Kessler's and Jack Kramer's testimonies about the money-laundering scheme were credible. Roettger then denied all the private claims on the Kramers' poker casino that the government had seized.

SEPTEMBER 10, 1991

SAMUEL COOPER

Between April and September, Greg Smith had come to take Samuel Cooper seriously. In later correspondence, Cooper sent Smith friendly letters that Kramer and one of Kramer's attorneys, Terry Forman (son of accountant Max Forman), had sent him.

On this day, Smith and Jerry Crawford traveled to Marion, Illinois, to see Cooper.

Cooper, aged thirty-nine, had been found guilty of robbing a Miami post office twice in 1985 and was sentenced the following year to forty-five years. Like every other prison snitch, he was looking for help to reduce his sentence.

Cooper had written that he knew more than what he had committed to paper. In person, he told Smith and Crawford that he had been Kramer's bodyguard at MCC Miami, and that the name of the guy from Oklahoma who Kramer was so nervous about was Bobby Young.

Cooper said that Kramer and Young were in contact with each other, through a lawyer who was Kramer's codefendant. [That was an apparent reference to Mel Kessler.] Kramer said he had set up legal representation for Young, but at the same time he had also arranged, through an inmate in the Dade County Jail, to kill Young so he couldn't implicate him.

Cooper didn't know the Dade County Jail inmate's

name but thought that he had been in jail a long time. [That also was an apparent corroboration of what Kessler had told Smith; Paul Thompson had been in custody ten years.]

Kramer told him he knew that one or two inmates at MCC Miami had snitched about his involvement in Aronow's murder. Without realizing that he was speaking to one of them, Kramer asked Cooper to either personally kill them or have them killed.

Cooper was also more precise about the dollar amount that Kramer said Aronow owed him: $600,000. The money was related to a boat business, he said. But money wasn't why Kramer said he had Aronow killed. It was disrespect: he had refused to pay the debt; plus, he was going to testify against him. On the other hand, Kramer said, he had been good to Aronow.

There was one change in Cooper's story: the man he knew as Saccenti *wasn't* part of the plan to kill Aronow, but he had unwittingly put his friend in position to be killed.

OCTOBER 1991

Brock Yates, a columnist in *Boating*, reflected on *Blue Thunder* and the *Motor Boating & Sailing* story:

"As for all the nonsense passed along in the stewpot of speculation called *Blue Thunder*, I can tell you this much. Don Aronow never dealt in drugs. He never smuggled them, sold them or dealt directly with people who did."

Yates wrote that Lillian Aronow called him just after *Blue Thunder* came out, claiming that the whole book was a pile of lies and that the author had distorted what she had said to him. But Yates thought there was some truth to the *Motor Boating & Sailing* story—or at least to the part that Ben Kramer had ordered the murder.

"Don openly disliked Kramer. He thought him an amoral goon. I have always believed that Kramer was the culprit, as have many of Aronow's friends. The often-heard theory is that Kramer had him killed out of pathological envy and the knowledge that no one could ever replace the charismatic Aronow as the king of offshore powerboat-racing as long as he lived.''

Yates wrote that Aronow wouldn't hesitate to fleece "poseurs" in the boat business. "But to his everlasting credit, he always picked on people his own size. He was the antithesis of a bully. If Aronow was going to elbow somebody, it would always be a guy who could fight back. That was the fun of it. That was why Aronow loved life. And why he liked to tweak bozos like Ben Kramer. And that, sadly, is what got him killed.''

OCTOBER 17, 1991

MELVYN KESSLER
(CONTINUED INTERVIEW)

After almost a year of reprieve before he had to begin serving his prison term, Mel Kessler had been ordered to surrender on September 20. Greg Smith went to visit him at MCC Miami.

Kessler had a hot lead: he said that Terry Forman had visited Paul Thompson; then, just two weeks ago, Forman visited Kramer. Terry's father, Max Forman, told him this, Kessler said.

OCTOBER 22, 1991

PAUL THOMPSON

Following up quickly, Greg Smith located Paul Thompson at Glades Correctional Institute, a Florida state prison. He and John LeClaire went there to interview him. LeClaire had investigated and charged Thompson for murder in 1980.

First, however, they checked the visitor log and found both Terry and Max Forman's names under the date September 23, 1991. The visit with Thompson had lasted an hour and twenty minutes.

Thompson talked; he said he had met Kramer once in prison, and Kramer occasionally put small amounts of money into his prison commissary account—money Thompson generally used to buy stamps or snacks.

However, since Kramer had gotten to MCC Miami, they had set up several calls to an attorney's office so they could talk on a three-way. Thompson thought Kramer was checking up on Bobby Young through him.

In addition, Kramer sent Thompson written notes through people who had come to visit him at the Dade County Jail. One of those messengers was Mel Kessler. However, Thompson hadn't kept any of the notes.

"In Ben's mind, he wanted Bobby Young killed and probably wanted me to handle it," he said. Thompson was upset about the solicitation.

He said he'd only met Young once, in a holding cell at the Dade County Jail, and he knew that Young had been part of the "St. Louis gun gang."

When Smith asked about the September 23 visit, Thompson said that only Terry Forman was present that day. Nor did they even discuss that Kramer wanted to kill Young. Instead, they talked about Kramer and "the old gangster days."

OCTOBER 24, 1991

LETTER FROM YOUNG TO THOMPSON

Two days after Smith interviewed Thompson, he mailed Smith a letter that Bobby Young had written him, dated September 6, 1991:

[Grammar and spelling left uncorrected]

Hi Paul!

I hope this finds you well as can be expected. I heard your call on I.C.T.V. [Dade County Jail's inmate-run closed-circuit TV station] and would like you to do me a favor. I plead guilty to 2nd [degree] murder (co-terminus) on my last beef, now I talk with Tallahassee from time to time and

*because of my murder conviction I am ineligible
for [early] release (I ask Mel and Billy about this
but they aren't really up on the prison rules) and
again I may have to go to court. Judge Sepe had
the case but the way I see it the judge wanted my
sentence to be exactly like my original which I
would of been eligible for the big gain time but
they naturally say I am not because of the conviction (sad but true).*

*Now can you do a little research on this for me
... I go to trial Nov 12th [a date that was later
postponed], can't hardly wait (looks good).*

Well take care bro

*Respectfully
Bobby*

NOVEMBER 26, 1991

MELVYN KESSLER
(CONTINUED INTERVIEW)

This time, Kessler spoke in detail of what he said
Bobby Young had admitted to him about how he had
killed Don Aronow.

Young said that earlier on that day, he went to
Aronow's office, alone. Afterward, he put on new
clothes, used makeup to change his appearance, and as
well altered the numbers of his Lincoln's license plate.

To shoot Aronow in his car, he had to "lean over and
pull the trigger." Then he called "Big Steve" [Romano,
apparently], who was waiting at a telephone down the
block. Later still, he tossed the gun he had used.

Kessler said Young's biggest concerns were whether
Aronow's secretary could identify him, and that Rick
Fidlin and Paul Silverman were cooperating with police.
He had also gotten extremely angry when he heard that
Carl Davis and Skip Walton had given statements, but
stopped worrying after he spoke directly to both of them.

14

JANUARY 15, 1992

Largely based on information Mel Kessler had supplied, prosecutors executed search warrants on the law and accounting offices of Terry and Max Forman. They seized Billy Thomas's tax records and receipts for legal work performed; FBI 302 investigative reports referring to the case that the state didn't have; and a handwritten note [later identified as written by Max Forman] reading:

1. Bob is back on 5 floor. He is still vacillating. If Paul can, he will
2. Never heard from Randy
3. Keith & Dwayne are O.K.
4. Mike has spoken to case mgr. He will see what he can do

JANUARY 22 AND 24, 1992

TERRY FORMAN
SWORN STATEMENT

Under subpoena, and therefore immunized against criminal prosecution for what he might say, Terry Forman told Gary Rosenberg that he had represented Ben Kramer as an attorney, and that his accounting firm did the books for both Apache Boats entities, Jack Kramer, Mel Kessler, and Billy Thomas.

Further, "Robter Consulting Corporation" was a Forman family account that his parents controlled, he said. From it, Terry received travel expense reimbursements for when he visited Kramer or Lanier in prison. Sometimes his father, Max, went with him on those trips.

Forman said Apache Boats had deposited money into the Robter account to pay those expenses—specifically, Mark McManus [who was running the Kramers' government-seized Apache Powerboats business] had done it. A few years back, Apache [McManus] had agreed to pay Robter a $2,500 royalty for vessels that were sold from Kramer's molds—even though Kramer no longer owned them; they had been seized by the government along with all the rest of his marine assets. From that money, Forman understood that "small items (for Kramer) were, shall we say, to be accommodated."

Forman visited Kramer in prison three times, and Lanier twice. During his second visit to Lanier, in September 1990, Lanier gave him written instructions to contact a European bank officer and have him draft a $100,000 cashiers' check. Forman said he tried to contact the banker—using pay phones, at Lanier's suggestion—but he never did make contact; therefore, the money never got withdrawn.

Forman also said he let Kramer and Lanier use his office phone's three-way calling capacity to talk to each other; however, he didn't eavesdrop on any of the conversations. [Later he said Kramer set up about half a dozen three-way calls, to talk with Lanier and others.]

The FBI 302, he said, was for Kramer to see. Mel Kessler had given it to his father.

Forman said his father also told him that he had hired Billy Thomas in 1991 to do legal work, and paid him $5,000 cash. "My father said it was from Ben, that he (Max) was paying certain expenses out in his (Ben's) behalf."

"Including the expenses involved with the representation of Mr. Young by Mr. Thomas?'' asked prosecutor Abe Laeser.

"He didn't say so, but that was my impression.''

"As close as you can remember, what did he say to you was the purpose of the $5,000 that was being transmitted from Mr. Kramer through your father to Mr. Thomas?''

"That Ben had asked him to do so.''

Laeser also asked whether Kramer, during visits, had ever asked him to pull out other inmates at the same time so Kramer could talk to them. Forman said yes, he had done that for Sam Cooper, Stanley Diamond, and Anthony Accetturo.

[Anthony Accetturo was reputed to be the top *capo* in the south Florida mob, a member of the New Jersey Lucchese family. He was charged with, but never convicted of, being the mastermind of a scheme to fix races at Miami's Calder Race Course between 1975 and 1977, by slipping drugs into the water of the favored horses.

The Lucchese family was also alleged to have imported tons of marijuana into south Florida between 1979 and 1983, under Accetturo's supervision, and then branched out into cocaine.

The Miami Herald reported a prosecutor saying in 1990, when both Accetturo and Kramer were at MCC Miami, that when Accetturo's name is announced on the prison loudspeaker, "the other prisoners get up and salute."]

FEBRUARY 7, 1992

MAX FORMAN
SWORN STATEMENT

Max Forman said he first met Ben Kramer in 1984, when Mel Kessler introduced them. Kessler had been his accounting client since 1960.

Max did Apache's taxes from 1984 to 1987, when Kramer was arrested. Even after, when the government made Mark McManus manager of Apache Powerboats, Forman remained the company accountant. In addition, Kramer had introduced him to Bobby Saccenti in 1985, and he had become Saccenti's company accountant as well.

Forman confirmed the royalty arrangement. After Kramer was arrested, Max set it up through the Robter account between himself and McManus—and Saccenti, too. When either Apache would deposit royalties, Kramer would call Max and tell him what to do with it.

The royalties normally were paid by check, but once, in 1989, Jack Kramer gave him the money in cash—either $25,000 or $30,000. From that, Forman gave $5,000 to Billy Thomas, plus amounts he couldn't recall to Mel Kessler and Ben's wife, Terri, in New York.

In addition to that cash payment, he paid Billy Thomas (through Robter) $6,500 in two checks in 1991, for legal work. Five thousand came from royalties from McManus's company; $1,500 came from Saccenti's company. Forman insisted that Thomas submit logged bills for services rendered to Robter to cover those amounts.

"The bills that William Thomas writes out, is that actual work he had done for Robter, or are those just bills so no one would know that the $5,000 and $1,500 amounts came from Ben Kramer?" asked Abe Lacser.

"To avoid detection," Forman answered.

"Those bills are not for work that he did for you?"

"No."

"Those bills are so no one would know that Ben Kramer had paid him $6,500 through Robter?"

"Correct."

Forman said he knew that Billy Thomas was representing Bobby Young at the time he wrote the checks, but Kramer hadn't specified that the money was to pay Thomas for representing Young.

"He didn't mention anything. He just said, 'Give it to Billy.' "

Forman volunteered that had Kramer kept USA Racing, he would have done the tax work for it. "I heard conversations about the passing of some cash. The exact amount I never knew, never heard, but I did—I heard the words 'six figures.' "

"Now when you say to me 'passing of cash,' I imagine that means a certain amount of money on paper for the purchase, and then under-the-table cash is given—"

"Correct."

"—that would not be in the purchase agreement?"

"Correct."

"Did you ever get any information concerning the resale of the business back to Donald Aronow about whether or not this cash was part of the deal on the resale?"

"No. I don't have any information to that extent."

FEBRUARY 10, 1992

In federal prisons, all phone calls prisoners make are routinely—and legally—taped. At Leavenworth Prison, in Kansas, where Ben Kramer was, a multitrack tape recorder in the basement runs continually during hours that prisoners are allowed access to the phones.

On this day, Smith and Crawford executed an order allowing them to cull Ben Kramer's telephone conversations from the master tape. Because Kramer was such a prolific user of the phone, they eventually filled forty-seven ninety-minute tapes and took two weeks to complete the job. And although on some days there were blizzard conditions outside, it was hellishly saunalike in the steam-heated prison basement because the air conditioning had broken. The detectives stripped to their skivvies and reviewed the tapes, sometimes for twenty hours at a stretch.

Kramer had called his attorneys on some of the tapes, and private attorney-client correspondences are privileged. However, since Kramer had made these calls on the prison's public phones, which were clearly marked as being surveilled, it was later argued successfully that Kramer had knowingly allowed a third person to overhear, so these conversations *weren't* privileged. Prisons also have special phones specifically for calls to attorneys that aren't tapped—phones which, annoyingly, need to be reserved in advance.

Among the many calls to Don Ferguson, he advised Kramer not to pay Young's attorney fees. "It's evidence—they'll nail you," he said.

FEBRUARY 12, 1992

CLEVELAND MILLER

Another federal prisoner at Leavenworth, named Cleveland Miller, had contacted an FBI agent on his case with information: Ben Kramer had told him about murdering someone whose name Miller pronounced "Arno." Miller had never heard of the man and had asked the agent if the murder had ever happened.

The agent was George Chmiel, of the FBI's Annapolis, Maryland, office. He found Greg Smith, so while Smith was at Leavenworth, Chmiel met him there to interview the sixty-year-old Miller.

Like every other Leavenworth prisoner, Miller was of pretty dubious background. He had been arrested in February 1988 in Baltimore for murdering a federal witness the year before. Instead of going to trial, he pled to twenty years and testified against two codefendants, both of whom were convicted. That sentence was later reduced by two years after he saved the life of another inmate who had hung himself in a shower.

Kramer was already at Leavenworth when Miller arrived in September 1990. After a week, he was assigned a bed in Kramer's unit.

Miller said that one day, Kramer saw an auto-racing magazine in Miller's room and asked if he knew Randy Lanier, who Kramer said was a racer and a friend of his.

From there, they started chatting. Miller told him he was in prison for killing a federal witness; Kramer seemed impressed, then added that he had also killed a federal witness, but he hadn't been charged, nor would he ever be convicted for it. The witness was a boatbuilder named "Don Arno," and he had had someone named Robert Young do the murder.

Kramer said that the hit was supposed to have occurred on February 1 or 2, 1987, but it actually happened February 3.

That was funny, Miller said; he had used the name Robert Young as a street alias, and his birthday was February 2. Suddenly, Kramer raised his defenses and accused him of being a snitch. He didn't calm down until Miller showed him legal papers proving what he had said.

Then, once Kramer saw that Miller was telling him the truth, he opened up with further confidences:

"Arno" had been working against him by building "Cigarette boats" for the government, which they used to catch Kramer's drug boats. (Miller told Smith he didn't know what a Cigarette boat was.)

At some point, Kramer told "Arno" that he should compensate him for his losses. "Arno" laughed at him. Then Kramer asked "Arno" to work with him in his drug business. "Arno" flat-out refused.

Kramer also said that "Arno" was friends with George Bush, which Miller didn't believe. When Kramer asked "Arno" to introduce him to Bush, "Arno" laughed at him again. All that laughing "pissed off" Kramer, he said.

Kramer said "Arno" was a snitch. He knew because government cars had been seen parked at his business; in addition, Metro-Dade police officers had verified it to him.

Kramer admitted that he and Robert Young had personally planned the murder. Kramer was to pay Young $25,000 for it, with a $25,000 bonus if "Arno" was killed instantly. "Arno" had a phone in his car, and Kramer didn't want him to be able to speak after the shooting.

Further, Young's deal was that he'd get a kilo of cocaine for every bullet that struck "Arno."

Young had a big car and waited for "Arno," in his white Mercedes, to approach him. When he did, Young got his attention by doing something like flashing his lights. Young then pulled up next to him, window to window, and shot "Arno" with a large-caliber gun.

For his own alibi, Kramer made sure he was inside his business at the time, where people would see him.

Later that night, Kramer met with Young at a bar across a causeway. Young said he shot "Arno" five times. Kramer said he heard he was shot three times, so they agreed on four. Kramer said he paid Young the $25,000 bonus plus four kilos of cocaine.

Kramer said there was someone else involved in the murder, but he didn't take part in the shooting; Kramer didn't name him. Concerned about getting charged with the murder, he contacted Kramer; Kramer told him to cooperate, but only against Young. Young, he said, was "stand-up" and would not flip.

March 5, 1992

TERRY FORMAN
SWORN STATEMENT

After a judge ruled that Terry Forman had no attorney-client privilege during his conversations with Ben Kramer, Forman added to his earlier sworn statements. Now he said that Kramer told him more than once, in person, that the royalty money paid to Robter was to go to Billy Thomas to represent Bobby Young.

April 8, 1992

STANLEY DIAMOND

Since Terry Forman had corroborated Stanley Diamond's May 1990 story that Forman had brought him out to MCC Miami's visiting area at the same time as Kramer so the two of them could talk alone, Greg Smith decided to drop in on Diamond—now back at MCC again—to see if he'd say anything.

Diamond repeated most of what he had told Detective

Saladrigas two years before: Kramer was petrified that Young would flip; he could send him to the electric chair. Back then, he had solicited Diamond to kill Young because he thought Diamond had the Mob connections to do it.

Now Diamond added that Kramer had admitted to him that he had hired Young to kill Aronow because Aronow had ripped him off in a business deal.

Diamond said he had just talked with Jack Kramer the night before. Jack was also fearful that Ben would be charged with the murder. Then he added that Ben was still trying to kill Young; now he was using a man named Paul, who used to be part of Ricky Cravero's Miami drug gang. Kessler had been helping Ben with this, Jack told him.

MARCH 31, 1992

KATHLEEN KUNZIG YOUNG
SWORN STATEMENT

Back under subpoena with immunity, Kathy Young still wouldn't admit much. She said she and Bobby Young had gotten divorced four months before, and she no longer wanted anything to do with him.

Gary Rosenberg asked her if she had been in contact recently with others in the investigation; she denied ever speaking to Skip Walton, having much to say to Carl Davis, or having anything to do with trying to get money to attorney Billy Thomas to pay his fee for representing Bobby Young.

And except to inform Young two weeks before that she had been subpoenaed, she hadn't talked to him for a full year, she said.

"I don't want to speak to Bobby anymore. This whole thing is upsetting me. It really irritates me. I'm being asked about something I had nothing to do with. I just want it done and over with. It just really irritates me."

Kathy said she had known Kramer since she was sixteen, hanging out with him and others on Hollywood

Beach. In the past year, she had talked with him twice, by phone.

"Did you and Robert Young ever see him during the time period when you were—"

"As far as I know, Bob doesn't know Ben Kramer," Kathy cut Rosenberg off.

"Did Ben Kramer know William Thomas?"

"Yes, I believe so."

"Where did you get that information that you believe so?"

"Because he knew Mel [Kessler]. Mel was with Ben on a criminal case."

"Well, did you ever have a conversation with Ben in which he told you—"

"Not that I remember."

"In which he told you—"

"Let him finish the question," Kathy's counsel, Jack Blumenfeld, told her.

"Did you ever have a conversation with Ben in which he asked you to get in contact with William Thomas?"

"Not that I remember."

"During the period of time when Robert Young was arrested in a first-degree murder after the Oklahoma case, did you have conversations with Ben Kramer concerning Robert Young?"

"Not that I remember."

"Have you ever discussed Robert Young's involvement in the death of Donald Aronow with Ben Kramer?"

"No."

April 13, 1992

BOBBY SACCENTI
SWORN STATEMENT

Saccenti admitted that he had an ongoing royalty agreement with Mark McManus at Apache Powerboats: McManus let him build thirty-six-foot boats from one of his molds, and Saccenti would pay him $2,000 per boat sold and delivered. He sold three and gave the money in checks to Max Forman—possibly written to Robter, he said.

"That is the way they wanted it. They made the agreement up that the royalties would go to the accountant."

"Did Ben Kramer figure into the agreement at all?" Greg Smith asked.

"I haven't got the faintest idea, sir."

MARK MCMANUS
SWORN STATEMENT

McManus volunteered to talk about his relationship with Aronow.

McManus had been working at USA Racing when Aronow sold the company to the Kramers. That's when Aronow told him he had negotiated a two-year contract for him to stay on at USA Racing as well as work for the Kramers' Apache shop in Hollywood. He did so, for additional compensation, starting work at USA Racing at 6 A.M. every day, then leaving for Apache at eleven o'clock and working there until eight. Even after the USA Racing deal fell through, McManus's arrangement continued.

Then, three months before Aronow was killed, "I was told to leave USA Racing by Mr. Aronow, and I would like to have the opportunity to explain that to you."

"Go ahead," said Rosenberg.

"Mr. Aronow came in one day, and he told me that I wouldn't believe it, but that he's got another sale for the company. It was a Mideastern client. I did not ask him who it was. He did not tell me. 'Now we have a problem. You are under a two-year contract with Mr. Kramer.'

"So he says, 'You go run the facility for Mr. Kramer exclusively. What I have to do is the following: I have to put together a new company of new people to sell as a package deal to my new client. I'm going to get out of the boatbuilding business for six or eight months, then I'm taking over Apache, Apache Marine, and we will all be together building deep-vees. We have to get immediately going on a twenty-four-foot catamaran, forty-foot deep-vee, and a whole package of boats to present to these people.' "

McManus said Aronow had already bought a vacant shop next to USA Racing, and told him to hire a boat designer and a salesman. Said Aronow, "'But you can't be part of the operation because you [would] be on contract with the new owner for five years. You can't have two contracts. You go work for Mr. Kramer. Whatever day you want to leave is fine. I'm telling the employees that we had a dispute.'

"'That is what we did."

McManus said all the boats he built for the Kramers carried Don Aronow's name. [When Cigarette Racing Team sued Aronow in July 1986, they complained that Aronow had improperly loaned his name and assistance to Apache despite their five-year non-compete agreement starting March 1982. An Apache magazine ad quoted in the suit bragged that their boat was "a race breed descendant from the legendary stables of Don Aronow, the industry's trendsetter for the past twenty years."]

"Were you aware of any problems prior to Mr. Aronow's death between Mr. Aronow and Ben Kramer or Jack Kramer?" Rosenberg asked.

"No, sir. I'm not aware of any problems."

"Did you ever discuss with Ben Kramer the death of Don Aronow?"

"Yes, the day after it happened. He asked me, 'Did I know who Don had a problem with? Why would someone kill him?' "

"Did you tell him you knew of any?"

"I told him I didn't know he had a problem with anyone and I was very scared for myself, because if someone was unhappy with a boat or something I built, it was me that built the boat, not Don. So I didn't know if I was going to have a problem."

Rosenberg probed into the royalty deal, which was the reason he had subpoenaed McManus. McManus confirmed the arrangement. Although it was the government, not the Kramers, who now controlled Apache, he said that Jack Kramer had initiated it, telling him to send

$3,000 royalties per boat sold to Ben's wife.

McManus added that he had written two or three Apache company checks to Robter after boats were sold, but said that that money was to pay Max Forman's accounting fees, not royalties.

MAY 21, 1992

BILLY THOMAS
SWORN STATEMENT

Thomas reluctantly admitted that Mel Kessler had given him $5,000 cash in an envelope to represent Bobby Young. Later, he said, the Formans gave him another $5,000 in cash, plus two Robter checks equalling $6,500. He knew that the money had come indirectly from the Kramers, through Apache royalties. Therefore, his bills that appeared to be for legal work done for Robter Consulting Corporation were not quite accurate, he conceded.

He also contradicted Kathy Young when she had said she hadn't tried to get additional money to Thomas to pay for Bobby Young's defense.

However, Thomas denied that his job was to keep Kramer from getting indicted, nor had he intentionally acted as a "pipeline" to keep Kramer informed about Young.

"Did you ever discuss with any person—by that, I mean Kessler, Kramer, Forman—why it was that Mr. Kramer or a member of the Kramer family was paying for the representation of Robert Young?" asked Abe Laeser.

"If I discussed it with anyone, it would have been Mel Kessler. The only discussions—for some reason they wanted to assist in his defense, and that's fine."

SEPTEMBER 3, 1992

"Blue Thunder, the sleek smuggler-chasing speedboat, is a white elephant," reported the *Sun-Sentinel.* United

States Customs planned to sell nine of their thirteen at a public auction later in the month.

A Customs spokesman said the boats were sturdy and maneuverable—not the fastest, but fast enough.

However, smuggling had since changed. Smugglers no longer simply tried to outrun patrol boats; instead, they now hid their drugs in secret compartments of less-obvious pleasure craft, or they loaded cocaine as cargo in containers aboard freighters.

" 'If the Customs Service is now selling these boats, at least it's a recognition that they're not going to waste money any longer in that program,' said Eric Sterling, president of the Criminal Justice Policy Foundation.

" 'But maritime drug interdiction is always a dumb strategy from a cost-effective or drug-interdiction point of view. Anybody could do an economic analysis and know it wasn't going to hurt traffickers because cheap drugs can always replace whatever drugs are seized off the coast of Florida,' he said."

15

MAX FORMAN

Early on a Sunday morning, the day before the case would return to a grand jury, Gary Rosenberg and Abe Laeser had Max Forman come to the state attorney's office to review his testimony.

"Did you ever discuss with Mr. Kramer why he was being so kind as to pay money for Mr. Young's defense?" Laeser asked.

"He once indicated to me that Young and he had done some business together in the narcotics field. I don't know the nuances of the conversation. The fact of the matter is that they have done business together. Kessler had represented both of them at one point or another. There was a common thread, several common threads there.

"And I do know that at one point, Kramer was looking for monies for himself and was reaching out to people he did business with in the past. So, the fact that Young was asking Kramer for help in his defense seemed to tie into the overall procedure of how these things go on."

Laeser asked Forman to discuss the seized note in his handwriting with a reference to Paul Thompson on it.

"One morning shortly before I was scheduled to see Mr. Kramer—I forgot what institution he was at. At the time, Kessler met me for breakfast and dictated the in-

272

formation on that note and said, 'Show it to Ben and then destroy it.'

"I showed it to Mr. Kramer. Gave it back to me. I put it in his file that I have with me and I forgot to take it out."

MARCH 1, 1993

BILLY THOMAS

The prosecutors played Thomas a tape of a Leavenworth-recorded call on which Thomas told Kramer that Bobby Young's problem was that he was always shooting off his mouth, which could get him into further trouble.

Thomas admitted that Kramer may have asked him whether Young was cooperating with police or not.

"How about language such as him being in trouble if Robert Young tells what he knows?" Laeser coaxed.

"He may very well have. But again, I just can't remember. He may very well have done so."

Late that afternoon, the Dade County grand jury returned a sealed first-degree murder indictment against Ben Kramer and a similar superseding indictment against Bobby Young. Both would face the death penalty if convicted.

MARCH 3, 1993

SKIP WALTON

Greg Smith and Jerry Crawford traveled to the Tallahassee federal prison to see Skip Walton, but once they were there, Walton told them to get lost, then demanded a guard take him away.

MARCH 24, 1993

Ben Kramer was transferred from Leavenworth federal prison to Dade County custody. That afternoon, Metro-Dade police announced the unsealing of the grand jury indictments.

MARCH 25, 1993

The Miami Herald: "A gangland-style ambush that has stumped police and captivated Miami for six years is solved, police say: Powerboat legend Don Aronow was murdered by two men, one a drug smuggler who might have been angered by a business deal gone bad."

The story didn't even make the front page.

MARCH 26, 1993

The *Sun-Sentinel* interviewed John Crouse:

"A party was made when Aronow walked into the room, usually with a beautiful woman on his arm. In business, though, he was ruthless."

Crouse said Aronow and Kramer had turned into bitter enemies after the USA Racing deal soured because Aronow wouldn't return all of Kramer's money.

"I can't tell you why. He was just that kind of guy."

APRIL 1, 1993

Kramer was arraigned amidst the heaviest security in the history of the Dade County courthouse—considering his past escape attempt from federal prison.

First, the courtroom was cleared for a bomb squad to inspect it. Then, to get inside, everyone—visitors, attorneys, even bailiffs—had to go through a metal detector and have their bags searched.

Nearby, in the judge's chambers, police kept gas

masks and "stun grenades" ready. On the street below, dozens of local officers and federal agents surrounded the courthouse building.

At the hearing itself, Kramer pled not guilty.

May 27, 1993

Kramer was in a Dade County Jail elevator, on his way back from court, when Captain Denise Bendross entered. She wrote in an incident report:

"Kramer said something to the effect that, you mean, you're going to get in the elevator with a dangerous inmate like me? As the elevator continued to travel to the sixth floor, Kramer said something to the effect that things are going to be different when the rabbit has the gun . . . Miami is a small town, and there are plenty of rabbits out there."

August 18, 1993

MIKE BRITTON
DEPOSITION

In Florida state criminal cases, defense attorneys have the right to interview all the state's witnesses on the record in advance of trial. Representing Kramer as his lead attorney was Don Ferguson of Boca Raton, a former federal prosecutor whose voice had been heard on the Leavenworth phone call tapes. He had previously represented two of the state's witnesses against Kramer: Skip Walton, in his 1989 murder on the high seas case, and Tommy Teagle, when he had violated his federal probation in November 1989.

The first to be deposed was Mike Britton, who had contradicted himself in statements to two different officers on the day of the murder. He told the first officer that he had seen the shooting, but he told the second that he had only heard it. At the deposition, he maintained that he had heard it.

But now, Britton contradicted himself even more seriously. Back on the day of the murder, he had said that Aronow "asked me if I could help him find some molding and some trim work for his house and for one of his boats. After we finished the discussion, I said that I had to leave and so did he."

Britton had said that he then walked to his pickup truck and began to drive away. At that point, "I happened to look in my rearview mirror and noticed Mr. Aronow coming out of the building." After passing the Lincoln and making eye contact with its driver, he turned into the driveway at Fort Apache Marina and heard a gunshot.

However, to Don Ferguson, Britton gave a very different story. He said Aronow "asked me to go with him to his home in reference to look at some other work for him at his residence. He wanted some brass work done on his staircase."

Britton said he agreed to go with him. "From there he said, 'If you're ready, we'll go to the house.' And I said, 'That's fine.' He asked me—if I recall correctly, he asked me if I wanted to drive myself or I wanted to ride with him. I said I would drive myself and then leave from there to my next appointment. So I said, 'If you want, I'll just follow you to the house.' He said okay."

Ferguson asked Britton if he talked to Aronow on the way to their vehicles.

"Yes, I did. I spoke to him and said I needed to drop off some paperwork or some parts—I don't recall at the time what it was—at Fort Apache before we proceeded on to his house."

Britton then described how Aronow followed him on the way to Fort Apache Marina, just a few hundred yards west. He pulled into Fort Apache's driveway and then heard the gunshots.

Ferguson also asked if he had seen Kramer and Aronow together prior to that day. Britton, who subcontracted work to both USA Racing and Apache, said he in fact had, on a number of occasions including about a week before the murder. The three would then talk together.

"Did Ben Kramer and Don Aronow appear in your presence to be friends?" Ferguson asked.

"Yes."

"Did it appear to you that Aronow expressed an interest in the boats that Ben Kramer was building?"

"Yes. Don was interested in the boats that Ben was producing mainly because Don at that time could not produce a V-bottom. He was under restrictions, I think, from Cigarette. So he would, I would imagine, often stop and see what new things they were coming up with in reference to the racing end and the pleasure boats."

AUGUST 27, 1993

ILENE (TAYLOR) CARY
DEPOSITION

Despite Patty Lezaca's June 1988 sworn statement to the contrary, Ilene Cary insisted she had never had an affair with Don Aronow. She admitted going to see him at USA Racing three times a week for about a year and a half, but they had only talked about horses and race handicapping, she said.

"Are you telling me that your relationship with Mr. Aronow was platonic in nature only?" Ferguson asked.

"We were friends," Cary answered.

"Did you ever tell Patty Lezaca that you loved Don Aronow very much and that you just didn't know what to do about him?"

"No."

"You read the part of the affidavit wherein Patty Lezaca swears that when you found out that Aronow's wife was pregnant, you became hysterical? Do you disagree with that statement?"

"I disagree."

Ilene said Aronow introduced her to Ben Kramer once, at the USA Racing office, about a year before the murder.

"They were just talking, and there was no friction in the room," she said.

"Did Don Aronow ever make statements to you about Ben Kramer out of Ben Kramer's presence?"

"Yes, once."

"What would he have said?"

"He was a punky kid."

Ferguson asked about the police report of her interview which read that she stated Aronow "had again been associating himself with Ben Kramer as recently as Monday, February 2, 1987"—the day before the murder.

"I don't remember this."

"Do you remember Aronow telling you that he was to have a meeting with Ben Kramer?"

"No."

"Within a month of Aronow's death, did he ever make a statement to you that he was concerned about something, like his personal safety or anything?"

"No."

SEPTEMBER 2, 1993

MURRAY WEIL
DEPOSITION

Weil was Don Aronow's attorney, and he had handled the closure of his estate. Pursuant to Ferguson's subpoena, he brought with him the records of the sale of USA Racing to the Kramers.

The agreements were elaborate and looked like lawyers had drawn them up. The sale price for USA Racing, as agreed to and signed by Aronow and Jack Kramer on August 29, 1985, was $700,000. $100,000 of that was paid on signing, leaving a mortgage of $600,000 at 18 percent interest. Seven thousand dollars was to be due each month; then, after five years, the remainder of the mortgage was due.

In addition, Jack Kramer signed a note promising to repay Aronow personally for $473,600 he said he put into the business earlier that year. That money had to be paid in full in one year.

Papers dated three months later showed the cancellation of the sale, as well as the Kramers' mortgage indebtedness of $600,000. Weil said Aronow kept the down payment of $100,000.

"Now, at the time of the sale of USA Racing Team, Inc., did Jack Kramer or any other individual on behalf of Super Chief South [the Kramers' company], or on behalf of anyone, tender in your presence cash to Mr. Aronow which is not reflected on that closing statement?" Ferguson asked.

"No."

"Commonly referred to as cash under the table?"

"I know what you mean."

"Did it ever come to your attention that Mr. Aronow received cash under the table for the sale of USA Racing Team, Inc.?"

"He never told me."

"Would you have participated in this particular closing had you had knowledge there was cash under the table paid to Mr. Aronow?"

"I would not have, because it creates problems."

"Such as?"

"With the bar, among other things, with Internal Revenue."

"Do you know why the $100,000 was not being returned?"

"Yes. Because Mr. Aronow did not want, when he sold the business, to take it back."

"Do you remember him telling you that?"

"Yes. I remember what he was doing at the time, and he wanted to quit."

[There were no papers recrediting the Kramers for $473,600—that is, if they ever paid it to Aronow in the first place—or canceling their promissory note indebtedness for that amount, nor did Ferguson even ask about it.

But at the Kramers' money-laundering trial in 1990, their Los Angeles banker testified for the prosecution about a document of his that had accounted for monies disbursed to Jack Kramer. On it was a reference to "Team USA," which he said he thought referred to Aronow.

It read "Land, $600,000" and "$476,000." There were also two checks to Fort Lauderdale attorney Emerson Allsworth, totalling $105,000. Allsworth, since disbarred, had negotiated the USA deal on behalf of the Kramers.

Was the banker's $476,000 the cash under the-table that Mike Aronow was referring to? Probably not. Mike said the money was paid in marijuana-scented cash. The banker's role was to help clean dirty cash, so his money would have been in a check. Besides, at trial, the banker said he never sent Jack the $476,000.]

OCTOBER 4, 1993

DAVID McCALLISTER
DEPOSITION

McCallister's interview with police had been one of the first breaks in the case against Bobby Young. He had been indicted as part of Young's coke ring, but by pleading guilty and cooperating against his codefendants, he got only an eighteen-month sentence. Therefore, he was free by the time he was subpoenaed for deposition.

McCallister said he had been a pilot flying charters, then freight, for Purolator Courier, before he contracted himself out to fly marijuana from Jamaica to the United States. Skip Walton had hired him to lease an airplane and keep it airworthy so it could haul cocaine, but he had already dropped out of the ring before the others were arrested.

Young's Fort Lauderdale counsel, Dohn Williams, asked McCallister to name the others indicted in Oklahoma with him. McCallister said because his role was peripheral, he didn't know them all; he knew Walton, Young, Vann Wilson, Wimpy, and a guy named Cowboy.

[Williams didn't follow up on Cowboy, but that name had arisen before; two days after the murder, February 5, someone had anonymously called the FBI's office in Lansdale, Pennsylvania, saying that a man named Cowboy had admitted killing Aronow. According to the caller, Cowboy's real name was Carol Thompson, and he sold weapons and drugs and lived north of Philadelphia. A man with that name had an FBI record, but there was a deluge of leads at that time, and this one never went anywhere. A later check of the federal Bureau of Prisons showed no incarceration history for a person of that name.]

McCallister described Young and Walton as the leaders of the ring. Although he met Walton first, he came to know Young better, staying at his house for a few weeks in late 1986.

"I was riding with Bobby in [his] Corvette one day, and Bobby told me that he had been offered $30,000 to do a hit on a man, a big man down here in Miami, quote unquote."

"And where were you going or where were you coming from that all of a sudden this conversation comes up?" Williams asked.

"Bobby was desperate for money," McCallister said. "He had some problems with a cocaine deal, and he needed money real bad because he had a bunch of people in Colombia that were hot on him."

"Where were you going or coming from?"

"We were coming from his house, and we were going to look at a sailboat. It was my understanding Bobby had just brought in a load of cocaine on it and was going to do some business with the people and look into repairs that were being done."

Williams asked about the anonymous tip McCallister had given to Metro-Dade Police in April 1987—that Robert Scott might have been involved in the murder. McCallister explained he had just read about the killing in a two-month-old *Time* magazine at his dad's house in Texas.

"Were you concerned you might be implicated in the murder?"

"No. I was kind of—outraged is the wrong word to use, but it was just—I was disgusted by it."

"Well, you're a thousand miles away at that point in time."

"That's right. I smuggled pot, and then it just, like, clicked, and I thought, 'That is murder,' and Bobby had told me he had killed fourteen people prior, so I thought, 'This man needs to be off the streets.' "

Williams asked if McCallister had used cocaine during that time.

"On occasion."

"During the period of time that you knew Bobby Young, do you know, did he smoke cocaine?"

"Yes. Probably every day for a couple of days and then not for several days, something like that."

OCTOBER 4–5, 1993

SAMUEL COOPER
DEPOSITION

Don Ferguson skirted Cooper's information against Kramer, except for one contradiction he was able to bring out. Cooper told Ferguson that Kramer had paid Bobby Young $50,000 to kill Aronow. He had told Greg Smith that the price was $250,000.

Instead, the two-day deposition concerned Cooper's own criminal record; Cooper admitted that he had spent about eighteen of his previous twenty years in prison. The defense began by asking Cooper to describe his August 1985 armed robbery of a post office in Allapattah, a black neighborhood in the city of Miami.

"Basically, I was there around ten seconds. I went there, threw down on the clerk, and had a guy that jumped across the counter. We got maybe $10,000, $15,000, and was gone." A month later, he said, he and his partner hit the same post office again and got another $10,000.

Cooper said he was first arrested at age eighteen, in 1970, for drug possession; then in 1971, for possession of a firearm. That same year, he pled guilty to aggravated assault, his first felony conviction.

In 1972, he began boxing professionally, as a local light-heavyweight, managed by Miami Beach promoter Chris Dundee. His record was 11–0. But the same year, he and a gang broke into a warehouse to steal color television sets, and he was the only one caught. Out on bond, he robbed a lunch wagon of a few hundred dollars and was apprehended immediately. He got ten years for the robbery, plus eighteen months for violating probation.

In 1982, he was arrested for having a shotgun in his car, then, "They got me for all the unsolved shotgun robberies once I was at the county jail."

"They charged you with all the unsolved shotgun robberies?" Ferguson asked.

"That fit someone tall, my size, my height, my complexion."

At his first trial, Cooper said he was found guilty of the shotgun possession charge and of using a firearm in the commission of a robbery, but, illogically, not guilty of armed robbery. He was sentenced to ten years. However, he was acquitted in his next three armed-robbery trials.

Out again in 1984 thanks to Florida prisons' early release policy [since changed], Cooper committed his post office robberies the next year, worth forty-five years. That's when he began writing to prosecutors and law enforcement agents, offering to trade information for help in reducing his sentence.

He wrote first to the FBI and U.S. Postal Service investigators. He admitted to two crimes he said he committed but was never charged with: robbing a bank in Hialeah of $100,000 and robbing another post office in Dade County of $12,000. Later he wrote to the U.S. attorney with information about the Yahweh murder case, and to the state attorney about other murders that Metro-Dade Police was investigating.

"So we are clear, your focus in this whole thing was

to get your sentence reduced?'' Ferguson asked.

"And straighten out my life," Cooper answered.

"The first step toward getting your life together is getting your sentences reduced?''

"Well, I do not look at it like that. The way I look at it is showing the people or showing the system I am willing to be on their side. Always been off their side, always been against them. There's no rehabilitation in prison. Prison is all about surviving. I can stay in this game. I can try to do forty-five years. I can hurt someone or get hurt. But I want to take the first step. I know there is no looking back. I know I cannot turn around, that I cannot be my old self anymore. I cannot go back to no prison, no more prison. I am taking the first step, and getting the sentence reduction is another."

OCTOBER 14 AND DECEMBER 20, 1993

CLEVELAND MILLER
DEPOSITION

As Don Ferguson had begun Cooper's deposition by asking about his past criminal record, he did the same with Cleveland Miller.

Miller, now aged sixty-one, said he dropped out of school in 1948 and joined the Army at sixteen, only to be discharged ten months later for fraudulently misstating his age. When he returned to civilian life, he went to Baltimore, stole a car, and promptly got arrested.

Given probation for a first offense, Miller violated it by leaving Baltimore. On his way to Missouri, he burglarized a restaurant in Covington, Virginia, on August 1, 1950.

"I walked in a restaurant and grabbed some money out of the cash register and ran," he said.

"Did you have a gun?" Ferguson asked.

"No, sir."

"How were you armed?"

"I wasn't armed."

Miller went to trial and lost, and was sentenced to five

years, but he didn't get out of the Virginia penitentiary for seventeen years, until 1967.

"Could you explain to me how it is that you did seventeen years on a five-year sentence?"

"I escaped from the road camps four times and collected more time each time I escaped," he said. One time he was arrested after breaking into a dry cleaning store to steal some clothes; another time, in 1953, he stole a car in San Angelo, Texas, then used a gun to rob a gas station in San Diego. He was arrested on federal charges of crossing state lines in a stolen vehicle, served four years on that, then was returned to Virginia to finish his term there.

In the middle '70s, Miller robbed banks in North Carolina and Pennsylvania, disguising himself by putting women's nylon hose over his head. In one robbery, he got $28,000, which he used to purchase a bar in Baltimore. There, FBI agents came to speak to him.

"Did you lie to those agents at all during that interview?" Ferguson asked.

"I'm not much given for lying, I don't think so. Because I will tell you, I won't answer you or I'll tell you the truth. I don't think I lied to them."

"What are you saying: you're not given much for lying, you don't like to lie, or you are not a good liar?"

"I was raised not to lie. I wasn't raised to do anything else wrong, you know, bank robberies, et cetera, but I was raised that if we ain't got a word, we ain't got nothing."

"You've always been of the opinion that a man has to have a word or he has nothing?"

"I have a reputation for telling the truth."

"Inside the prison, or—"

"It's with my friends, in and outside the prison."

"Where would you have had the opportunity to tell the truth if you've been in prison for almost all of your adult life?"

"Well, you're respected even in the penitentiary if you tell the truth."

"And you've always told the truth?"

"Yes, sir. That's the only thing I've got to be proud of."

Miller was arrested in 1976 for both bank robberies, pled guilty, and wasn't released until 1984. Then, in June 1987, he got involved in the killing of a federal witness in Baltimore. Miller said he was paid $500 to drive his car to a place where two other men wanted someone named Leon Vitkauskas beaten up. But the scheme turned into murder, and as it was, Miller pulled the trigger.

At trial, Miller pled guilty and testified against his co-defendants. Because he cooperated, a judge gave him twenty years.

"Here you sit," said Ferguson. "Why are you testifying on behalf of the state in this case?"

"Your client is a pretty vain and—he's a vain person."

"My client's a vain person?"

"Vain and glorious person. He's a braggart."

"That's why you're testifying against him, because he's vain and he's a braggart?"

"I just—first right thing I've ever done in my life."

Ferguson tried to get Miller to concede that he was testifying in order to get some sort of sentence reduction. But Miller insisted that he hadn't been promised anything, and his federal parole board had already determined that he do all of his time, less statutory good time and credit for working in the prison furniture factory.

Ferguson asked him to detail his conversations with Kramer, starting with the first. Miller recalled, as he had told Greg Smith, that he and Kramer were in the same cell unit at Leavenworth, and Kramer noticed that he had a race car magazine.

The first conversation was short, as Kramer was on his way to spending a couple weeks in "the hole" as discipline for having drug residue found in his urine.

Miller had used the name Robert Young when he was arrested in Independence, Missouri, after one of his escapes. When he told Kramer that, plus that he had killed a federal witness in 1987—the same year Kramer admitted killing one (Miller reported), Kramer asked, "Are you a plant?"

Miller said Kramer admitted the murder a second time when they were together watching a Dolphins football game on TV.

"He told me he'd gone out with Dan Marino and knew Dan Marino's sister and been out with her. 'I've had the whole team out. I give him cocaine. I've given that one cocaine.'

"I said, 'Ben, if you hadn't killed that man, you wouldn't be here today.' 'I'm not in here for that. I'm not convicted of that yet. They'll never convict me of that. No one knows anything about it. Robert Young is not going to roll over.'

"I would always pretend we were all in here for murder. He said, 'I'm in here for selling marijuana in Illinois.' That's what he told me. Whether that's true or not, I don't know."

"Did he explain to you who this government witness was?"

"Yes, sir. He said he was a boatbuilder named Donald Aronow, whom I never heard of in my life, and he would tell me that—he bragged that he'd go fishing with the president. And I said, 'You're a bullshitter. You're the biggest liar I ever known.' He said, 'I'm serious.' "

"Where does the government witness come in at?"

"What government witness? He said that he had snitched on him for hauling drugs. And beat him in a big boat deal out of a bunch of money, about a million dollars or something."

Noting the similarity between that and the *Motor Boating & Sailing* story, Ferguson asked Miller if he had ever read it, or the book *Blue Thunder*. Miller denied knowing about either.

Sometime in early 1991—after *Blue Thunder* but before *Motor Boating & Sailing*—Miller said he phoned the FBI agent on his Baltimore case, George Chmiel.

"I asked him to find out if there was anybody named Don Aronow had ever been killed in Miami. He was a big boatbuilder and a friend of the president, and he said he could find out. I said 'There's a guy in here telling me that he hired that to be done by a guy.' I said, 'Find out if it's true or not.' I said, 'If it's true, it's still unsolved, but I think it's a bunch of bullshit.'

"In about a week, I called him back. He said, 'That's a hot case.' He said, 'Just stay with it.' "

"Did Ben ever tell you why he had Don Aronow killed?"

"He fucked him up out of some money. It was a couple or two or three different things. You want the story?"

"Yes, sir," Ferguson replied.

"First of all, he wanted Don to fly a plane and he wanted—I mean, he had a good known name down here and he wanted him to bring drugs in. And when Don would introduce himself to the tower out here, he would have carte blanche to pass—you know, he could get by, by being Don Aronow. He said he turned him down.

"He said he also got down on him because you'd see a lot of cars out around in front of his shops and he'd run the tag numbers through the police department and it would be government cars, and he used to say Don Aronow was snitching on him. But more important is he fucked him around out of a million dollars on a boat deal."

"What kind of boat deal?"

"He didn't really elaborate on that. He just fucked him around out of some boats and out of a business amounting to about a million dollars. He bought the business and Don took the business back from him. He fucked him around out of about a million dollars. Wouldn't pay him."

"And just exactly how was it that Ben knew that Aronow was snitching on Ben Kramer?"

"Because the police was coming down on him and the police had come to Ben and told him that 'We're getting information on you, slow down a little bit,' things like that."

"Did you tell Detective Smith that Ben told you that he wanted Don Aronow to introduce Ben to President Bush?"

"He said he wouldn't introduce him to President Bush. He said he wanted to go fishing with him one time. And Aronow wouldn't take him along."

"Did you ever tell Detective Smith that Ben Kramer told you that he personally planned Don Aronow's murder with Robert Young?"

"Yes, I did. He asked me what did I get for killing— he thought mine was a contract murder. He said, 'What did you get for killing yours?'

"I said, 'Five hundred dollars and a six-pack of Budweiser.' I said, 'What did you give for killing yours?' And he said, 'Ninety to a hundred thousand dollars,' but he said it was $25,000 in cash and he said every shot over one would be a kilo of cocaine. He said it amounted to about $100,000. And I told him I would have done it cheaper than that.

"I said, 'Why did you choose Robert Young?' He said, 'He had bodies, it wasn't his first hit. He had other bodies laying around.' "

OCTOBER 15, 1993

JERRY ENGELMAN
DEPOSITION

Engelman had been one of Tom Burdick's best sources for *Blue Thunder*. However, he said, Burdick didn't play fair with his information.

"Many things that are attributed to me are wholly false. Some things are wholly accurate. Other things are slanted wholly out of context. I think whenever he needed a source, he said, 'According to Jerry Engelman . . . ' There are numerous, numerous things in there that were attributed to me that I did not say at all, or things that I said that I had heard somebody [say] sometime that were attributed to me.

"I now see from reading the book that Tom Burdick had his own agenda. He had his theory. He thought he was going to solve this murder. The police did not know what they were doing and he was going to solve the murder, and he was convinced that two guys from Chicago were the hit men. I think he let the thing go crazy on him, and he tried to force the facts to meet his own personal agenda.

"He was out to prove that Don was heavily involved in the Mafia, and he was out to prove that Don was involved in drug smuggling, possibly drug smuggling with Ben Kramer. He was out to prove that marijuana was off-loaded at the back of the old Cigarette factory.

"He kept talking about his fundamental source. I had no knowledge of any of this stuff. It was all in the past. Burdick kept on me about Aronow being involved in drugs, and I never saw any evidence of it. I never heard any whispers in the street of anything about him.

"I frankly never believed it. Aronow was a real bright guy, and I frankly found it hard to believe that he would permit drugs to be off-loaded at the back of his [factory]. It's just too crazy. I just don't think he was that stupid, and I told Burdick this consistently over and over and over and over again."

Dohn Williams pointed out a page in the book where Burdick had attributed to Engelman a story that Aronow kept hashish in his desk at work.

[The passage read, in Engelman's quotes, "It was just another of those hush-hush things for Don that we weren't ever supposed to talk about, like these enormous chunks of hashish he used to keep in his desk upstairs when his girlfriends came over."]

"This is an example of how he distorted. He kept asking me over and over again about drugs. He finally said, 'Did you ever hear anything about even smoking a little pot, anything?' "

Finally, Engelman said, he broke down and told him a secondhand story that had happened prior to the time he began work there, about hashish being found in Aronow's desk—which may well have belonged to a former employee.

"In the book, he makes it sound like I personally found a chunk of hashish—I knew that Don Aronow kept hashish in this drawer and went upstairs with his girlfriends and smoked dope and did whatever. Absolutely not true.''

The girlfriend reference reminded Williams to ask about Ilene Taylor Cary.

"Is it fair to say he was having an affair with her, for lack of a better term?''

"Yes.''

"Would he take her upstairs in the office on occasion?''

"Yes.''

Williams also asked about Aronow's relationship with Kramer. Engelman said he saw them speaking together only once or twice, plus Kramer called a few times. However, "In the months before Aronow was murdered, there seemed to be more phone calls between Kramer and Aronow.''

"Do you have any idea what the reason was that there was an increase in the number of communications?''

"I figured they must be doing some kind of deal.''

NOVEMBER 29, 1993

SKIP WALTON
DEPOSITION

As evidenced by Skip Walton's last contact with Greg Smith, he had since changed his tune about cooperating with the state. At deposition, he claimed he didn't know what he was saying when he offered information that he supposedly knew Bobby Young was involved in the murder.

Walton explained: he has diabetes, and when his blood sugar gets low, he loses the ability to function. In June 1989, when Mike DeCora and Gary Rosenberg took him from the federal prison in Oklahoma to a nearby city jail so they could talk, his condition worsened. He was under a lot of stress, the city jail didn't meet his medical needs, and the investigators took him to restaurants, where he binged on pizza, steak, and Coca-Cola—further upsetting his blood sugar balance.

[Since Don Ferguson had represented Walton on his murder on the high seas case (and had since gotten Walton to sign a release waiving their attorney-client privilege), he wasn't present. Dohn Williams asked the questions.]

"What was your state of mind when you were giving them that statement?"

"I was a mess," Walton said. "You know, I was, like, I was taking insulin and the food, I don't, I don't really know what happened up there."

"Well, in that statement you implicated Robert Young in the death of Donald Aronow. Do you have knowledge that Robert Young was involved in the death of Donald Aronow?"

"No."

"Has Robert Young ever made any admissions to you that he was involved in the death of Donald Aronow?"

"Well—he has never come out and said directly that he killed Don Aronow to me. That I remember. Of course, he's kind of a braggart, you know. You know what I mean? He's a little guy and he's got a little guy complex." [That was the first-ever reference to Young, six feet tall and 180 pounds, as small.]

"Well, has he ever bragged about doing stuff that you know he did not do?"

"Of course."

"To make himself be bigger than he is?"

"That is why I took it with a grain of salt, you know. He brags. More mouth than—more show than go."

"Did you hint to Detective DeCora and the federal agents that you could provide them the motive, who hired the killer, who the trigger man was, the weapon, the vehicle used in it, and give them an eyewitness concerning Aronow's death?"

"Yes."

"And that was based on secondhand knowledge that someone had related to you?"

"Tommy Teagle and all the other deals I was—"

"Was part of your knowledge based on conversations with Rick Fidlin?"

"No."

"Just what Teagle was feeding you?"

"Just what Teagle was feeding me."

"Has Teagle repeatedly talked to you about wanting to cash in on this $100,000 reward?"

"He has, yes. I refused."

"Does that appear to be his primary motivation, hopefully to get this $100,000?"

"I believe so, yes."

"Does Teagle appear to be the kind of person that would lie in order to collect $100,000?"

"Yes. I believe Tommy Teagle would do anything to anybody, do anything just for money or to better himself or to cut his time."

When Carl Davis came to Oklahoma, Walton said he planned to lead police to believe that Davis was in the car with Young when Aronow was killed.

"But, in fact, Carl really was not with Young when Aronow was killed?" Williams asked.

"I don't remember all the details of the conversation. But I remember vaguely, very vaguely, that they wanted Carl in the car."

"They wanted?"

"Yes."

"The wool was going to be kind of put over their eyes that Carl was an eyewitness to this thing, correct?" Williams led.

"I remember, yes, I remember that Carl was supposed to be in the car. I really don't remember that. Honestly, I cannot recollect how it arose. I really don't."

"The truth of the matter is, Carl was not in the car, was he?"

"I don't think he was, no."

16

PATTY LEZACA
DEPOSITION

Patty Lezaca, Aronow's longtime secretary and office manager, recalled the day when a U.S. Customs agent came to the factory and told Aronow they wouldn't follow through with the Blue Thunder contract because the Kramers now owned the company.

"Don said, 'No, it wasn't sold to the Kramers.' But [the agent] just laughed." Then Aronow admitted, "Well, he didn't sell it to Ben, he sold it to Jack. They're not really bad people. Ben had changed, he had been in jail, he changed, he was a different person."

"This is what Don said?" asked Dohn Williams.

"They just laughed, yeah, Customs just laughed. Don had to get the company back before they could get the bid. He had to show that he still owned the company."

"Without the government contract, there was no business for USA Racing, it wasn't selling boats?" Ferguson asked.

"Right."

Lezaca said that after the sale to the Kramers, little changed at the office. Jack Kramer would drop in about once a week, and Ben Kramer came over only a little bit more often. "But again, it wasn't like he was there working."

"When Ben Kramer would come over to USA, what
would he do?"

"He would just look around and talk to Don."

"Was he pleasant enough to you?"

"Yes, he was always pleasant to me."

"Ben Kramer looked up to Don Aronow just as everyone else looked up to Don Aronow; isn't that true?"

"That's an opinion."

"Apache Boats had Don Aronow's name on the side
of them, did they not?"

"Yes."

"Why?"

"They weren't supposed to."

"They did."

"They weren't supposed to."

"Ben Kramer put Don Aronow's name on the side of
the boats without Don Aronow's permission?"

"Because Ben Kramer wanted to be Don Aronow,"
she said.

Lezaca said Aronow didn't want anyone to know about
the sale; he told her but still kept the deal's details a
secret.

"He told me it was better I didn't know."

"Did Ben Kramer ever express to you any dissatisfac-
tion about Mr. Aronow having to take the company back
over?" asked Williams.

"No."

"How about Jack Kramer?"

"No."

"Prior to February 3, 1987, had you ever heard Ben
Kramer utter anything that you would consider to be a
threat as to Mr. Aronow?"

"Yes, he did to me once. He said, 'I'll kill the son of
a bitch, I'm not afraid of him.' "

Lezaca explained that Kramer had said that during a
telephone call she made to him while he was in Key West
for a boat race. [That may have been the Key West World
Championship, run November 12–16, 1985, just before
the papers returning USA Racing to Aronow were

signed.] She said she called him because Aronow had said that Ben wanted her to work for him at Apache, and therefore she would have to go.

"I got real upset about it. And I said that I wouldn't work for the Kramers. And when I told Ben, you know, Ben said it wasn't true, that I was still working there for Don and he got mad, you know, and then Don got mad because I called Ben. Ben got mad when I said Don had made the remark, he said that Don was starting trouble, and that's when he said, 'I'll kill the son of a bitch, I'm not afraid of him.'"

"Did you relate that remark to Don?"

"No, I didn't."

"You laugh and shake your head no."

"I wouldn't make a remark like that to Don Aronow. I mean, knowing Ben for the little time that I knew him, something like that coming from him, I just wouldn't cause any more problems."

"You kind of left me lost," said Williams. "Supposedly Ben has threatened to hurt your longtime employer? That's what you told me, correct?"

"Yes. No, I wouldn't say that to Don. I guess I didn't take him serious."

"Didn't take Ben serious?" interjected Don Ferguson.

"I didn't take Ben serious," she said.

"In the prior context you had had with Ben, did Ben fly off the handle?" Williams asked.

"Yes."

"I guess for lack of a better word, you, took him with a grain of salt?"

"I wouldn't say really with a grain of salt because, personally, Ben Kramer scared me. His personality scared me."

Williams asked if Aronow had ever told her whether either Kramer had threatened him. She said no.

"Is it fair for me to say that you never had a conversation with Ben Kramer concerning his purchase of USA from Don Aronow?" Ferguson asked.

"Correct. I spoke to him as little as possible."

* * *

Lezaca also said she knew that cash under the table had passed when the USA Racing sale closed, but she didn't remember Aronow telling her that.

"I knew there was cash, undocumented cash, and I can't remember how I knew, but I knew it was undocumented cash, yes."

Ferguson asked whether Lezaca knew Aronow had had affairs with married women over the years, using a private room upstairs over the USA Racing office, as well as rooms in other buildings he had worked in. Lezaca said yes.

Ferguson asked for names, besides Ilene Taylor.

"Some of them came in the back door. I didn't know. There was one I wasn't allowed to know her name because she had a lot of money."

Ferguson asked if any of the women's husbands or boyfriends ever found out.

"If he was ever caught—yes. Yes, one time. Somebody in New York."

"Can't wait to hear this," Ferguson said. "You have a smile on your face. What happened?"

"Supposedly he put a hit out on Don Aronow."

"Was this gentleman from New York one of the boys, a connected individual from New York?"

"He was Jewish."

"He put a contract out on Don Aronow for fooling around with his wife?"

"Early '70s, yes, but it was straightened out. Some men came down to talk to Don about it, and they straightened it out."

Lezaca said she had overheard their conversation: "He denied it and promised them that it was a lie." Then Aronow never saw the woman again.

"Miss Lezaca, while Don Aronow was married, how many women would you say he had affairs with? Just give me your best estimate, the number over the years. You were with him for, like, fifteen years?"

"Yes."

"Do you need a calculator?" offered Williams.

"Probably a few. He was terrible, he really was."

"While he was married?" Ferguson prompted.

"As soon as he left Shirley, he married Lillian. And he was with that Missy for a long, long time, but he even cheated on her. Don even cheated on his mistresses. Twenty-five to be kind."

"Lillian was the previous girlfriend of King Hussein from Jordan?"

"Yes."

"Was there any resentment that Aronow stole Lillian from King Hussein of Jordan?"

"No. He didn't steal her. Lillian didn't want to marry King Hussein because she, like—"

"He was too short?"

"No, he had too many wives. King Hussein was a very good friend of Don's."

Toward the end of the deposition, Ferguson had Lezaca cover a few final areas: Aronow never trusted Mark McManus, she said, and he never kept drugs on his premises for his personal use.

"He was against drugs," she said.

And one last item: "So if Ilene Taylor would have said to us that she never had an affair with Don Aronow, she would be lying?"

"Yes."

JANUARY 18, 1994

GREG SMITH
DEPOSITION

Most of Greg Smith's deposition was an excruciating review of his police reports, but Don Ferguson also pursued a big question first raised in *Blue Thunder*:

"Did it ever come to your attention, Detective Smith, that Don Aronow was under subpoena to appear before a federal grand jury?"

"No," said Smith.

"Had he been served, sir?"

"No, he had not been served."

"Did it come to your attention that a subpoena had been issued but not served upon him?"

"Yes, sir."

"What was your information as to what the return date of that subpoena was?"

"I don't know that there was even a date, a specific date given. I'm not privy to that information, but I was told by the U.S. attorney's office that he was to be subpoenaed before a grand jury."

"Was there any particular assistant U.S. attorney that you spoke with at the U.S. attorney's office?"

"Yes, sir."

"Who would that have been?"

"Robert Bondi."

[Bondi was the lead prosecutor in the money-laundering case against the Kramers, Kessler, et al.]

"Did he say it had not been issued, but it was going to be issued?"

"Correct."

"Was Bondi the person that was going to issue it?"

"Yes."

MARCH 24, 1994

STANLEY DIAMOND
DEPOSITION

Diamond, now aged fifty-five and in failing health, was also no longer anxious to assist the state's case. He said Gary Rosenberg had promised to help him at a sentence reduction hearing in 1990, but he didn't show. He got the reduction anyway and was now out on federal parole.

"I just said, 'I'll help you if you help me.' He got all the time in the world. I need his help in sixty days. If that was very important for him, why didn't he help me? Nobody can answer that, right? Meanwhile, I can't remember nothing. So I got a worse memory than him as far as he's concerned."

Don Ferguson read Diamond the Metro-Dade police

reports having to do with him. In 1987, they wrote, he told a detective that for $5,000, he could try to find out if Kramer was involved in the murder.

At first, he said he didn't remember. Then Ferguson jogged his memory: "Let me ask you this: was this a scam that you were trying to pull on the police officers for money?"

"Oh, I always—yes, it could have been that, too. Like I said, it could have been to benefit myself."

"You used the word 'always,'" Ferguson noted.

"Yes. I have done a lot of time. I have not gotten any breaks from them, from anybody, so I'm out to help myself if I can."

"The report goes on to say that Mr. Diamond [in 1989] advised that when Ben Kramer was arrested by the federal government, he had been running from a group of Colombians who he had ripped off for approximately $30 million."

"Oh, the kid ripped it off. That was common knowledge. That was in the street."

"You did not say that from any type of personal knowledge or anything?"

"No. Everyone knew that."

"Why were you speaking to the police? Were you just being a good citizen?"

"I'm not a good citizen. It was strictly, I think, to help myself at one point."

As Ferguson read aloud further what Diamond told the police that Kramer allegedly said, he stopped him.

"Listen, I don't want to make a problem with Ben Kramer; you understand what I'm saying?"

Ferguson continued: "This police officer alleges that you told that Kramer solicited you to murder a man by the name of Robert Young. Allegedly, according to this police officer, Kramer told you that if Young flipped and testified for the government, that Young could put Kramer in the electric chair."

"Well, he did say that to me," Diamond said. "Kramer did say that to me."

"Did you say that to the police officer?"

"No, but Kramer did say it to me, and he must have said it to a few other people, too."

"They are saying that you're allegedly saying that Kramer asked you to murder Robert Young, which is pretty serious. Are you saying you did not tell them that, or you did tell them that?"

"I don't think I did tell them that. I really don't know."

"It isn't true, is that what you're saying?"

"Yes. Off the top of my head, I don't remember that. That is something I would remember."

"So you are saying that is not true?"

"There was talk about having trouble and this and that. He did call me out many times to the visiting room, but it was just Benny liked to talk. That's all."

JUNE 1, 1994

FRANK MEADE
DEPOSITION

Frank Meade—who didn't seem to mind his nickname, Filthy Fucking Frank—had helped set up Bobby Young's capture in 1988. He had worked for Young as an enforcer but had since turned paid informant for a number of state and federal law enforcement agencies. He had a lengthy criminal record for drugs, assaults, and gun violations.

Dohn Williams asked Meade what Young had said to him about the Aronow case.

"He told me that there was a reward out for him and that they had upped the reward. I didn't even know who Don Aronow was.

"We were in the backyard, shooting guns and talking. And now I'm trying to think of how it came about. If I was Bob and you were somebody that screwed up in the organization, his exact words were, 'I'm going to kill you like I did that fucking Aronow punk.' He said that many, many times."

That was new information. Williams asked Meade if he had told that before to the prosecutors.

"I don't think so. I just—the last few days I have been rerunning the tape of what happened years back and [I] recall[ed] that conversation."

"In fact, this is the first time you've told anybody this, isn't it?"

"Second time. I just told [assistant state's attorney] Mr. [Gary] Winston that in the office probably forty minutes ago."

"Why didn't you tell the police when you brought Mr. Schaab here in November of 1988 to tell what he knew about Mr. Young's involvement in the Aronow case? Why didn't you tell the police then about your conversation with Mr. Young?"

"I just didn't think. Like I said, I didn't think of it then, or maybe I had said it, I don't know. I don't remember what I said then, but I recollect it now."

"Don't you think that Mr. Young admitting to you that he killed Mr. Aronow would have been an important piece of evidence in the police investigation?"

"Mr. Young has admitted to me of committing thirty-four murders that I know of."

Meade described some of his duties for Young. "If Bob was out of town, I would make sure Cat Dancer was protected. If there was money to be collected, I would collect it. I would do whatever Bob said, more or less." That, he said, included ripping off dope dealers who had ripped off Young, beating people up, and threatening them.

One of his cleverest and most successful intimidation techniques was giving someone a bulletproof vest and telling him to run around Young's backyard. Then Meade began shooting at him with a .22, his lowest-caliber gun. He also kept pistols up to .45s in plain sight.

The first time he tried it, "I shot him two feet away, and 'All right, motherfucker, see all of these guns? We are going to go through them until you tell us what I want.'

"And I only had to use that interrogation technique one time, and the word got out, Hey, if they ask you to put the vest on . . .''

"You seem like you were doing a lot of things for him," Williams noted. "Did he ever solicit you to participate in the killing of Don Aronow?"

"No. Don Aronow was killed before I even knew Bob, I believe. I really don't know the date Don Aronow was killed."

Meade said he knew Carl Davis—"Crazy Carl"—through Young. "Carl was an enforcer somewhat like me. I don't know when Carl and Bob got together, but he had been working for Bob longer than I had."

[In November 1989, a West Palm Beach–based FBI agent had told Metro-Dade Police that he had investigated Davis a few years before as someone who had collected drug debts in Palm Beach County.]

"Well, along those lines that Carl was an enforcer somewhat like you, were you and Carl involved in a conspiracy to commit a murder in the New Orleans area?"

"Yes, sir."

"What was that all about?"

"Bob handed us $2,500 in expense money, told us to go to New Orleans, that the hit was paying $250,000. He was a witness in the federal witness protection program."

Meade said Young gave them a bomb to use in New Orleans.

"We were surveilling a house and we were going to plant it, and it didn't seem like we ever got the right opportunity to do that, and we ended up coming back."

Meade said he couldn't remember the name of the intended victim.

During the time they were planning the New Orleans hit, Young repeated his admission about killing Aronow.

"Bob would get real aggravated. In fact, I can tell you the exact guy that he used one of those phrases on was a guy named Mark. Mark, this thing was going down with that New Orleans deal and we're sitting outside on the table, like a picnic table by the pool where we always go, guns laying on the tables, targets over there. Mark was saying, 'Let me go, let me go, let me go.'

"Bob always carried a nine millimeter, I can't tell you what brand it was. Mark is sitting across like these two are, the length of the table. Picked up a gun and shot it by Mark's head, I'm talking inches, and told him, 'You fucking punk, I'll kill you like I did that Aronow fucker. Don't even think you have the balls or the gumption to do something like that.' ''

JULY 21, AUGUST 5, AUGUST 10,
AND AUGUST 15, 1994

MELVYN KESSLER
DEPOSITION

Bobby Young's attorneys had asked the court to order Kessler not to testify about his conversations with Young—even at a deposition—because they were privileged attorney-client communications, they said, and Dade County Circuit Court judge Michael Chavies had granted the motion.

However, Chavies had rejected Kramer's argument that an attorney-client privilege existed between him and Kessler. Therefore, Kessler could relay whatever he said Kramer told him.

"What is it that Ben Kramer told you, if anything, regarding his involvement, if any, in the homicide?'' Don Ferguson asked.

"He told me that he participated to the extent that he hired Robert Young to murder Aronow.''

"Best you can recall, Mr. Kessler, what were his exact words?''

"The first time that he discussed it with me was at a dinner. That evening, he was talking about Aronow in a very strange way. It was sometime in the spring of 1987, and it's only by reflection really that I recall it. At the time I did not pay any attention to it.''

"What did Ben say?''

"He said something to the effect, 'That cocksucker stole my money and made me look like an ass.' ''

"Any other statements that he might have made, sir, that evening?''

"He talked about—the conversation related to the

Blue Thunder boats. That is how the conversation began. The Blue Thunder boats are the boats that were being produced by Aronow, and one of the bases for Ben to buy the Aronow name and plant was this contract, this alleged contract that Aronow had with Customs to build X number of those Blue Thunder boats. We were talking about the boat, the physical boat itself, without anything to do with the government or anything else. During the course of that conversation, Ben made a remark like I said."

Ferguson asked if Kessler had somehow prompted that remark.

"Ben was aware of my feelings about Aronow and his business dealings before Ben ever got involved with Mr. Aronow."

"Your feelings?"

"I did not particularly care for Mr. Aronow. I did not care for his business dealings. I thought he was a thief, and I still think he's a thief. That is what I told Ben."

"Did you in any way warn or caution Mr. Kramer against doing business with Mr. Aronow?" asked Dohn Williams.

"Yes, but I did not find out about Ben's involvement with Aronow in terms of buying Aronow out until after it was done. Ben mentioned to me that he was considering it. When Ben said to me he was considering buying the Aronow plant out, it was already a *fait accompli*. But he did not say that to me. He said it was something that was going to happen in the future. Right at that moment, I told him he was out of his mind and out of his league."

Ferguson asked how Kessler responded when Kramer called Aronow an ass.

"I probably nodded and the discussion ended. I mean, Aronow *was* a cocksucker, and he did steal his money."

"What money?"

"Ben's, part of Ben's investment in the company."

"How do you know that?"

"Anyone that knows Aronow knew that was going to happen. It was a *fait accompli*."

"Did you know it, Mr. Kessler?"

"At the time I don't think I did. I just assumed."

"Did there ever come a time when you knew it for real?"

"Later on."

"When later on?"

"Ben was in jail already when we discussed it."

Kessler said he and Kramer talked both on the telephone and in person about Bobby Young and Aronow, "up to and including the day [Kramer] was arrested. Almost the day he was arrested."

Ferguson asked him to recall when the next discussion was after the dinner meeting.

"Probably the next day. If not the next day, the day after that. Ben called my office practically daily. I didn't speak to him daily, don't misunderstand me when I say that. He called practically daily if not every day, every other day if he was in Miami. If he wasn't in Miami, that's a different story, then he didn't call me. But when he was in Miami, if he wasn't out on a race or something like that, he called all the time."

"What was the subject?"

"I didn't speak to him. Usually bullshit, but on occasion more so than not, he would ask me about Young. 'What's he doing? How's he handling it? Is he going to cooperate?' On many of these occasions he repeated the remark, 'Do you think Young is going—I'm worried about Young bringing me into this case.' He also said many times to me, more than twenty occasions probably, 'You know, Mel, I never met this man. I never saw him face-to-face. He wouldn't know me if we passed each other out on the street. Never met him. Never talked to him.' Which I pretty much knew myself anyway."

"Am I to assume from your response, then, that Mr. Kramer, between the time period of the first conversation at the restaurant up to the day of his arrest never said, 'Mel, I did it, I hired him, I hired Bob Young to kill Don Aronow?' "

"He never said that to me."

Kessler said he visited Kramer at a number of different prisons, both before and after his smuggling trial. Even after Kessler was indicted himself, as Kramer's codefendant in the money-laundering trial, he visited him in the fall of 1988 in Marion County Jail. He said they talked about Randy Lanier; Ferguson asked for specifics.

"That Randy was supposed to come up with money and was not coming up with it; I should talk to Randy and make arrangements with Randy to get some money."

"Randy was supposed to come up with money for whom, sir?"

"For Robert Young and for Melvyn Kessler."

"To be used how?"

"Robert Young had some family problems, and he needed some money to handle his family problems."

"What quantity of money are we talking about, or was Ben talking about?"

"Over $200,000."

"How were you to obtain $200,000 from Randy Lanier if he was in jail?"

"Through one of Randy's people."

"How much of the $200,000 was to go to Melvyn Kessler?"

"Around fifty."

"What for, sir?"

"For the representation of Mr. Young."

"In which case?"

"In the Oklahoma case."

"Who was to get the rest of the money?"

"It was to be earmarked for Robert Young."

Kessler said Kramer wanted him to see Lanier in person to ask for the money. Ferguson asked why Kramer would need any money from Lanier.

"Mr. Kramer told me to talk to Randy, that Ben Kramer did not have access to ready cash, and that the only one that had access to ready cash was Randy Lanier, and that he wanted Randy Lanier to come up with that money."

"Had you met Randy Lanier prior to that meeting with Ben Kramer?"

"I had known Randy Lanier probably since 1977, 1978."

"Have you ever provided any type of legal services for him?"

"Yes. Criminal, with regard to criminal, potential criminal. When Mr. Ingold was arrested in Illinois, who was a driver for Randy Lanier, Mr. Lanier retained me to investigate the facts of the Ingold arrest and whether or not he was a suspect in what became the Illinois case."

Kessler said Lanier eventually gave him $300,000, in a number of deliveries to his office; it was all cash, wrapped and sealed in white sacks, some of it dropped off by Lanier's girlfriend. Fifty thousand was for him to represent Young in Oklahoma, plus $200,000 was "to me personally for money that I would have put aside so, when and if I ever got out of jail, I would have some cash." From the last delivery, he gave ten or fifteen thousand in a lump sum to Billy Thomas to defend Young in the Aronow case. The remainder he used to reimburse expenses and bills he had paid for Kramer.

Kessler said at his second meeting with Kramer at Marion County Jail, Kramer suggested hiring a private investigator to interview Carl Davis, Tommy Teagle, and Skip Walton. Ferguson asked why.

"He wanted to make sure that he was able to get affidavits from those people, that those people knew that Robert Young committed murder and Ben had nothing to do with it."

"He did not say he wanted them for Bobby Young; he wanted them for himself?"

"Absolutely."

Also, Kessler said Kramer told him he was trying to bribe a juror in his smuggling trial, and that he was having the jail guards bring him food and liquor every night.

"Anything else?" Ferguson asked.

"If you want me to tell you how he was screwing his wife in the closet."

Ferguson stopped him. "We have all heard that story," he said.

* * *

The next time Kessler said he saw Kramer, it was at a prison hospital in Springfield, Missouri, after Kramer had broken his leg during his 1989 escape attempt.

"What was the purpose of the trip there?" Ferguson asked.

"Only one thing: Robert Young."

Ferguson asked what was spoken.

"Basically, Ben was very much concerned with whether or not Bobby Young was going to be 'stand up,' [and] what my feelings were.

"I had had a conversation with Paul Thompson, I think, already by then. There was a letter from Ben to Paul where—I mean, he does not say so in words; you have to read between the lines—he wanted Robert Young moved up to Paul's floor, and then Paul should kill him or have someone kill him and then claim the same insanity defense that [Thompson] did in his case."

[At that time, Young was in the Dade County Jail on the Panzavecchia murder charge. His indictment for Aronow's murder was still a year away.]

"What indication did you have that a murder indictment was imminent, if it was?"

"Well, to be honest with you, I did not think there was going to be one. I really did not believe Bobby was going to be indicted for that murder, not from my knowledge of what the state's case was.

"I expressed that opinion to him many times. I felt that the state's case against Bobby Young at that point in time as I knew it—I am not telling you I knew everything about it—but as I knew it, I felt the state's case against him was very circumstantial and very weak."

"Has not changed much since then, has it?" Ferguson goaded.

"I don't believe it has."

Ferguson asked about Kessler's phone conversations with Kramer between prison visits.

"Anytime Ben had access to a telephone, regardless of where he was, [he] would call me. And each of the calls related to 'What's Mr. Young doing? Do you think he's going to cooperate? Is he bothering you? Is he a pain in the ass? Tell him that "Look, I can't help it but all my money and all my property were confiscated by the government, and I have to get it from somebody else." ' "

As the deposition went on, Ferguson's strategy was to ask Kessler about criminal acts he may have committed while acting as an attorney. His intention was to use those answers against him at trial, to impugn his character.

Kessler said sometimes his clients left cash in his office safe, so when they or their associates got arrested, they'd have money for bail or investigators immediately available.

"Have you ever been hired by a client or clients to represent members of his or their smuggling operation?" Ferguson asked.

"Yes, sir."

"You ever have any advance knowledge that the smuggling operation was afoot, underway?"

"Sometimes."

"How many occasions?"

"With Ben, twice as an example . . . on two separate occasions, Ben called me and Ben said to me the following: 'Mel, can you keep yourself open for next weekend,' and I assumed that to mean that Ben or somebody that Ben was involved with was going to be committing an illegal act. He never said to me, 'Mel, I am smuggling, bringing in X number of pounds of marijuana or cocaine on March 1 in Atlantic City,' or anything like that."

Ferguson asked Kessler what he had told federal investigators about his prior criminal acts.

"I told them that I had used cocaine, partied with it over a lengthy period of time." [Kessler said that was between 1980 and 1983; in November 1983, he had an operation for a deviated septum—a hole in his nasal membrane—a classic symptom of heavy cocaine use.]

"What type of frequency?"

"Just party with it."

"How many times a week would you have used it?"

"That's difficult to answer. There were weeks I would never use any. Just partied with it."

"Where would you obtain cocaine for use?"

"Mostly from Sal and Willie."

"Sal Magluta and Willie Falcón?"

"Yes."

[As Kessler had turned witness against Kramer and Young, he had also given information against boat racers Magluta and Falcón. In 1996, Kessler had been scheduled to testify against them at their federal drug-smuggling trial in Miami, but was never called.]

Kessler said Magluta sometimes gave him half an ounce of coke to pass around to other attorneys who worked with him.

"Usually I went to Sal to pick up money. When I picked up money from him, he always gave me a small little bag to give to the guys."

"Did you keep any of the cocaine for yourself?"

"Sometimes. Most of the times, if not all of the times."

"When you received the cocaine from either Sal or Willie, did you see other quantities of cocaine in your physical presence at the time you did that?"

"Yes."

"What kind of quantities are we talking about?"

"On several occasions there were duffel bags full of it. Several, eight, nine, ten duffel bags full of it."

"How did you know the duffel bags were full of cocaine?"

"They told me."

"Did you know that you were violating the law, Mr. Kessler, by taking cocaine and giving it to those individuals?"

"Yes."

"Why did you do it, then?"

"That's a difficult question to answer. I really don't have an answer for it. No logical answer, anyway."

Ferguson asked Kessler whether he had ever bribed a judge. He said he had, once.

He couldn't remember the name of the client, except that he was Colombian. The client had skipped his $85,000 bond, leaving Kessler, who had personally guaranteed the money, responsible.

He said he made a deal with a Miami bail bondsman connected to the presiding Dade County Circuit Court judge, Ellen Morphonios: he paid the bondsman $25,000, and the judge granted either a motion to suppress or a motion to dismiss. As a result, the bond was discharged.

"What did [the bondsman] tell you that he was capable of doing?"

"Exactly what happened. I told [him] that I had—it was a good motion, but I just wanted the insurance of getting it granted."

"So what did [the bondsman] tell you that he was capable of doing?"

"He was able to bribe Judge Morphonios."

"Did he tell you that he gave it to her?"

"Yes, he did."

"Did you ever speak directly with Morphonios about the payoff to her?

"No, never."

[In 1992, *The Miami Herald* had reported that the U.S. attorney's office in Miami said Judge Morphonios was the target of a bribery investigation; there were allegations that she took bribes to keep the state from collecting bonds that should have been forfeited after drug traffickers had skipped before trial.

Morphonios, who already had written her autobiography, *Maximum Morphonios*, describing herself as a former beauty queen and a no-nonsense hanging judge, and had been featured on *60 Minutes*, denied the allegations. But she had left the bench just months before the investigation began. Other Dade County judges were later indicted in federal court and convicted for bribery, but Morphonios was never charged. In 1997, she returned to the bench as an honorary senior judge, part-time, then resigned her commission months later.]

*   *   *

"Have you ever committed perjury?" Ferguson asked.

"Yes," Kessler answered.

"When?"

"In a case involving Ben, where Ben was arrested in his vehicle with Richard Portnoy. And in the vehicle was a little bit over $100,000 in cash in small bills."

[Kramer had been stopped for speeding in his white Porsche 928S, doing fifty in a thirty-five miles per hour zone near his apartment in north Dade on the evening of October 2, 1985. The officer smelled pot, and Kramer freely admitted to him that he and his cousin, Richard, had been smoking a joint. When they saw his flashing lights, they threw it out the window.

"Yeah, I was smoking marijuana," Kramer was quoted as saying. "Is that a crime? What are you going to do? Arrest me?"

(Detective Jerry Crawford had spoken to Portnoy on the day after the murder; he said he was Apache's advertising manager.)

The officer shined his flashlight inside the Porsche. He saw a garbage bag in the back seat, stuffed so densely that he could tell it contained stacks of money. The officer took the men to the nearby Metro-Dade Police substation, but after Kessler arrived, they decided not to make any arrests. However, they did keep the cash on suspicion that it was drug money.]

"In what forum did you commit perjury?"

"The day of—earlier [that day], Jack called me in the office and told me that he had a client or customer that was going to make a cash deposit for the purchase of a boat, and do I have any of the cash-reporting forms. And I shipped up to Jack the cash-reporting forms.

"Late that evening, or maybe early, very early in the morning, Jack called me and told me Ben was in jail, if I would just do him a big favor and go get him because [Jack] didn't have a car and he didn't want to go down there. I agreed to, and I met with Ben and I met with the two officers involved. And at that time they asked me about the money. I told them—I said, 'There's really no problem about the money as far as I know. It was a deposit on a boat and that the paperwork will show that.'

"It became a lie later on where I created a fictitious individual by the name of Sean something or other as the purchaser of the vessel, to protect Ben."

"The Sean guy, is he a real-life, living person?"

"No, he doesn't exist. Before I had made him up, Jack created a file with a set of plans for a—I think it was a forty-six- or forty-seven-foot Apache. And a contract for it. And I signed it on behalf of the client to create a file to protect Ben."

[Nine months after the incident, Kessler took the witness stand in Dade County Circuit Court and testified that Sean Gordon was a British Columbian living in Argentina, and that he wasn't available to appear in court. Placing his trust in testimony from a longtime member of the local bar, the judge ordered the county to return Kramer's seized money.]

"It wasn't a protection of Ben so much for money, it was the fact if he [had lost], it would have violated his parole. And I had a conversation—Jack just, I mean, begged me to do it. He just didn't stop until I agreed to do it. And I agreed and I did it. I testified, I gave a deposition, and I testified under oath. And I lied."

"And you committed perjury?"

"I also lied in my own trial, too."

"How many times did you lie under oath in that trial?"

"When I testified. I denied knowledge of Ben and of Ben's money. That's the crux of it, really."

Kessler said Kramer had used him another time before to keep someone from cooperating with the Feds against him—Charles Podesta. When Podesta was arrested in the first wave of smuggling indictments in 1986, Kessler said Kramer asked him to go visit him.

"Ben asked me to talk to Chuck about Chuck cooperating and not getting stuck—Ben felt that there was going to be another indictment and that they would all be charged with life felonies. [Podesta] didn't have to implicate anybody, didn't have to implicate Ben, but give them some type of partial cooperation, just enough to be

necessary to do as quickly as possible a plea of guilty to
the present charges, to avoid what they felt was going to
be a life felony.''

And even before that, when Conrad Ingold was arrested in New Orleans, Kessler said Kramer told him to
''do a favor for Randy, to check out this fellow and see
what happened with his case.

''I know I flew up to Chicago one time as a result of
that investigation. I tried to hire a former FBI agent as
an investigator on behalf of Randy in that particular case,
so Randy had not been arrested [yet] or was a fugitive
even at that point in time.''

Ferguson asked what had happened to Ingold.

''He was arrested in New Orleans and was put in pro-
tective custody almost immediately.''

''He was cooperative?''

''Yes, sir.''

''You had subsequent conversations with Ben Kramer
concerning him?''

''Yes, sir.''

''What was the substance of the conversations?''

''Ben told me that he had—on behalf of Randy, he
put out a contract to have this man murdered.''

''Who would the contract have been put out with?''

''Robert Young. I didn't know at the time and I did
not ask and I didn't—I personally thought he was full of
shit. Just bullshit. Excuse my language. That he was just
plain bullshitting. I didn't really pay any attention to it
at all at the time.''

''When was it that you found out that Robert Young
supposedly had some participation?''

''I can't tell you exactly when it was. Ben was at MCC
when I had the conversation with him and I believe it
was before the escape attempt. I don't remember him
being on crutches or anything like that.

''Ben told me Robert Young, and he mentioned two
other names but I don't recall—I think I know who he
said, but I wouldn't swear to it. I don't know for sure,
so I'd rather not mention any names.

''And [the] two others got within shooting distance of

this individual and the only reason that he wasn't murdered, there were too many U.S. Marshals around him and it would have been a bloodbath. Those are pretty much his exact words.''

[When Frank Meade had described what sounded like the same job, he said Young had sent him and Carl Davis to do the murder.]

Kessler said Kramer never admitted being involved in Aronow's murder until he visited him at MCC Miami sometime after his escape attempt. Kessler didn't remember the exact date, but recalled that Kramer was in segregation at MCC—"the hole"—and that he had his leg in a cast.

"What did he say, sir?" Ferguson asked.

"He was writing a letter to Paul [Thompson] regarding Bobby. We were talking about Paul. He was talking, and I'm just sitting and listening to him. He was talking about Paul keeping an eye out or stuff like that. We had already discussed this on several occasions. And during the course of that conversation he said to me—I don't remember the exact words, but again, to the best of my knowledge, he said that 'You know, I never met Bobby. There's no way he can pin this on me. And I should have never paid him the money.'

"I think that's pretty close to what he said. Ben and I had had conversations earlier on about the money that he had paid Bobby Young and the reasons why he paid him; Ben told me what they were.''

"Which reasons?"

"Ben told me that Bobby had come to him after the murder and demanded that he give him the hundred thousand dollars, or a hundred thousand dollars.

"And that Ben was afraid of him because the guy was crazy on dope, and he paid him the hundred. He got it from Chuck Podesta, and Chuck got it from Randy, or he had got it from Randy and Chuck delivered it to him, and he gave it to Steve Romano and Steve Romano gave it to Bobby Young.''

"Who's Steve Romano?"

"Steve Romano was someone who worked for Ben.''

"How was the demand for the $100,000 made?" asked Dohn Williams.

"I have no idea."

"You don't know whether it was supposedly made through an intermediary, or what?"

"No. Ben mentioned an intermediary, but not in that context. I didn't ask him how the demand was made. I didn't care how the demand was made. I didn't want to know how the demand was made."

"Go ahead. He's writing a letter," prompted Don Ferguson.

"In segregation, he's writing a letter to Paul, and he's asking me to deliver this letter to Paul Thompson regarding Bobby Young. He had asked me previously to talk to Paul, to ask Paul to keep an eye out for him, you know, just to make him comfortable, so to speak.

"He had also told me that Young was afraid of Paul and that Young, knowing that Paul and Ben were very tight, would keep, help keep Young in line. And I gave Paul those messages.

"I gave Paul the letter; I read the letter with Paul. The letter basically stated that Paul should get him transferred up to I think it was the sixth floor or the fifth floor [of the Dade County Jail], one or the other. And kill him and then claim insanity as he did in his old murder case."

"And Paul Thompson was supposed to get Bobby Young transferred up to his floor?"

"Yes. But at that point in time, Paul Thompson had pretty much the run of the jail [he had been there five years, an unusually long time because the jail was primarily used to hold defendants awaiting trial]. Dade County Jail, the old jail, had and still does have a TV station. And he worked in that office.

"I didn't read the letter until I read it with Paul. [Kramer] put it in an envelope, sealed it, and gave it to me, and I stuck it in a book or something and I took it out when I left MCC, and the next week, or three days, or eight days later, I went to see Paul over at Dade County Jail."

"What did Paul Thompson say?"

"Said, 'No way.' He said, 'Ben's out of his fucking mind,' in those words. Again, please excuse me."

"Those were the exact words he used?"

"I will never forget Paul's face ever in my lifetime."

"Did he say anything else that you can recall?"

"Yes. He said, 'Look, you know, just tell Ben that I'll handle—I'll keep him cool,' or something like that. I don't remember exactly what it was, but some kind of story to keep Ben quiet."

"Where is that letter that Ben Kramer wrote?"

"Paul destroyed it. I don't remember if he destroyed it in my presence or not, and he told me that he's not going to do anything like that; that's bullshit, that Ben is nuts."

"But he destroyed it, not you," Ferguson probed.

"I believe he destroyed it. I know I was not very happy with the contents of the letter, and he certainly wasn't happy with it, either."

Asked Ferguson, "You've made a statement previously, Mr. Kessler, that Ben Kramer told you that he had paid $100,000 to have Don Aronow murdered. When did Ben Kramer make that statement to you?"

"He made it several times."

"I'm sure the first time would stand out in your mind as being an admission by Ben Kramer as to having ordered the homicide. Do you remember when?"

"The first time he said anything to me, again, to the best of my recollection, Ben was in jail, I seem to remember him being at MCC Miami when he discussed that. His discussion with me was in a very positive sense that he was, you know, being put in a position by Young; that he was afraid of Young because Young was crazy on drugs; that he was going to get implicated in something that he had nothing to do with and he had nothing to do with it."

"That Ben had nothing to do with it?"

"Yes. And that he was giving him the money or had given him the money because he didn't want to be involved. Again, he had nothing to do with it and he didn't want to get involved, but it was just cheap insurance.''

"You're saying it was hush money, is what he told you basically?'' asked Dohn Williams.

"That's a good expression for it.''

"So apparently that was not the money that had been agreed upon for the contract to begin with?'' Ferguson asked.

"I don't know what the agreed amount was. You may know better than I do,'' Kessler tweaked his opponents, "but I don't know what it was.''

"Then the $100,000 was more hush money to Bobby Young because Ben was afraid of him?''

"That's how—that's what he said in the beginning. He said it more than once, maybe twenty times.''

Ferguson tried to straighten out the story.

"Just so I'm clear, $100,000, you're certain Ben said, was paid to Bobby Young as hush money; you're not familiar with or aware of how much money was paid for the actual contract for murder itself?''

"Not at that time.''

"Not at that time? Did there come a time that you did become aware of how much was paid?''

"Only from what Ben said.''

"When was that?''

"It's when I first learned that Steve Romano was the intermediary. Whenever that conversation took place. And what Ben said to me is that he had given Romano— he had given Big Steve—that's the term he used—the hundred grand for the Aronow hit. Again, those are pretty much his words.''

Kessler tried to clarify that he never saw the money.

"Mr. Kessler, if I understand you correctly, are you saying that the story changed from that the $100,000 payment was hush money to that the $100,000 was for actually having the deed performed?'' Williams asked.

"Yes.''

"Where did the conversation take place when he first told you that the purpose of the $100,000 was to have Mr. Aronow killed?'' cocounsel Ken Kukec asked.

"It was when Ben, I think, was in E unit at MCC. It was shortly before his escape."

[A long few moments earlier, Kessler said the admission had come *after* the escape, when Ben's leg was in a cast.]

"Did you have prior knowledge of that escape attempt?"

"I had a good idea that he was going to try something."

Although Kramer was scared of Bobby Young, Kessler said Kramer was more spooked by Young's wife, Kathleen.

"Cat Young had become involved in talking to Skip Walton and Carl Davis and Tommy Teagle. Again, this is what Ben is telling me."

"About what?" asked Ferguson.

"About them not cooperating or stopping their cooperation or changing their story in the murder case."

"How was Cat going to stop Carl Davis and Skip Walton from cooperating?"

"Threatening them."

"This is what Ben is saying to you?" asked Dohn Williams.

"Yes. What Ben said to me was that Cat was going to dissuade Skip Walton and Carl Davis and Tommy Teagle from cooperating. If it meant doing something, that's what was going to be done. He didn't use quite those words."

"That Cat was going to do this?"

"Oh, yes. I think Ben was more afraid of Cat, physically more afraid of Cat than any other person I ever met that Ben had associated with in my life."

"How was Cat going to effect this threat?"

"That I don't know."

"Ben ever mention it to you?"

"Not that I recall. Maybe herself."

"Did it ever happen?"

"No, not—yes, I know Cat spoke to Davis and Walton. I don't know about Teagle."

"How do you know that?"

"Because she told me."

Kessler explained: "We went in my office and in the back, and she sat down and we talked, and she told me that she had spoken to Walton and spoken to Davis and there was just no problem, what was going to happen with their testimony as it relates to Robert Young."

"Did she say anything else?"

"That's what it all boiled down to. That she had spoken to Walton, she had spoken to Davis, both of them had assured her that they would never hurt Bobby. I remember what my responses were to her."

"Which were?"

"That they're full of shit. Again, excuse my language."

"That she's full of shit?"

"No, not she, Walton and Carl Davis."

"What was her response?"

"She said that Young has no problem. 'No worries' were the words she used."

Kessler recalled another meeting with Kramer at MCC Miami after Kramer had just talked to Kathy Young.

"He was literally jumping up and down. I mean, figuratively and literally jumping up and down, it seemed. Can I say what Cat said? What Bobby said?"

"You can say what Ben—no. You can say what Ben said to you," Ferguson responded.

"I understand. As a result of whatever Cat said to Ben, Ben was very agitated. He was petrified that Young was going to cooperate and give Ben up."

"In other words, implicate him in the Aronow death?"

"Yes. Those were Ben's words, that 'He was going to give me up.' That I had to go and see him [Young] or speak to him or do something."

During a different conversation at MCC Miami, Kessler said Kramer revealed who Bobby Young had called immediately after the murder.

"What he told me was that Young had called Big

Steve at the telephone booth and that he was concerned because the cellular phone that Young had used could be traced.''

''Are you saying that he told you that Big Steve was called at a pay phone?''

''Yes. He didn't use the word 'pay phone.' He said he called him in the shopping center, words like that. I assumed it was a pay phone. I don't recall exactly. I only remember him saying something about a shopping center.''

That was also about the time Kessler said he and Kramer addressed who they should hire as new counsel for Young, since Kessler was under indictment in Kramer's money-laundering case, and it was about to go to trial.

''I discussed with him the need in my mind that I felt Robert Young needed an extremely strong personality. That was number one. To keep him from cooperating. That a weak-personality lawyer would not stop or inhibit Young from cooperating. That Young's M.O. was to get to the end of the line, and then at the end of the line work out a plea. That Young's M.O., his *modus operandi,* was that if he had to make a deal, especially where it affected Cat, that he would make a deal and step all over or screw anybody else that was in his way at the time.

''I think Cat was already subpoenaed at this time, or there were discussions about it. The conversation was to the effect—with Ben, was that she was the connection between Ben and Robert Young, and Cat was the one that paid the contract.

''We discussed this problem about Cat at length. I told him that if Cat was put in any type of position where she was indicted or may be indicted, that Robert Young will cooperate in a heartbeat, in a New York second; that he will not permit under any circumstances Cat to go to jail.

''We talked about the evidence that Cat was the go-between between him and Young.

''Ben then tells me—I think it was the second time he mentions Big Steve's name. He didn't go into detail about Big Steve's role, but it was intimated it was really simple, that it was Steve who was the go-between.

"He had mentioned once before, probably 1986, give or take, it may even have been a little earlier than that, that Steve was friendly with—I don't remember if he used the [name] Bobby Young. I don't recall that exactly. But that Steve had—was friends with these people who did the—who were going to set up the murder of this witness in the Randy Lanier case and participated in two other murders. And then Steve was the person who set up these other murders for Randy Lanier. And Ben—"

"Let's just finish that one conversation," Ferguson cut him off. "Does that finish that lengthy conversation?"

"No, there was more," Kessler insisted. "Ben didn't want to spend the money [to retain another attorney for Young]. He wanted to get away with spending nothing. He wanted to get away with a story is really what he wanted to do."

"Story what, that his funds were tied up?"

"He just didn't want to do anything, really, if he could avoid it. And he talked to me about 'Why can't he use a public defender?' And I told him very pointedly, 'If a public defender got involved in this case, you're dead meat. You would last fifteen minutes before you'd be sitting next to him, hand in hand.'

"And he said, 'Why?' 'Because the public defender is not going to work. It's not the results that Bobby concerns himself with, but rather the fight. That if he feels if somebody is fighting for him and on his behalf only, Bobby will stand up. But anything short of that, it's just not going to work.'

"I told him at that point in time that unless matters changed drastically, the possibilities of Mr. Young standing up were remote. I felt that it was imminent, if not—not necessarily in the near future but closer to an indictment, closer to an arraignment, closer to a trial, that he was going to cooperate. And that he was going to implicate you and other people."

Kessler said Kramer told him he had someone in Colombia who could connect him with his stash of money, but when Kessler probed for details, he got vague.

"I felt that was a story. I didn't think he was going to try to call him, contact him, or in any way get any of his money, if, in fact, he had any money in Colombia."

"Are you saying you yourself did not know whether he had money?"

"No. Ben always talked about millions and trillions, but to get money out of Ben Kramer, I got to tell you something, you had to fight for it. He never voluntarily gave up a nickel."

At another visit at MCC, Kessler said Kramer talked about the getaway car used in the murder.

"We talked about the car and the color of the car and the individual who was employed at the car rental agency. Apparently this individual was supposed to have been a relative of Walton's or Davis's. I don't remember which one it is now. I believe it to be Walton, but I'm not positive. And they told him, or he told Ben not to worry, that he had this kid—that was the word he used—'under control.' And he didn't have to worry about the car, is what it was. That the car had been returned and repainted and moved out of the state."

Ferguson didn't follow up that answer, leaving unsaid the make and color of the car, as Kessler apparently knew it.

Around that time, Kramer also wanted Kessler to revisit Randy Lanier to get more money. Kessler said he did, twice, first traveling to the federal prison in Marianna, Florida, then Oxford, Wisconsin.

"Randy felt that Ben was abusing him; that this was Ben's obligation; that Ben had to start spending his own money and not spending Randy's money; that Ben was indebted to Randy or something like that. But he would see what he can do and if he can—he said, 'You have to bear in mind, my money is not in the United States, it's in Europe and I have a hard time getting at it. I'll do what I can as quickly as I can, and I'll try to get it to you.' "

Kessler relayed that message back to Kramer. He

wasn't pleased. For Kessler's next trip to see Lanier, Kramer's instruction was:

"Basically, you remind Randy that there were two more incidences that he—meaning Ben—did on behalf of Randy Lanier. And that if Ben goes down, Randy is going to go with him. And he doesn't want to hear any more bullshit about no money, the money is in Europe or the money's in France or the money's here or the money's there. That was the message."

"Then you went to Oxford. Did you deliver that message?" Williams asked.

"I sure did."

"What was Mr. Lanier's response?"

"Well, he turned black, blue, red, green, and orange. Jumped up off—he was sitting like you were sitting right now, just like I'm sitting slouched down in the chair. Randy is kind of a small guy. He was slouched down, and he jumped off the chair and started jumping up and down and started hollering and realized that the guard was right behind him, and he shut up and he says, 'I don't want to hear about that, I don't want to hear about these kind of things. That's not my problem. I don't want to know from it, I don't want to hear this garbage, and I'll see what I can do,' and words like that. 'I'll try my best.' And walked out, and I left."

Ferguson asked Kessler if he felt he was giving Kramer legal advice regarding potential murder charges against him during those meetings. Kessler said no.

"What capacity were you in at the time you saw Ben?"

"A friend."

"Were you committing any criminal activities by meeting with Ben and having these types of discussions?"

"I guess you could—"

"In your opinion?"

"I didn't think so, but I guess you could consider it that way. I wasn't doing anything to hinder the investigation. At least, I felt I wasn't. It's possible, I guess you can consider that maybe I was aiding and abetting something or other.''

''Aiding or abetting what?''

''Obstruction of justice.''

''In what form, keeping Bobby Young from cooperating?''

''Sure.''

''Were you doing that?''

''No. In fact, I advised Bobby Young to cooperate.''

17

February 1994

FIRST PERSON

I had no idea why *Boating* magazine would have left a message for me. I was eminently unqualified to write about boats—a landlubber, I knew nothing about them.

No, no, no, we want you to write about murder, said Hanna Rubin, the executive editor. Ah, now that was something I did know how to write,

Then again, I was deflated to hear that the murder case she wanted me to follow was Don Aronow's. I had been trying to ignore it for the previous seven years because it had touched a sensitive spot. Besides the day Hurricane Andrew had struck here, I could not point to any single scarier afternoon in Miami than the one when Aronow was killed in broad daylight, in between my current and former neighborhoods, which aren't far apart. Even though this is Dade County—known during most of the twentieth century for sun and fun, then in the '80s for glitz and violence—there remain safe and boring neighborhoods here. I happen to prefer those to live in.

But Hanna waxed poetic about Aronow. She wanted an elegy to him, and to an era since lost in powerboating. He was the Elvis of the sport, and he had a sexuality both raw and refined. The mere mention of his name to her readers recalled a '60s playboy lifestyle-of-leisure complete with speed and beautiful women hangers-on, and James Bond's masculinity, sense of adventure, and youthful energy. Everyone missed him terribly. True, she said, we were discovering that he was more of a rogue than we had known, but that only added to his lore.

In the next few days, I discovered that I had an unusual connection into the story, one that helped me decide to take it on. Paul Luskin knew Jack Kramer. Quite well, in fact. In the book that would become *Flowers for Mrs. Luskin*, I wrote about Luskin, the CEO of a chain of Miami TV and stereo stores, convicted for the attempted murder of his wife during their incredible divorce. Until a few months before, Jack and Paul had been incarcerated together, at federal prison in Jesup, Georgia—a familiar place to that book's readers. While inevitably discussing each other's cases, Paul had mentioned me to Jack and had shown him my 1991 cover story about Paul in *The Miami Herald*'s Sunday magazine.

Jewish geography? In prison? It's a small world, my high school friend in Baltimore used to remind me, annoyingly. Paul gave me a phone number and an address in Los Angeles for Jack, who he said would be pleased to talk with me.

APRIL 25, 1994

JACK KRAMER

Jack had made the same decision as Mel Kessler to help the Feds in their asset-seizure case following the money-laundering conviction, but unlike Kessler, he had refused to assist the state's murder investigation.

Jack's reward came in July 1993; the court reduced his sentence from nineteen years to five years and ten months. On October 15, 1993, after doing just over three and a half years, he was released. Further, his $200,000 fine was later expunged on verification that he had relinquished his entire interest in Apache.

I called him to say hello and that I was reading up on the case. Paul Luskin had already written to him to say I would call. We chatted, and he told me that he and Ben were at arm's length, which I later understood was because Jack had made the deal to testify that he did. Ben did not approve of any deals with prosecutors that would involve testimony.

I already knew from Paul that Jack believed his son innocent of the murder charge, but Jack freely admitted that Ben was guilty of smuggling, and that they were both guilty of laundering the profits. Despite that, Jack was still proud of his son.

"He succeeded in anything he wanted to do. Unfortunately, it was smuggling." He remembered that when Ben was arrested, "two kids owed him $500,000. He told them, 'Keep it for your attorneys.' "

May 27, 1994

Then, a month later, Jack called me; he had moved back to south Florida, which saved me a trip to California. We met a day later at his office; he was back in the lighting business—strictly aboveboard, he said.

Jack was tall and stocky, sixty-four, with a square jaw compared to the oval face his son has. He struck me as avuncular, vigorous but with a weary edge from his last tumultuous years. Since I come from an extended family of very charming salesmen whom I like a lot, I recognized Jack as such, but put up my same guard as I do for my own uncles.

In the movie _The Graduate_, one of Dustin Hoffman's family friends offers him advice for how to conduct himself in his anticipated business career—coming undoubtedly from someone who knew: "You've got to have a little _gonif_ in you." That's Yiddish for thief, and it was real-life advice that rang true, not a suggestion to go and stick up somebody. When Ben had offered Jack the chance to be around the tremendous smuggling profits he was earning, Jack wasn't able to say no.

But Ben had been accused of murder. None of my uncles had reared such rough businessmen-sons; in fact, many of my cousins, like myself, had rejected our fathers' entrepreneurial callings as repugnant, like Dustin Hoffman's character had, and found our ways into the arts. In my extended family in my generation, the biggest successes in business were daughters.

Jack didn't have any girls. Perhaps that's where things first went wrong.

Don Aronow had a little *gonif* in him, too, Jack said, without using the word. But that didn't detract from their friendship.

"There's no possibility there was any bad blood between Don and Ben," he told me right off the bat. Don used to come over to Fort Apache Marina two or three times a week to chat with them, and had even advised them on how to build it, falling back on his experience in the construction business.

"Don was very quick with figures. And he could smell money," Jack said.

We talked about the USA Racing deal. Jack said Ben wasn't a businessman, so he relied on him for advice; it was Jack's signature, as company president, on the sale papers. Jack had anticipated that U.S. Customs might nix the Blue Thunder contract once they discovered that Ben had purchased the company, so he insisted on a proviso that in that event, they could undo the sale because most of USA Racing's value was in that contract. Aronow was sympathetic; "He said, 'Don't worry about it. I'll guarantee it to you,' " Jack said.

When Customs did speak up, both he and Aronow called their attorneys and told them to rip up the papers. There were no hard feelings, Jack said, nor had there been any under-the-table money paid or unreturned. Nor had they negotiated the sale price; they paid the full price Aronow had written on a yellow sheet of paper.

The obvious question, then—so obvious that I didn't have to ask it—was if Ben didn't have Aronow killed, who did?

Jack thought the murderer was someone's jealous husband. "Don was a stud, but Lillian had him on a short string," he said. An obscure part of the USA Racing deal was a leaseback to Aronow for his second-story bachelor pad above the factory. [I had noticed that while reading through the contract—it was referred to simply as a "one-room office."] Aronow would pay $10 a month for it.

Or maybe, he thought, it had something to do with the Colombian mob-hit story, along the lines that Skip Walton had offered.

Another obvious question Jack anticipated was whether Ben's marijuana-smuggling empire had ever expanded into cocaine. It hadn't, he said. He remembered how much Ben disliked coke; right in front of Jack, he fired someone for using it and told his father not to defend him. Cocaine made a boat pilot lose his edge, and you couldn't risk that at speeds of 100 miles per hour and higher.

I asked about the day of the murder. Jack said he and Ben were among the first to get to Aronow after he was shot. They were there so quickly that he saw Don's Rolex still on his wrist. Its later absence that day had become a small mystery of its own.

"I saw the doctor keep him from swallowing his tongue and choking on blood. It was an extremely bloody scene. There was nothing we could do." They watched the airlift, then went back to the waterside bar at Fort Apache and had soft drinks. A few days later, when the cops wanted to interview him, they knew that he was under federal investigation and asked if he wanted an attorney present. He said no.

I asked about Greg Smith's deposition, a few months before, at which time he said that Aronow had been subpoenaed to a grand jury, but was murdered before he could be served. Smith didn't say, but the grand jury apparently was the one investigating the Kramers' money-laundering.

Jack responded, cranking up his volume and acting hurt. That had come up once before, he said, at the money-laundering trial in 1990, and federal prosecutor Robert Bondi had then *denied* that Aronow had ever been subpoenaed. "That's on the trial record," he said.

June 17, 1994

DON FERGUSON

Jack had volunteered to call Don Ferguson for me, to set up an appointment. When I first met Ferguson and cocounsel Ken Kukec at their Boca Raton office, Ferguson said they didn't usually meet with journalists before a trial, but they broke their rule this time because Jack asked them.

Ferguson went straight to the problems they had in the case. First, and perhaps most difficult to overcome, was the Jerry Jacoby issue: that was the name given by the man who entered Aronow's office, as well as Bobby Young's shipmate off the Cuban coast. The defense had nothing to soften that.

Nor would they be able to rebut much of the evidence that Ben had paid for some of Young's attorney's fees. The prosecution would call that "consciousness of guilt"—that by paying, Ben was trying to keep Young silent.

However, the two prison snitches, Cooper and Miller, were easily neutralized. Neither, said Ferguson, had a clean record of honesty. They had brought that out in deposition.

The biggest battle at trial would be against Mel Kessler, he said. At deposition, Kessler had admitted lying under oath at his own trial. But the assault on Kessler would be no-holds barred and personal. When Ferguson had been an assistant U.S. attorney in the Southern District of Florida between 1973 and 1976, Kessler once told the court that Ferguson had approved a sentence reduction for his client, handed the judge an unsigned motion, and said it was only a matter of substituting a signed, executed copy. In fact, Ferguson said, he had never agreed to the reduction. Ferguson brought him before the bar for it. Since then, he had considered Kessler "the worst."

There was also the message seized from Max Forman's office that read "Bob is back on 5 floor. He is still vacillating. If Paul can, he will."

Kessler had interpreted the messages between Ben and Paul Thompson to mean that Ben wanted Thompson to whack Young in Dade County Jail. But was the note itself really as clear as all that? Ferguson suggested.

There was also the matter of the failed identifications. Mike Britton had had the closest look at the man inside the Lincoln, but he didn't recognize Young at the live police lineup.

And as for the group of witnesses that first pointed cops in Young and Kramer's direction, none agreed with each other on crucial points. Skip Walton was now denying most of what he had originally said; Tommy Teagle was obviously inventing; and Richard Fidlin got nervous and stuttered when he lied, Ferguson said.

Meanwhile, on the affirmative side for the defense, Mark McManus—who had worked for both the Kramers and Aronow at the same time—would testify that Ben and Don got along, all the way to the end.

AUGUST 15, 1994

BROCK YATES

Since I was now affiliated with *Boating*, I felt it cricket to call Brock Yates, a Buffalo-based columnist with the magazine, who had commented about the 1991 *Motor Boating & Sailing* story a short time after it had appeared.

What caught my eye now was a line Yates had written: he knew "a much-decorated senior agent with DEA in Miami [who] says that not only did Aronow not deal with the bad guys, but [he] cooperated as an informer for many years."

Yates hadn't named the friend in the story, but on the phone, he told me: he was D.J. Lane, and he wasn't at DEA, he had worked for U.S. Customs. Lané had since died of Crohn's disease, an intestinal defect possibly caused by stress, he thought.

Yates said Lane had told him that Aronow had been a major source of information for a long time. He had been reliable and a good guy, and Customs had liked him.

Yates had some other Aronow stories. He had known him for fifteen years.

About a year before the murder, Yates remembered that Aronow showed him a piece of land at the end of 188th Street, adjacent to Apache, that Kramer wanted to buy. But Aronow wouldn't sell to him; he called Kramer an ''asshole.''

''It was implicit there was a lot of bitterness between them,'' Yates said.

Yates had written that he had always thought Ben Kramer was behind the murder, but to me, he said his first thoughts were that a cuckolded husband might have been behind it. Aronow was a ''ravenous womanizer'' and ''a world-class cocksman'' who liked people to know that about him. But, Yates added, Don and Lillian were close, and he had slowed down his womanizing.

AUGUST 18, 1994

JACK KRAMER

My interview with Jack was an ongoing thing. Brock Yates's observations about Aronow, vis-à-vis Ben, in the last year of his life had contradicted what Jack had said, so I brought it up, without revealing my source.

''People who don't realize how tight we were with Aronow don't know what the hell they're talking about,'' Jack responded.

AUGUST 19, 1994

MIKE ARONOW

Boating had been kind to Don Aronow's sons over the years. In March 1993, they published a photo spread of a publicity stunt; they sent Mike to Washington to lobby the Postal Service for a commemorative Don Aronow stamp. They even had an artist do a mock-up of his portrait—it was based on John Crouse's photo of Don smirking (and/or grimacing) after winning a race. In

April 1994, they devoted five pages entitled "Family Secrets of The Don," an excerpt from Mike's self-published paean to his father, *Don Aronow: King of Thunderboat Row*. Then, a month later, the magazine publisher used his column to promote David Aronow's new boat business.

Knowing that everyone else named Aronow had long since stopped talking to the press after the murder, Hanna dished me Mike and David's phone numbers, and suggested I hope for the best. David spoke to me briefly, said nothing of substance, and made an appointment to meet me at his boat shop, in Hollywood. At the appropriate time, I tried to find it, but the address didn't exist. I checked my answering machine to find an apology from him; he couldn't make it and we'd reschedule, but despite a number of attempts, I could never reach him again.

Mike, in New York, was more cordial. To warm him up, I encouraged him to talk about fond memories.

He reminisced about the summers in the late '60s when he was a teenager and his dad took him cavorting through Europe, winning boat races in France, Italy, Sweden, and elsewhere.

"When you're right there, it doesn't seem so dangerous. The parties the night before took away the dangerousness of the race. But 75 to 95 percent of the entrants didn't take the risks, and they didn't win.

"My dad was so proud of his accomplishments, and his boats. Nobody had ever come close to dominating a sport and an industry like he did."

After Mike's car crash in 1970, which left him unable to walk, Don put Mike in the horse racing business. At the end of his life, Mike said, his father wanted a Kentucky Derby winner more than anything.

"He would dedicate himself to accomplish the victory, and when he won, there would be such a rush of accomplishment, he'd want to feel it again. I felt it myself about making an animal into a victorious animal. A boat or a horse was the tool to do it."

Then I edged my way into a question of what his family thought about the murder investigation.

"It's difficult bringing up the subject of Don," he said. "For my mother and my sister, it ended February 3, 1987. They don't like to talk about it."

Then the real question: about the money-under-the-table story.

"Don't believe it," he said.

"But that's what you and your brother told police, the night of the murder," I insisted. "The cash stank of marijuana. It's in the police report."

"Is my signature on it?" he asked. No, I said. Police reports don't have signatures from witnesses.

"If I didn't sign it, I didn't read it, and it means nothing to me," he said.

The interview was going downhill fast. I got in one last topic before I knew he was going to excuse himself from the phone: what about the Kramer theory of the murder?

"I never knew Kramer. I never met him. His name never came up in conversations with Dad. Kramer idolized him—but he was one of many."

AUGUST 26, 1994

KEN KUKEC

Ken Kukec, cocounsel to Don Ferguson, was the backroom guy who knew every detail about the case—and there were a lot of details.

I got him talking about the pros and cons of the case. Kukec had been at the smuggling trial in Illinois, and one big con, he said, was that Kramer "looked the part of a thug."

But there was a new big pro. Judge Chavies had just excluded a number of state witnesses in one fell swoop because prosecutor Gary Rosenberg hadn't produced them for the defense to depose: Bobby Young's associates Wayne Shehan, Paul Silverman, and Billy Schaab, plus witness-at-the-scene Bobby Ralph.

Kukec said the defense had told the judge that they had had to notice all of those witnesses in care of the state attorney's office—repeatedly—and that Rosenberg had never produced them after almost two years. It all seemed to imply that either the state's case was falling apart because some of the witnesses who had originally set them on Young and Kramer's trail were now getting reluctant; or the state just couldn't find them; or that the state for some reason now considered them useless and had intentionally dropped them.

AUGUST 29, 1994

DENNIS FAGAN

Now that I had D.J. Lane's name, I could try to run down the Aronow-as-Customs-informant story. I reached Dennis Fagan, deputy special agent-in-charge (DSAC) for U.S. Customs' Office of Enforcement, in Miami. He had worked in the office for almost all of the previous fifteen years.

Fagan told me that just after the murder, the FBI investigated whether Aronow's murder had a connection either to Customs' Blue Thunder contract or just to Aronow providing information to Customs. It's the FBI's job, he said, to investigate if a federal employee or a government witness is killed. But Fagan said the FBI had decided there was no connection.

Fagan said he could not officially confirm nor deny that Aronow was a Customs informant, but it sounded to me like he just _had_ confirmed it. "I've heard the stories, but I have no personal knowledge of it. Then again," he added, "knowledge of an informant's name would have been on a need-to-know basis." Lane was a supervisor, he said.

He admitted that Aronow might have been able to provide information regarding Kramer. "There are a lot of possible confidential informants in the boating industry," he explained. Oftentimes, Customs identifies them by number for their protection. Sometimes they become witnesses to be used in court, but other times their tips must be developed so traceable sources can be used.

August 30, 1994

RON BLISS

Fagan suggested that I also speak to Ron Bliss, the office's assistant special agent-in-charge, because he had dealt with Aronow on the Blue Thunder contract. Bliss remembered Aronow as a blustery, impatient, straightforward guy.

He said Aronow argued with Customs all the time over the boats. Aronow insisted they set up their own maintenance shop because the boats would break all the time.

"He would talk like this: 'If you don't do it right, get the fuck out of the business. If you don't want to listen to me, don't do it.' He was funny. He was a funny guy. He didn't take shit from anybody."

"Did he annoy people?" I asked.

"Did he ever. He had an attitude."

Bliss remembered when Aronow took him, some other Customs officers, and Mark McManus out for a demonstration run on Blue Thunder.

"He only knew one speed—full throttle. I remember hanging on as it was popping out of the water."

But the boat was "top-shelf," Bliss said. "We got a good hull—of course, we paid for it." None of the hulls ever cracked, nor were there ever electrical problems. They required so much maintenance, he said, because "we put twenty years in five years on them."

I asked what Customs knew at the time about Aronow's reputation for selling boats to smugglers.

"He wasn't a stupid man. He knew smugglers were buying his boats." But Bliss didn't think he specifically constructed boats to order for carrying dope.

Bliss also knew something about Aronow's connection to George Bush. He speculated that Aronow met Bush when he had built boats for the CIA, and Bush was its head.

"When George Bush and Aronow were together, they were always close. I remember, when George Bush visited his mother in Hobe Sound [north of Palm Beach], Aronow flew there by helicopter."

"Why would Aronow sell USA Racing and its Blue Thunder contract to the Kramers, when everyone at Customs knew Kramer was a smuggler?" I tossed out.

"He was just that way," Bliss answered.

SEPTEMBER 1, 1994

RALPH JOHNSON

Bliss made an introduction for me to Ralph Johnson, who had worked for Aronow as a rigger and a mechanic for ten years, beginning at Cigarette. When I met him at his office at Port Everglades, in Fort Lauderdale, I spotted a model of Blue Thunder on his cabinet shelf.

Johnson, a blond, husky man wearing a mechanic's blue uniform, said he was one of the first people to reach Aronow at his car after he was shot. When he heard the shots, "I thought it was a pack of firecrackers that the Cubans were letting off." Most of the skilled-laborer boatbuilders were Cubans.

Then, half an hour later, at four o'clock, Johnson said he saw Ben Kramer at the Fort Apache bar, laughing.

That led him to a conclusion about who was behind the murder: "I'm a hundred percent sure it was Ben Kramer," he said.

I knew that police had talked to Johnson, but if he had told them the bar story, it wasn't in any police report, I said. No, he admitted, he hadn't told that to police.

He also told me he had overheard arguments between Aronow and Kramer. "Before the murder, I thought Kramer was capable of murder. He was mostly a blowhard, but if you were there and saw the arguments, you'd think so, too."

Again, that was something Johnson hadn't told police. He said a lot of other people had heard the arguments, too.

"That kid wanted everything. I stayed as far away from him, as far away as I could from that crowd." Johnson also agreed with the *Motor Boating & Sailing* story that Kramer wanted to replace Aronow as "king of the street."

It was obvious that Kramer's Apache empire was not a moneymaking proposition, he said. He built Fort Apache for $7–10 million to "hold his toys, his friends' boats. He didn't make money selling boats. He had no customers."

I asked Johnson what Aronow had thought of Ben Kramer.

"He was a joke. He didn't consider him a threat."

"Then why would Aronow sell USA Racing to him?"

"Aronow knew he would get USA back, so he didn't mind selling it. Don was a businessperson; he didn't care who he sold to, if they could pay—or he could take the company back."

I raised the suit that Cigarette had filed against Aronow in 1986, and their five-year non-compete agreement that was about to expire a month after the murder, in 1987.

All that was true, Johnson said; Cigarette was afraid of Aronow getting back in business and competing against them. In advance of the agreement's expiration, Aronow had begun to prepare V-hull molds for later sale. In fact, he and Dick Genth were going to introduce a new forty-five-footer in June 1987 at the Miami-Nassau race—John Crouse's event. When Aronow was killed, the plug work was 99 percent done, Johnson said; then he completed the work at the orders of Lillian and Mike Aronow. Eventually, the boat was marketed under the label of Aronow Powerboats, the company that succeeded USA Racing. Johnson showed me a picture.

Johnson theorized that Aronow knew his killer. "Don wouldn't stop in his car if he didn't know you." But he had stopped for the killer; the automatic transmission in his car was in neutral. Otherwise, when his dead foot jammed the pedal (gunning the engine full throttle, his final action a screaming metaphor for how he lived his life), the car would have taken off.

SEPTEMBER 6, 1994

WILLIE MEYERS

Johnson was good friends with Willie Meyers, another Aronow insider, and he set up an interview for me. I found him at a Fort Lauderdale marina mechanical shop, rebuilding a very large workboat that Customs had seized.

Meyers had connections to George Bush, too, but that was far from the only thing interesting about him. As a younger and more reckless man, he had worked as an underwater stunt man on the TV show *Flipper* and the James Bond flick *Thunderball*, and had been a commercial deep-sea diver.

He had also raced boats all over the world. In 1967, he competed against Aronow in the Bahamas 500, a 539-mile race in shark-infested and reef-strewn uncharted waters. That was the race that knocked Knocky House unconscious, and Aronow had had to slap him to bring him to.

Meyers had his own crazy story about that day: his twenty-three-foot Formula ruptured a fuel line with Nassau on the horizon. Racing with his father-in-law, a Bahamian senator, they limped into port and pilfered a fuel line from a parked taxicab. They replaced their leaking one fast enough to finish fourth in the race, two boats behind Aronow, earning $5,000. The taxi driver probably wasn't nearly as pleased.

Months later, Meyers beat Aronow in the Round Nassau race and set a then–world record average speed of 61.8 miles per hour. In 1971, he won the United States outboard championship, and he continued racing into the '80s.

In the early '70s, working for Aronow on 188th Street, he had sold Bush a Cigarette.

"He still has it. It does fifty miles per hour, which he thinks is fast," Meyers teased.

Meyers had stayed close to the Bushes over the years. Besides sharing some of their very informal pizza dinners at Barbara's invitation, Meyers had been in the prototype

Blue Thunder with Aronow and George when he came to Miami in 1984 to test it out—a photo op for the news.

Meyers had also since concluded that Ben Kramer was the source of the Aronow murder. For him as well, the *Motor Boating & Sailing* story settled it.

"Kramer was an obnoxious kid who wanted to be king of the street—except no one liked him," he echoed Ralph Johnson.

Meyers said he, too, had overheard arguments between Kramer and Aronow, but he couldn't be specific either about what was said.

"I stayed away from Ben Kramer. I thought he was a snotty, know-it-all kid. I remember I took him for a ride on Blue Thunder, with a washed-out blonde. He wanted it to go faster.

"Kramer always wanted Don to introduce him to George Bush. Imagine, introducing him to George Bush."

Meyers said Kramer wanted USA Racing as a means to wash his drug money. Since boats were largely a cash business, it was an ideal vehicle to use.

Again, I asked why Aronow would sell it to him.

"Aronow would sell any company he had, then start up a new one down the street," he said. "Don disliked Kramer, but he kept the upper hand with him. Kramer bought all of Don's [boat] molds. He would have bought a mold of Don's turds, if he would have sold them."

I got Willie talking about Aronow's women. "He had a lot of women. He got the cream. Me and John Crouse got the leftovers. He'd take 'em upstairs in his bachelor pad over the business.

"At a party, he once said to me, 'I've balled five of the women here.' All of them were with their husbands or boyfriends. He loved women. He didn't care if they were married or not."

CIVIL COURT FILES

I also buried myself in Dade County civil court files around this time. There were a few legal actions that were date-sensitive to the murder.

Aronow's friend Elton Cary—and later, husband to Aronow's (said-to-be) mistress Ilene Taylor—was getting a divorce from his wealthy wife, Frances (Frankie) Wolfson, heiress to her family-owned business, Wometco, which had owned Miami television station WTVJ, the Miami Seaquarium (famous for its dolphin shows), movie theaters, and a soft-drink-bottling plant.

Cary ran a south Florida bank, Financial Federal, and Miami Beach–based General Insurance Company (GIC). Frances had refinanced it all in 1978, and both spouses afterward each owned half the stock.

But the couple split in 1983, and a year later, Cary had tried to stack the board of directors with his friends—including Aronow—and they voted to issue three new shares of stock, giving Cary the permanent voting majority he wanted. Meanwhile, the insurance company posted losses of $6.9 million from 1983 to 1985. Frances, in a suit against her husband, Aronow, and others, charged that Cary personally had "removed" more than $3 million from the company.

By 1986, Frances began winning in court. In May, the three shares of stock were voided. In August, the court appointed an overseer to break the newly re-created fifty-fifty deadlock. In November, Cary's salary as CEO was cut almost in half.

On the morning of the day Aronow was murdered, he attended a Financial Federal board of directors meeting—something he rarely did. Two weeks after the murder, the court-appointed overseer removed Cary as chairman of the board and suggested that Cary be required to pledge his GIC stock as security to the company for his indebtedness.

I also checked Aronow's probate file.

After all his assets were liquidated, Aronow left $15,629,794. The estate paid $3.6 million taxes; $981,000 in legal fees—$263,000 to Murray Weil; and $396,000 in claims. Most of those had to do with the redesign of the Miami Beach house on N. Bay Road, which he and Lillian were just about to move into:

$12,630 for a burglar alarm; $30,000 for painting; $13,788 for gardening; $177,000 for decorating; $33,000 for shelves and cabinets; $11,000 for landscaping; and $17,500 for an 18-karat gold Bulgari watch.

From the remainder, as of August 1992, Lillian had already received $4.9 million; trust funds for Gavin and Wylie, her two young boys by Aronow, got a million each; Aronow's three grown children by his first wife, Shirley, got $569,000 each; and Aronow's two sisters each got $100,000. That still left almost $1.3 million, and all that was designated for Lillian and her two children. However, Lillian decided to split up that amount between the older kids, Michael, Claudia, and David.

Still, totalling up the money controlled by Lillian, that made $6.9 million.

Meanwhile, Lillian had remarried in October 1990, her fourth marriage.

The new man was Gregory Lovaas, her plastic surgeon, a Minnesota native, four years older than her. But first, the marriage had to wait for Lovaas's divorce from his wife.

The Lovaas divorce in May 1990 provided an intimate glimpse of Lillian Aronow, post-Don.

Like Lillian, Charlotte Lovaas had been a professional model. The couple separated in April 1988.

Lillian testified that was the same month she came into his office, as a patient. She had known Greg and Charlotte socially before that.

In May 1988, Lillian said, she and Greg traveled to New York together; she paid. By June, they were living together—she paid the $5,000-a-month rent on the home they shared; he paid for groceries. Over the next year or so, they traveled to Europe, Italy, Monte Carlo, Brazil, and London together. In Amman, Jordan, King Hussein and his wife had them as palace guests for three days.

In December 1992, a daughter was born of Lillian's union with Greg, but thirteen months later, Lillian initiated a divorce. This time there were few details in the files; a separation agreement that was signed within two months required Greg to pay no alimony, nor child support beyond a "voluntary contribution."

When Lillian changed her name from Lovaas, she went back to Lillian Aronow.

SEPTEMBER 9, 1994

JACK KRAMER

I told Jack about Aronow's estate, that he had left almost $16 million. Jack was amazed at the number.

"He didn't show it. He didn't spend it," he said.

"No one really knew how much money Aronow had. He said the house [he was building] was tapping all his financial resources.

"He came to me and asked if I would buy Cigarette Ranch [his horse farm in central Florida]. I said, 'What the hell do I need something like that for?'

"He said, 'Answer the same question for me—what do I need it for? I bought it to get away, and my wife can't stand it.' "

Jack said he asked Aronow why he didn't buy a yacht and get away that way.

"He said, 'I hate boating, you know that.' It was a hard thing to get him into a normal size boat—he hated it."

GREG SMITH

When I got Greg Smith on the telephone, he told me he didn't usually speak to authors, especially after Tom Burdick. He was proud that his name wasn't mentioned even once in *Blue Thunder*. Then, as he warmed up, he told me a story Burdick hadn't written in his book: Metro-Dade detectives had granted him an interview at headquarters, and Burdick taped it, without their knowledge—until his concealed recorder clicked off at the end of the tape. It didn't take long for detectives to hustle him out of the building, permanently.

Speaking of tapes, after listening to so many hours of

Ben Kramer's (legally) wiretapped conversations, Smith felt he had some insight into him.

"He's one of the most arrogant, self-centered persons I have ever come across. He's a piece of work. He'll latch onto you if you can help—and then he'll drop you."

An unintended consequence of those tapes, he said, was that Don Ferguson, Kramer's counsel, was now a witness for the state since he hadn't been able to convince a court that Kramer's taped conversations with him were privileged. That was likely to lead to Ferguson's disqualification from further representing him. Smith said he had had a problem with Ferguson anyway in that he had previously represented Tommy Teagle and Skip Walton. In fact, he said, Ferguson had represented Teagle yet again very recently, when he had applied for Lillian Aronow's still-unclaimed $100,000 reward money.

I cut to the chase. "So, did Kramer do it?"

"Absolutely," Smith replied.

"Are you going to win the case?"

"Yup. And if things work out on what we're still working on, it would be a lock." That was all he'd tell me about that.

Leaving that, I asked about other specifics of the case. Was Aronow subpoenaed, as Smith had said at deposition? Yes, he said. Detectives had heard about it the first week after the murder, but the Feds then denied it. Later, they said yes. Yes, he thought the subpoena had something to do with the murder, and no, he didn't think Aronow would have balked at testifying.

"What's always bothered me is, how did Ben Kramer know about the subpoena?" he asked me.

"Was Aronow an informant?"

"I had heard that, but it was never confirmed."

I reviewed some of the problems in the case, as Don Ferguson had seen them. When I suggested that Samuel Cooper and Cleveland Miller, the jailhouse snitches, might not be very credible to a jury, he stopped me.

"Don't underestimate Cooper and Miller as witnesses," he said.

MIKE KANDROVICZ

Willie Meyers had said that "Old Mike" Kandrovicz had been at the USA Racing office when the person who said his name was Jerry Jacoby entered. However, the police hadn't mentioned him anywhere in their reports, and when I had asked Greg Smith, he specifically told me that Kandrovicz was not present.

I got Kandrovicz on the telephone; true to his nickname, he was an older man with a gravelly voice. He said he *had* been there.

"He said he'd kill for his boss. Don had a grin on his face, he didn't think nothing of it. So I didn't think nothing of it," he said.

He described "Jacoby" as a "big, strong guy who looked like a bodyguard. He didn't look like a killer." He had a day or two of tourist-sunburn, and hairy legs underneath his khaki shorts. He wasn't a local, he said; maybe he was from the Northeast, like Massachusetts, or maybe Chicago. He had seen Bobby Young's picture printed in the paper; "It was nowhere near him," he said.

The Chicago reference was a tip-off; Tom Burdick had used Mike as one of his major sources. Burdick had written that the cops had gotten it all wrong; the killers were two Mob guys from the Windy City. Mike was the only person in the story who thought that theory had any credibility at all.

"So why haven't the cops used you as a witness?" I asked.

"I couldn't understand it," he said. He told both Mike DeCora and Archie Moore that he had seen it, but "I guess they didn't believe me."

After USA was sold, Mike went to work for the Kramers.

"Kramer wasn't the guy. Don and Ben were friends. Ben used to call Don 'Uncle Don.' "

"Right to the end?" I asked.

"Yeah," he said.

Mike said he was Aronow's closest confidant. He had worked for him for seventeen years, starting as a ma-

chinist and jack-of-all-trades at Cigarette. At the end, he
was a gofer and often carried Aronow's cash to put in a
safe-deposit box.

"There was no room in it," he said. "He needed another box. He asked me to find him one."

[If that was so, safe-deposit-box money was never specifically reported as an asset of Aronow's estate. There
was a listing for "cash on hand and in bank accounts"
of $122,572, but that sounded like something else.]

I asked if he knew whether the USA sale to Kramer
involved under-the-table cash.

"Sure there was under-the-table money."

"Did you ever see it?"

"No, I didn't see it. Patty never saw it, either. You
can't go by Patty. Half the time, she didn't know what
she was talking about."

"Did Aronow give it back?"

"I don't think he ever did."

Mike said that when the USA deal was first made,
Aronow told him not to tell anybody about it. But everybody else already knew, and told him, he said.

I also asked about the subpoena. There were two, he
said. The first one was for an appearance that was eventually postponed. "I seen the subpoena. Patty had the
subpoena. She didn't know what it was for, though."

"Was he an informant?"

"I don't think so. But he used to sell to smugglers.
They'd come in with cold cash and buy two boats. It was
obvious. That's why the boat business is dead today,"
he said, suggesting that with the demise of smuggling by
fast boat, the whole fast-boat business lost its main market.

He remembered, "One guy lost his boat in a smuggling run. The next day, the guy bought another. They'd
come in with valises attached to their wrists."

Mike speculated that had Aronow lived, once George
Bush became president, he would have appointed
Aronow an ambassadorship.

And he corroborated Ralph Johnson in that Aronow

would never stop his car if he didn't know the person. "Whoever done it, he must have known him."

SEPTEMBER 13, 1994

JACK KRAMER

I invited Jack to dinner at Unicorn Village, an airy, California-reminiscent, natural foods restaurant about twenty blocks from 188th Street. Unsaid was that less than a year before, Jack wouldn't have been able to make the appointment; he was still incarcerated. And even as we ordered, his son was doing life without parole—and faced possibly worse.

We talked about Ben. Jack said that the cards had fallen all the wrong ways for him. The two federal districts that were investigating him had competed to see who would try him first. He was sent to Illinois, but the Fort Lauderdale judge, Norman Roettger, writted him back—which the judge in Illinois ignored. In a Florida trial, Ben wouldn't have gotten life, he thought; marijuana smuggling is common here, and Ben wasn't that big (or so Jack felt). But in southern Illinois, he was very big.

As a child, Ben had a high IQ, and the ability to think things out and plan, Jack said. He was a leader, even as a boy. On parents' visiting day at Seneca Lake camp in upstate New York one summer, Ben's counselors asked Jack to please try to convince Ben to do as they said, because then all his followers would go along.

"He was a good boy. Now he's a good man. I just wanted him to be successful. And he was."

Even though his business was illegal, I thought it my place to fill in the blank.

Criminal or not, Jack clearly had a father's anguish about losing the ability to enjoy his son. Sometimes, he explained, he'd still spot someone in a crowd who he thought was Ben, until he got closer. Driving and seeing hitchhikers, he still slowed down, thinking and hoping one was Ben.

I had to say this for Jack: there was no question I asked him that he wouldn't answer. That was in marked contrast to the sons of the victim.

In an earlier conversation, he had told me that the ten years before his conviction "were the best part of my life."

"For a while, you were one of the richest men in America," I said.

"That's right."

I also playfully complimented him for making such a large contribution to reduce the federal deficit. His southern California card casino that the government had seized and still continued to operate was now worth $200 million, producing profits at a rate of $3 million a month. It was the largest U.S. government seizure in history, and who knows? Maybe the most moneymaking item in the government's portfolio.

I also noted to myself that I was buying dinner—well, actually, the magazine was.

We talked about those ten good years. Jack said Apache Boats competed directly with Cigarette; he traveled to Europe frequently and got Cigarette dealers in places like St. Tropez and Majorca, Spain, to stock Apaches. They sold boats to King Juan Carlos, television producer Chuck Barris, and actor James Caan. On the racing circuit, the Kramers partied with the international jet set.

And despite what Ralph Johnson had told me, Apache did make money selling boats, Jack said, even after Ben was arrested in 1987. That year, they made $800,000. In the next two years, the company did more business than ever before. In 1988, he sold almost thirty boats and told customers he wouldn't be able to fill their orders for months.

Apache's profits and smuggling profits were kept separate, he said. Ben kept his own books.

Jack said he advised Ben against starting a racing team because it was so expensive, but Ben wanted to do it. It cost $500,000 for the boat, plus $250,000 per race. "Eighty-five percent of the racers were smugglers. Who else could afford it?'' he said. In prison, Jack saw seven or eight guys who were associated with racers.

I asked Jack if he sold boats to smugglers.

"Never," he said. Aronow, however, "sold to everyone with money in their jeans."

"Aronow knew he was selling to smugglers," I half stated, half asked.

"Of course."

Jack repeated that there was no under-the-table money in the USA Racing sale. He recalled that the day they closed the deal, at Aronow's attorney Murray Weil's office, as an afterthought Jack said it had to be predicated on the Customs contract going through. Aronow agreed.

"No one knew about the sale; then, five to six weeks after, I notice that USA is losing money. I ask Mark McManus 'What's going on?' and he answers, 'Pop, I don't have any purchase orders.' People weren't buying cats."

Jack said he called Aronow to ask about the lack of orders as well as the Customs contract. He told Jack he'd get back to him later in the day, and at four o'clock, he called and said, "The deal's off. They know about your record."

"What do we do?" Jack asked. Aronow told him to meet at Weil's office the next day, and there they rescinded the contract. Each side was left only with attorney's fees—and Aronow paid Weil "fishcakes." That's to say, not very much.

"Aronow was an honorable guy, to a fault. He gave you his word, and that was it."

"Didn't you think Customs would figure out that they were buying enforcement boats from a smuggler?"

"In the back of my mind, I thought Customs would know."

"Wasn't there a certain irony in that?"

"I did get a certain kick out of it."

Given that, I asked why he thought Aronow sold them USA in the first place. Jack said that the only way to make money in the boat business was to sell companies, not boats. For Apache, the deal made sense even without the Blue Thunder contract because it included the land USA sat on, plus they could get Mark McManus. "He was the best builder and salesman in the whole fucking industry."

I asked Jack to detail what he had seen on the day of the murder.

He said he and Ben were drinking Cokes at the Fort Apache bar when their secretary, Edythe, ran in, shouting, "Somebody's been shot."

"All I remember is her tits up and down," he said. Jack and Ben ran out together to the Mercedes, about forty or fifty yards away. They saw Don, his face white, being supported by Dr. Wesley King. The car was full of blood—it was "gruesome."

"What happened, doctor?" Jack had asked.

"He's been shot."

Jack said they stayed until after the first emergency vehicle arrived, which was quickly, although Jack couldn't say just how long. I asked if he could remember anyone else there, like Mike Britton. He said he never saw Britton there at all.

He said he and Ben went back inside Fort Apache, then came out later to watch. I asked if he and Ben had discussed what had happened, and Jack said Ben felt "terror—he thought this could never happen to a man like that." Ben was "morose, if anything."

Back then, Jack said he thought the murder had something to do with a woman. He remembered one day when Aronow was with four women. "He brought them all to see me. The first one was twenty-four, down to nineteen or twenty. 'This is my new niece, Jack.' God bless him.

"He was the biggest womanizer I ever knew." Then Jack stopped. "I don't want it to appear like I'm knocking him. I admired him. I genuinely liked him. He was okay, Donnie."

Jack said Ben would testify in his own defense, whatever the lawyers told him. "Juries assume you're guilty if you don't."

Then, in the parking lot, he asked me how I saw the case. I mentioned that I had learned from reading depositions that the state was trying to get Randy Lanier to testify. Jack said he wondered what Randy Lanier could know, that he was just helping himself.

SEPTEMBER 19, 1994

KNOCKY HOUSE

I met Norris "Knocky" House at his propeller repair shop in Hollywood, a business Aronow had helped him start. At age seventy-four, he looked like Popeye the Sailor Man incarnate. A college wrestler, said to be the only man who could stay in a boat with Don Aronow during a race, he seemed to have lost little of his strength with age, and he wanted to prove it to me with a hard, hard handshake. He still had bright blue eyes—he was of Dutch ancestry—and blond hair, with only some gray in it, and tattoos up his arms in the maritime tradition. He said he had only quit racing in 1980, at age sixty.

"I once brawled with Don, right in the middle of his shop," he said. They were arguing over an improvement to a boat. "He could be very intimidating. He would fight, but so would I. He was bigger than I, but I was stronger."

The fight lasted all of thirty seconds. "I put him down. That was it. I won the fight. He walked into his office and said, 'I think we ought to have a beer.' He wasn't much of a drinker. I said, 'I think you're right.'

"He had a brilliant mind—he was much smarter than I. He had determination. He had no fear.

"Only one time were we scared," he said. That was during the 1968 Miami-Nassau race, when their boat burned. "Ten minutes later, he was making jokes in the lifeboat."

Aronow had a reputation as a gentleman competitor, and once lost a race so he could rescue two other racers who had gone overboard. But in this race, when Aronow and Knocky went in the drink, the boat behind them passed.

"Motherfucking bastards," House remembered Aronow

telling those racers later. In the end, they were rescued by a fishing boat.

Aronow was an "animal," Knocky said, but no wilder than he. "We complemented each other. He never liked to be second banana. He wanted to win—we both wanted to win. We went through hell together, and when it was all over, we were successful. Man to man, he was one of the greatest guys I ever met in my life."

And like Aronow, who beat up his body fiercely, Knocky had his lumps, too. In college, he had broken his neck, wrestling. Now he had a battery-powered heart pacemaker, an artificial left hip, and metal in his right hand. He said he was taking a huge amount of calcium to help repair his bones. "Otherwise, I'm doing fine," he said.

Unlike Aronow, he was a survivor.

I asked him to describe the psychology of winning by risking one's body. "I can't," he said.

Knocky said he knew Ben Kramer from racing. Oddly, he also knew Bobby Young, before his name arose in connection with the murder. "He was a coke-addicted smuggler," he said. As for Kramer, "he was a son of a bitch." He didn't want to point the finger at him, but he did think the state had a strong position, charging him.

"Don didn't do anything wrong," he said. "I think he was killed for jealousy."

Did Knocky subscribe to the popular "Kramer as king of the street" theory? "No. If anybody was going to be the new king of the street, it would have been George Morales. He was a gentleman." Morales, of course, had been indicted as a coke smuggler and pled guilty.

Knocky liked Lillian and had kind words for her, although he admitted, Lillian didn't like Knocky back. Yes, Don was a womanizer. "For the first year of his marriage to Lillian, he didn't fool around. But while he was alive, she didn't know he fooled around."

SEPTEMBER 21, 1994

DAN CASSIDY

To attempt to settle the issue of whether Aronow was subpoenaed, I went to the source: Dan Cassidy, the assistant United States attorney who got the Fort Lauderdale federal grand jury to indict the Kramers and Mel Kessler for money-laundering.

Tom Burdick had written that Cassidy was mysteriously "shipped out" of Miami, to the Denver office of the U.S. attorney, after Aronow's murder and before the money-laundering case came to trial. I knew that assistant United States attorneys are usually pretty silent people when it comes to talking with journalists, but I called anyway. I didn't get much from him, but I got something.

Cassidy laughed about his so-called banishment to Denver. Denver had snowy winters, but it was hardly the Gulag. "If we were exiled, we should get a check for moving expenses from someone at the U.S. government," he said. He called Burdick's book "a joke."

Greg Smith had said he couldn't figure how Kramer knew about Aronow's subpoena. Cassidy wouldn't talk specifically about the Kramer case, but he could quite understand how a grand jury target would know about witness subpoenas.

"When you're sending out subpoenas and interviewing, everybody knows what you're doing, that there's an investigation. Especially in a place like Miami. That's what I tell my class of investigators that I lecture."

As for Jack Kramer's reference that prosecutor Robert Bondi had said on the trial record that Aronow had never been subpoenaed, Cassidy said, "I don't think he [Bondi] knows. Just me and the investigators know. When Bondi got the case, there had already been indictments."

OCTOBER 8, 1994

WILLIE MEYERS

"I'm surprised Old Mike Kandrovicz didn't say that Ben Kramer was a jerk," said Willie Meyers. As for Ben calling Aronow "Uncle Don," he said, "Ben may have called him 'Uncle Don,' but it was a joke.' "

I asked Willie again about arguments between Ben and Don that he said he had overheard. This time he said he never actually heard them, but had walked past the two men a few times and knew that they had just argued. The real source for specifics, he said, was Patty Lezaca. "She could tell you every argument they ever had."

But Patty Lezaca wasn't talking, and at deposition, she had mentioned only one incident when Kramer had said something that sounded like he threatened Aronow—and that, Kramer had said to her, not to Don. The defense attorneys never asked her directly about arguments the two men might have had.

OCTOBER 12, 1994

BILL NORRIS

Bill Norris had been the assistant U.S. attorney who was Dan Cassidy's supervisor on the money-laundering case. Tom Burdick had interviewed him; he quoted him saying that Aronow was going to be subpoenaed, and that Cassidy had just signed the papers when they heard about the murder on the radio. Norris was now in private practice, and freer to talk than Cassidy.

To me, Norris denied saying that, and denied knowing about the subpoena at the time—which was consistent with what Cassidy told me, that Norris wouldn't have known. However, he did seem to imply that he knew now that Aronow had been subpoenaed.

"I don't know there's any reason to believe Aronow would have any direct knowledge of Ben Kramer's smuggling activity," he said. However, "there was reason to believe that he would have knowledge of Kramer's financial empire.

"But was he murdered because he was subpoenaed? What was the bridge—was he cooperating?" he asked.

That was a good question; a grand jury subpoena

meant that he would have had immunity from prosecution for whatever he would have truthfully testified to about himself, but on the other hand, getting subpoenaed doesn't mean that someone is necessarily a willing or cooperative witness.

Did the answer have anything to do with Aronow being a confidential informant against smugglers for United States Customs investigations, as Brock Yates wrote?

Or was it, as Burdick suggested, that when the local Mob heard about the subpoena, they got worried that Aronow would expose his own smuggling links to them?

GREG SMITH

Preparing for my meeting with Greg Smith, at his office at Metro-Dade Police headquarters, I remembered *not* to bring my tape recorder.

Smith was a tall blond man with a darker-colored mustache, in his early forties, who had spent twelve years on the "cold case squad"—a desirable assignment for a sleuth. For most of the last four years he had worked just three old, unsolved murders, of which Aronow was one.

He showed me a prize picture of Ben Kramer, posing for a *Miami Herald* photographer by giving him the finger. Near it in his cubicle was a photo of Smith and Jerry Crawford shoveling a grave after dark. Posted was the caption:

> *God grant me the serenity to accept the things I*
> *   cannot change;*
> *The courage to change the things I can;*
> *And the wisdom to hide the bodies of those people*
> *I had to kill because they pissed me off.*

Smith said that he had discussed the same subject of cooperation with Bobby Young in the past two years. But, he said, it wasn't likely that the state would consent to flip him.

November 5, 1994

JOHN CROUSE

After the murder, John Crouse left the boating business and opened an antique store on the main drag in rural Homestead, just south of Miami. Over the years, he had always been good for a quote, and often a pretty blustery one. But more than anyone else, Crouse was the man who had helped mold Aronow's image for the public. And, in fact, Kramer had hired him to promote himself, too.

So, he said, when Kramer was implicated, he was both surprised and not surprised.

"He's a complete coward," he said. "I never thought he had the brains or the guts for something like this. He was always a loose cannon, but nobody was ever scared of him.

"Unless he could make a phone call."

I met Crouse at his store, then followed him home to his 1928 house on five acres, which he claimed that Al Capone had used as a brothel—or so the lore went. In his sixties, Crouse was still handsome, a little bit burlier than in his boating days, with straw-colored blond hair and a moustache—a face with which he had adorned the cover of his 1989 book *Searace*, which documented the sport year by year and race by race. Perhaps it was the bible of the sport.

"The first time Ben Kramer surfaced, I was doing PR for Don. Jack Kramer asked Bobby Saccenti to hire him, to get him off the street. I thought Jack Kramer was the power in the family, but it turns out he was fearful of the kid."

The Kramers hired Crouse in 1982. "Ben Kramer told me, 'We don't like the drug guys. We're clean. My uncle's Joe Sonken.' I chuckled to myself; Sonken's Mafia."

[Sonken owned a locally famous seafood restaurant on Hollywood Beach called Joe Sonken's Gold Coast Restaurant, reputed to be a longtime Mafia hangout by the 1980 Pennsylvania Crime Commission. In May 1986, Kramer made news for rescuing the heavyset seventy-nine-year-old Sonken from the Intracoastal Waterway behind the restaurant, where late one evening he had inadvertently driven his station wagon off the dock. Kramer dove into the water, then helped squeeze him through an open window to safety.

The *Sun-Sentinel* wrote the next day that Kramer had known Sonken since he was 10, when his parents first took him to the restaurant.

Sonken, who decorated his restaurant with kitsch from his earlier days in Chicago, died in 1990, denying any Mob affiliation to the end.]

After a few months of working for the Kramers, Crouse said he talked to Aronow about Ben. "The kid's a crook. He's still a drug smuggler," Aronow told him. Nor did Aronow like it that Crouse was promoting Kramer.

Nor, in fact, did Crouse like doing it, either. He remembered that Kramer liked to show off in front of his friend James Caan by putting Crouse down. "I don't get put down too easily. I quit."

In 1985, Crouse said he brought some Italian boating magazines to show Kramer.

"What do you want, Crouse? You always want something," Kramer sneered.

"Fuck you, Kramer, you want a fight, I'll give you a fight. I just came here to give you something."

Crouse said Ben called him at home twice that night to apologize. Given that story, Crouse added that both Ben and Jack liked him.

"(Ben) Kramer called me from prison and asked for a copy of *Searace*," he said. "I told him, 'You're not going to like it.' "

Kramer asked why not, and Crouse said because he had referred to him as a drug smuggler.

"But I was framed by the FBI!" Kramer protested.

"Jesus, Ben, three times?"

Crouse said he never saw Aronow and Kramer together. He did think that Kramer admired Aronow, but that Aronow treated Kramer with contempt at the end.

JACK KRAMER

Jack agreed with my theory that Aronow and Ben were like father and son. I qualified that to say I believed so for at least most of the time of their relationship.

"Positively. No question. They were mentor/protégé," he said.

"Don constantly was going over to give advice, and Ben would go over and see him. Don had ideas for building the marina. The man was fantastic about merchandising. When *Warpath* won the world championship, he came over and said, 'Now is the time to make sales. Now advertise you're a world champion. Forget national champion—world champion is what counts.'

"That's when we put an ad in the *Robb Report* [an upscale leisure magazine], we'd make ten *Warpaths*, and then we'd destroy the mold."

"Did you sell all ten?" I asked.

"We sold four or five—so we never destroyed the mold," he said.

"How about up to the end? Were they still close?"

"It was a constant thing—up to the last day. They were hugging each other, punching each other in the arm. Aronow was a man's man—and Ben wanted to emulate him completely."

I asked if Ben had ever bought any boats from Aronow, and Jack remembered that he had bought three, between 1975 and 1976.

I paused to recall my time line. "But Ben was a fugitive then."

Jack laughed at me. "That didn't make any difference. Where do you think he was? In Spain?" Actually, he said, he was in Tampa.

"Aronow knew he was a smuggler. Don't believe anybody when they tell you Aronow didn't sell to smugglers. He knew them by first name. I know that firsthand.

"I don't want to knock him, to the advantage of my son, but the public image of Aronow was far from the reality of what it was—from my dealings with him. His image, it was manufactured. He was a tremendous promoter, equal to those guys selling bonds.''

"You mean like Michael Milken?''

"Yeah. He merchandised his name and his reputation. His fans, the magazines, they could only look at the veneer. They couldn't see through it.

"I'd say 65 to 70 percent of Aronow's total production was for smugglers. He always had three boats ready to go for cash. They were completely ready to run and had no interiors. A thirty-six-foot boat with the cabin completely empty. What was that for, if not for smugglers?

"He knew every big smuggler on the coast. Much to his surprise, his boat became a generic name because so many smugglers were caught in them.''

We moved on to Ben's chances of acquittal. "It was ridiculous, indicting these people,'' he said. "Young—there are two or three convicted felons concerned only in their own benefit. I was in prison; I know that.'' He pointed out what I already knew, that all federal prisoners convicted under "new law'' in effect since 1987 have to do 85 percent of their sentences, and the only way to shorten their time is to give "substantial assistance'' to prosecutors on another case. "Under normal conditions, they wouldn't have a case,'' he said, meaning that the snitches wouldn't have come out of the woodwork.

Then I mentioned the issue of Mel Kessler, and I could hear Jack's ire get up and his voice quickened and rose. "People will take what this rat–son of a bitch says. You know what he said to people in prison, who told me? He'd do anything or say anything about anyone to get out of there—whether it's real or not real, he doesn't care.

"Bob Bondi [who prosecuted the money-laundering case] said he's a liar. He's going to be a witness for the defense.''

When Kessler would eventually make it to the witness stand, Jack promised that his cross-examination would be something to watch.

"They will rip this man's ass out. They have the

proof—six inches thick of false assertions he's made in the past. They will knock this guy's jockstrap off. Ken Kukec can't wait to get to him. After they're finished, the jury won't believe anything he says.

"If they're relying on Kessler, they're up the stream without a paddle."

Jack said Ben wasn't the lead defendant in the money-laundering case—it was Kessler, a thirty-year criminal defense attorney.

"They really just wanted Kessler. We could have gotten a deal with Cassidy." He said that their lawyer, David Bogenschutz, was friendly with Pat Sullivan, one of Cassidy's bosses, and could have arranged a deal. "They said if Ben would testify against Kessler, they'd give Ben twelve to seventeen, and he'd serve about seven—which is what he's done already."

"But how about the Illinois case?"

"He would have never gotten Illinois. They would have kept the case in Florida."

"So why didn't he take it?"

"My son is an idiot. He has this *omertà* thing in his mind. He will never testify against someone."

Then Jack lamented, "This boy did nothing, *nothing* to warrant what's happened. He told me he didn't do it. He's not a child who lies. As far as I'm concerned, he's innocent."

I asked again about the under-the-table money in the USA deal.

"It's bullshit. If this animosity existed, why would he let me out? He didn't have to—he had it all signed."

"So there was no cash involved at all?"

"I would have known about it. I'll take a lie detector test. If it was, his attorney would have known about it."

During depositions, Murray Weil had agreed there was no cash in the deal. But Patty Lezaca said there was.

"Lezaca wasn't privy to the deal," he answered.

Jack said that Aronow just wanted out from USA Racing and didn't want to be in the boat business anymore, except for the new "surface effects" boats he was finishing at the end of his life.

"Before the Blue Thunder contract, he sold a couple of thirty-nines. The people who bought them complained to Don, 'How could you sell me something like this?' The boat was a piece of shit. They just romanced the whole thing up.''

"So you were going to buy a company that you knew produced a bad boat?''

"I didn't care, as long as people were going to buy them.''

Then, before we got off the phone, Jack offered me a wonderful piece of gossip that I knew I'd never be able to confirm:

"Did you know that King Hussein offered Don a million dollars in a briefcase *not* to marry Lillian? You know, Hussein bought USA after Don died for a huge amount of money—$6 million—just to give her money.

"Aronow told me this story. He could always smell money. Hussein brought in a briefcase filled with cash. Don asked, 'How much is in it?' A million dollars. He said he'd think about it. I'm sure he didn't, but he told me he did. He said it wasn't enough; she was worth more.''

NOVEMBER 7, 1994

HANNA RUBIN

My editor, Hanna, had been getting emotionally involved in the story as I had provided her with running details. Still at the office in the no-longer-early evening, she called me; throughout the day, she had been staring at a T-shirt she had placed on a chair. It was David Aronow's promotional shirt for the company he was trying to start up, and someone at the magazine had just brought it back for her from a boat show.

She sent it to me the next day, perhaps to be rid of the distraction: on the front, it had a pocket with a red "A" in a blue circle, a white five-pointed star cut out of the "A", making it reminiscent of Texaco's logo. The same artwork appeared on the back, only larger, and encircled with the name "Aronow Marine."

"It looks like a bull's-eye target," she said. And when I got the shirt and draped it over my own chair, I realized that the bull's-eye was right over the heart.

"This makes me sad. I feel Don's sitting there in the shirt. I miss him something terrible—he was the best the sport had to offer. I feel so angry. He had more life to lose than the rest of us."

This was not the first time Hanna had said something like this to me. I already knew from asking that she had never met Aronow, and at the time he was killed, she was working in New York as an editor at a magazine that had nothing to do with boats.

"He is almost a symbol. But these people are invariably flawed. His death was larger than life, but what in him got him killed?" she pondered.

"I suppose people shape their own destinies, to a large degree."

NOVEMBER 10, 1994

MELISSA

Jack had told me that Ben was close to Rabbi Moshe Horn, in charge of Jewish prisoner services for an organization called Aleph, run by the orthodox Lubavitch sect. Not entirely coincidentally, Paul Luskin was also close to Rabbi Horn. I was getting it from both sides to speak to the rabbi, so I put in a call and found his assistant far more interesting.

I'll call her Melissa, although that is not her true name. She was in her early twenties, a law student, and had a model's body. She also had the most unusual link between the Kramers and the Aronows—she talked to Ben on the phone quite often, and had dated and lived with David Aronow for the previous year. They were just in the process of breaking up.

I told her I admired her ability to get right into the center of a story.

She called Ben "a great guy" and believed that he was innocent of the murder charge. She also agreed with me that Don had thought of Ben as his son—and she had picked up resentment from David that his father's relationship with Ben was to the exclusion of his relationship with David.

Melissa even knew who I was from my fruitless attempt to meet and interview David.

"He was paranoid; he called his mother and sister in New York and asked if he should talk to you," she said. "They were nonchalant about it. But he told me he never gave you a quote. [That was true enough.] I'm embarrassed he just didn't return your calls."

I told her about the T-shirt, and Hanna's and my observations about the bull's-eye over the heart. She laughed. She said she had designed the shirt but hadn't realized that.

She had a few insights, from David, about Don and his family. She knew that Don had built boats with empty interiors, for smugglers. He had always worried that if one of his boats failed and a smuggler died, "it would come back to him."

David had hung around the boat shop in the '70s—that's where he met Ben—although he got the impression that his father had always tried to get rid of him, by giving him errands to run. "David thought that was because Don didn't want him to see who came in the door," she said.

David also saw pot at his father's office once, she said. "Don said he didn't use it; it was for his girls. I wouldn't be surprised if he had kept coke there, too. One of his girlfriends back then was a coke whore."

Discussing the case, she said Rabbi Horn had told her that there was a prostitute in the car with Don when he was shot. That must have come from Ben Kramer, I thought to myself. "I thought that was in the police reports," she said. It wasn't, I told her.

NOVEMBER 11, 1994

CRAIG DAVIS

Craig Davis had covered powerboating for the *Sun-Sentinel* in the '70s and '80s, and was still on the paper's sports staff. When I reached him on the phone, he was willing to talk about the bad old days on 188th Street.

"Kramer was a punk," he said. "Clearly a hood. He looked like he could be set off without doing much. Anything was possible with him."

He never saw Kramer and Aronow together, but he viewed Aronow in similar terms as Kramer, except that Aronow had a "Teflon character."

"He kept the bad people away from him. Publicly, he was fairly clean. But you knew he walked both sides of the line and was keeping it in balance somehow. You sensed it. It was like he had a second life."

NOVEMBER 14, 1994

DICK GENTH

Dick Genth was one of Aronow's oldest friends and competitors in racing and boatbuilding, going back to the early '60s. He bought Formula boats from Aronow in 1964, and Donzi in 1965.

Suddenly I realized that I could name a list of people who believed they had been Aronow's closest confidant. It might include both of his wives, Ilene Taylor and Missy Allen, Mike Aronow, Knocky House, Mike Kandrovicz, Patty Lezaca, Murray Weil, and perhaps even Ben Kramer.

Genth said he and Don were very close as well, but "I don't think he ever had a real buddy. He was so damn competitive, it created a lot of problems with people in the same circle with him."

Genth said he had talked to Aronow just three or four days before his murder. "Don always wanted to go into business with me. He was great at starting businesses, but he wasn't worth a shit in the marketing. He knew that. Like Formula—I took what Don had created and built on it.

"He wanted to do one more thing. His non-compete with Cigarette was ending. We were going to put Don's and Genth's names together. We had been talking for six months about it. Don had a joke about it—'You being German, me being Jewish, what a company we could make.'

"I got a call from him: 'You got to get your butt right over here. Drop whatever you're doing,' he said. I protested that I had a boat show in Philadelphia I had to go to. He said, 'But I need to do it right now.'

" 'Don, I'll be back in a week.'

" 'It won't wait for a week.'

" 'The hell it won't,' I said. 'As soon as I come back from Philadelphia, I'll come down and see you.'

"I was staying in a Hyatt Hotel in Philadelphia, and the manager called me. He asked, 'Weren't you once the president of Donzi?' I was.

" 'Well, you were just killed.' The news said the owner of Donzi had just been shot.

"At the boat show the next day, they thought it was me. People looked like ghosts when they saw me."

I asked about Aronow's business dealings.

"Don walked a very tight line—and the older he got, the tighter it got," he said. "He sold all his boats for cash. He never took a check. Don liked cash. He'd give you a receipt on a legal tablet sheet."

All the fast-boatbuilders knew they were selling to smugglers—indirectly, at the very least, he said.

"Dealers would ask us if we could build the front hatch a little bigger—so you knew what was happening.

"Don would sell to anybody. I'd go over there and meet some shady people. Some real, real shady people. I saw a lot of people from New Jersey, New York— cigar-smoking types."

"Mafia types?" I asked.

"None of this was a secret," he said.

Genth also had an opinion about the Blue Thunder

boats. He explained that catamarans are very sophisti-
cated boats, but Aronow merely split one of his deep-
vees in half and connected them.

"I said to him, 'Jesus, how in the hell can you do what
you're doing?' Blue Thunders were absolute pieces of
junk. He just laughed."

Genth said his first impression after the murder was
that a jealous husband was to blame. "Don had a lot of
enemies." Then he added, "I liked Don, of course."

I asked if he knew Kramer well. "I never got ac-
quainted with the guy. I kept my distance from those
guys. That whole bunch was a different breed."

"Do you agree with the Kramer theory?"

"I don't know what to think. I don't think I want to
know what happened. Kramer, as we all know, is very
capable of doing anything."

NOVEMBER 14, 1994

JACK KRAMER

Ben had called Jack the night before, and they had
discussed how Lillian possibly had arranged the murder.
Jack asked me if I had seen the will. I said I had, but I
didn't think that was the source of the crime.

Jack again recalled the time Aronow had tried to sell
him his horse farm. "He said, 'I got to sell it. She don't
like it up there. No ifs, ands, or buts, I got to sell it, even
at a loss.'

"You'd think that Aronow would be the last one to
be pussy-whipped."

Jack also thought that King Hussein was "up to his
ears in this.

"He had a burn for Don after Don turned him down
[to pass on marrying Lillian]. He didn't even come back
to him with a counteroffer. He [King Hussein] is a pretty
goddamned poor loser."

NOVEMBER 14, 1994

KEN KUKEC

Kukec admitted it would be hard to prove an alternative solution to the murder because "the trail was pretty cold by the time we caught it." But the theory that Kramer murdered Aronow fourteen months after the USA Racing deal fell through didn't make sense, he said. "Especially for as volatile a person as Ben.

"There were a lot of people who he rubbed the wrong way. But that's different than connecting him to murder." He laughed. "I don't think I'll be calling any character witnesses."

DECEMBER 1, 1994

RABBI MOSHE HORN

I took two notebooks to my interview of Rabbi Horn; one was the Aronow book, the other was the Luskin book. If only all my interviews could be so time-efficient.

In addition to being a rabbi, Horn was also an attorney. But he looked more like a rabbi; he had a curly red beard and wore a blue skullcap held on his head with a hairpin. He appeared to be about thirty-five years old.

Horn said he visited Ben an average of four hours every week. He described the security in the Dade County Jail: between Ben and the rest of the jail population, there were three secure doors, a twenty-four-hour-a-day guard that faced him, and a video camera overhead as well. It sounded oddly like the security for Hannibal Lecter. And as if the guards needed to be reminded, a sign was posted outside his cell: HIGH SECURITY ESCAPE RISK. Because of his nearly successful escape, Kramer is considered the most dangerous criminal in the federal prison system, Horn said—"or at least in the top ten."

Horn, like his assistant, Melissa, thought Kramer innocent of murder, and believed in his goodness.

"I appreciate his honesty and sincerity. I believe if Ben walked out today, he would be a religious person, a spokesman. He realizes that all the things that have happened to him are to make him change the world.''

Horn said Kramer's crime against God was that he hadn't fulfilled his potential. ''Such a young man, so smart. He could have used his business skills in legitimate business. He could have helped people.''

But I asked Horn, if Kramer was guilty of the murder and got convicted, would he support the death penalty for him?

There Horn paused to defer to a higher authority. ''Judaism has a death penalty. Sometimes death is justified. If the proper course for his full rectification is to die, then I would support it. Who gives anyone the right to take another's life? Every life is equal,'' he said.

DECEMBER 2, 1994

BOB GOWENS

Bob Gowens had been president and CEO of Cigarette at the time of Aronow's death. He was now in charge of sales and marketing for MerCruiser, in Stillwater, Oklahoma.

Gowens said he did everything he could to avoid the racers on 188th Street. ''They weren't my style. I was too busy trying to turn around a company in dire straits.''

But Aronow he knew, and, in fact, he was the one who sued him in 1986, alleging that he had violated their five-year non-compete agreement.

''He denied it at the time. We now have proof. Of course, it's a moot point now.''

Gowens said that although there was a conflict between their businesses, he and Aronow were personally friendly.

''Aronow was a very clever guy. You had to admire his chutzpah. He was nobody's dummy.

''He didn't hand out compliments easily. We heard that he had said to many people that he would buy Cigarette back for ten cents on the dollar. But I think he was shocked when we turned the company around and made it more famous than in his day."

Gowens said he considered it a great personal compliment when Aronow had asked to see him. "He said, 'When you came here, I didn't think you had it in you to succeed.' He said I had carried on the tradition of Cigarette like he had hoped it would be carried on. From that, he and I developed a business relationship that was based on mutual respect.

"Aronow had a real sensitive spot—like a lot of guys who are tough on the surface. He could be as charming as anybody, but he was real talented at turning it on and off. He had the ability to endear himself to people, but he was, number one, a businessman. He was driven for business reasons for most of what he did."

Gowens remembered hearing the "pops" of the bullets on the day of the murder. He was sitting in his office.

"I have to believe the cops didn't know how to begin. It didn't matter which way you turned, there was a plausible motive—the businesses he had dealt with, women who wanted to get back at him.

"A cop asked me, 'Where the hell do you start?' "

Gowens also admitted that he himself had been under suspicion at the beginning because of the conflicts and legal actions between his company and Aronow. But after the police spoke to him a few times, they dropped that notion.

"I talked to a cop, I think it was DeCora, a few days after. I said I thought the hit was amateurish—there were so many people around, it was a one-way street.

"The cop said, 'Absolutely not. Just the opposite. It's as professional as they get. The best hits are in broad daylight. Our problem is there are fifty-plus witnesses, and at trial, they'll inevitably disagree, and they'll get off.' "

Gowens said he had every reason to believe, in retrospect, that Aronow knew something was going to happen to him in the last weeks or months of his life.

"He talked to me more. It was out of character, a little

strange to me. His manner was quite sensitive, reflective, different than in the past.

"I didn't make any sense out of it at the time, then someone else said to me the same thing, and I thought about it. He never said anything about being in danger.

"The last time I saw him, I was in the back of his shop and he offered me a Cuban cigar. I was smoking a Partagas, which is the best domestic cigar. He reached into my mouth, pulled out my cigar, and threw it in the water. Then he gave me a half dozen real Cuban cigars, that he could get somehow."

That story was astoundingly similar to the one about Ben Kramer yanking tobacco cigarettes out of people's mouths at rock concerts in the early '70s, then encouraging them to smoke pot. I told that to Gowens, and he laughed.

"Aronow told me, 'I think I want to get out of this, and get into something else.' He was building his forty-five-foot mold, and he asked me if I wanted it. That was strange because, months before, he was pounding his chest about the boats.

"It seemed out of character. His whole personality changed in his last few weeks. It was as if he was saying, 'The hell with it.' "

Gowens explained that Aronow's competitors on 188th Street had changed as the years went by, and so had the rules of doing business. In the early years, his rivals were good-natured, and Aronow could get away with how he liked to do business, which was cutthroat. That was the way he treated Cigarette's new owners in the beginning, hoping they would fail—and attempting to tip the balance if he could—so he could buy back the company for a profit.

Cigarette's new owners were legit people, he said, but many other fast-boat builders weren't. Meanwhile, Aronow practiced business like he always had.

"I think he was shocked by the new Miami standard," Gowens said. And considering the violent way he was murdered, "I believe he underestimated his foe."

DECEMBER 22, 1994

JACK KRAMER

Jack had been ruminating more about the million-dollar cash under the table story:

"Why in the world would anyone give Aronow that kind of money for that fa-cockta company?" All USA Racing had was the Blue Thunder contract, he said; besides that, no one had bought the catamaran save a few of his regular customers.

"I took the numbers through on my PC. I figured that if the company's not worth a shit, I've got the land. Six hundred thousand was high priced for it; it was probably worth three or four hundred thousand."

JANUARY 29, 1995

KEN KUKEC

"I don't see how the prosecution can go under the subpoena theory," said Ken Kukec. "There's no one on their witness list to prove it."

In fact, Kukec said, the *defense* wanted to depose two of the men most likely to know whether or not a subpoena had been issued: Dave Borah, the DEA agent who had co-led the money-laundering investigation, and assistant U.S. attorney Robert Bondi, who prosecuted it. But to do that, the federal Department of Justice had to approve, which they hadn't so far.

"Bondi is on *our* witness list. We have a letter from Bondi to a defense lawyer on another case saying that Kessler perjured himself."

Kukec, cocounsel for Ben Kramer in the money-laundering case as well, said Aronow's name never surfaced in that investigation.

"If the Feds thought he had murdered Don Aronow, Ben would have been indicted in federal court for obstruction of justice. You think they'd sit on their hands with something like this? They would not have hesitated. They would have used it at his [laundering] trial as consciousness of guilt, and to muddy up the waters."

We also discussed the logic of subpoenaing Aronow. "It doesn't have the ring of truth to it," he said. "If he's a rat, he doesn't need a grand jury subpoena. If he's unwilling to testify, he claims five [the Fifth Amendment].

"Was there an immunity offer prepared, to force him to talk? And what's he going to say that's going to get Kramer to want to kill him?

"A grand jury subpoena means they're getting no place. If he's a cooperating witness, he comes in and talks. If he's not talking, he needs a subpoena."

Kukec added that Mel Kessler had never linked an Aronow subpoena with the murder. In fact, Kukec said, "He's never come up with any motive."

"Motives are less necessary when you have an explosive personality," I suggested.

"If you're explosive," Kukec retorted, "you don't wait a year and a half to do it. I can tell you, if there's something on Kramer's mind, he doesn't wait a year and a half to tell you."

FEBRUARY 1995

BOATING

My article appeared, headlined "Why Don Aronow Had to Die." The magazine titled it, and although it posed the most compelling question of the story, I wasn't sure I knew the answer yet myself.

Maybe they didn't think I did, either. Since it began on page 174, and there was no mention of it on the cover, I got the feeling they had buried it. I think, in the end, they were disappointed that it didn't have any shattering new insights like the *Motor Boating & Sailing* story or *Blue Thunder*.

Although the month of publication was the eighth anniversary of the murder, I had written that the trial was still a vague few months off. By the time the story hit the newsstand, the trial date had been postponed indefinitely once again, pending pretrial rulings from the appeals court. Would this case ever get resolved?

MAY 8, 1995

FOIA FROM THE DRUG ENFORCEMENT ADMINISTRATION

My Freedom of Information Act requests to agencies of the federal government had largely been a washout. Under federal law, you have all sorts of privacy rights to keep buttinskies like me away from the files that the federal government collects on you—unless I get your signature to let me see them. That's usually a pretty difficult question to ask.

However, dead people have none of those rights. Normally, all that's required for the Feds to open wide their files, without a signature, is proof of death. That can be demonstrated by death certificate, newspaper obituary, or, in Don Aronow's case, a front page headline.

But denials of FOIA information can speak loudly, too. The U.S. attorney's office confirmed that they had information on Aronow but couldn't release it yet because that would interfere with still-pending enforcement proceedings. Interesting, considering Kukec had said that Aronow's name had never come up in Kramer's money-laundering investigation.

The FBI and U.S. Customs confirmed that they, too, had material on Aronow, but the FBI is infamous for its years-long waiting list, and Customs was backlogged as well. The CIA and Secret Service responded promptly with material, but there was nothing in either small batch to write about. The CIA had conducted some sort of investigation of Aronow in 1984, but all I got was copies of index cards and punch cards—nothing of actual intelligence reports, if there were any. The date suggested to me that it had something to do with the Blue Thunder contract.

However, the DEA sent me a few documents full of blackouts that were interesting, on close scrutiny. Their

Fort Lauderdale office had called the Metro-Dade Police homicide unit on the same day as the murder, once they heard about it.

Also, the DEA's case file number began with the numeral 86; that meant the case had been opened prior to the murder. On another page, it appeared that the DEA's program code for the file was "Operation Man," also known as Operation Isle of Man, the money-laundering investigation of the Kramers.

There was more that struck me as funny on the page, information that had been compiled the same day as the murder:

"According to [blackout], Aronow, prior to the shooting, had walked from his USA Racing office on N.E. 188th Street to the Fort Apache Marina, also on N.E. 188th Street.

"Aronow attended a short meeting at Fort Apache Marina with [blackout] and then returned on foot to the USA Racing offices.

"A short time later, Aronow returned to Fort Apache Marina in his white Mercedes for a second meeting.

"As Aronow left the second meeting and pulled his car onto N.E. 188th Street, a second vehicle, described as a dark-colored four-door Lincoln, pulled alongside Aronow's car.

"According to [blackout], Aronow rolled down his driver's-side window as the driver of the Lincoln motioned for Aronow to stop.

"The driver of the Lincoln also pulled his driver's window down, at which time the driver of the Lincoln shot Aronow at least five times with a .45-caliber weapon. Aronow subsequently died from the gunshot wounds on 2/3/87."

At the end of the report, there were three names for indexing; one was Aronow, and two were blacked out. However, the second name was not completely blacked out; I could read that it said "Saccenti, Robert."

Some of this information contradicted what I had come to accept as a result of reading police reports and witness statements.

First, I had never been led to believe that Aronow had had a meeting that day at Fort Apache Marina—owned by the Kramers—much less two. But actually, there were some obscure references to it; Mike Aronow told Detective Sheldon Merritt that Don had called his house in New York at about two o'clock that day and talked to Ellen Aronow, Mike's wife. Mike passed on what Ellen had told him: Don had been in a good mood and said he was about to have a meeting at the Apache Marina.

Also, Ilene Taylor, at her police interview a week later, referred to a meeting between Don and Ben Kramer the day *before* the murder; she said she didn't know if it had taken place. She knew Don had sold USA Racing to Kramer in about 1985 and then bought it back. But just recently before the murder, she said, he and Ben had begun talking about it again.

And for that matter, former Fort Apache Marina employee Scott Deering—who had written a letter to police from a Broward County jail in 1990—said Aronow had met with Kramer at Fort Apache the day of the murder, and that they had argued. However, he couldn't remember who had told him that.

According to witnesses, Aronow walked into his office at about two o'clock, and a few minutes later, the Jerry Jacoby incident occurred. A few minutes after that, Aronow left the office. Then Patty Lezaca said Ben Kramer called for him. She thought Don had left for the day.

But Don walked back in ten minutes later. USA Racing employee Mike Peters said they had been talking about Peters's salary. Lezaca gave Don the message from Kramer, but Don didn't seem interested in talking to him. He walked out again, saying he would stop by to see Bobby Saccenti, then go home.

Another ten minutes later, Ben Kramer called again, Lezaca said.

At Saccenti's shop, Aronow found Saccenti, metalwork subcontractor Mike Britton, and Saccenti's customer, George Bacher. Here, the record was extremely muddy.

The problem was Britton. When he gave police a taped

statement on the evening of the murder, he said Aronow had asked him about finding some molding for his new house and a boat. Then Britton said he had to go, and Aronow said the same thing.

But at his 1993 deposition to defense attorneys, Britton said Aronow had asked him to come to his house right then to look at a brass staircase. He agreed, and off they went in separate cars, Britton in the lead, only Britton said he first had to drop off something at Fort Apache Marina.

Which was it? And why the contradiction?

Even besides that, Britton had severely contradicted himself earlier on other major points. Ten minutes after the shooting, Officer Oscar Plasencia wrote that Britton told him he had seen the Lincoln's driver lower his window and fire five shots. But later that evening, Britton said he had only heard the shots—and there had been three, not five.

Clearly, the third blackout name on the index was Britton's. "According to [Britton?], Aronow rolled down his driver's side window as the driver of the Lincoln motioned for Aronow to stop."

Britton was consistent in saying that he had passed the Lincoln and gotten an eye-contact look at its occupant. But that first night, asked whether he could identify the man in the Lincoln if he would ever see him again, Britton answered, "I honestly don't know, you know, it's very hard."

And, in fact, at the police's live lineup, he failed to identify Bobby Young.

And what of Saccenti? Was he the source of information that Aronow had met twice at Fort Apache Marina that day? Tom Burdick had quoted Aronow asking Saccenti at his shop, "So what do you think—is Ben in? Maybe I'll stop by and see him. Well, see you later, kid." Burdick wasn't crystal clear on who had told him that, Saccenti or Britton, but more likely it was Saccenti. (I had tried to get Saccenti to talk months before, but with absolutely no success.) So that made for three additional references to at least one Aronow meeting that day at

Fort Apache, plus a fourth to a meeting the day before.
Very curious.

May 31, 1995

JACK KRAMER

Jack called to tell me that the state had lost its appeal
regarding the attorney-client privilege between Mel Kessler and Bobby Young. Kessler would be prohibited from
testifying to whatever Young had told him, even though
he said Young knew he had shared much of it with Ben.

However, the court affirmed that Kessler would still
be able to testify to whatever he said Ben told him, because no attorney-client privilege existed between them.
Regardless of that concession, the ruling was a huge set-
back for the state's case.

Jack also said he had tried to investigate for himself
whether Aronow was subpoenaed. Since Jack had given
substantial assistance to the Feds a few years before and
gotten his sentence reduced, he was now on close terms
with DEA agent Dave Borah and IRS agent Roger Edwards, both of whom had opposed him previously.

"I took it upon myself to ask these people whether
Aronow was going to testify at a grand jury against
Ben," he said. "Edwards said he checked every agency
to see if Aronow was ever subpoenaed, and he didn't
find any. Borah said the same thing."

June 5, 1995

DON FERGUSON

Back in September 1994, DEA and U.S. Customs
agents, holding search warrants, raided the office of Don
Ferguson and other criminal defense attorneys who represented members of the Cali drug cartel. They gathered
up files, computer disks, and even computers themselves,
looking for evidence that those attorneys might have ob-
structed justice through witness tampering, jury tampering, and money-laundering.

Then, on this day, a federal grand jury in Miami indicted Ferguson, five other attorneys, and fifty-six others. Ferguson was charged with racketeering, conspiracy to import and distribute cocaine, and money-laundering. Further, he was accused of notarizing signatures of drug smugglers on fake affidavits; using drug money for bail; and threatening smugglers not to cooperate with the government.

A month before, three of the other five attorneys had pled guilty to obstruction of justice.

One of the other two attorneys who had denied the allegations was William Moran, who at times had represented leaders of both the competing Cali and Medellin Colombian cartels. One of his clients was Miguel Rodriguez Orejuela, a head of a branch of the Cali cartel (until his capture by Colombian authorities). According to the indictment, Rodriguez Orejuela paid $115,000 for the murder in October 1990 of the secret DEA informant whose work had led to George Morales's 1986 arrest.

The indictment further read that Moran confirmed to Morales who the informant was. Freed after a sentence reduction for assisting the Feds to convict another top Cali cartel member, Morales then allegedly asked Rodriguez Orejuela to order a hit. (Morales himself died in Colombia in 1991. Perhaps it was a car accident—he was speeding on a rainy night, drinking champagne with a young woman, when his car smashed into a truck. Or perhaps it was a set-up murder.)

[A month later, Ferguson pled guilty to charges of obstruction and laundering, carrying seven to nine years of prison time. His attorney said Ferguson didn't want to risk losing at trial and getting life without parole, all the while paying for a very expensive defense. Part of his plea agreement included an offer to enter the witness protection program.]

The case came to trial in May 1997. Ferguson testified for the government, but after five months, including three weeks of deliberation, a jury acquitted the remaining two attorney/defendants, Moran and Michael Abbell, of racketeering and hung on the cocaine and money laundering charges.

JUNE 15, 1995

JUDGE'S RULING

Once again, Bobby Young's defense won a major pre-trial victory in court. Circuit judge Michael Chavies ruled that the prosecution could not introduce Greg Smith's testimony of his interviews with Young in 1990, both in jail and on the day of the police lineup. Smith had said Young told him, just after the lineup, that he was surprised the secretary in Aronow's office [Lezaca] hadn't recognized him, because she had gotten the best look.

But Young had set the ground rules for the interview in advance. He had told Smith he would only talk "off the record" if Smith wouldn't administer his Miranda rights; if he did, he wouldn't utter a word. Smith agreed; then Young talked.

That was enough, Chavies wrote, to disqualify use of the interview.

JUNE 28, 1995

NEWCOMB AND FRAN GREEN

Since my entrée into this story had come from a marine magazine, I hadn't chased Aronow's horse-racing enterprises much. So, kind of picking up loose ends, I found Newcomb Green, who had trained many of Aronow's horses and, in fact, took one of them to the Kentucky Derby.

Green wasn't a betting man, and he knew very little about that side of Aronow. In fact, Aronow's finest quality, to him, was that he had left him alone to do his work and had never second-guessed him.

"I always considered Don to be the best owner I ever had," he said. "I trained horses six years for him. In that time, he came out to the track in the morning twice. Once, *Turf & Sport Digest* wanted pictures, and the other, he wanted to show one of his lady friends his horses."

Green said he had a complete photo collection of each time an Aronow horse had made it into the winner's circle—and that Aronow was in almost every one of the shots. That alone induced me to go meet him and his wife, Fran, at their home in Hallandale, not far from Gulfstream Park race track—which itself was not far from 188th Street.

When I got there, I found a treasure trove: about ten albums full of winner's circle pictures, and clips and videos about Aronow in life and death that Fran had collected and wanted to share with me, as Aronow's biographer—or, and I'm not sure if I'm inventing a new word, his necrographer.

Fran and Newcomb, in their seventies but youthful, were not jet-setter types, but they had been friends with Don and Lillian. "He had a charm about him, a smile. You just believed him," she said. "He had a smile that could close a deal."

However, neither of them harbored any illusions about Aronow. They knew he was a tough businessman and that he fooled around on the side, but he had some redeeming values, too. He had always been kind and generous to the Greens, never tried to take the least bit advantage of them, and was never late in paying his bills. In fact, one of the reasons they were comfortable in their later years, and had the money to take annual summer bicycle trips to Europe, was that Aronow had helped provide for them.

Fran played a video of a 1986 race that Don's horse My Prince Charming had run at Gulfstream, in the ironically named Fountain of Youth Stakes. ESPN had broadcast it, and before it went off, Pete Axthelm called the horse the "long shot of the day." In fact, it came from behind to win.

Although I had seen many still pictures of Aronow, I realized I had never heard him speak, and here he was in the winner's circle, with Lillian. Don wore a blue sportcoat and a pink shirt, open at the collar, while Lillian wore a green dress and pearls. At every pause after Don's responses, she looked poised to answer a question herself, but her chance never came.

What Don said in the interview was irrelevant. What

was interesting was listening to his remainder of a Brooklyn accent, and, as Fran pointed out, his rough edges but warm, easygoing way. Every tale I had heard about Aronow made him out to be invulnerable, a mad sports hero, but here was something human, something very vulnerable about him. He stumbled over his words, and his banal responses showed an absolute lack of preparation or polish. Nor did it matter to him.

I spent the whole evening discussing the case with the couple, even though Newcomb had to wake up the next morning at 3:30 to get to the barn, like every morning. Near the end of the evening, Fran volunteered that Aronow would have liked me. I was flattered, but I had long begun to lose it for Aronow, after learning so much about him.

"But would I have liked him?" I asked her.

"Definitely, yes, as long as you didn't do any business with him."

I thought about it later. The Aronow I saw on the video was not a complex man, just a very driven one. He needed to win, needed to crush others, needed the world's adulation, needed women's adulation. Nor did I think he was as handsome a man as everyone had said—I thought he was coarse, and I wondered why so many delicate-in-appearance women were attracted to him. Money? Maybe they wanted to see if they were up to the task of taming the savage beast. Who had money.

I wouldn't have liked him.

But the Greens had liked him, and he treated them wonderfully. "What was there not to like about him?" Fran said. Everyone else I had talked to had seen Aronow in full-competition mode. But if he wasn't competing against you, he was human. Nobody else had been able to show me that side of him.

Fran asked me to return another night, after she could make a copy of her collection of Aronow stories on video. It began with local news reports beginning just an hour and a half after the shooting. Fran had been quick on the record button, recording for posterity.

When I came back, she had found an NBC News segment on the story, aired in April 1991 on their magazine show *Exposé*. We watched it together, and my mouth dropped open.

NBC's reporter Noah Nelson had interviewed Tom Cash, then special agent-in-charge of the DEA's Miami office:

"The IRS was looking at Aronow very closely at the time of his death, as was DEA," Cash said. "And indeed, it now is known that there were strong reasons to believe that the boat business was a beautiful money-laundering scam."

Nelson: "Investigators tell *Exposé* that Aronow *knowingly* received hundreds of thousands of dollars in laundered drug money for the sale of his company. And that Aronow raked in lots of cash for boats he'd never built.

"In January 1987, the IRS seized records of Aronow's sale of his company to the Kramers. Just one day before he would have been subpoenaed to appear before a grand jury, Aronow was murdered."

Things were starting to make sense. The DEA case file reporting Aronow's murder had an 86 case number and a reference to Operation Man, which had been breathing down the Kramers' necks since mid-1986, investigating their money-laundering. The day of the murder, the DEA wrote that Aronow had two meetings at Fort Apache Marina. Patty Lezaca said Ben Kramer called USA Racing twice, looking for Don, in the half hour before the murder.

When Greg Smith was deposed by the defense in 1994, he had surprised them by saying he had since learned that Aronow was going to be subpoenaed to testify to a federal grand jury, implying that it was the one investigating the Kramers' money-laundering. He was vague then on his source, and vague to me when I had asked him. Smith had also appeared on the show, talking to Noah Nelson at the crime scene; however, he said little beyond that he was looking into the connection between Kramer and the murder—which was then a scoop.

But after I had watched *Exposé*, Smith admitted to me

that the show's interview of Tom Cash was in fact his first confirmation that the subpoena had been ready to go. True, Tom Burdick had reported the same thing in his book six months earlier, but Burdick didn't write that Aronow himself was a potential target of criminal investigation.

Cash: "He certainly had known felons as his associates, and those felons were without question deeply involved in not [just] any drug trafficking, [but] world-class drug trafficking. Now then Mr. Aronow, was he so naive that he wouldn't have known? I find that hard to believe."

Nelson also asked William Von Raab, commissioner of United States Customs during the time that his agency contracted with Aronow to build Blue Thunder, if he was bothered by knowledge that Aronow had a "spotty background, that he associated with underworld figures."

"I think it's embarrassing. I was shocked and surprised at two things. One, that we had dealings with an individual with as questionable a past as he did. And secondly, that that information hadn't been made known to me as head of the agency."

I couldn't help thinking that the story had been broadcast about a year and a half before the presidential election of 1992.

Nelson: "By the time drug agents on the trail put it all together, the Kramers and the government were already partners." At the end of the piece, Tom Brokaw, anchoring the show, concluded: "That's right, the boats the Customs Service uses to catch drug smugglers were built for Customs by convicted drug dealers who used laundered drug money to buy the boat company. And you thought you'd heard everything."

That was a great line, but it wasn't true. Customs had caught onto the scheme in time, so you couldn't say that the Kramers and the government had ever been married.

I also recalled something Bob Gowens had told me: that a great many investigating agencies were crawling all over 188th Street at the time. I guessed aloud which they might be, and he confirmed all of them: Metro-Dade Police (obviously), FBI, and IRS. An IRS investigation, I thought back, might have been the reason Aronow had the blues in the last months of his life, as Gowens had noticed.

"Old Mike" Kandrovicz had confirmed that Aronow kept cash in safe-deposit boxes, and numerous people had told me that Aronow liked to be paid for his boats in cash. "A beautiful money-laundering scam," Tom Cash had called it.

Returning to Ken Kukec's logic, Aronow may not have been a willing witness against Kramer, but he also might have been unable to afford to "claim five" at a grand jury because the IRS had the goods on him. Did the Feds present Aronow, approaching age sixty in a month, with a Hobson's choice: an untenable number of years in prison as a relative bit player for tax evasion and money-laundering, or testimony against Kramer? Perhaps he figured he had no chance against the Feds, and would try his lifelong good luck against Kramer.

Meanwhile, how did the Feds react that first week? They insisted to Metro-Dade that the rumors of an Aronow subpoena were not true. And almost nine years later, despite Tom Cash's looser lips, they hadn't ever changed their official position.

I thought back to Aronow's will. He had placed an unusual codicil in it, requiring that all his businesses be liquidated within a year of his demise. No one in the press could understand it; nor could Burdick, who was certain it meant something.

Now I could speculate; nobody else could run his boat business because nobody else would run it like he did, as a cash business. He had to figure that the IRS might catch up with the business sometime, as they apparently did. And by liquidating within a year, that would lessen the possibility the IRS would follow through, and limit the exposure of anyone in the family who would otherwise try to take it over.

I also thought of something my editor, Hanna, at *Boating* had said: she was mad at Mike Aronow for denying the money-under-the-table story that the police said he had told them on the night of the murder. They were protecting their father's estate—of which they were beneficiaries—from the IRS at the expense of hurting the state's murder investigation, she thought.

AUGUST 24, 1995

KEN KUKEC

"The case has really fallen apart since the appeals," said Ken Kukec. Without Kessler's testimony regarding what Young allegedly told him, and without Young's admission to Greg Smith at the live lineup, the state had inquired whether they could settle both cases with pleas, and avoid trial.

"They think it's a loser," he said. Young was offered no additional prison time (on top of his previous sentences) in exchange for a no-contest plea. Kukec wouldn't say what they offered Kramer, but they had turned it down. However, he expected they'd try again.

OCTOBER 25, 1995

JACK KRAMER

"Bobby Young has pled," Jack Kramer called to tell me. "He's back in federal custody. The plea is coterminous with his other sentences."

Although Jack hadn't talked to his son for a while, he said Ben had called his mother, and she called Jack.

Checking my calendar, I saw that there was a status hearing on Kramer's case that afternoon. I ran downtown to the courthouse, only to find that it had been postponed. But checking the court file in the courtroom, I confirmed the deal, dated October 20. Young had pled nolo contendere, which translates to "I will not contest it." That was tantamount to a guilty plea, without admitting anything. It read:

"First-degree murder—reduced to second-degree murder with a deadly weapon.'' In open court, but with media unalerted, Young had appeared so he could accept the deal. Judge Chavies gave him nineteen years, concurrent with his two other state cases: the Panzavecchia murder and the Marshall attempted murder.

But, a court clerk told me, Young repeatedly said, ''I will not testify for the state.'' In return for the plea, he would not be forced to testify against his codefendant.

OCTOBER 26, 1995

The Miami Herald had found out about the deal, too. They interviewed assistant state attorney Penny Brill, who said Gary Rosenberg explained the reason for the deal to the judge: the family wanted closure in their lives, and important testimony had been ruled inadmissible.

As for Kramer, Brill said, ''We have a very good case.''

Kayo Morgan, Young's cocounsel, told the *Herald*, ''Bobby is not a rat. He is not a cheese-eater.'' He said Young's previous state time was about to expire, which meant the new concurrent time would expire then, too, although he still had his federal time for drugs in Oklahoma.

''It was a good deal. Say he went to trial and got convicted on second-degree murder, the judge could depart from the sentencing guidelines and give Bobby life. I think he would have died in jail.''

The *Herald* also interviewed Greg Smith: ''Bobby Young was hired, and he did his job. I am not happy with the plea but I accept it, because the family was in agreement to it. This thing has been dragging on for almost nine years. It just seems to be never-ending. It's sad that Bobby [now aged forty-seven] may be out when he's sixty.''

Jack Kramer called me back, angry. Ben had called him the night before, extremely upset. I thought he would have been thrilled that Bobby could make a deal without having to rat on him; instead, the deal also precluded Young from testifying *for* him.

The cases had been arranged so that Young's would have gone first, and if he were acquitted, he would have testified at the second that he didn't know Kramer at all. In fact, Young had already written an affidavit exonerating Kramer. Before the deal, the state would have been prohibited from marching in Kessler in rebuttal to tell his story of confidences between himself and Young. But now, the deal was, if Young testified, he would void his attorney-client privilege with Kessler, which would open up Pandora's box for the jury.

Jack thought that Young had just four years remaining to serve in actual time. "He's laughing all the way," he said.

NOVEMBER 8, 1995

MIKE BOLÉ

An FBI agent had tied Ben Kramer and Randy Lanier to the 1985 murder of Tommy Felts, shot while driving his truck on a main street in Hollywood. The agent had testified at Kramer's bond hearing in August 1987 that they had Felts murdered to avenge his murder of Ted Richards, who the agent believed was a cocaine customer of Kramer and Lanier. Ten years later, the case remained unsolved.

Months before, I discovered that the cold case detective on it was someone I had written about in a story I had published years before in *The Miami Herald*'s Sunday magazine: Broward Sheriff's Office detective Mike Bolé. (I wrote that BSO had made a deal to cooperate with one of a pair of girls who had shot a man in the head during a robbery. She said the other girl was the shooter; she didn't know she was going to do it. But weeks later, when the victim awoke from his coma, he identified the shooter as the *cooperating* girl. Undaunted, the state attorney continued his prosecution theory as before, which produced a nightmare at trial. Just before the

Herald published it, the prosecutor insisted on meeting with my editors, hoping they'd kill the story. After he railed on about me for an unrebutted hour, as calmly as I could I shoved at him two Florida statutes on victim's rights I had found that I felt he had violated, for subverting the victims by failing to tell them about an important pretrial court date when they could have told the judge they objected that the first girl should get a favorable plea deal. In absence of their input, the judge had approved it. The prosecutor was totally shocked and unprepared to respond. Back to Bolé, he and I had become, and stayed, friends throughout it all.

A day earlier, I had run into Bolé's lieutenant in the Broward County Courthouse office of my old friend Brian Cavanagh (the prosecutor in my book *Until Proven Innocent*), and he had told me that something was up on the Felts case, and it had to do with Bobby Young.

I called Bolé; he told me he had talked to a number of people connected to Kramer and Lanier, but if they knew anything about Felts's murder, they weren't saying.

However, Bolé still thought Young was their man, and he volunteered that in the next three months, he was going to approach Young to admit to it and take a plea. They wouldn't insist on a deal any more constrictive than the Aronow plea—that is, no additional jail time.

I asked what Young's motivation would be to take it. Bolé explained; should someone who knew Young's guilt get into criminal trouble sometime in the future and need information to give away in order to lessen his sentence, then Young wouldn't get the same deal he'd be offered now.

GREG SMITH

When I had called Bolé, he had been talking to Greg Smith. Bolé called me back first; then Smith called me a half hour later, ending my conversation with Bolé.

I asked Smith if Kramer was going to get a plea offer similar to Young's, as it sounded like things were going, which would mean that neither case would ever go to trial. He confirmed that one might be worked out.

"Personally, I'd hate for that to happen. Our case against Young crumpled, just went to shit. Our chances of winning were slim. But we have a much better case against Kramer," he said.

Smith said he was "sickened" by Young's deal, except the part that they could keep him off the stand against them.

"Young was going to be Kramer's star witness," he said. "He could have sabotaged our case. Still, as necessary as it was, I'll never be happy about the plea."

Smith said certain members of Aronow's family okayed Young's deal because they just wanted the whole thing over. Mike Aronow was one of them, but Lillian had disagreed. But she said that if the rest of the family said yes, she would, too.

Smith said he would agree with a Kramer deal concurrent to his federal time only if he pled to life in prison. "I'd just like to see justice done. But if the family wants it to away, it'll go away."

DECEMBER 20, 1995

JACK KRAMER

"The state has offered Ben the same deal as they gave Young," Jack called to tell me after speaking to his son the night before. If he would take a plea of nolo contendere, he'd get four years concurrent with his federal sentence. Plus, Jack said, the state would promise to see what they could do about keeping Ben out of one of the new highest-security federal prisons open or opening soon in Colorado and Pennsylvania.

"You never leave your cell in those places. Visiting is by television." That was no way to live, he said.

To discuss the deal, the state offered to bring Ben to the state sttorney's office, with his lawyer, for lunch. Jack said Ben's new lead attorney, Jose Quiñon, responded that they owed him more than that, considering he had spent the last three years in solitary confinement at the county jail. Ben's answer to the olive branch, reported Jack: "Stick your lunch up your ass."

Although a trial date had been set for July 1996, "the state doesn't want it for nothing," Jack said. He repeated what Greg Smith had told me: that the Aronow family was tired of the whole thing. And tomorrow, Jack said, the defense was going to motion the court to vacate the death penalty qualification upon conviction. [Although the judge later denied the motion, Greg Smith explained to me that Young's sentence would make it impossible to win death against Kramer. At a penalty-phase hearing, Kramer's defense could present the mitigating factor that the shooter had pled to nineteen years. None of the state's aggravating factors arguing for death would be able to override that.]

Jack thought that Ben still wanted to roll the dice to "keep his name clear." But if they offered him manslaughter—which they did to Young—then he might take it. All of his money had gone to pay attorneys, and he didn't have any left—"and that's the *emmess*," Jack added, invoking the Yiddish word for truth.

During this conversation with Jack, as well as the previous one, we talked about Ben's new defense theory that the Colombians had ordered Young to murder Aronow, as Skip Walton had changed his story to—the last time anyone had bothered to listen to him. Now, with Young's plea as the shooter, Ben could say that was that.

After we talked, I thought back to the *Motor Boating & Sailing* story, which said that Ben had gone through an elaborate rigamarole to convince his so-called Colombian bosses to okay the hit. There were so many things clearly wrong and disreputable about that story that both prosecution and defense had dismissed it.

But what if the basic story line was right—that Kramer got the Colombians to do it, and they hired Young? Federal prisoner Charles Kelvin Smith, the author, intimated that Randy Lanier had given him much of his information, but when Greg Smith had tried to check it all out, he found that Charles Smith and Lanier had never been in the same prison at the same time.

But now I thought back; Charles Smith had been in FCI (federal prison), Danbury, Connecticut, and so had another obscure character: Jerry Kilpatrick, who had bought some of Aronow's land in 1981 and then sold it two months later to Kramer's money launderers—an obscure transaction that Smith might have inaccurately made a reference to. Kilpatrick had won a 1981 race in an Aronow-built Squadron XII called *Apache*.

I checked the federal prison inmate locator service and found that Kilpatrick had been at FCI Danbury through mid-1989, which meant that he could have been Charles Smith's source.

What did Kilpatrick know? He had clear connections to both Aronow and Kramer. His name had surfaced just two days after the murder, when Metro-Dade detectives told Mike DeCora that Aronow had testified against him at a Virginia federal grand jury in 1985. DeCora talked to a Virginia State Police investigator who told him that Aronow had testified only about a land purchase Kilpatrick had made from him, and that both men remained friends after the testimony.

The inmate locator also listed the charges Kilpatrick was then convicted for: they all had to do with conspiracy to import and distribute marijuana. Why bring Aronow to Virginia to testify to a land purchase if Kilpatrick wasn't charged with anything having to do with it? Was a better answer that Aronow had testified to knowing of Kilpatrick's marijuana ring? When Charles Kelvin Smith said that he had chucked bales for Kramer and Lanier in the early '80s, was it possible that he had really worked directly for Kilpatrick, which would explain why he may have opened up to Smith behind bars?

And, getting back to a larger issue, did this prove that Aronow was a federal informant or, at least, that he had a track record (that Kramer certainly would know about) of willingness to testify against smugglers? Smith had written that Kramer started a rumor that Aronow was an informant.

I also recalled what Paul Silverman had told detectives the first time they talked to him. He recounted drinking coffee with Bobby Young at Fort Apache Marina's bar on a Sunday afternoon before the murder. He said Young had told him that the marina's owner was having some sort of problem with Don Aronow, to include a problem in New Orleans and possible testimony by Aronow. But the New Orleans problem was the smuggling investigation, not money-laundering. Did someone get confused as the story got passed down, or was Aronow involved in testifying against Kramer in that case, too?

There was yet another problem in New Orleans about that time that resulted in a Colombian hit: the machine-gun murder of federal drug informant Barry Seal, on February 19, 1986. He was mixed up in Colombian drug trafficking, and allegedly worked for the CIA as part of the scheme to supply the contras with weapons, and to pay for them by selling drugs in the U.S.

[In 1987, Ben Kramer's racing pal George Morales told the Senate Iran-contra committee that he had gotten caught up in that as well. After the DEA arrested Morales in June 1986 as a result of a cocaine-transporting sting from January of that year, the U.S. attorney's office said that at least three people were in the witness protection program because of him. Seal had refused entry into the same program.

One of Morales's attorneys on his 1986 charges was Kate Bonner—one of Kramer's counsel in his money-laundering case.]

I gathered newspaper clips: the DEA said Seal was "the key player in the government's top drug cases," as reported by *The Washington Post*. He had testified to a federal grand jury that indicted no less than three of the top Medellin cartel kingpins: Carlos Lehder, Pablo Escobar, and Jorge Ochoa. In response, Colombian traffickers let it be known that they had put out contracts on the heads of top DEA officials. The DEA called Seal the first victim of that Colombian-financed hit squad.

Lehder was arrested February 4, 1987—the day after

Aronow was killed. A month later, *The Miami Herald* reported the Feds had learned that the Colombians were plotting to kill Leon Kellner, U.S. attorney for the Southern District of Florida. That threat was taken very seriously.

In footnotes of Leslie Cockburn's 1987 book *Out of Control*, documenting the gist of charges that came out in the Senate investigation, she wrote about Seal's murder:

"During his illustrious drug career, Seal worked for both the CIA and DEA, in between runs for his own profit. He was the pilot used for the famous Sandinista sting, contrived by the CIA to pin drug-smuggling charges on the Sandinista government.

"What is not common knowledge about this sting effort is that representatives of the Colombian cocaine cartel had previously met with [a pseudonymous] CIA antiterrorism expert in a Miami restaurant to offer the cartel's services to sting the Sandinistas directly.

"This offer came with other perks: use of the cartel's two-thousand-man guerrilla army and hundreds of millions in cash to overthrow the Sandinistas. The CIA failed to tell the cartel about the Seal operation in progress. When the druglords discovered the agency's duplicity, they killed Seal 'to teach them a lesson.' "

Fair to say is that the Colombian cartel back then was pissed off and in the mood to take action. Could that possibly have extended to Aronow?

Kramer's ring was a big customer of the Colombians. Aronow was apparently going to testify against him. Could Kramer's pleas of innocence be a matter of semantics—that it *was* the Colombians who killed Aronow, but with Kramer's knowledge and prodding, and to their mutual benefit? It was obvious that the Colombians were bigger players than Kramer; could that have made for a boss-employee relationship between them, as written by Charles Kelvin Smith? And then, were Kramer's boasts allegedly made to Kessler and the jailhouse snitches that he had Aronow killed, just that—boasts, in Kramer's well-documented blowhard style?

When Tommy Teagle first spoke to homicide detectives, he said he knew firsthand that Bobby Young used his ranch in Jupiter, Florida, to shelter mercenaries and store weapons such as C-4 explosives, grenades, handguns, and rifles.

Mercenaries? Storing C-4 and grenades? That's the stuff of soldiers of fortune, which is exactly how one of Young's attorney's described him in the press. With so many characters playing dual roles as smugglers and patriots, could Young have been involved with the contras, too, as well as (allegedly) the Colombians, Morales, Seal?

And Aronow, as well; wasn't he the king of playing both sides, selling fast boats both to smugglers and to the government to catch them? He even tried to sell the Blue Thunder contract to Kramer. His ties to the CIA went back to George Bush, maybe even before, when Miami boatbuilders in the '60s had constructed dull-black fast boats for a possible clandestine invasion of Cuba from the U.S. mainland. My public records request confirmed that the CIA had reopened a file on him in 1984—although it didn't confirm any more than that.

Was 1984 a significant date because the CIA was keeping tabs on the Blue Thunder contract? Or could it have had anything to do with the contras?

Willie Meyers had told me that Kramer wanted Aronow to introduce him to George Bush. "Imagine, introducing him to George Bush," Meyers huffed. If what Morales told Iran-contra was true, maybe Kramer felt he could get in on the same deal by talking to Bush, and guessed (or knew) that Aronow could arrange it for him. Or maybe when Kramer asked Aronow, he needed the same insulation from federal charges that Morales said he got from those "high-level Washington people"— specifically, Morales said, George Bush. When Aronow refused to intervene, maybe this was not just *a* fight between them, but *the* fight.

Twigs of the same branch.

TOMMY FELTS

Months earlier, when I had asked Detective Mike Bolé if he would share with me the still-open cold-case investigative file on Tommy Felts's 1985 murder, he had declined. But a week earlier to this day, while I was visiting his lieutenant at the Broward Sheriff's Office, Bolé tossed me a manila folder

"It's the Felts statements," he said. Pleased but a little surprised, I thanked him.

Then on this day, as I sat with him outside a grand jury room, he asked if I had read them, implying that he had given them to me because the Felts case had been resolved. He thought I knew that, and I didn't.

"Bobby Young pled two months ago," he said. Bolé explained that when he had approached Young's attorney, H. Dohn Williams, with the offer he had mentioned to me in November—plead now, clear the books, no additional prison time—Young had jumped at it Nor had Young been forced to make any statement about his complicity.

But now that the case was closed, the file was public record. And although the witnesses' statements hadn't been enough to bring Young to trial, they did fill in more of the whole Kramer-Lanier picture.

First, as background, Felts had already been established as a loan-shark enforcer and bodybuilding partner of Gil Fernandez Jr., a one-time Mr. USA national bodybuilding contestant, vocal born-again Christian, and former Metro-Dade cop who left the force in 1983 with a personnel file that indicated volatility. That year, Fernandez began running the Apollo Gym in Hollywood, known among local bodybuilders for its rowdy members and steroid use. Also that year, according to a 1990 indictment, he and Hubert Christie committed a drug-rip-off, execution-style triple murder, dumping their bound, gagged, and shot-in-the-head victims near a fish camp in the Everglades.

The Apollo Gym, police said, was a front for drug dealing and gambling, adding that Christie was working for organized crime, collecting loan-shark and gambling-debt money. Further, a federally protected witness accused him of carrying out three contract Mob murders between 1980 and 1982.

In 1983, Christie hired some muscle from among his gym members—Fernandez and Felts. They allegedly extorted drug dealers by shooting up their homes, then came around later to sell them protection. They set up cocaine deals, then stole drugs at gunpoint, threatening their victims not to complain.

Police also linked Fernandez and Christie to at least six other murders. In 1991, they were convicted of the triple murder and sentenced to life in prison.

As the trial had played out, the 1984 murder of Ted Richards in Fort Lauderdale arose. Police said that Felts had set up Richards, whom he knew from high school in Hollywood, and who was connected in the marijuana business to Randy Lanier. After Felts's murder, his brother, William Felts, told police what he said Tommy had told him about Richards's murder: "Gilbert Fernandez shot Richards in the head."

That all led police to speculate that Felts was murdered by someone connected to Lanier and Kramer, to revenge Richards.

Bolé had taken the statements in 1994. The centerpiece interview had been with Lee Ethridge[1], who had been thirty-three years old in 1985. He said he knew Ted Richards and admitted having been in the drug trade himself, but said he had gotten out of it by 1985.

Ethridge remembered a Saturday morning in September 1985 when Felts—whom he knew from high school as well—and Gil Fernandez came to his home, unannounced.

"He [Felts] said, 'Um, Lee, there's something—something I have to talk to you about,' and he suggested,

---

[1] Not his real name

'Let's step outside.' And this is when he told that they knew—they knew the people that had killed Ted—Ted Richards. And then he said, the same people want to kill you.

"I was obviously shocked at the time; I questioned what he could be talking about. He said, 'Well, we can't go into a lot; we can't tell you who it is or anything, but I'm just telling you, these people want to kill you—but if you can get us two hundred thousand dollars, we can take care of it for you.' "

Felts told Ethridge there were other friends of his on the same list, including Ronald Hartenburg[2], who also had a marijuana connection to Randy Lanier, and Keith Phinney[3], who had worked with Ted Richards. "That's when Fernandez stepped in and said something to the effect of, um, 'Look, you have twenty-four hours or you're dead—your choice.' " Then both Felts and Fernandez dramatically marched out the door without further discussion.

Ethridge told Hartenburg, who sloughed off the threat. Hartenburg, a boat captain, then left to pilot Lanier's boat on a trip to the Bahamas. But Ethridge and Phinney moved their families to a Howard Johnson's. That night, both of their houses were sprayed with gunfire.

Days later, when Lanier arrived on the boat, he told Hartenburg he had an emergency at home, and to phone his sister. Calling, Hartenburg found out that his house and car had been machine-gunned as well.

At home, Hartenburg told police about the extortion attempt. Detectives wanted to give him the money to pay it, and to wear a wire, but Hartenburg decided he had too many family members around town to risk that.

When Hartenburg told Lanier what had happened, Lanier took him to see Mel Kessler, who advised him to get out of town. Hartenburg then left for his father's home in Tennessee.

Ethridge said he met with Felts once more, this time

---

[2] Same

[3] Same

at a restaurant at Miami International Airport. By this time he had guessed that Felts and Fernandez were probably referring to themselves when they were talking about the people who had wanted him dead. And, he thought, they very well might have been Ted Richards's killers as well.

Ethridge said he asked Felts why this was happening. "He says, 'Lee, what can I tell you, what can I tell you.' And I said, 'I know it's you, it's gotta be you and Fernandez,' and he was just like, 'Hey, what can I tell you'—it was almost like he was just doing his job." Not long after that meeting, Ethridge flew his family and himself to Europe to live. Phinney left for Clearwater, in central Florida.

About a week later, October 6, 1985, Felts was murdered. He was driving at 5:20 on a Sunday afternoon on Stirling Road, a main street in Hollywood, headed for the Apollo Gym. He was shot several times by someone in a passing pickup truck.

After the murder, Hartenburg came back but didn't want to live in his house anymore. Instead he rented a house from Jeff Tuchband—who was later convicted in the same Illinois drug trial with Kramer and Lanier. Hartenburg tried to sell his house but found that no one was especially interested in buying a place that had just been shot up.

Bolé, with Greg Smith, also interviewed Tuchband, who was then in federal prison in Tallahassee. Tuchband described how Ted Richards and Ronald Hartenburg fit into the Lanier-Kramer smuggling operation.

Hartenburg, he said, began in the business by working with Richards, off-loading other people's marijuana, which both Lanier and Tuchband bought. Richards, he said, later "was either purchasing marijuana from my partner and myself, or, on occasion when he had some to sell, he could sell to us, and he was also selling cocaine at the same time."

Tuchband said his partner had told him that Richards was murdered during a drug rip-off. Yet that hadn't been the first such incident involving Lanier's friends. A number had been preyed upon, mostly getting ripped off, but one other had been killed: Dickie Robertson, one of the three 1983 victims that Fernandez and Christie were convicted of murdering.

The extortion attempt on Hartenburg "was a natural progression," he said. Every time the group doing it made a score, they learned from their victims the names of other drug dealers they could do the same to.

Tuchband remembered a conversation with Randy Lanier after Felts's murder. They were driving together in Tuchband's car, after playing racquetball, when they passed the spot where Felts had been shot.

"So we're driving by, and I remark, 'Is this the spot right here?' I go, 'What did you do, did you guys get them whacked out, did you take care of the problem for Ronald [Hartenburg]?' And then, clearly, his remark was, 'Well, you'd be surprised what you can get done for fifty grand.' "

"And you, took that to mean?" asked Bolé.

"That in some way, he participated in it, getting these guys taken care of."

"And clearly," asked Bolé, "it was referred to the Felts murder?"

"There was nobody else that we were talking about, we were talking about the two guys that killed Ted [Richards] and that were trying to do Ronald [Hartenburg], okay, and that probably everybody else felt, including Randy, that if Ronald [Hartenburg] went, then he [Lanier] would be next."

Tuchband said he didn't ask Lanier for any details, but in jail, he speculated with Charles Podesta—Lanier's bookkeeper and the Feds' star witness at the Illinois trial—that "Lanier, with the help of Ben Kramer, would be capable of doing it."

Tuchband said the rip-off threats ended after Felts was killed.

"Was there a collective sigh of relief from the group [then]?" Bolé asked.

"Yeah, things were better," he said.

* * *

In south Florida's most ruthless era, perhaps the most ruthless, scary guys out there were Gil Fernandez, Hubert Christie, and, until his own murder, Tommy Felts. To be a knowing target of theirs was clearly petrifying.

A number of people have said this to me, including Bolé and Greg Smith: marijuana smuggling was a gentlemanly business in the '70s when Kramer and Lanier got into it. But in the '80s, when the really big money went into cocaine, the business became bloody.

For Kramer and Lanier to have Felts murdered to physically defend themselves made sense. There's even a law-of-the-jungle morality to it. Given Bobby Young's plea to Felts's murder, I recall what Young said in 1988 to Fort Lauderdale detective Steve Robitaille: "Just remember, Steve, I never did anyone who didn't deserve it."

Felts was 1985. In 1986 and 1987, there was a new and different kind of mortal assault on Kramer and Lanier's organization: two federal investigations and likely informant testimony by Don Aronow. Given the availability of a weapon like Young and the emotions of the moment, was it a far reach to believe that he was employed once again for self-preservation?

And perhaps that the law of the jungle might even still apply?

A number of prisoners have told me over the years that the cops or the Feds don't always get you for your precise crime—but when you're guilty, they get you for something. Applying this, when the Feds got Kramer and Lanier for smuggling, they didn't sentence them for Aronow's (or anybody else's) murder, but by giving them life without parole, in effect you could say they did.

And although a trial date for September 30, 1996, remained on the clerk's computer, I think everyone realized that by now.

SEPTEMBER 11, 1996

Ben Kramer had just made *The Miami Herald*; he had been charged for possessing marijuana in a Jif peanut butter jar, while in the Dade County Jail's maximum security.

That incident in itself seemed pointless. But the story also said that his September 30 court date was still on.

I called Greg Smith. "The case will be resolved sooner than you think," he said. Monday or Tuesday, Kramer was going to take a plea.

I didn't ask to what. It didn't seem to matter. I told Smith what I had joked with Jack Kramer, that the state at this point would accept a plea to a parking ticket.

"Absolutely," Smith said.

It had been almost ten years, and the case was ending with a whimper, he noted. I tried to cheer him up.

"When the Feds enacted their drug-kingpin statute— that gave life without parole—what they were saying in effect was that these guys commit murders in the process of doing business. We may not ever be able to pin a murder on you, but we're going to give you the maximum penalty, short of death. So Kramer in effect already has been convicted of murder, at least as far as his sentence goes. Another conviction is pointless."

Smith agreed with me. "When we gave Bobby Young nineteen years for being the shooter, there wasn't any way we could argue for the death penalty against Kramer. And you're right, Kramer has already got life."

Smith calculated Young's release in about twelve years. "He owes the Feds ten. He'll be out of state in three or so; then he'll have to do 85 percent of the ten, eight and a half. He'll be sixty when he gets out."

I said it was just as well there wouldn't be a trial; I agreed with the defense attorneys that the state didn't have much of a case left. The Feds had decided not even to bring Mel Kessler to the stand in the Willie Falcón and Sal Magluta drug case—which the Feds lost. After that, it was hard to base a case on two jailhouse snitches.

"Well, I think it was a coin flip whether we'd win. We have those tapes of Kramer's phone calls from Leavenworth, and juries love stuff like that. We were trying to prove that Kramer was trying to keep Young from testifying against him, by paying for his attorney and asking about him.

"When we executed a search warrant for his accountant and his lawyer (the Formans), we found out that Ben had called while we were there. The secretary kept telling him, 'Max can't talk, don't call back.' He called Max that night at home and found out about the search warrant.

"While he was waiting for Max to accept the collect call, we could hear talk in the background. Someone was asking Ben, 'Did Bobby flip?' 'I don't know, I'll find out.' Then after he talks to Max, his next call is to Cat Dancer (Young's wife).

"That's just the sort of thing we were trying to show."

SEPTEMBER 25, 1996

Although it took a week longer than Greg Smith had expected, the state and Ben Kramer worked out a deal similar to Bobby Young's; he pled to manslaughter and was sentenced to nineteen years.

Concurrent, of course, to his life without parole in federal prison.

Kramer said he was pleading no contest just so he could get out of the Dade County Jail. It was a plea of convenience, as far as he was concerned.

"I've lost teeth in here"—eleven, he told *The Miami Herald*, the only newspaper to cover the anticlimactic conclusion to perhaps Miami's most sensational crime, which took just short of ten years to close. "I haven't seen a doctor in years. That was the decision—or don't take the plea and die."

Kramer was now forty-one years old. It wasn't that he looked so much older than his age, but his body appeared decrepit after eight years of incarceration.

Even so, the Metro-Dade Police SWAT team surrounded the courtroom. And Kramer himself, inside court, had to wear a chain wrapped around his waist connected through his handcuffs and latched with a padlock, as well as shackles around his ankles.

The security hearkened back to his 1990 escape attempt from the federal Metropolitan Correctional Center in south Dade.

OCTOBER 4, 1996

About a week after Kramer's plea, I went to the same prison—now deemed the Federal Correctional Institute— to visit Paul Luskin. I had never been there before.

I asked Luskin where the helicopter had swooped down to pick up Kramer. He pointed. Then he had me look up: there were thin wires running diagonally from poles all over the compound. I wouldn't have noticed if he hadn't mentioned them. That was Ben's legacy.

Kramer wires.